**The Academic Canon of Arts
and Humanities, and Science**

The Rissho International Journal
of Academic Research
in Culture and Society **2**

The Academic Canon of Arts and Humanities, and Science

Edited by The Rissho University
International Journal Committee

RISSHO University

Editing / Publishing: Rissho University
4-2-16 Osaki, Shinagawa Ward, Tokyo 141-8602, Japan
Sales: Heibonsha Limited, Publishers
3-29 Kandajinbo-cho, Chiyoda Ward, Tokyo 101-0051, Japan

The Rissho International Journal of Academic Research in Culture and Society 2
The Academic Canon of Arts and Humanities, and Science
Edited by The Rissho University International Journal Committee

© Rissho University 2019
All rights reserved.
Printed in Japan

Contents

Message From the President
Noboru Saito 7

1 The Greater East Asia Co-Prosperity Sphere and Archaeology in Japan
  Hideichi Sakazume 9

2 The Techniques and Tools of Kazusabori Well-Boring
  Hiroki Takamura 37

3 A Study on Scripture Worship in the Kathmandu Valley: An Interim Review with a Prospect of a New Approach for the Philological Study of Sanskrit Buddhism
  Kazunori Sasaki, Fumio Shoji 63

4 On Academic Training in the Early Nichiren Sect: With a Focus on Cases from the Nikkō Lineage
  Shumbun Homma 83

5 Gentrification and the Spatial Polarization in Eastern Inner-City Tokyo: The Restructuring of the Kyojima Area in Sumida Ward
  Fumiko Kohama 119

6 A Study on the Prosperity and Decline of Buddhist Sites in Northern Bactria: Kara Tepe and Zurmala
  Atsushi Iwamoto 151

7 The Influence of *The Sketch Book* on Longfellow's *Outre-Mer*
  Mika Takiguchi 179

8 Penal Reform for Drug Offenses in Japan
  Yasuhiro Maruyama 197

9 Is Social Security Reform Really Willing to Deal with Poverty?
  Ju Kaneko 223

10 How Do Parents Communicate with Their Infants?: The Function of
   Parental Proxy Talk in Pre-Verbal Communication
   *Yoriko Okamoto, Yukie Sugano, Reika Shouji, Chie Takahashi,
   Akiko Yagishita-Kawata, Yayoi Aoki, Ayuchi Ishikawa, Miyako Kamei,
   Manabu Kawata, Osamu Suda*   243

11 The abc Conjecture of the Derived Logarithmic Functions of Euler's
   Function and Its Computer Verification
   Michinori Yamashita, Daisuke Miyata, Natsumi Fujita   275

12 Characteristics of the Potential Temperature Distribution Along
   Mountain Slopes Experiencing Cross-Mountain Air Currents in the
   Winter Season
   Yasushi Watarai, Yoshinori Shigeta, Kiyotaka Nakagawa   293

13 The Promotion of Social Inclusion by Adoption of the Private
   Finance Initiative on a Correctional Institution
   Yumiko Kamise, Naoya Takahashi, Emi Yano   313

14 Mental Health in Local Public Employees Affected by the Great East
   Japan Earthquake
   Naoya Takahashi, Takeshi Furuya, Shigeki Sakata   343

Contributors   369

Message From The President: The Rissho International Journal of Academic Research in Culture and Society

Rissho University's roots go back to the year 1580, when the Iidaka Danrin seminary was established in Sosa, in what is now Chiba Prefecture. It was an educational institution of the Nichiren School of Buddhism, which was founded by Nichiren (1222 – 1282) around the middle of the Kamakura period in Japan. Today, Rissho's history and traditions are among the most illustrious of all of the nearly 800 universities in Japan. Our university is one of the largest in Japan, too, with a student body of more than 10,000.

As an educational institution we have developed steadfastly over the centuries, while experiencing the vicissitudes of history. Maintaining optimism for the future, Rissho University actively promotes a wide range of original, forward-looking academic research projects, publishing and promulgating research results, thereby fostering the global advancement of knowledge and contributing to sustainable social development.

Rissho is a multi-disciplinary university with eight undergraduate faculties and seven graduate school research departments. Taking advantage of its strengths in various academic fields and its unique characteristics, the university has restructured advanced data intelligence systems that store the results of our research activities. To promote comprehensive and integrated innovative thinking in the humanities, social sciences and natural sciences, we are enhancing our research systems to make them more effective. We intend of course to continue enriching the practical and sustainable nature of those systems, while also contributing to the development and communication of an even more extensive store of knowledge for Japan and the world at large. With these goals in mind, we have decided to publish *The Rissho International Journal of Academic Research in Culture and Society* as a compendium of outstanding and influential research results.

At Rissho University, our pedagogical and research reforms are alert to world standards. At the heart of those reforms lies an ideal espoused by

Ishibashi Tanzan, who served as the 16th president of our university and also Japan's 55th Prime Minister. He was a man with a great soul, famed for his integrity as an individual, his lionhearted style as an orator, and his rare skills as a journalist and politician espousing the Small Japan policy (or "Small Japanism"). But above all else he was a principled philosopher and a great thinker who synthesized theory and practice. He always prized world peace and order, and as an upright man of learning he dedicated himself to the ennoblement of the human spirit, always exhibiting a glimmer of hope for the future. His emphasis on philosophical anthropology lives on today as part of the enlightenment pedagogical ideals of Rissho University.

Rissho University intends to use the opportunity provided by publication of this *Journal* to instill further intellectual momentum into the trends driving this tumultuous age of globalization. But even more, as an educational and academic research institution, we shall pursue a bold mission: contributing through our university's various pedagogical endeavors to the creation and development of sustainable human communities for a brighter tomorrow. This will help us to continue our own sustainable growth. These ideals are in keeping with the 2030 Agenda for Sustainable Development, adopted at the UN Summit in 2015, and promoting these ideals has a direct positive impact on improving quality assurance in each area covered by the Goals.

Noboru Saito
The 33rd President of Rissho University

The Greater East Asia Co-Prosperity Sphere and Archaeology in Japan

Hideichi Sakazume

Abstract

Research regarding Japanese archaeological history up until now has been advanced with a central focus on investigation and research in the Japanese archipelago (the *naichi* ["domestic territory"] or Japan proper.) Meanwhile, archaeological research in the *gaichi* ("overseas territories")—areas outside the Japanese archipelago that were temporarily made territories of Japan—has hardly been taken up as a matter of consideration. This paper, taking archaeological history to be a part of modern Japanese history, summarizes the significance of research in the overseas territories.

The "Greater East Asia Co-Prosperity Sphere" was a concept that came to be espoused in 1932 for the sake of establishing the framework for a new order in East Asia, and throughout East Asia there was archaeological research carried out in connection with the policy. Following the annexation of Korea in 1910, the post of Governor-General was established on the Korean Peninsula, and research was conducted throughout the region, with research locations established in Pyongyang, Gyeongju and Buyeo under the Government-General Museum of Chosen. Research on Han dynasty tombs in the Lelang region is specially noted.

With the establishment in 1932 of Manchukuo in northeastern China, the Far-Eastern Archaeological Society, organized in Japan proper, independently carried out archaeological research. The northern region of China was called Hokushi ("North China"), and the Far-Eastern Archaeological Society took on research in this region as well, researching sites that included Han dynasty tombs and the Yungang Grottoes. In the southern region of China, research on matters such as artifacts excavated at Yinxu in the Nanjing area was carried out by Japanese scholars as well.

That is to say, in the early Showa period (1926–1945), following the Sino-Japanese war that began in 1937, archaeological research was conducted primarily by Japanese official scholars in colonies that were occupied under the framework of the Greater East Asia Co-Prosperity Sphere; and this point is verifiable as a characteristic feature in the archaeological history of the era.

Introduction

Currently, there is a move to develop research on the history of Japanese archaeology based on new perspectives and methods.[1] That trend is steadily enriching the academic field of Japanese archaeology as a science, while simultaneously offering advancements in the direction of the systemization of Japanese archaeology.

As is well known, historical study of Japanese archaeology has maintained, examined and systematized historical documents by persons such as Jiujiro Nakaya,[2] Seiichi Wajima,[3] Kenji Kiyono,[4] Yukio Kobayashi,[5] Yoshiro Kondo,[6] Tadashi Saito,[7] Mitsunori Tozawa,[8] Masaki Kudo[9] and Akira Teshigawara.[10] Meanwhile, views on those archaeological studies are regularly being published every year.

Based on this state of archaeological studies, the author has continued exploring the history of Japanese archaeology using the approach of linking it to the development of modern history in Japan.[11] During this time, the author has especially focused on how archaeology in the Showa period (1926–1989) developed based on a connection with the Greater East Asia Co-Prosperity Sphere.

The term "Greater East Asia Co-Prosperity Sphere" is said to have been coined by Yosuke Matsuoka, the Minister of Foreign Affairs in the second cabinet of Prime Minster Fumimaro Konoe formed in July 1940. However, its roots lie in the declaration for the establishment of a New Order in East Asia announced on November 3, 1938, by Konoe's first Cabinet. The declaration of a New Order in East Asia was presented as Japan's desire to build a new order that would enable attainment of permanent security in East Asia.

The Greater East Asia Co-Prosperity Sphere and Archaeology in Japan

Fig. 1 Thematic Map of Japan and Relevant Asisn Countries During Pacific War

Matsuoka's subsequent concept of the Greater East Asia Co-Prosperity Sphere stated that, under the rule of His Imperial Majesty the Emperor of Japan, Japan's immediate diplomatic policy would seek to form a Greater East Asia Co-Prosperity Sphere including Japan, Manchuria and China. Thereafter, that concept established Japan's path forward.

The formation, development and collapse of the Greater East Asia Co-Prosperity Sphere were closely related to the colonial rule of Japan's Imperialism, and overlapped with the 15 Year War.

In *Dai Toa Kyoeiken no Keisei to Hokai* ("The Rise and Fall of the Greater East Asia Co-Prosperity Sphere," 1975), Hideo Kobayashi divided the campaign into stage 1 (1931–1937), stage 2 (1937–1941) and stage 3 (1941–1945), and presented a comprehensive approach to understanding it.

His establishment of three stages was an ambitious endeavor, treating first the economic and military aspects that hinged on military occupation, then unification of the monetary system, and then the evolution of industry and development policy.

Fig. 2 1 *ARCHAEOLOGIA ORIENTAUS* (Series A-1, 1929)
2 *Koseki Chosa Hokoku* (Research on Ancient Sites: an Annual Report, 1937)

While inspired by research on the Greater East Asia Co-Prosperity Sphere epitomized by Kobayashi, this paper attempts to look at how the world of archaeology in Japan behaved with reference to a number of materials that touch on the author's own views.

The approach of linking archaeological trends in Japanese archaeological history to the Greater East Asia Co-Prosperity Sphere is highly unusual. Traditionally, and even today, research on archaeological history within Japan proper is predominant. In most instances of discussion on archaeology outside Japan, retrospectives by academics who directly furthered "outside" archaeology and assignation of meaning are commonplace, and statements based on the awareness of those involved are central.[12] Without a doubt, archaeology "outside" of Japan was developed by the best minds and technologies in Japanese archaeology at the time, and their academic outcomes can be judged above reproach.

A look at Japanese archaeological history from the perspective of archaeological research by Japanese people can be categorized by two approaches: an archaeology of a narrow region focused on the Japanese archipelago, and archaeological studies targeting a broad region defined by the concept of the Greater East Asia Co-Prosperity Sphere. Archaeology outside Japan spanning the Meiji period (1868–1912), Taisho period (1912–1926) and into the Showa period (1926–1989) takes an archaeological view that casts archaeological sites as colonies. Perhaps it can be called the equivalent of targeting locales such as British India.

An especially typical illustration is the state of archaeological studies under colonial rule in the Korean Peninsula through the Taisho period to the first half of the Showa period, following Japan's annexation of Korea on August 22, 1910.

Archaeology outside of Japan was the archaeology of colonies, pure and simple. In particular, the field collectively called archaeology of East Asia progressed along with the New Order in East Asia and the Greater East Asia Co-Prosperity Sphere. Archaeology of the Greater East Asia Co-Prosperity Sphere was launched in the colonies as a national policy.

Just as modern history studies in Japan are deeply entwined with the issue of colonies, this relationship in Japanese archaeological history cannot be ignored.

A point of view now being called for is an approach to the archaeological history as a perspective on Japanese archaeology that surpasses the locality of archaeology in places such as the Korean Peninsula, Mainland China and Taiwan.

Archaeology in the Greater East Asia Co-Prosperity Sphere was a process in which archaeological studies of East Asia peaked and then declined. It should be explored as an aspect of the historical study of Japanese archaeology in the first half of the Showa period.[13]

According to a perspective that divides archaeology in the Showa period into an early stage (1926–1945), middle stage (1946–1965) and late stage (1966–1989),[14] the early stage exactly corresponds to the New Order in East Asia and Greater East Asia Co-Prosperity Sphere.

This paper selects several matters that shaped the archaeology of the Greater East Asia Co-Prosperity Sphere as an historical aspect of Japanese archaeology in the early Showa period and considers their significance.

1. Korea and the Society for Studying Historic Sites in Korea

The signing of the Japan-Korea Annexation Treaty on August 22, 1910 led to Japan's annexation of Korea, and the Governor-General of Korea was established on October 1. With the installation of the Governor-General and simultaneous jurisdiction given to the First Regional Office of Domestic Affairs, a research system for historic buildings and ruins was developed. Its central figure was Tadashi Sekino, who had already gotten the endeavor underway. It was completed in 1913 and results compiled in the *Chosen Koseki Zufu* ("Collection of Ancient Korean Sites and Monuments," 15 volumes) and distributed within and outside Japan.

In addition, Ryuzo Torii studied ruins primarily related to the Stone Age for a research project for the Domestic Affairs Bureau of Academic Affairs, Office of the Governor General, from 1911 until 1920.

This study was a major tour accompanied by a team consisting of technicians who took survey photos, interpreters and even military police. It was said to be more than a simple trip to gather data[15]; at the time, a study under direct control of the Governor-General was unusual.

In 1915, the Museum of the Korea Governor-General's Office was opened. It publicly displayed history and materials from the Stone Age to the Joseon Dynasty. Starting the following year, research on historic sites throughout the Korean Peninsula was conducted according to an annual plan. Research committee members included Tadashi Sekino, Katsumi Kuroita, Ryu Imanishi, Ryuzo Torii, Shogo Oda, Saiichi Tanii, and later, Yoshito Harada, Kosaku Hamada, Sueji Umehara and Ryosaku Fujita. The results were published annually in the *Koseki Chosa Hokoku* ("Research Report on Ancient Sites"). The *Koseki Chosa Tokubetsu Hokoku* ("Special Research Report on Ancient Sites") was also published.

This kind of research project under direct control of the Governor-General dwindled from the last years of the Taisho period to the early Showa period. This is said to have been due to budgeting difficulties for archaeological research.

Katsumi Kuroita determined the necessity of organizing a research body as a replacement. He wanted to establish a research organization through donations, and presented an approach that set up an external body to the Governor-General.

In August 1931, the Chosen Koseki Kenkyukai (Society for Studying Historic Sites in Korea) was launched. This research society was not just a group of like-minded individuals, but was in charge of a department researching historic sites and treasures as part of the Governor-General. It was an extra-governmental organization that assisted Governor-General projects by providing researchers and excavation costs.

Operational funds came from sources including grants from the Japan Society for the Promotion of Science. These funds made it possible to manage three research institutes (Pyongyang, Gyeongju, Buyeo), pay research costs and publish research reports. The office was located in the Museum of the Korea Governor-General's Office, while the Pyongyang Research Institute was established in the Pyongyang Museum, the Gyeongju Research Institute in the Gyeongju Branch Museum, and the Baekje Research Institute in the Buyeo Museum.

Beginning with research on the ancient tombs of the Lelang Commandery in Namjeong-ri, Seokam-ri and Jongbaek-ri, the Pyongyang Research Institute carried out research on Lelang tombs and flat earthen wall ruins in the vicinity of Pyongyang. Furthermore, research was conducted on Goguryeo tombs, flat earthen wall ruins and temple ruins located in Taedong, Pyongwon, Kangso, Ryonggang and Nyongbyon. Notably, the 1931 excavation of Lelang Ch'ae hy p-ch'ong and 1932 excavation of the tomb of Wang Kuang of Lo-Lang discovered a completely intact wooden burial chamber with a wooden coffin and an array of grave goods, causing a global stir in the world of archaeology. The finds were reported in the *Koseki Chosa Hokoku* with the first issue titled, "Select Specimens of the Remains Found in the Tomb of Painted Basket of Lo-Lang" (1934) and the second issue titled, "The Tomb of Wang Kuang of Lo-Lang" (1935).

Table 1—List of aid and donations to the Society for Studying Historic Sites in Korea

1931: Baron Yataro Iwasaki (7,000 yen donation)
1932: Marquis Moritatsu Hosokawa (6,000 yen donation)
1933: Japan Society for the Promotion of Science (15,000 yen subsidy); Ministry of the Imperial Household (5,000 yen grant)
1934: Japan Society for the Promotion of Science (12,000 yen subsidy); Ministry of the Imperial Household (5,000 yen grant); Yi Imperial Family (5,000 yen grant)
1935: Japan Society for the Promotion of Science (8,000 yen subsidy); Ministry of the Imperial Household (5,000 yen grant); Yi Imperial Family (5,000 yen grant)
1936–1938: Japan Society for the Promotion of Science (yearly 8,000 yen subsidy); Ministry of the Imperial Household (5,000 yen grant); Yi Imperial Family (5,000 yen grant)

Table 2—List of directors in the Society for Studying Historic Sites in Korea

Chairman: Parliamentary Commissioner
Councilors: Katsumi Kuroita, Shogo Oda, Yoshito Harada, Hiroshi Ikeuchi, Sueiji Umehara, and the Director General of Special School Affairs
Secretary: Ryosaku Fujita

In addition, research on ancient tombs and flat earthen walls in the Lelang Commandery of the Han Dynasty conducted from 1933 to 1935 was published each year in three issues as *Kofun Chosa Gaiho* ("Summary Report on Studies of Ancient Tombs") so that the research content was made public. Also, research conducted from 1936 to 1938 was compiled annually in the *Kofun Chosa Hokoku* ("Research Report on Ancient Sites").[16]

The Gyeongju Research Institute implemented research on sites such as ancient tombs, castle ruins and temple ruins from Silla/Unified Silla, and published the outcomes annually in the *Koseki Chosa Hokoku*.

The first volume of the *Chosen Homotsu Zuroku* ("Illustrated Book of Korean Treasures"), entitled *"Bukkokuji to Sekkutsuan"* ("Bukkoku-ji Temple and Sekkutsuan Cave," 1938) and the second volume, entitled "*Keishu*

Namsan no Busseki" ("Buddhist Ruins of Mt. Namsan in Gyeongju," 1940) both became publications of the Korea Governor-General, but were reports on work in which the Gyeongju Research Institute was actively involved.

The Baekje Research Institute conducted research on sites including ancient tombs and temple ruins in Gongju, Iksan, and Han Nam. The results were presented annually in the *Koseki Chosa Hokoku*.

The activities of the Society for Studying Historic Sites in Korea replaced research on historic sites by the Governor-General. All of the three established research institutes were housed in museums, and the society's office was located within the Museum of the Korea Governor-General's Office in Gyeongseong. They were inextricably linked to the Governor-General. Expenses for operation were provided by donation, but a majority was funded by the Japan Society for the Promotion of Science, the Ministry of the Imperial Household and the Yi Imperial Family. Thus, the society was not a non-government affiliated research body.

In addition to researchers, people engaged in studying the Lelang ruins in 1935 included part-time employees of the Office of Archaeological Research, Korea Governor-General's Office. Furthermore, from 1937 to 1938 employees other than researchers participated, with titles including "part-time employee of the Museum of the Korea Governor-General's Office." Researchers and research assistants were persons involved with the Governor-General's Office, or researchers belonging to Imperial Universities and the Imperial Museum in Japan. These were the types of individuals who made up the members.

This was only natural because the work of excavating ruins in the era of the Governor-General was limited to members appointed by the Governor-General or relevant government officials. Very few instances remained in which research was conducted by civilian researchers of archaeology. However, the one exception applied to ruins related to the Stone Age.

Viewed in this light, it becomes clear that the Society for Studying Historic Sites in Korea was similar to the Toa Koko Gakkai (Far-Eastern Archaeological Society).[17] Furthermore, it was operated by subsidies, grants and Imperial donations. The state (government) was constantly involved. While the Far-Eastern Archaeological Society was oriented towards archaeology in East Asia, the Society for Studying Historic Sites in Korea undertook archaeology studies in Korea. Kyoto Imperial University, Tokyo Imperial University and government archaeologists assigned to the Imperial Museum were directly involved in both societies, and the names of people common to them all can be found.

The Far-Eastern Archaeological Society joined with the Pekin Daigaku Koko Gakkai (Peking University Archaeology Society) to form the Toho Kokogaku Kyokai (Association of East Archaeology), which held meetings, planned lectures and created society field uniforms. In contrast, the Society for Studying Historic Sites in Korea operated by changing the names of Governor-General archaeological projects and implementing them as is. Therefore, although a look at the activities of these two societies reveals similarities, in essence they were entirely different.

The Society for Studying Historic Sites in Korea promoted archaeological research in the Korean Peninsula from June 1931 to August 1945, and was clearly an organization that undertook archaeological studies in the Greater East Asia Co-Prosperity Sphere.

2. Manchuria and the Far-Eastern Archaeological Society

The Northeast area of China comprises three northeastern provinces in China—Liaoning, Jilin and Heilongjiang—and the region covering Inner Mongolia. The Japanese colony of Manchukuo was founded there in March 1932 with Puyi as a puppet ruler, and ultimately dismantled in 1945. The era name at the time of its establishment was Datong, followed three years later by Kangde. Datong lasted two years, and Kangde twelve.

Archaeological research in the Manchurian region had already been initiated by Ryuzo Torii from 1887–1896. From then on research occurred repeatedly until the Taisho period (1912–1926). In addition, Kosaku Hamada traveled to Manchuria from 1910 and Sozaburo Yagi from 1918, and research in the region was gradually carried out in earnest.

However, that work was principally superficial study and did not reach the level of all-out excavation.[18]

Organized, full-blown excavation was realized by the inception of the Far-Eastern Archaeological Society.[19] Excavations that took place in succession, such as P'i-tzu-wo (1927), Mu-yang-cheng (1928), Nang-shan-ri (1929) and Ying-cheng-tzu (1931), are representative of this time.

The Far-Eastern Archaeological Society was an organization that held an inaugural ceremony in March 1927 and aimed to conduct archaeological research in the East Asian region. The society conducted an excavation right away in the vicinity of Pulandian in the year of its launch. The society had already been eyeing organizing in the fall of 1925. In fact, in August 1926 a request for a government grant to study P'i-tzu-wo addressed to the Minister of Foreign Affairs (Baron Kijuro Shidehara) had already been submitted by the Far-Eastern Archaeological Society (Standing Committee: Kosaku Hamada, Yoshito Harada; Secretary: Kozaburo Shimamura).

Moreover, Manchukuo, which was formed in 1932, enacted and publicly announced the Historic Sites Preservation Act two years after the state's establishment on July 1, 1933. This act was revised in March 1934 and thereafter perpetually applied in Manchukuo.

In addition, in 1936 and beyond the Manchukuo State Council Culture Department conducted national research on historic sites and antiquities. Reports on that research reached as many as 80 volumes, but only the following five were published.

Manshukoku Koseki Kobutsu Chosa Hokokusho ("Research Report on Historic Sites and Antiquities in Manchukuo")
Vol. 1 "Historic Sites in Jinzhou Province" (Sozaburo Yagi)
Vol. 2 "Rehe from an Archaeological Perspective" (Sadahiko Shimada)
Vol. 3 "Research Report on Historic Sites in Jiandao Province" (Kiichi Toriyama, Ryosaku Fujita)
Vol. 4 "Historic Remains from the Jin Dynasty in Jilin and Binjiang Provinces" (Kazuki Sonoda)
Vol. 5 "Research Report on Ying Zi Historic Ruins in Yanji Province" (Ryosaku Fujita)

The administration of cultural assets in Manchukuo was carried out based on the Historic Sites Preservation Act, but jurisdiction belonged to the Public Welfare Department (later, the Culture Department). From 1940, Shunjo Miyake became involved as an investigator of cultural assets (and simultaneously held the post of Preservation Association Director).

The Far-Eastern Archaeological Society continued with active research even after the establishment of Manchukuo, and excavated at sites including Yang-téca-wa and Tung-ching-Ghéng (first stage: 1933), Tung-ching-Chéng (second stage: 1934) and Hung-Shan-han, Chin-feng (1935).

After the state's formation, archaeological studies were conducted in various locations in Manchuria by the Manchukuo State Council Public Welfare

Department (Culture Department), various provinces, museums, the Far-Eastern Archaeological Society and research groups organized through the sponsorship of people central to Japanese government, including Manmo Gakujutsu Chosa Kenkyudan (Manchuria and Mongolia Academic Research Group), Nichiman Bunka Kyokai (Japan-Manchuria Culture Association) and the Japan Society for the Promotion of Science.[20]

Among these various research groups, the Far-Eastern Archaeological Society played a large role.[21] In addition, research in Warman under the sponsorship of the Japan-Manchuria Culture Association on the three Liao tombs (Emperor Shengzong, Emperor Xingzong, Emperor Daozong) was conducted by scholars belonging to Kyoto Imperial University.[22]

Thus, archaeology in Manchukuo was conducted based on the leadership of Japanese government and academia, and carried out by the Far-Eastern Archaeological Society. The same was true for the operations of preservation institutions established in the different locations, including the Mukden Branch of the National Central Museum, Lüshunkou Museum and Harbin Museum (Liaoyang, Fushun, Dongjingcheng Mudanjiang Province, Lin Dong), local museums (Jinzhou) and galleries of treasures (Rehe). In particular, Sadahiko Shimada[23] (previously an assistant and teacher at Kyoto Imperial University Archaeology Department), who was director of the Lüshunkou Museum, played a significant role in archaeological exchange between Manchukuo and Japan, which was in command. Moreover, close attention must be paid to the fact that, similarly to Korea, the Japan Society for the Promotion of Science was deeply involved in archaeological research.

3. Northern China and Mengjiang Archaeology

The former provinces of Chahar and Suiyuan and the northern area of Shanxi were called Mengjiang or Hokushi (Northern China).

Japanese scholars were involved in archaeology studies in this area as far back as 1908 in a study conducted by Ryuzo Torii. It then fell outside the sphere of interest for a long time, but in 1930 Seiichi Mizuno and Namio Egami, exchange students from the Far-Eastern Archaeological Society, explored Mongolia and the northern extremities of China. Having gained knowledge related to microlith/bronze and cord-marked pottery,[24] on the suggestion of Egami, the Far-Eastern Archaeological Society dispatched a research group comprised of members in the fields of geology, paleontology, anthropology and archaeology to Silin-Gol and Ulan-Chap.[25] This study was aided by the Ministry of Foreign Affairs Cultural Affairs Department, the Harada Sekizenkai Foundation and Marquis Hosokawa.

The Far-Eastern Archaeological Society subsequently conducted an excavation of Shangto in Duolun in 1937.[26] This study headed by Yoshito Harada and Kazuchika Komai was entirely funded by the Ministry of Foreign Affairs Cultural Affairs Department.

From 1941 to 1943, tombs from the Han Dynasty were excavated in Yanggao Province, Mengjiang. They are Pei-cha-tch'eng, Wan-ngan and Ku-chéng-Pu, Yang-kao. These grave mounds, the former called *karyotai* and the latter *koryotai*, have legends about fanciful mountains of foods, but lore about the tombs did not exist.

Seiichi Mizuno, who studied the Yungang Grottoes in Datong, focused on these mounds and conducted excavations as projects for the Far-Eastern Archaeological Society.

The excavation of Pei-cha-tch'eng, Wan-ngan was headed by Mizuno. It targeted three tombs and confirmed that they dated from the Han Dynasty.[27] This excavation was sponsored by the Daido Sekibutsu Hozon Kyokai (Datong Association for the Preservation of Stone Buddhist Images) and funded by the Mongolian government at the request of the Far-Eastern Archaeological Society.

Excavation of Ku-chéng-Pu, Yang-kao targeted three foundations. It took place from 1942 to 1943 and was headed by Katsutoshi Ono, Takeo Hibino and Seiichi Mizuno.[28] The organizers were the Daido Sekibutsu Hozon Kyosankai (Datong Support Association for the Preservation of Stone Buddhist Images) and the Yanggaoken Shiseki Hozon Kyokai (Yanggao Province Society for the Preservation of Historic Sites).

Archaeological digs at Pei-cha-tch'eng and the old castle fortifications determined the sites to be tombs from the Han Dynasty. However, notably, the discovery of an abundance of grave goods in the old castle fortifications not only increased people's amazement about the world of archaeology, but also provided such a satisfying result that it caught the attention of relevant individuals in Japan. The outcomes of this excavation of old castle fortifications immediately led to a meeting in Kyoto.

At that meeting, Hibino and Mizuno gave lectures at the second conference of the Greater East Asia Academic Association. The lecture held on December

19, 1942 was titled, "Recent Archaeological Discoveries in Mengjiang," and its content was published as *Daitoa Gakujutsu Soshi* 1 ("Academic Records of Greater East Asia").[29] The Greater East Asia Academic Association was founded in June 1942 to research the natural features, ethnic groups, and cultures of the Greater East Asia Co-Prosperity Sphere, and generally to make known the research results with the aim of aiding the construction of a new culture of Greater East Asia. Therefore, the results of the excavation on the old castle fortifications were truly appropriate to generally making known and expanding the outcomes of various academic research on the Greater East Asia Co-Prosperity Sphere during the building of Greater East Asia. It was truly deeply significant for being conducted in Mengjiang, and furthermore, by the Japanese, where academic research on ancient burial mounds had yet to be conducted in mainland China.

Hibino and Ono, who were in charge of the excavation and report, were government scholars dispatched by Toho Bunka Kenkyusho (Research Institute for Cultural Treasures of the East) after an invitation from the Mongolian government.

Research on the Yungang Grottoes was an archaeological study in Mengjiang that garnered further attention.

Grottoes from the Northern Wei Dynasty that exist in Yungang in the west of Datong Prefecture, Shanxi Province (21 large caves, 20 medium-sized caves, and countless small Buddhist altar niches) were introduced by Chuta Ito in 1902, but this study, conducted from 1938 to 1944, was undertaken by researchers belonging to Toho Bunka Gakuin Kyoto Kenkyusho (Toho Culture Academy Kyoto Research Institute) headed by Seiichi Mizuno and Toshio Nagahiro.[30] The study clarified the actual state of the Yungang Grottoes, such as the five caves of Tanyao.

Prior to studying the Yungang Grottoes, Mizuno and Nagahiro studied caves in The Buddhist Cave-Templer of Hsang-T'arg-sso[31] and Longmen[32] in March-May 1936 as part of research on caves in Northern China in the lead up to full-out study on the Yungang Grottoes. However, that research was quite eventful as it took place in unfavorable conditions. During work at Xiang-tang-shan shi-ku carried out April 10-15, the Ci County and Pengcheng police provided guard and were on constant patrol; while at Luoyang during research April 24-29, the locals were inhospitable, security was insufficient, and government officials and police exhibited an anti-Japanese attitude. Particularly when researching Longmen, they were accompanied by several police on bicycles as escorts who kept watch.

The study of the Yungang Grottoes was carried out within this environment.[33]

Archaeology in Mengjiang focused on excavations of Han Dynasty tombs implemented by persons related to the Far-Eastern Archaeological Society, and research on caves in Northern China by scholars belonging to Toho Culture Academy Kyoto Research Institute (Toho Culture Research Institute).

4. Archaeology in the Battlegrounds of Central China

After the Marco Polo Bridge Incident on July 7, 1937 (which led to the Second Sino Japanese War), Japan expanded the war and seized Nanjing on December 13. Nanjing was abandoned, and an immense volume of archaeological finds from Yinxu, Yin-mu and other places in Anyang in Henan Province related to research by the Institute of History and Philology were put into order.[34] Sueji Umehara was placed in charge of the archaeology department.

Along with these organizational activities by Umehara, of note is the dispatch of a party of scholars to the Chinese continent from Keio University. This planned academic tour was proposed by Joe Shibata and implemented in three groups lead by Kashiwa Oyama (Datong, Zhang Wei, Beijing), Shibata (Central Shina (China)) and Nobuhiro Matsumoto (various locations in Central China).

The report by the Central China group, *Konan Tosa*[35] ("Archaeological Studies at Nanking and Hangchac," FY1938) paints a vivid picture of the actual circumstances of the expedition. Shinzo Koizumi, who contributed the forward, wrote, "In late 1938, Nanjing fell and, shortly after entering a new phase in which the state of the war became significant, historians at Keio University Faculty of Letters proposed that immediately going to China to conduct academic study and archaeological digs for ancient ruins was imperative. As a result of deliberations, three groups were dispatched for an academic tour in May 1938. At the time, although the hostilities had not long been over, it felt good for the scholars to vie to explain the necessity of academic study." In the Central Shina group, Saburo Hosaka (graduate school) and Hideo Nishioka (student) participated under Matsumoto and went to Nanjing, Hangzhou (Gudang Shihushan ruins) and Shanghai. The initial plan was primarily to conduct an excavation, and the organization of existing specimens in Chinese museums was not really under consideration. However, in the end, the tour became an endeavor to organize the Institute of History and Philology, Ceramic Research Institute, and Institute for the Preservation of Antiquities in Nanjing, conduct exploratory digs at the Gudang Shihushan ruins in Hangzhou, and inspect the Asian Society Museum. Exploratory digging at the Gudang Shihushan ruins in Hangzhou turned up brick tomb chambers from the late Han Dynasty in the early period of the Six Dynasties, and insight was gained into the chronological view of Hei-tao pottery.

Umehara went to Nanjing and engaged in organizational activities immediately after Nanjing was seized, and Shibata very quickly proposed sending an academic research team to the continent of China. These two scholars were directly and indirectly connected to the "state." Umehara was an assistant professor at Kyoto Imperial University; Shibata was an assistant at Tokyo Imperial University, held positions in the Home Ministry and Ministry of Education, and also worked as a teacher at Keio University.

After the seizure, other archaeological schemes (an expression by Umehara) that were a part of pacification work were naturally implemented under government leadership.

This kind of movement was accepted in every region of the Greater East Asia Co-Prosperity Sphere. Moreover, it was not at all uncommon for archaeology researchers in the private sector to be enlisted and sent outside of Japan.

It is difficult to know what it feels like for a researcher to deal with a battleground as a soldier, but there is documentation on an archaeological experience that happened to a certain archaeologist on the battlefield.[36]

The *Asahi Shimbun* ("Asahi Newspaper") dated December 16, 1943, carried a two-column article titled, "Well done, soldier-scholar."

Special dispatch from Nanjing on the 14th: In the midst of battling anti-Japanese forces, a single soldier by chance dug up a nearly intact jar-shaped vessel from 3,000 years ago, providing an artifact valuable to the study of culture in Central China in the Neolithic Age. Private Teruya Esaka from the Central China XX Unit (from 1042 Akatsutsumi-cho, Setagaya-ku, Tokyo) studied archaeology under the guidance of his teacher, Ichiro Yawata at the Department of Cultural Anthropology at the University of Tokyo. Furthermore, after working as a junior assistant at the Department of Earth Science at Bunri University, he is now conducting research in archaeology at the Department of History, Faculty of Letters, Keio University. He is a young and energetic student who came to the battlefront after being drafted, and participated in XX military operations at the end of this past November. While marching near Matsuryoseki in the Jiangning District approx. 25 km south of Nanjing, he keenly spotted a piece of a jar along a loess cliff facing northwest in the suburb of Shoshyanteo. He dug it out, carried it home, and researched literature to find that this jar dates from around the late Neolithic Age to the Spring and Autumn period and the Warring States period, and is at least 3,000 years old.

This article in Tokyo's *Asahi Newspaper* was a special dispatch widely reported as news from the Continent in Nanjing at the time.

In 1943, the expanded battle lines of the Japanese forces had to be increasingly walked back after Japan's withdrawal from Guadalcanal in February, the complete destruction of the Attu garrison in May, and the country's September retreat from the absolute defense perimeter strategy, which necessitated falling back from the line of defense that ran from the Mariana Islands to the Caroline Islands and West New Guinea. Meanwhile, around the time these dark clouds were gathering, articles on soldier-scholars were run in daily newspapers that communicated news such as a farewell party held on October 21 at the outer garden of Meiji-jingu Shrine for students before they departed to the battlefront.

The news reporting on the jar discovered to the south of Nanjing by Esaka, a soldier in the 101st detached unit to China (Nanjing Defense Command), was useful in suggesting the military operation in the Nanjing region was going well, and could be described as effectively communicating that there was a sense of calm in the region.

This news favorably impressed the top ranks in the army, and on December 25 and 26 Esaka was able to once again research the site where the jar was excavated. His re-examination was conducted together with individuals such as Isao Taki and Etsuji Tanida from the Research Division of the Government Committee for the Preservation of Cultural Artifacts, and Seiichi Wajima from the Tokyo Imperial University Department of Cultural Anthropology. Earthenware fragments identical to the jar were collected in the vicinity.

Esaka immediately wrote about the outcome and submitted it to

Jinruigaku Zasshi ("Journal of Anthropology"), a bulletin of the Society of Anthropology in Tokyo. The paper, entitled "Ancient Earthenware Discovered in Matsuryoseki," was completed on December 28. It was also published in the March 1944 issue of the *Journal of Anthropology* Vol. 59 No. 3.

The jar discovered in Shoshyanteo outside of Matsuryoseki in the Jiangning District of Jiangsu Province was a black ceramic vessel. The opening measured 12.5 cm in diameter, the height 14 cm, and the bottom diameter 16.5 cm. Earthenware fragments collected nearby were also of the same marked earthenware. The discovery of the Shoshyanteo ruins southwest of Matsuryoseki was reported to academia.

The end of the report states, "I am sincerely grateful to the local military authorities who provided diverse support, and particularly to Chief of Staff Yamashita and Captain Sakata." This speaks to the fact it was written while serving in the military in the Jiangnan (Nanjing) Tobirokuichi Command.

Around this time, Esaka wrote an essay while in Jiangnan, entitled "Archaeology Viewed from the Battle Lines." This essay was published in the June 1944 issue of *Kobijutsu* ("Antiques") Vol. 14 No. 6 (Tsukan No. 161). Though a short article of two, A5-sized pages, the text expresses his evident joy at focusing on archaeology for a moment while in the field of war. He wrote, "Imperial Army stations in the Greater East Asian War are located nearly over the entire Greater East Asia Co-Prosperity Sphere. The majority of these places are uneducated." The text concludes, "Just as we cannot be neglectful of military service in the current battlefront, we students of archaeology stationed on the battle lines hope to carry out our duty of aiding the ethnic policy in the Greater East Asia War by being vigilant at all times in our endeavor to gather artifacts." This communicated the thoughts of an archaeology researcher who found himself on the battlefield. Of course, this was Esaka's impression, but it goes without saying that his profound daily thoughts compelled the discovery of the Shoshyanteo ruins. Esaka said, "There are museums of varying sizes in cities in each area of the Co-Prosperity Sphere. The archaeological artifacts from the areas housed in these museums were roughly organized and reported on by Western scholars in the past." However, he points out that, "If we who live in East Asia and are researching the ancient culture of this region can view them, we may discover many research aspects not comprehended by Western scholars." That sentiment can be said to have once inspired the research team from Keio University headed by Nobuhiro Matsumoto to explore the Jiangnan region and obtain comparable outcomes.

Afterword

Archaeology in Japan in the early Showa period corresponds to a time when steps were taken to supersede even the highest level of enlightenment based on archaeological outcomes from the Taisho period. These included chronological research on Jomon pottery, basic research on the wet-rice farming theory of Yayoi culture, establishing Yayoi pottery chronology, and research on the four-period chronology of ancient Imperial graves, temple ruins from the Asuka period, and tile designs. That was a steady step toward establishing archaeology as a science represented by the Minerva debate, which is founded on the outcomes of Jomon pottery chronology. It was also a time when, along with the rise of archaeological research in the private sector represented by the launch of the Tokyo Koko Gakkai (Tokyo Archaeology Society), publications impacted the world of archaeology in Japan. In addition to the already existing *Kokogaku Zasshi* ("Journal of the Archaeological Society," published by the Archaeology Society) and *Jinruigaku Zasshi* ("Journal of Anthropology") and *Tokyo Jinruigaku* ("Tokyo Anthropology"), both published by The Anthropological Society of Nippon), other publications were also launched. These included *Kokogaku* ("Archaeology"), the bulletin of the Tokyo Archaeology Society; *Kokogaku Ronso* ("Collection of Essays on Archaeology," published by the Society of Archaeological Studies); *Shizengaku Zasshi* ("Paleethnology Journal," published by Shizen Gakkai (Society of Paleethnology); and *Senshi Kokogaku* ("Prehistoric Archaeology"; published by Senshi Koko Gakkai [Prehistoric Archaeology Society]).

However, after the Second Sino-Japanese War of 1937, the concept of a New Order in East Asia, followed by the Greater East Asia Co-Prosperity Sphere, gradually took hold in the world of archaeology as well. It was a way for Japan to extend its reach toward colonies, and a movement that symbolized the systemization and activities of the Far-Eastern Archaeological Society/Association of East Archaeology with archaeological studies by the Imperial universities at the core.

Manchuria and the Far-Eastern Archaeological Society/Japan-Manchuria Culture Association, Korea and the Society for Studying Historic Sites in

Korea, and Manchuria/Korea and the Japan Society for the Promotion of Science were directly connected to archaeology in the colonies as associations; they were linked to archaeology in the Greater East Asia Co-Prosperity Sphere. It was the same for Mengjiang.[37] The expenses necessary for those "archaeological schemes" were funded by bodies such as the Ministry of Foreign Affairs (Cultural Affairs Department), the Ministry of the Imperial Household and the Japan Society for the Promotion of Science. Their existence truly contributed to national policy.

This trend reached not only archaeology at the Imperial universities, but also archaeology in private universities. In addition, three archaeology research groups in the private sector (Tokyo Archaeology Society, Society of Archaeological Studies, Chubu Archaeology Society) merged to create the Nihon Kodai Bunka Gakkai (Japan Society of Ancient Culture).

In the early Showa period, many new perspectives were academically presented in fields of individual research, but archaeology was not unrelated to the tides of the times.

The Japanese people's comprehension of the history of archaeology in Japan has tended to focus on the boundaries of Japan proper. However, we can understand the macroscopic history of archaeology in Japan by also turning our attention overseas.

Notes

1. For example, this includes the publication of *Studies on the History of Japanese Archaeology* by the Kyoto Mokuyo Club (first issued in 1992; historical research on archaeological publications by Seiichi Yanagisawa ("The Minerva Debate & Archaeology in the Founding of a State—A Slice of Archaeological History Viewed from the History of Publication"; *The Lives of Our Ancestors* and other publications by Shuichi Goto; *Senshi Kokogaku Kenkyu* ("Prehistoric Archaeology Study") 3, 1990; critical biographies by Wako Anasawa ("The Path of Dr. Yukio Kobayashi" and "A Discussion on Sueji Umehara," *Kokogaku Kyoto Gakuha* (Kyoto University Archaeology), edited by Bunei Tsunoda, 1944).
2. Jiujiro Nakaya. *Nihon Senshigakujoshi* ("Prehistory of Japan," 1935).
3. Seiichi Wajima. *"Nihon Kokogaku no Hattatsu to Kagakuteki Seishin"* ("The Development of Japanese Archaeology and the Scientific Spirit"), *Yuibutsuron Kenkyu* ("Study of Materialism") 60/62, 1937), "Nihon Kokogaku no Hattatsu— Hattatsu no Shodankai" ("The Development of Japanese Archaeology—The

Many Stages of Development"), (*Nihon Kokogaku Koza* ("Studies on Archaeology in Japan") 2, 1955).
4. Kenji Kiyono. *Nihon Kokogaku/Jinruigakushi* ("Japanese Archaeology & Anthropology," Vol. 1, 2, 1954, 1956) and *Nihon Jinshuron Hensenshi* ("History of Japanese Theory of Race," 1944).
5. Yukio Kobayashi. "*Kokogakushi/Nihon*" ("History of Archaeology in Japan") (*Sekai Kokogaku Taikei* ("Summary of World Archaeology") 16, 1962).
6. Yoshiro Kondo. "*Sengo Nihon Kokogaku no Hansei to Kadai*" ("Post-war Archaeology in Japan: Reflection and Issues"), *Nihon Kokogaku no Shomondai* ("Issues in Japanese Archaeology," 1964).
7. Tadashi Saito. *Nihon no Hakkutsu* ("Japanese Excavations," 1963; expanded edition 1982), *Nihon Kokogakushi* ("History of Japanese Archaeology," 1974); *Nihon Kokogakushi Shiryo Shusei* ("Compilation of Historic Documents on Japanese Archaeology," 1979); *Nenpyo de Miru Nihon no Hakkutsu/Hakkenshi* ("History of Japanese Excavations & Discoveries Viewed Chronologically") (1) Nara period–Taisho period, (2) Showa period," 1980, 1982; *Nihon Kokogakushi Jiten* ("Lexicon of Japanese Archaeology," 1984), *Kokogakushi no Hitobito* ("Figures in the History of Archaeology," 1985); *Nihon Kokogakushi no Tenkai* ("Historical Development of Japanese Archaeology"; *Nihon Kokogaku Kenkyu* ("Japanese Archaeology Research") 3, 1990); *Nihon Kokogaku Yogo Jiten* ("Dictionary of Terminology for Japanese Archaeology," 1992); *Nihon Kokogakushi Nenpyo* ("Chronology Table of Japanese Archaeology," 1993), etc. For texts by Sakazume on Saito's academic research, refer to: "*Saito Tadashi-sensei no Nihon Kokogakushi Kenkyu*" ("Research on Japanese Archaeology by Tadashi Saito"); *Kokogaku Soko* ("Thoughts on Archaeology," Vol. 2, 1988); "*Nihon Kokogakushi Kenkyu Kinkyo*" ("Recent State of Historical Research on Japanese Archaeology"), later revised to *Nihon Kokogaku no Churyo* ("Trends in Japanese Archaeology," 1990).
8. Mitsunori Tozawa. "*Nihon Kokogakushi to Sono Haikei*" ("History & Background of Japanese Archaeology") (*Nihon Kokogaku wo Manabu* ("Learn About Japanese Archaeology") 1, 1978).
9. Masaki Kudo. *Kenkyushi/Nihon Jinshuron* ("Historical Study on Japanese Theory of Race," 1979).
10. Akira Teshigawara. *Nihon Kokogakushi—Nenpyo to Kaisetsu* ("History of Japanese Archaeology—Chronology & Explanation," 1988).
11. Hideichi Sakazume. *Manshukoku/Kotoku Juichi Nen no Koko Jijo* ("Manchukuo 1945: The State of Archaeology," *Kobunka Danso* ("Journal of Ancient Cultural Studies," 30 Vol. 2, 1993); "*Nihon Kokogakushi Shui—Toa Koko Gakkai/Toho Kokogaku Kyokai to Nihon Kodai Bunka Gakkai*" ("Insights on the History of Japanese Archaeology—The Far-Eastern Archaeological Society/Association of East Archaeology & Japan Society of Ancient Culture"), *The Journal of the Department of Literature, Rissho University* 99, 1994), etc.

12. An example can be seen in *Toa Kokogaku Gaikan* ("Outline of Far-Eastern Archaeological," 1950) by Sueji Umehara. In this work, the author writes primarily about lecture content conducted in various places in French Indochina as "a Japan-Vietnam exchange professor" in December 1942; it was completed in July 1945. The aim of the lectures was to introduce "achievements in Far-Eastern Archaeological by past Japanese academics." There were nine volumes of recorded text, including "*Chosen ni okeru Kandai Iseki no Chosa & Sono Gyoseki*" ("Studies of Han Dynasty Ruins in Korea & Their Achievements"); "*Chosen Jodai Iseki no Chosa—Tokuni Kokuri no Hekiga ni tsuite*" ("Studies on Ancient Ruins in Korea—Particularly Wall Paintings in Goguryeo"); "*Minami Manshu toki ni Kantoshu no Shizen Bunbutsu ni kansuru Shinkenkai*" ("A New View on Prehistoric Cultural Assets in Kwantung in South Manchuria"); and "*Saikin Nihongakusha no Okonatta Shina no Kokogaku Chosa nit suite*" ("Recent Archaeological Studies on China by Japanese Academics").
13. Concerning this issue, Yoshiro Kondo succinctly pointed out that archaeological research in Korea, China, etc. by Japanese academics came about and developed in close relation to Japan's invasion of Asia. With aid from the invading government, archaeology was carried out with help and protection from military authorities and governing institutions in each area. (See literature cited in Note 6.)
14. This classification is by Sakazume. The early stage spans from the start of the Showa period until the end of the Asia-Pacific War. The middle stage spans from the year after the war until around the publication of *Nihon no Kokogaku* ("Archaeology in Japan"), which is described as a post-war summarization of research results in Japanese archaeology. The subsequent late stage lasted until the end of the Showa period. The time from around the end of the middle stage and the start of the late stage was particularly a period when "preliminary excavations" according to "development" became large in scale, and "government excavations" became commonplace. Therefore, the period was provisionally extended to 1965, but there was a transition between the middle and late stages up until around 1970.
15. Ryosaku Fujita. "*Chosen Koseki Chosa*" ("Research on Historic Sites in Korea," *Kobunka no Hozon to Kenkyu* ("Preserving and Researching Ancient Cultures," 1953), later *Chosengaku Ronko* ("Discussion on Korean Studies," 1963). Regarding the Society for Studying Historic Sites in Korea, in addition to its issued reports and research papers published by Kyoichi Arimitsu in *Arimitsu Kyoichi Chosakushu* ("Collection of Works by Kyoichi Arimitsu," Vol. 2, 1992), refer to works such as *Chosen Kodai Iseki no Henreki* ("Traveling to Ancient Sites in Korea," 1986) by Akio Koizumi and *Toa Kokogaku no Hattatsu* (Development of Archaeology in the Far East," 1948) by Seiichi Mizuno.
16. The annual *Koseki Chosa Hokoku* was published three times from FY1936–FY1938. It was not published after FY1939.

17. Refer to Note 11 for information including the circumstances of the establishment of the Far-Eastern Archaeological Society.
18. The history of archaeology in Manchuria is detailed in *Manshu Kokogaku Gaisetsu* ("Outline of Archaeology in Manchuria," 1944) by Shunjo Miyaki; *Chugoku Tohoku Chiku Kokogaku Gaisetsu* ("Outline of Archaeology in the Northeast Region of China," 1989) by Li Lian Yi; *Tohoku Ajia Kokogaku no Kenkyu* ("Research on Archaeology in Northeast Asia," 1975); *Zai—Man Nijuroku Nen—Iseki Tansa to Waga Jinsei no Kaiso* ("Twenty-Six Years—A Refection on Exploring Archaeological Ruins and Our Life," 1985); and *Chugoku Tohoku Iseki Tanbo* ("Searching for Archaeological Ruins in Northeast China," 1992). However, *Toa Kokogaku no Hattatsu* ("Development of Archaeology in the Far East," noted earlier) by Seiichi Mizuno contains even more detail.
19. The Far-Eastern Archaeological Society's report, *Toho Kokogaku Sokan* ("Archaeologia Orientalis") published 5 class A booklets and 8 class B booklets.
20. The achievements of Shunjo Miyake are known as independent investigations, but *Hanrajo—Bokkai no Iseki Chosa—* ("Ban-la-cheng—Research on Bohai Archaeological Ruins," 1942) by Jinpei Saito and *Hanrajo to Hoka no Shiseki* ("Ban-la-cheng & Other Historic Sites," 1973) cannot be ignored.
21. As for Far-Eastern Archaeological, in addition to excavation studies in Machukuo, the Mongolia research group was dispatched to the Ulanqab region and Xilinhot region in Inner Mongolia twice, once in 1931 and again in 1935. *Moko Kogen Odanki* ("Diary of Travels Across the Mongolian Highlands," 1937; revised edition 1941) is a record of that. Observations during this exploration (Namio Egami) directly prompted the Qing-ling study of the three Liao tombs by the Japan-Manchuria Culture Association.
22. Jitsuzo Tamura, Yukio Kobayashi. *Keiryo* ("Qing-ling," 1953); Jitsuzo Tamura *Keiryo no Hekiga* ("Qing-ling Wall Paintings," 1972), *Keiryo Chosa Kiko* ("Travelogue of the Qing-ling Investigation," 1994).
23. *Koko Zuihitsu Keikanko* ("Archaeological Essays on Cockscomb Jars," 1936) by Sadahiko Shimada is an important writing that conveys a glimpse into the circumstances of archaeology of Manchukuo at that time, along with *Manshuu Kokogaku Gaisetsu* ("Outline of Archaeology in Manchuria"; previously cited in Note 18) by Shunjo Miyake. It is touched on in Hideichi Sakazume's *Manshukoku/Kotoku Juichi Nen no Koko Jijyo* ("Manchukuo 1945: The State of Archaeology"), *Kobunka Danso* ("Journal of Ancient Cultural Studies," 30 Vol. 2, 1993).
24. Namio Egami, Seiichi Mizuno. *Uchimoko/Chojo Chitai* ("Inner Mongolia and the Great Wall Area," *Toho Kokogaku Sokan* ("Archaeologia Orientalis," class B, 1 booklet, 1935).
25. Reports on the fields of geology, paleontology and anthropology were publicized as *Moko Kogen* ("The Mongolian Highlands," Vol. 1), *Toho Kokogaku Sokan* ("Archaeologia Orientalis," class B, 4 booklets, 1943).

26. Yoshito Harada, Kazuchika Komai. *Shangtu* (*Toho Kokogaku Sokan* ("Archaeologia Orientalis," class B, 2 booklets, 1941).
27. Seiichi Mizuno, Uichi Okazaki. *Pei-cha-tch'eng, Wan-ngan, Toho Kokogaku Sokan* ("Archaeologia Orientalis," class B, 5 booklets, 1946).
28. Katsutoshi Ono, Takeo Hibino. *"Ku-Chéng-Pu-Yang-kao"* ("Old Castle Fortifications in Ku-Chend-Pu Yanggao"), *Toho Kokogaku Sokan* ("Archaeologia Orientalis," class B, 8 booklets, 1990).
29. Research on old castle fortifications was made public by the research group in *Mocho Yokoken Kanbocho Chosa Ryakuho* ("Brief Summary of Research on Han Dynasty Tombs in Yanggao, Mengjiang," 1943; published by Osaka/Yamato Shoin), and by Ono and Hibino who were in charge of research in *Mocho Kokoki* ("Archaeology Diaries on Mengjiang," 1946) based primarily on research diaries. The official report (Note 28) was published in the 48th year after the excavation.
30. Seiichi Mizuno, Toshio Nagahiro. *Unko Sekkutsu* ("Yum-Kang," 16 volumes, 1951–1957).
31. Toshio Nagahiro, Seiichi Mizuno. *Kahoku Jiken, Kanan-buankyo Dosan Sekkutsu* ("Xiangtangshan Caves in Tzu-hsien Prefecture in Hebei and Wu'an in Henan," 1937).
32. Seiichi Mizuno, Toshio Nagahiro. *Konan Rakuyo Ryumon Sekkutsu no Kenkyu* ("Research on the Longmen Caves in Luoyang, Henan," 1941).
33. Concerning research on the Yungkang Grottoes, Seiichi Mizuno published *Unko Sekibutsugun—Toho Bunka Kenkyusho Unko Sekkutsu Chosa Gaiho* ("Yungkang Stone Buddhist Images—Toho Culture Research Institute Yungkang Grottoes Research Summary Report," 1944) ahead of the official report (Note 30), but publications on research also include: *Unko no Sekkutsu to Sono Jidai* ("The Yun-gkang kshika & That Period," 1939; partially revised in 1952) by Mizuno; *Daido no Sekibutsu* ("Stone Buddhist Images in Datong," 1946) by Mizuno and Nagahiro; *Unko Sekkutsu* ("Yungang Grottoes"; 2 volumes in *Chugoku Bunka Shiseki* ("Historic Cultural Sites in China," 1976) by Nagahiro; and *Unko Nikki—Taisenchuu no Bukkyo Sekkutsu Chosa* ("Yungang Diary—Study of Buddhist Caves During the Great War," 1988). In particular, Yungang Diary is Nagahiro's record of the research in 1939, 1941, 1942 and 1944, and readers can gain an understanding of the state of Mengjiang from 1935 to 1944.
34. Sueji Umehara. *"Kinnen Waga Gakusha no Okonauta Shina no Kokogakuteki Chosa ni tsuite"* ("Recent Archaeological Studies on China Conducted by Japanese Academics"), *Toa Kokogaku Gaikan* ("Outline of Far-Eastern Archaeological"), previously cited.
35. Nobuhiro Matsumoto, Saburo Hosaka, Hideo Nishioka. *Konan Tosa* ("Field Investigation of Jiangnan"; FY1938) (research report, Department of History, Faculty of Letters, Keio University, class A, 1 booklet, 1941).
36. This was the experience of Teruya Esaka who was directly asked about it, but

at the outset there was a problem involving "*Sekkosho Jikeiken Joshotomongai Iseki*" ("Ruins Outside the East Castle Gate in Cixi District, Zhejiang," *Shigaku* ("Historical Science," 26-1/2, 1952). That is, in the same text a survey drawing of stoneware was presented, but in regard to earthenware only a description was given, so the issue was whether earthenware existed. The topic was then shifted to the Matsuryoseki ruins in the Jiangning District of Jiangsu, and Esaka provided information on the background of the excavation. At that time, his name was presented in the *Asahi News*, etc. It is an extremely valuable experience of how one enlisted archaeologist handled archaeology in the battlefield, and with his permission his insights should be made note of.
37. In addition to Korea, Manchuria, Mengjiang, and north and central China, Hu Wan, Southeast Asia, and Sakhalin should also be examined.

References

Egami, N. and Mizuno, S. (1935). Uchimoko/Chojo Chitai (Inner Mongolia and the Great Wall Area). *Toho Kokogaku Sokan* (Archaeologia Orientalis) *class B, 1 booklet.* Shinjidaisha.
Fujita, R. (1953). Chosen Koseki Chosa (Research on Historic Sites in Korea). *Kobunka no Hozon to Kenkyu* (Preserving and Researching Ancient Cultures). Kuroita hakushi kinenkai.
Fujita, R. (1963). *Chosengaku Ronko* (Discussion on Korean Studies). Fujita sensei kinen jigyokai.
Harada, Y. and Komai, K. (1941). Shangdu. *Toho Kokogaku Sokan* (Archaeologia Orientalis) *class B, 2 booklets.* Toa kokogakkai.
Kiyono, K. (1954, 1956). *Nihon Kokogaku/Jinruigakushi 1, 2* (Japanese Archaeology & Anthropology). Iwanami shoten.
Kiyono, K. (1944). *Nihon Jinshuron Hensenshi* (History of Japanese Theory of Race).
Kobayashi, Y. (1962). Kokogakushi/Nihon (History of Archaeology in Japan). *Sekai Kokogaku Taikei* (Summary of World Archaeology) *16*. Heibonsha.
Koizumi, A. (1986). *Chosen Kodai Iseki no Henreki* (Traveling to Ancient Sites in Korea). Rokko shuppan.
Kondo, Y. (1964). Sengo Nihon Kokogaku no Hansei to Kadai (Post-war Archaeology in Japan: Reflection and Issues). *Nihon Kokogaku no Shomondai* (Issues in Japanese Archaeology). Kokogaku kenkyukai jyussyunen kinenronbun kankokai
Kudo, M. (1979). *Kenkyushi/Nihon Jinshuron* (Historical Study on Japanese Theory of Race).
Li. L. Y. (1989). *Chugoku Tohoku Chiku Kokogaku Gaisetsu* (Outline of Archaeology in the Northeast Region of China).
Li. L.Y. (1975). *Tohoku Ajia Kokogaku no Kenkyu* (Research on Archaeology in

Northeast Asia). Tohoku Ajia kobunka kenkyujyo.
Matsumoto, N., Hosaka, S., and Nishioka, H. (1941). *Konan Tosa* (Field Investigation of Jiangnan; FY1938). (Research report, Department of History, Faculty of Letters, Keio University, class A, 1 booklet). Mita shigakkai.
Miyake, S. (1944). *Manshu Kokogaku Gaisetsu* (Outline of Archaeology in Manchuria). Manshu jijyo annaijyo.
Miyake, S. (1985). *Zai—Man Nijuroku Nen—Iseki Tansa to Waga Jinsei no Kaiso* (Twenty-Six Years—A Refection on Exploring Archaeological Ruins and Our Life). Miyake chugoku kodaibunka chosashitsu.
Miyake, S. (1992). *Chugoku Tohoku Iseki Tanbo* (Searching for Archaeological Ruins in Northeast China). Tohoku Ajia kobunka kenkyujyo.
Mizuno, S. (1939). *Unko no Sekkutsu to Sono Jidai* (The Yungkang Grottoes & That Period). Fuzambo.
Mizuno, S. and Nagahiro, T. (1941). *Konan Rakuyo Ryumon Sekkutsu no Kenkyu* (Research on the Longmen Caves in Luoyang, Henan). Zauhoukankokai.
Mizuno, S. (1944). *Unko Sekibutsugun—Toho Bunka Kenkyusho Unko Sekkutsu Chosa Gaiho* (Yungkang Stone Buddhist Images—Toho Culture Research Institute Yungkang Grottoes Research Summary Report). Asahi shimbun Osaka honsha.
Mizuno, S. and Okazaki, U. (1946). *Pei-cha-tch'eng, Wan-ngan*, in *Toho Kokogaku Sokan* (Archaeologia Orientalis) *class B, 5 booklets*. Zauhokankokai.
Mizuno, S. and Nagahiro, T. (1946). *Daido no Sekibutsu* (Stone Buddhist Images in Datong). Zauhokankokai.
Mizuno, S. (1948). *Toa Kokogaku no Hattatsu* (Development of Archaeology in the Far East). Oyashima shuppan.
Mizuno, S. and Nagahiro, T. (1951-1957). *Unko Sekkutsu* (Yum-Kang) *16 volumes*. Kyotodaigaku jinbunkagaku kenkyujyo.
Mizuno, S. and Nagahiro, T. (1976). Unko Sekkutsu (Yungang Grottoes). *2 volumes in Chugoku Bunka Shiseki* (Historic Cultural Sites in China).
Nagahiro, T. and Mizuno, S. (1937). *Kahoku Jiken, Kananbuankyo Dosan Sekkutsu* (Xiangtangshan Caves in Tzu-hsien Prefecture in Hebei and Wu'an in Henan). Tohobunkagakuin Kyoto kenkyujyo.
Nagahiro, T. (1988). *Unko Nikki—Taisenchuu no Bukkyo Sekkutsu Chosa* (Yungang Diary—Study of Buddhist Caves During the Great War). NHK books.
Nakaya, J. Mizuno, S. and Nagahiro, T. (1941). *Konan Rakuyo Ryumon Sekkutsu no Kenkyu* (Research on the Longmen Caves in Luoyang, Henan).
Nakaya, J. (1935). *Nihon Senshigakujoshi* (Prehistory of Japan). Iwanami shoten.
Ono, K. and Hibino, T. (1990). Yoko Kojoho (Old Castle Fortifications in Yanggao). *Toho Kokogaku Sokan* (Archaeologia Orientalis). *class B, 8 booklets*. Rokko shuppan.
Saito, J. (1942). *Hanrajo—Bokkai no Iseki Chosa—* (Ban-la-cheng—Research on Bohai Archaeological Ruins). Hunchun County Public Office.

Saito, J. (1973). *Hanrajo to Hoka no Shiseki* (Ban-la-cheng & Other Historic Sites). Hanrajoshi kankokai.
Saito, T. (1974). *Nihon Kokogakushi* (History of Japanese Archaeology). Yoshikawa kobunkan.
Saito, T. (1979). *Nihon Kokogakushi Shiryo Shusei* (Compilation of Historic Documents on Japanese Archaeology).Yoshikawa kobunkan.
Saito, T. (1980, 1982). *Nenpyo de Miru Nihon no Hakkutsu/Hakkenshi (1) Nara period–Taisho period, (2) Showa period* (History of Japanese Excavations & Discoveries Viewed Chronologically). NHK books.
Saito, T. (1982). *Nihon no Hakkutsu* (Japanese Excavations). Tokyodaigaku shuppankai.
Saito, T. (1984). *Nihon Kokogakushi Jiten* (Lexicon of Japanese Archaeology). Tokyodo shuppan.
Saito, T. (1985). *Kokogakushi no Hitobito* (Figures in the History of Archaeology). Daiichi shobo.
Saito, T. (1990). *Nihon Kokogakushi no Tenkai* (Historical Development of Japanese Archaeology). Gakuseisha.
Saito, T. (1990). *Nihon Kokogaku Kenkyu* (Japanese Archaeology Research) *3*. Gakuseisha.
Saito, T. (1992). *Nihon Kokogaku Yogo Jiten* (Dictionary of Terminology for Japanese Archaeology). Gakuseisha.
Saito, T. (1993). *Nihon Kokogakushi Nenpyo* (Chronology Table of Japanese Archaeology). Gakuseisha.
Sakazume, H. (1990). Nihon Kokogakushi Kenkyu Kinkyo (Recent State of Historical Research on Japanese Archaeology). *Nihon Kokogaku no Churyu* (Trends in Japanese Archaeology). Gakuseisha.
Sakazume, H. (1993). Manshukoku/Kotoku Juichi Nen no Koko Jijyo (Manchukuo 1945: The State of Archaeology), *Kobunka Danso* (Journal of Ancient Cultural Studies) *30 Vol. 2.* Kyushu kobunka kenkyukai.
Sakazume, H. (1994). Nihon Kokogakushi Shui—Toa Koko Gakkai/Toho Kokogaku Kyokai to Nihon Kodai Bunka Gakkai (Insights on the History of Japanese Archaeology—The Far-Eastern Archaeological Society/Association of East Archaeology & Japan Society of Ancient Culture), *The Journal of the Department of Literature, Rissho University 99*. Risshodaigaku bunkakubu.
Shimada, S. (1936). *Koko Zuihitsu Keikanko* (Archaeological Essays on Cockscomb Jars). Manshu jidaisha.
Tamura, J. and Kobayashi, Y. (1953). *Keiryo* (Qing-ling). Kyotodaigaku bungakubu.
Tamura, J. (1972). *Keiryo no Hekiga* (Qing-ling Wall Paintings). Dohosha.
Tamura, J. (1994). *Keiryo Chosa Kiko* (Travelogue of the Qing-ling Investigation). Heibonsha.
Teshigawara, A. (1988). *Nihon Kokogakushi—Nenpyo to Kaisetsu* (History of Japanese Archaeology—Chronology & Explanation).

Tozawa, M. (1978). Nihon Kokogakushi to Sono Haikei (History & Background of Japanese Archaeology). *Nihon Kokogaku wo Manabu* (Learn About Japanese Archaeology) *1*.

Umehara, S. (1950). *Toa Kokogaku Gaikan* (Outline of Far-Eastern Archaeological). Hoshino shoten.

Wajima, S. (1973). Nihon Kokogaku no Hattatsu to Kagakuteki Seishin (The Development of Japanese Archaeology and the Scientific Spirit). *Yuibutsuron Kenkyu* (Study of Materialism). Wajima Seiichi chosakusyu kankokai.

Wajima, S. (1955). Nihon Kokogaku no Hattatsu—Hattatsu no Shodanki (The Development of Japanese Archaeology—The Many Stages of Development). *Nihon Kokogaku Koza* (Studies on Archaeology in Japan) *2*. Kawade shobo.

The Techniques and Tools of Kazusabori Well-boring

Hiroki Takamura

Abstract

The Kazusabori method of well-boring originated during the Bunka era years (1804 – 1818) of the Edo period in the area now called Kimitsu-gun, Chiba Prefecture. This method was used to bore a large number of flowing wells, which supplied water for the local community and farming. In the 25th year of the Meiji period (1892), Kazusabori was even utilized to develop oil wells in Niigata and Akita and was introduced outside of Japan (in India particularly) as the Kazusa System. It was the most advanced well-boring technique of the time in Japan.

Kazusabori well-boring is designated as an important cultural asset in Japan's List of Important Tangible Folk Cultural Properties (Occupations), and the tools associated with this method are archived at the Chiba Prefectural Kazusa Museum. However, few studies have been done on the development of and tools used for this technique.

In February 1981, the author had the opportunity to observe a reenactment of the Kazusabori method by a master borer working to keep the technique alive. The author utilized the occasion to conduct research on the technical details of the Kazusabori method, the tools used, and the history of its development.

As a result, much light was shed on the technical details of Kazusabori well-boring and the actual tools used in the process. Some questions still remain regarding the origin of this method and the use of clayey water. A document in FAO library indicates that Chinese Drilling bears a close resemblance to Kazusabori well-boring, and could provide clues for further research.

Introduction

Kazusabori, a well-boring technology developed in the area now called Kimitsu-gun, Chiba Prefecture, has contributed to construction of numerous flowing (artesian) wells for non-commercial and farming water supply, since its birth during the Bunka period (1804 - 1818) in the Edo era. In 1892, this method was employed even in oil well development in Niigata and Akita Prefectures. It was also introduced to the international community, to India in particular, as the Kazusa System. It was Japan's most advanced well-boring technology of the time.

However, in the wake of the introduction of the rotary boring technology and the spread of waterworks, the Kazusabori method began losing its prevalence since the mid-1950s, and today, it is no longer used at all.

The Kazusabori technology is designated as an important folk-cultural asset, and the tools involved are kept in the Chiba Prefectural Kazusa Museum. Although Nagami (1948), Hishida (1955, 1960), and Hida (1973) studied its development and the tools, very few studies have been conducted so far on the technology itself.

In February 1981, the author had an opportunity of seeing reproduced Kazusabori processes demonstrated by Mr. Haruji Kondo (at Abe 12, Sodegaura-machi, Kimitsu-gun, Chiba), a well borer who inherited and passes on the Kazusabori technology. Making much of that opportunity, Hisahiro Ishiwatari (Rissho University) and the author carried out studies on the details of the technical aspects, tools and history of Kazusabori.

1. Geological Considerations on the History of Kazusabori

The Kazusa district occupies the central part of Chiba Prefecture, bordering on the Shimofusa district on the north, on Awa on the south, facing Tokyo Bay on the west and the Pacific Ocean on the east. In the southern area, a mountain range forms a border between Kazusa and Awa, from Mt. Kiyosumi (383 m) to Mt. Nokogiri (228 m). Having their headwaters in this area, the Yoro, Obitsu, Koito and Minato Rivers pour into the Tokyo Bay while the Ichinomiya and Isumi Rivers flow into the Pacific Ocean.

This district resides on the foundation of marine deposits that belong to the Mizuho series formed in the later Tertiary Era. Sedimentation continued from the Paleozoic Era through the Cenozoic Era. As a result of crustal movements at the end of the Mesozoic Era, the entire Kazusa district bulged. In particular, the area around the present district-bordering mountain range drastically bulged to emerge above the sea. Those movements formed the monoclinal structure that is sloping northwestward, as we see today. In the Quaternary Era, sedimentation of gravels, sand, and clay in the shallow-water zone to form the Narita group. Meanwhile, sedimentation and decomposition of volcanic ashes from activities of the volcanoes in the Kanto district formed a loam, which bulged due to the Kanto basin-forming movements. These movements along with development of alluvial formations of sand and clay produced the current topographic features of the Kazusa district.

Kimitsu-gun, the birthplace of Kazusabori, has a monoclinal structure that inclines northwestward. Presumably, its geological structure is founded around Mt. Kano (352 m). The aquifer resides in the Miura group formed in the Tertiary Era. As for the inclinations of these formations, the farther from Mt. Kano, the sharper the inclination becomes.

At Tawarada in Obitsumura located in the river basin of the Obitsu River, paddy cultivation was impossible since the shallow riverbed could not allow irrigation from the river, which caused this area to suffer a severe poverty level. However, once the pit well technology called Kazusabori was introduced to this area, the monoclinal structure allowed construction of flowing wells utilizing confined groundwater, enabling paddy cultivation to be carried out. This technology spread across the Kazusa district including the river basin of the Yoro River.

2. The Origin and Development of Kazusabori

1) The origin of Kazusabori

The literature on the origin of Kazusabori includes *The History of Kimitsu-gun* (1927). In that, there is a statement as follows: "A person named Hisazo Ikeda, a resident at Nukata, Nakamura, started a well-boring business around the year 14 of the Bunka Era (1817). It is unknown who conveyed the well-boring technique to him ..." Supporting the fact, *The History of Well Boring*, kept at the Omiyaji temple located in the Nakamura area clearly indicates that a pit well was constructed on the premises of the Omiyaji temple in year 1 of the Bunsei Era (1818), in the following statement; "the Omiyaji temple completed a thrust-bored well, located at the end of Aza-Yarita, within the temple's enclosure that is neighboring Tsuneemon's property. Having shared the construction expenses, the parties shall share well water for drinking, and for irrigation in case the water supply from the well exceeds the parties' drinking water consumption. In that case, the parties shall use well water for farming once a day, on a day-to-day rotating basis, rain or shine."

The event that led to construction of pit wells in this area is introduced as follows; "According to an oral tradition in the Nakamura area, Nakamura is the cradle of Kazusabori, whose invention was stimulated by an incident in which a child playfully butted the ground with a bamboo stick, causing water to belch out." (Hishida, 1955). Probably, people in this area were empirically aware of the fact that confined groundwater existed in this area due to the monoclinal structure of the foundation. However, they did not have any established, structured well-boring technology. Although the pit well technology was established in Tokyo (then Edo) in year 2 of the Shotoku Era (1712), there is no evidence that the well-boring technology employed in Edo was transferred to Kazusa. As the Kazusabori technology resembles the excavating method used for well construction in the continent of China before World War II, it may have been conveyed from the continent.

2) Development of Kazusabori

Since year 14 of the Bunka Era (1817), when the pit well construction method was conveyed to the Kazusa district, the technology went through a number of improvements before it was perfected in the final form, which involves a *higo* unit, made of jointed split bamboo members, with an iron pipe attached at the bottom section, an up-and-down movement booster connected to the bamboo unit above the ground for driving boring operation, and a wheel called *higo-guruma* that raises the bamboo unit along with the iron pipe by rolling *higo* members up (see Fig. 1). The following section provides an overview of the development process of the boring technology inherited in the Kazusa district by roughly dividing the period into its development phase and establishment phase (see Table 1).

Table 1—Chronology of Kazusabori Technology

Year in Imperial Era	Dominical Year	Event Nakamura	Event Obitsumura
Bunka14	1817	Hisazo Ikeda bored wells using the pit well technology that he learnt from an unknown person.	
Bunsei1	1818	Thrust-bored wells were made at 13 locations including Omiyaji in Momiyama (for drinking/farming water supply). Eight wells among these wells naturally discharged water at the surface (e.i., flowing wells).	
Meiji12	1879		A well borer from Senju, Tokyo, delivered a pit well, to whom Yasunosuke Omura apprenticed himself.
Meiji14	1881		Omura purchased gas pipes.
Meiji15	1882	Tokuzo Ikeda tried the *Kashibo-tsuki* method.	Omura developed the *Kashibo-tsuki* method (a thrust boring method using oak rods).
Meiji16	1883		Omura developed the *Higo-tsuki* method (a thrust boring method using split bamboo).
Meiji19	1886	Minejiro Ishii developed *hanegi* (bow-type bamboo spring).	
Meiji26	1893	Kinjiro Sawada developed *tsukigi* (wooden thrust rod). Kinjiro Sawada developed *higo-guruma* (bamboo wheel).	

Development phase: Bunka14–Meiji16
Establishment phase: Meiji19–Meiji26

Peak	Meiji29	1896	Kazusabori spread across the country.
	Meiji35	1902	Kazusabori was introduced into India as "Kazusa System."
	Showa16	1941	Mechanical boring technology was developed.
Decline phase	Showa25	1950	The number of well borers was reported to be decreasing.
	Showa44	1969	Haruji Kondo retired from work as a well borer.
	Showa55	1980	Haruji Kondo re-performed the manual boring procedure.
	Showa56	1981	Haruji Kondo re-performed the manual boring procedure.
	Showa57	1982	The Asia Well Development Association transferred the Kazusabori technology to Philippines.

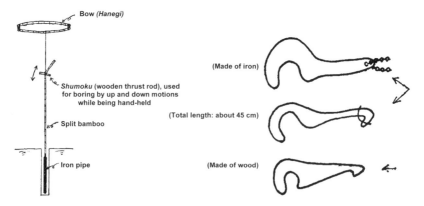

Fig.1 Kazusabori Schematic   Fig.2 Vise (source: Nagami's literature)

The development phase is when improvements were made to extend the boring depth. As for the boring method, improvements were made for 66 years between year 14 of the Bunka Era (1817) through year 16 of the Meiji Era (1883), starting with use of metal rods for butting, to be replaced with oak rods, and ultimately, with split bamboos. Thus, the initial boring limit of around 50 m was thus extended to 500 m or more.

The boring method inherited in the Kazusa district was referred to as *Kanabo-tsuki* (thrust boring with metal rods) according to *The History of Kimitsu-gun* (1927), as in the following statement; "In those days (around 1817, annotated by the author), they used boring tools composed of metal rods equipped with herringbone/octagonal ball-shaped metal fixtures..." They used a vice, as shown in Fig. 2, to raise the entire boring unit and then dropped it to produce boring force. With this method, it was difficult to continue boring vertically, and the vibration generated when dropping caused breakage of the metal rods' joints. Another problem was the limitation of the boring depth that was dependent on the weight of metal rods used, which was 27–28 *ken* (about 50 m) long. Although it may be questionable if they could construct a well that could supply required amounts of water under this limitation of the boring depth, no improvement was made before the Meiji Era. In year 12 of the Meiji Era (1879), a well borer came to Obitsumura from Senju, Tokyo, who started well construction in that area, after which Kazusabori started evolving around the two development centers, Nakamura and Obitsu.

In year 15 of the Meiji Era (1882), Yasunosuke Omura, working in Obitsumura as an apprentice under the well borer from Tokyo, invented the *Kashibo-tsuki* method (a thrust boring method using oak rods) and, in the same year, Tokuzo Ikeda, a resident in Nakamura, also tried this method. With the *Kashibo-tsuki* method, they installed scaffolding like the one in Fig. 3. The iron ring fixed on an oak rod joint was hooked onto the lever rod to enable the oak rod to be raised when the lever rod was operated. Then this oak rod was dropped to butt the ground for boring. This method solved the problem with heavy metal rods previously used and made it possible to extend the boring depth up to 50–60 *ken* (about 100 m).

For placing cleaning tools into the wellhole to remove the muck, Omura used split bamboo members joined together. In the year 18 of the Meiji Era (1885), he invented a boring method reusing these split bamboos for boring by attaching 5 to 6 m-long iron rods, with a diameter of 3.5 cm, on the bamboo tip. This was the birth of the *Higo-tsuki* method (a thrust boring method using split bamboo). Meanwhile, Tokuzo Ikeda of Nakamura used joined iron pipes, rather than iron rods used by Omura, for boring, that were equipped with a bit called *sentanrin-sakurin-ichi* (ring-type chisel at the tip section). These improvements helped extend the boring depth limit to around 1,000 m.

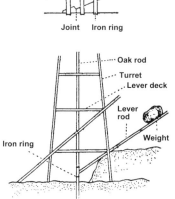  

Fig.3 Kashibo-tsuki method – Oak Rod Joints and Scaffolding (Source: Nagami's literature)

Phot. 1 Higo-guruma (Bamboo wheel)

Phot. 2 Turret and Hanegi (Spring bars)

With these developments by year 19 of the Meiji Era (1886), the improvement of the boring depth achieved with the Kazusabori method was completed with the invention of the *Higo-tsuki* method. Thereafter, the focus of improvement effort was placed on innovation for streamlining the operation. This period forms the establishment phase. First, in 1886, Minejiro Ishii of Nakamura invented *hanegi* (bow-type bamboo spring).

When excavating by moving up and down a split bamboo device with an iron pipe on the tip section, the resilience of *hanegi* was utilized to reduce manual labor. Additionally, in year 26 of the Meiji Era (1893), Kinjiro Sawada invented *shumoku* (wooden thrust rod) and *higo-guruma* (bamboo wheel). The invention of *shumoku* enabled well borers to change the operating manner from manually moving the *higo* (split bamboo) unit up and down it to holding it with both hands at a right angle to it, which contributed to higher efficiency. With the invention of *higo-guruma*, the operating efficiency of raising iron pipes also improved as a well borer could enter the wheel unit to turn it in a manner like a pet mouse revolving a wheel in a cage. This invention of *higo-guruma* perfected the Kazusabor technology that had been rooted in the Kazusa district since year 14 of the Bunka Era (1817).

3) Mechanization of Kazusabori and its decline

Perfected in 1893 as a well-boring technology, as described above, Kazusabori was also applied to oil well boring in Niitsu, Niigata Prefecture, leading to the discovery of some oil fields. In year 29 of the Meiji Era (1896), it was transferred to Taiwan, Kyushu, and Hokkaido to be widely applied in coal mining and boring for hot springs.

Around year 16 of the Showa Era (1941), the previous manual boring was replaced with mechanical excavation using engines. This improvement enabled reduction of the *higo-guruma* diameter to half of the initial dimension (to about 2 m). The wheel was now operated using a belt to roll up split bamboo members. A crank was also introduced to convert the rotary movement into up-and-down movement to drive excavation. The development of this mechanical excavation technology enabled to reduce the manpower involved to just one borer for most of the entire well-boring process, from two to three borers previously required for boring, operating *higo-guruma*, and shifting.

In the third decade of the Showa Era (after the mid-1950s), with the introduction of the rotary boring technology, Kazuzabori gradually lost opportunities to be used even though it had spread throughout the country. According to an old document in Mr. Haruji Kondo's collection, well borers around the Yokota area where he lives, organized a union named Suijin-ko (water-god union, literally) and set out arrangements twice a year (on the 5th of February and the 5th of October) concerning well prices. The union had twelve members at the beginning of the Showa Era (around the mid-1920s), but continued to decrease after World War II. Mr. Kondo continued to work as a well borer despite the trend of decreases in the number of well-boring job opportunities and the number of well borers. In year 44 of the Showa Era (1969), when the order placements for wells dropped to about three per year, he ended his career as a well borer. That marked the end of Kazusabori as an active technology, after being used for nearly 150 years.

3. Major Tools Used in Kazusabori and Their Structures

The major tools used in Kazusabori can be roughly classified into two categories: boring tools and power transmission devices used by well borers on the ground.

1) Boring tools

Iron pipe
An iron pipe is a tool used for breaking into the bottom layer by butting for boring in the Kazusabori technology. The iron pipe is complete with *sakiwa* (tip chisel) and claws, as shown in Fig. 4.

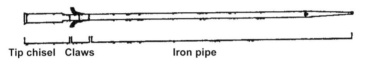

Tip chisel   Claws   Iron pipe

Fig.4 Iron Pipe Schematic

Sakiwa is the very tool that breaks the bottom layer of soil, whose tip is made of steel. This tool can be considered to be the core device in Kazusabori. There are three types of *sakiwa* for different soil properties (Table 2).

Table 2—Types of Sakiwa

Name	Purpose
Nagawa (double-ring)	For general-purpose boring into layers of clay/sand or rock mass
Ichimonji (bar-shaped chisel)	For general-purpose boring into layers of sand or rock mass
Gravel thrust-boring bar	For boring into layers of gravel

Among these, the gravel thrust iron rod is an independent 6.3 m-long iron rod, to be used separately to break gravel layers, and not to be equipped on any other iron pipe tip.

Inside the assembly of *nagawa* and *ichimonji* chisel, a device called *koshita* (component at the lower section with valve) is installed, which is used to suck out the muck from boring, which floats in clayey water through the discharge port provided on the iron pipe at its upper section. *Koshita* has a valve fixed on a frame made of oak.

At the tip of the iron pipe and at the back of *sakiwa*, two projections called claws are provided. These projections are made of steel and assist boring with a long iron pipe by creating an extra clearance between the iron pipe and the bore so that friction may be controlled and the muck be prevented from being stuck between the pipe and the bore, which may cause problems.

The length and the diameter of the iron pipe section vary depending on the well diameter, special usage of the well, and other requirements specific to the well. At the upper section of the iron pipe, *kama* (tapered hook) is provided to enable the pipe to be joined with split bamboo members so that the iron pipe can be suspended from the section above the ground.

Suiko (suction pipe)
The muck from excavation is let float in clayey water that is constantly poured into the bore during boring operation to settle over time. *Suiko* cleans up the muck by sucking and discharging them out of the bore.

The *suiko* is a light-weight device made of galvanized sheets. For protection from breakage due to water pressure, claddings made of galvanized sheets are wrapped around the iron pipe at a certain interval, called *hotai* (literally, bandage). Like the iron pipe, a *Koshita* valve is provided at the lower section and a discharge port at the upper section (Fig. 5). The length and the diameter of *suiko* are determined based on those of the iron pipe, as classified in Table 3.

▨ ⋮ *Hotai* (Cladding)

Fig.5 Suction Pipe Schematic

Operation using *suiko* is performed at the start and end of the day's operation, at every two to three meters of boring, or when boring operation has slowed down due to a massive amount of muck clogging the iron pipe when boring a layer of sand.

Table 3—Classification of Boring Tools
Iron pipes

Name	Diameter (cm)	Length (cm)	Weight (kg)	Claw (cm)	Remarks
Large iron pipe	7.5	630	28.0	4.5	
Iron pipe	4.5	900	28.0	3.0	
Hon (main) iron pipe	4.5	810	19.1	3.0	
Iron pipe	4.2	630	14.5	---	
Tateire (vertical setup) iron pipe	4.6	270	9.1	---	Used for starting boring
Uchizuki (inside thrusting) iron pipe	3.3	810	13.2	---	For boring inside vertical water duct (inner diameter: 4.8 cm)
Uchizuki (inside thrusting) iron pipe	2.7	540	6.2	---	For boring inside nested pipes (inner diameter: 3.3cm)
*Gravel thrust-boring bar	---	630	50.0	---	

* See the section describing *sakiwa*

Suiko (suction pipes)

Name	Diameter (cm)	Length (cm)	Weight (kg)	Claw (cm)	Remarks
Suiko	6.0	630	---		
Suiko	3.0	---	---		For cleaning inside vertical water duct
Suiko	2.7	---	---		For cleaning inside nested pipes
Suiko for cleaning	4.2	---	---		For cleaning inside completed wells

2) Power transmission devices

Higo (split bamboo)
Higo suspends the boring tools placed inside the wellhole and transmits the power for boring. Tapered hooks called *kama*, made of long-jointed bamboo stems, are provided as joints of *higo* members. To make a *kama* hook, a bamboo stem is shaved off, as shown in Fig. 6, in a width slightly less than 2 cm and cut in the length indicated in the figure, and the bamboo stem joints close to the cut end are utilized. With the joining method using *kama* (called *kama-tsugi*), two *kama* hooks are engaged and iron rings called *higo-wa* are installed from each end to completely fix the bamboo members with the tapered sections.

The depth already bored determines the length of the *higo* section. As explained in the "*Suiko*" section above, muck deposited inside the iron pipe might affect the boring efficiency due to an increase of the weight of the iron pipe. When that situation arises, the iron pipe is replaced with a *suiko* pipe to clean up inside the wellhole. One unit of boring depth is called one *sage*, which is about 1.8 m for manual boring. Each time boring is completed for a depth of one *sage*, *higo* is added to the existing *higo* section. Therefore, the unit length of *higo* members is also 1.8 m.

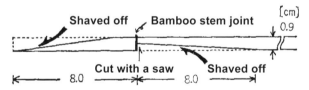

Fig.6 Preparation of Split Bamboo

As boring develops, additional *okkake-higo* (extension split bamboo) having that unit length is attached to the *higo*. As the joint is the weak point of *higo* that can lead to accidents if any joint is broken, *okkake-higo* is replaced with 5.4 m-long *hon-higo* (main split bamboo member) whenever three *okkake-higo* members have been added, reducing the number of junctions.

Kama hooks for engaging *higo* members are fabricated in symmetrical shapes at the ends for *okkake-higo* and *hon-higo*. This is an innovative idea with considerations given to the balance and strength of the bamboo members involved, allowing *higo* members to be joined using a *kama* hook with its thicker portion down and the back-side portion up. This way, when rolling up *higo* members around the *higo-guruma* wheel, the back of the bamboo stems face outward.

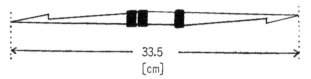

Fig.7 Kama (Tapered Hook) Made of Iron

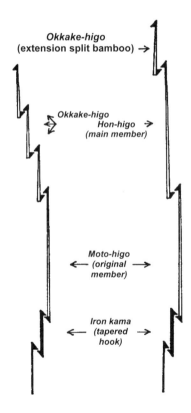

Fig.8 Higo Junctions

In addition to such arrangements, iron hooks (Fig. 7) are also employed to protect *higo* junctions from wear due to repeated operations to attach/detach to/from iron pipes or the *suiko* unit. The ends of this iron hook are made in the opposing orientation. To accommodate this design, one *higo* member called *moto-higo* (original split bamboo member) is used (Fig. 8) that is joined with a hook in the same orientation.

Hanegi (spring bars)
Hanegi is also referred to as *yumi* (bow). As shown in Fig. 1, it is connected to the *higo* unit that suspends an iron pipe with a rope. This power transmission unit utilizes the resilience of bamboo to drive up-and-down movements of the pipe for boring. Two long-jointed bamboo stems (with a diameter of 12 to 13 cm) are bound together with a straw rope, providing a certain distance between the connecting points, and mounted onto the uppermost section of the scaffold. The total length of the *hanegi* unit is about 5 to 6 m.

Shumoku (wooden thrust rod)
Shumoku is the section that the well borer holds to give thrust to the boring device. *Shumoku* units are made of oak, to the size of each borer's hand. It has a grove in the middle for fixing *higo* in place with a wedge. It is installed so that it comes just above the borer's knee when the iron pipe is driven down all the way. So the *shumoku* unit is moved downward as boring develops.

4. Boring Method in Kazusabori

This section summarizes the actual boring procedure used in Kazusabori, based on the manual boring performance reproduced by Mr. Haruji Kondo, an ex-well borer, demonstrated at the residence of Mr. Hiroshi Kamei, at Abe, Sodegaura-machi, Kimitsu-gun, Chiba Prefecture, along with the description of how the tools introduced in the previous chapter were actually used. Table 4 shows the flow of the processes.

Table 4—Flow of Kazusabori Processes

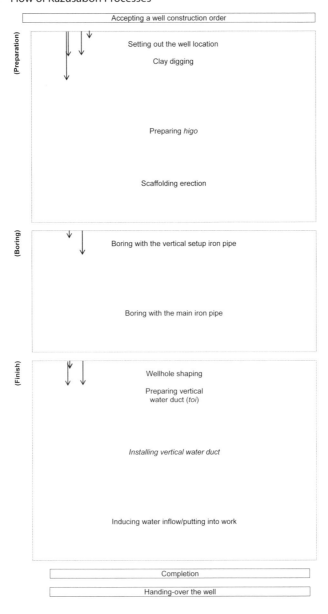

1) Scaffolding

In preparation for boring, a scaffold is set up that is unique to the Kazusabori method (Fig. 9). Logs with an average thickness at the bottom of 12 to 13 cm are used for the main members of the scaffold, with each node fixed with a rope.

First, three columns called *tateji* are erected in line, oriented in the east or south, at an interval appropriate for the diameter of the *higo-guruma* used. In parallel to them, another line of columns is installed 120 cm away from the original columns, on the opposite side of the wellhole position that is in between. Next, three rows of horizontal connection members called *yokonuno* are fixed in place with ropes for each line of *tateji* member.

The lowest *yokonuno* members are fixed at a level about 30 cm above the ground so that they can support a scaffold plate that functions as the working deck for boring operations. The middle *yokonuno* members are for supporting the *higo-guruma*, fixed at a level about 2.2 m above the ground, slightly higher than the radius of the *higo-guruma* wheel (2 m). Since this section takes the greatest load, particularly thick logs are used for this part. The uppermost members are for maintaining the scaffold's stability and for mounting the *hanegi* unit that is used for boring, and are fixed at a level about

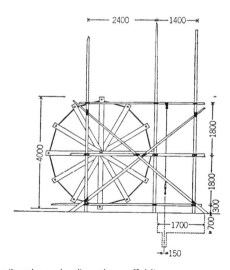

Fig.9 *Higo-guruma* (bamboo wheel) on the scaffolding

4 m above the ground.

At the position of the wellhole, a hole called *do-ana* is provided, whose approximate dimensions are 1.8 m in length, 0.8 m in width, and 0.7 m in depth. This *do-ana* contains clayey water for sucking up muck, protecting the wellhole wall from collapsing, and cooling bits used. As for the origin of clayey water used this way, no specific explanation is given in the related literature, except that it was already in use in year 12 of the Meiji Era (1879). As for the clay, black clay with relatively high viscosity was collected from around rice paddies in the area where well borers lived. It was mixed with water and the supernatant liquid was collected and stored in a barrel buried next to the scaffold.

2) Boring [1]

- Boring with tateire iron pipe (vertical setup pipe)

The first phase of boring is carried out by means of a *tateire* iron pipe of about 2.7 m in total length. A *sakiwa* is installed at the tip of the iron pipe, and *ok-kake-higo* (extension split bumboo) (2.7m) is joined with the *kama* (tapered hook) at the upper position. Then, this pipe assembly is made to stand *tateire* iron pipe in the *do-ana* in the wellhole.

The well borer installs the scaffold at the second stage of *yokonuno* to start the work. Boring is performed by vertical movement of the *higo* on which the iron pipe is suspended; the iron pipe end is made to hit the well bottom, to break ground. The *shumoku* serves as grip for this job. As shown in Fig. 10, the well borer sets it nearly at knee height, and holds it with both hands. The well borer continues the job, with the upper part of the *higo* put on the shoulder.

The muck generated by digging is made to float by the specific gravity of the clayey water, and it is discharged onto the ground through the outlet at the upper part of the pipe, by means of a *koshita* valve installed at the lower section of the iron pipe inside.

Along with the progress of the boring, the *shumoku* is displaced. When boring advances, with the whole of the pipe entered into ground, the work bench is moved to the 1st stage of *yokonuno*, and work is resumed.

When boring corresponding to one *okkake-higo* is completed, another *ok-kake-higo* is joined with the end of the *higo*.

Boring by the *tateire* iron pipe is carried out to the depth equal to the iron pipe length (2.7 m) plus two *okkake-higo* (2.7 m each), that is, 8.1 m.

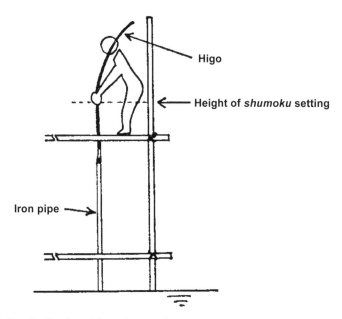

Fig.10 Sketch of boring with tateire iron pipe

3) Boring [2]

- **Boring with a hon iron pipe**

When ground is dug to a depth of 8.1 m, a *hon* (main) iron pipe whose total length is 8.1 m is used for well digging, instead of *tateire* iron pipe.

With the *hon* iron pipe that is heavier than *tateire* iron pipe, it is easier to break the wellhole bottom layer. However, the work efficiency becomes lower. To compensate, a rope is connected to the center of *hanegi* installed on the top of *yokonuno*, and the end of the rope is wound around the *shumoku*, to lift the iron pipe by utilizing the resilience of the bamboo.

The *hon* iron pipe is provided with two projections about 3 cm, called *tsume* (claws), at an interval of 180 degrees near the end (see IV 1) [Iron pipe], to prevent the work efficiency from lowering because of the friction between the iron pipe and wellhole wall. While vertical motions for boring are repeated 20 times, the claws alternately turn clockwise and counter-clockwise around the center line of the wellhole.

Boring is carried out at a rate of about 1.8 m per day. This job is continued, adding extension *higo*, while evaluating the nature of soil at the bottom by reactions transmitted to hands, and replacing *sakiwa*, until the target aquifer is reached.

4) Boring [3]

- Job with suiko (suction pipe)

Along with progress of boring, muck floating in the clayey water increases in amount, and begins to settle in the iron pipe and wellhole. Then, the iron pipe is lifted up by means of the *higo-guruma*, to be replaced with *suiko* to clean the wellhole.

The *suiko* is lowered into the wellhole, and moved vertically more than ten times, to suck the clayey water containing much muck in the bottom. Then, the *suiko* is lifted up, and moved vertically above ground to discharge the clayey water. This job is repeated several times. As a general rule, this job with the *suiko* is performed when ground is excavated about 2 to 3 m.

After cleaning the wellhole, the *suiko* is replaced with the iron pipe to resume boring.

5) Finishing process [1]

- Wellhole shaping

When boring reaches, through the clay layer, the sand layer, i.e., aquifer (called "*shikiba*" by well borers), which contains many shells, the well borer stops boring to proceed with the finishing process.

To smoothly insert the *toi* (vertical water duct) (see the next page), the wellhole is shaped. This job uses a hole shaping tool made of a cedar log around which nails are driven. The diameter of the *toi* is measured, and a margin is added to the measured diameter. Based on this dimension, the projecting length of the nails is adjusted so that the finished hole may have the desired diameter. Then, this tool is mounted at the tip of the *hon* iron pipe, and the *shumoku* (wooden thrust rod) is set as in the boring job, to shape the wellhole wall.

When the hole is shaped to the bottom, muck generated by shaping is removed by means of the *suiko*.

6) Finishing process [2]

- Placing toi (vertical water duct)

To prevent the wellhole from collapsing, a *toi* is inserted into the whole length of the wellhole (Fig. 11). The *toi* was initially made of *moso* bamboo (a species of bamboo of large diameter). Currently, PVC pipes are used. It is easy to connect *toi* of PVC pipes together, and also easy to make connected pipes straight. In contrast, with bamboo *toi*, rather difficult preparations are necessary, involving correction of bend, piercing nodes, and processing the jointed portion.

The bend of bamboo is corrected by warming its nodes of the bent portion over fire, and cooling down it to solidify. For allowing water to pass through the bamboo duct, its nodes are pierced by means of a rod about 1.2 m long with wavy projections. To connect the bamboos made straight, joints called

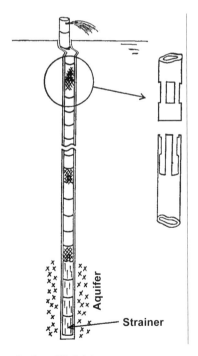

Fig.11 Toi (vertical water duct) and its joint

hane are provided.

After these preparations, four to eight water collecting ports, called *mado* (window), are made between nodes. These ports are designed to introduce groundwater contained in the aquifer into the *toi*. These ports are made in parallel with the bamboo fiber with a *tatebiki noko* (saw with teeth for cutting along the direction of grain). Except for flowing (artesian) wells, to prevent sand from entering through *mado* during pumping, two or three plies of palm barks are wound around the *mado*. The *toi* duct is introduced into the shaped wellhole, and their joints are wound with newspaper and palm barks to prevent intrusion of mud and sand. In the case of a flowing well, the *toi* is made to project about 50 cm on the surface, to provide a flowing port.

7) Finish process [3]

- Mizuyobi **(inducing water inflow),** *Ikashi* **(putting into work)**
During the jobs described above, groundwater springing is prevented by injecting clayey water of large specific gravity into the wellhole. At the final stage of well creation, the clayey water in the pit is discharged, and jobs for making groundwater spring start.

At first, *mizuyobi* (inducing water inflow) is carried out. For this purpose, a *suiko* thinner than the *suiko* for cleaning is lowered to the position of *mado*, which is lifted up about one meter per cycle. Generating zero water pressure at an instant, groundwater is made to flow into the well pit. This priming job is repeated several tens of times.

After priming, *ikashi* (putting into work) begins. This job is to pump up the clayey water in the wellhole to decrease the concentration of clayey water, thereby removing the clay sticking to the well wall, and making groundwater spring. Nowadays, a pump is used for this job, but once clayey water was pumped with the *suiko*.

After *mizuyobi* and *ikashi,* the creation of a well by the Kazusabori is completed, and the well is handed over by the well borers to the client.

Conclusions

This study has overviewed the Kazusabori manual well-boring method, its tools and the history of its development. However, there are still some facts yet to be revealed, including the origins of the Kazusabori technique and of the use of clayey water. With regard to the technical origin among others, a document in the FAO library shows that Chinese Drilling bears a close resemblance. The investigation should be left to future studies.

Triggered by this restoration of the technology, a second restoring demonstration was carried out in the city of Kimitsu by Mr. Haruji Kondo and Mr. Aoto Morooka (cinematographist), and this technology was exported to the Philippines through the Asia Well Development Association. As seen by this fact, this well boring technology is being reevaluated in developing countries. (Accepted on September 16, 1982)

Those wishing to conduct an in-depth research on distribution of Kazusabori wells and their status of use are advised to refer to Hiroki Takamura (1973) "*Jifuntai no Kotai to Jifunryo*" (Recession of the area of artesian flow and the flowing volume) in Isamu Kayane (ed.) *Chikasui Shigen Kaihatsu to Hozen* (Development and Conservation of Groundwater Resources), Water Science Research Institute, in addition to the following references.

Phot. 3 The monoclinal structure of the stratum allowing artesian well development

Phot. 4 Artesian wells for residential use

Phot. 5 Simple kazusabori well-boring method

Phot. 6 Bits at the tips of Kazusabori well-boring tools

References

Education Association of Kimitsu-gun, Chiba Prefecture (1927): *"History of Kimitsu-gun, Chiba Prefecture"* Part II, 1010–1011.
Shuzo Nagami (1948): *"Kazusabori no Kenkyu"* (Research on the Kazusabori Well-boring), Museum Research Collection.
Tadayoshi Hishida (1955): *"Kazusabori Ko"* (Study on the Kazusabori Well-boring) Part I, *Boso Tembo* (Boso Outlook), August 1955, 8–10.
Tadayoshi Hishida (1955): *"Kazusabori Ko"* (Study on the Kazusabori Well-boring) Part II, *Boso Tembo* (Boso Outlook), September 1955, 4–6.
Tadayoshi Hishida (1960): *"Kazusabori Ko"* (Study on the Kazusabori Well-boring), *Bunkazai Shiryo* (Materials on Cultural Assets), Chiba Prefecture.
Isamu Kayane (1973): *"Kazusabori no Hattatsu to Kazusabori I no Riyo"* (Development of the Kazusabori Well-boring and Utilization of Kazusabori Wells), *"Chikasui Shigen no Kaihatsu to Hozen" (Development and Conservation of Groundwater Resources)*, Water Science Research Institute, 200–208.
Nobuo Kurata (ed.) (1975): *"Chiiki Shakai no Naka no Chikasui"* (Groundwater in the Community), Groundwater Engineering Center.
Hiroki Takamura et al. (1975): *"Boso Hanto Chubu no Chikei Chishitsu to Chikasui"* (Topography, Geological Conditions and Groundwater in the Central Part of the Boso Peninsula), *(Junken Annai)* (Introduction to Site Surveys), the Association of Japanese Geographers, 11–13.

A Study on Scripture Worship in the Kathmandu Valley: An Interim Review with a Prospect of a New Approach for the Philological Study of Sanskrit Buddhism

Kazunori Sasaki
Fumio Shoji

Abstract

Even today the culture of Mahayana Buddhism, which originated in ancient India, still remains and is practiced daily in Kathmandu, the capital city of the Federal Democratic Republic of Nepal. Among the various cultural events associated with Buddhism that are carried out in Kathmandu, "scripture worship" is particularly of great interest as a subject of study, considering its development into a rite of Buddhist doctrine, it can also be viewed as a representative example that reveals the difficulty of studying a "living culture" that is routinely practiced.

This paper first looks at the example of a recitation ritual, *Prajñāpāramitā-paṭhana* that is conducted in a Buddhist temple named *Kwa Baha* in the city of Lalitpur (Patan) in the Kathmandu valley. Careful examination in multiple topics, mainly focusing on *Nava-Dharma*, reveals cultural meanings of this recitation ritual comparing with its doctrinal background. Related matters are also looked at to clarify the positioning of Scripture Worship in Nepalese Buddhism. Following that examination, it introduces a challenge that has been carried out by RNAP(: Rissho-University Nepal Academic-research Project) for pioneering new generation philological study of Nepal Buddhism, taking full advantage of digital format data of newly acquired huge database of unpublished Nepalese manuscripts, the *Thapa Collection*.

Nepal's Buddhist Sanskrit Manuscripts and the Birth of Modern Buddhist Studies

It was in the first half of the 19th century that Brian Houghton Hodgson (1801-1894), a British Resident officer of the Company[1] at Kathmandu and later recognized as a world-wide renowned pioneer naturalist and ethnologist on the Himalayan region, collected over 400 titles of Sanskrit manuscripts in his place of appointment. He sent them to Calcutta (now "Kolkata") and other places.[2] It was only in 1937, however, that he started serious study of those manuscripts after Eugene Burnouf (1801-1852) of the College de France firstly put them on the desk in his study. No orientalist at that time, other than Burnouf, even noticed the importance of those historical documents and undertook serious investigation of them until this French genius drew out the first portrait of Indian Buddhism with his truly epochal work, *Introduction a l'histoire du Buddhisme Indien* ("Introduction to the History of Indian Buddhism").

Burnouf picked out a Sanskrit manuscript of *the Saddharmapuṇḍarīka*, the so-called *Lotus Sutra*, from Hodgson's collection in the Bibliotheque Nationale, Paris. He translated it into French and published it along with the detailed introduction. This introduction was cut out and published independently with the title mentioned above. It was the first introduction of Mahayana-Buddhist scripture written in Sanskrit into the modern world.

Modern Buddhist studies made their first step exactly at this point. There is no doubt that the discovery of Sanskrit Buddhist manuscripts in Nepal, along with Burnouf's elaborated introduction, set up the contemporary academic study of Buddhism. Regarding the extreme importance of the Nepal manuscripts as the source of Buddhist studies, Friedrich Max Müller (1823-1900) commented as follows:

> It is this work (i.e., *Introduction a l'histoire du Buddhisme Indien*) which laid the foundation for a systematic study of the religion of the Buddha. Though acknowledging the great value of the research made in the Buddhist literatures of Tibet, Mongolia, China, and Ceylon, Burnouf showed that Buddhism, being of Indian origin, ought to be studied first of all in the original Sanskrit documents, preserved in Nepal.[3]

The Nepal manuscripts are important, as suggested by these words of the great pioneer scholar in the comparative study of religions, because they consist of texts written in the original language of Indian Buddhism. This should mean that they convey the original ideas and thoughts of Buddhists in India. Hence, it is expected that expert scholars can elucidate, through the study of those manuscripts, the whole picture of original Buddhism, which was totally lost and disappeared in its mother land, just as Burnouf attempted, to attain the first fruit.

Ritual Background of the Corpus of Nepal's Buddhist Sanskrit Manuscripts

After Hodgson's discovery and Burnouf's introduction, Nepal became recognized as the storehouse of Buddhist manuscripts. Kathmandu valley is situated in the middle of the main trade route connecting Madhyadeśa of India and the capital area of Tibet, and it has been prosperous because of the great traffic of traders between those two Buddhist Empires. Since the merchants and traders are mostly Buddhists, Buddhist culture along with related materials were brought into the valley since ancient times.

With regard to the Buddhist manuscripts, some manuscripts are said to have been brought there so long ago that they date back to the 2nd century,[4] as the oldest Buddhist manuscripts written on palm leaf found in the valley. However, the larger part of the manuscripts are relatively new, dated after the Muslim invasion of India when a flood of Buddhist monks took flight from their motherland and came to the valley with their arms full of manuscripts.

Buddhist monasteries in the valley could not afford sufficient accommodations for all those Indian refugees, according to Shanker Thapa of Tribhuvan University, so "Many of them had to support themselves by selling manuscripts, scriptures and antiquities which they carried at their arrival for personal use."[5] Besides, if the refugees died of an unexpected cause, for example a natural disaster like famine, the host could have confiscated their belongings. Due to these reasons, Sanskrit manuscripts gradually accumulated in Nepalese Buddhist monasteries as well as in the homes of wealthy people.

However, although the Sanskrit manuscripts were transmitted and preserved in Nepal, the larger part of the extant munuscripts are not the original copies brought from ancient India. They are copies duplicated by particular local workers, the scribes, in the Kathmandu valley. Traditional Buddhists in the Kathmandu valley, the members of which roughly overlap with the Newar people, accepted not only the materials of Indian Buddhism but also the customs and manners of it. They adopted Indian Buddhism as a whole and made it their own culture. They duplicated manuscripts instead of just preserving old ones which were passed down to them along the generations.

Copying and possessing manuscripts is, for the Nepalese Buddhist, believed to be a typical act of merit accumulation.[6] Some Buddhists copied or had a proper person copy appropriate scriptures for special occasions to commemorate a dead kinsman with auspicious *pūjā*s or rituals. Others did so on the death of a family member to accredit merit to the deceased on behalf of the dead person by himself. Unlike the case in Tibet and China, Nepalese Buddhists would not dare to utilize the woodblock printing method for duplicating sacred scriptures. This was no doubt not a matter of their poverty of woodworking skill. The Nepalese people were/are in fact superior artisans of wood carving. Why, then? It was probably due to the prohibition on the lower caste people using Sanskrit, the sacred language. Using Sanskrit is strictly limited to the upper castes, so the ordinary people could not even read it. There were so many opportunities requiring Sanskrit manuscripts, but only a few people understood and had the right to use Sanskrit. This is why being a scribe became one of the most popular occupations for intellectuals like Buddhist monks and the Brahmin caste, and copying manuscripts finally became a major industry in the valley. This propensity of the Nepalese people, the popularity of copying manuscripts, caused an inflation in the number of newly duplicated Sanskrit manuscripts, and they overwhelmed the original copies imported from India.

Thus, the manuscripts that Hodgson discovered and collected in the valley with the ready help of Amritananda Shakya (1774-1834), the eminent Nepalese Buddhist pandit who instructed Hodgson about Nepalese Buddhism, were also of recent duplication.

The case was the same with Ven. Ekai Kawaguchi, who first brought Sanskrit manuscripts of Buddhist scriptures to Japan. According to the Kawaguchi's famous memoirs of the journey into Tibet and Nepal, *Three Years in Tibet*, prime minister Chandra Shumsher Rana, who was the counter part of Ven. Kawaguchi in the negotiation to exchange scriptures, suggested that he would give, at first, copies of several titles of scripture that were available and currently not in use, and would give the remainings later when

Kawaguchi would come to Nepal again. The prime minister promised him that he would get certain persons to duplicate the wanting copies. This means that Nepalese people did not just store the manuscripts which their ancestors had received from India long ago, but also duplicated them quite freely to meet their needs. Duplication of Buddhist scripture is such an ordinal thing in the Kathmandu valley that there have been very many duplicated manuscripts in the valley in ancient times and in modern times also. Therefore, both Hodgson and Ven. Kawaguchi obtained mostly modern duplicated paper manuscripts of scriptures.

Manuscripts under Practical Use

I do not intend to imply that Nepal's Sanskrit manuscripts are less important because they are merely recent duplications and do not have the value of antiquity. What I want to point out here, however, is that having been recently duplicated seems to give some uniqueness to the corpus of the manuscript as a whole: The corpus would not be identical with that of the Indian original, simply because the corpus of manuscripts was composed under a unique ritualistic culture of Nepalese Buddhism.

In that case, the selection of scriptures to be duplicated depend on the needs of the ritualistic contexts, and the list of texts for duplication would not be identical to the list of texts ranked by doctrinal importance.

The focus on the ritual side is the most significant feature of Nepalese Buddhism, distinguishing it clearly from the situation of Tibet and China. In those countries, people put the priority on systematizing the doctrine: For that purpose, it was necessary for them to collect and translate all the concerning texts.

The Sanskrit language is not the mother tongue of the Nepalese people. The Newar language, which is the native language of the Newar people, belongs to the Tibeto-Burman language group and totally differs from the Indo-Arian language group, of which Sanskrit is an ancestor. This means the Newars had to take pains to learn Sanskrit. It would not seem an easy task for the Newar people, yet they did indeed learn Sanskrit. We need to know what motivated the Newar people to study this difficult foreign language and use Sanskrit manuscripts for rituals.

In fact, recent field research on Buddhism in Nepal, reveals that the library of Sanskrit Buddhist scriptures found in Nepal contains quite a lot of documents which are written/edited by Nepalese natives. It is also reported that manuscripts of texts with a theme related to Nepal tend to remain[7]; the Buddhist Sanskrit manuscripts found in Nepal have been duplicated and transmitted under the unique religious cultural sphere known as "Newar Buddhism."

The Buddhists in Kathmandu Valley as I mentioned above, did not just recieve and hand down the ideas and materials of the Indian originals; they also accepted and transmitted the whole culture. For example, take their practice of rituals. They practice daily rituals using a certain ritual cord, and in these rituals, they sometimes use real manuscripts in the process as a representation of the corresponding sacred matter.

The Nepalese people in general did not copy manuscripts for purposes of study. They did not necessarily read the manuscripts. They prepared them for merit accumulation: The major reason for duplicating manuscripts was to use them in rituals.

We can often see that cover board above manuscripts are stained with some colored powder. It is stained not because of ill maintenance, but because it was used in the ritual. That color powder was an offering. The stain that remains recalls those offerings.

As long as the tradition of scripture worship continues, manuscripts as the object of offering are required. The fact that they are used in rituals is a strong motivation to duplicate manuscripts.

I assume that they use Sanskrit because of a ritualistic reason. In ritual, what is important is the sound of the Sanskrit. What is not so important is to deliver the meaning.

The fact that there remain so many manuscripts in the Kathmandu valley suggests that the people accept Buddhism through rituals.

Nava-Dharma

The people of the Kathmandu valley practice unique customs of scripture worship, which have made the situation of Nepal's manuscripts different from that of any other places. I will introduce here two examples of rituals which indicates the uniqueness of Nepalese Buddhism: the Dharma Mandala in the *Aṣṭamīvrata* ritual and *Prajñāpāramitā Paṭhana* ritual which is practiced routinely in the Golden Temple (*Kwa Baha*).

Aṣṭamīvrata is a ritual practiced on the 8th of every month of the Nepalese calender. It is a fasting ceremony for lay believers with a *pūjā* (offering ritual) for Amoghapāśa Avalokiteśvara, the deity of rain-fall and fertility.[8]

In the process of the ceremony, Vajrācāryas, Buddhist priests in Nepalese Buddhism, are invited and give an offering rutual. Nine real manuscripts of Buddhist scriptures are set on the ground, making a wheel shape with eight spokes. This formation of scriptures is called *Dharma Maṇḍala*. *Prajñāpāramitā* is set in the center of the maṇḍala, and the other eight scriptures are put according to the four directions and four oblique directions. Those nine scriptures compose the set of *Dharma Maṇḍala* called "*Nava-(ratna-)Dharma*," or the "nine precious scriptures." The contents of this set of scriptures are as follows:

(1) *Aṣṭasāhasrikā Prajñāpāramitā*
(2) *Gaṇḍavyūha*
(3) *Daśabhūmika*
(4) *Samādhirāja*
(5) *Laṅkāvatāra*
(6) *Saddharmapuṇḍarīka*
(7) *Tathāgata Guhyaka*
(8) *Lalitavistara*
(9) *Suvarṇa Prabhāsottama Sūtrendra Ratnarāja*

Nava-Dharma is well-known among Nepalese Buddhists, especially to Vajrācāryas. Hodgson also noticed this set of scriptures through Amritananda soon after he started researching Nepalese Buddhism. He wrote about it in his *essays*[9]:

The nine Dharmas are as follows: 1. Ashta Sahasrika. 2. Ganda Vyuha. 3. Dasa Bhumeswara. 4. Samadhi Raja. 5. Lankavatara. 6. Sad Dharma Pundarika. 7. Tathagata Guhyaka. 8. Lalita Vistara. 9. Suvarna Prabhasa.

Divine worship is constantly offered to these nine works, as the "Nava Dharma," by the Bauddhas of Nepaul. The aggregation of the nine is now subservient to ritual fancies, but it was originally dictated by a just respect for the pre-eminent authority and importance of these works, which embrace, in the first, an abstract of the philosophy of Buddhism; ......

I esteem myself fortunate in having been first to discover and procure copies of these important works. To meditate and digest them is not for me; but I venture to hint that by so doing only can a knowledge of genuine Buddhism be acquired.
(underline is added by the present author)

Hodgson's description here is certainly a secondhand opinion of his instructor Amritananda. Amritananda is not a Vajrācārya but he is a extremely learned pandit and he must have introduced the Nava-Dharma collection as the most respected set of scriptures in Nepal. Thus Hodgson came to regard these nine scriptures as an authentic collection of Buddhist scriptures which contain the core of Buddhist philosophy.

His estimation was widely spread by Max Muller who took up his opinion of Nava-Dharma and introduced it in his essay comparing it to the authentic *Tripiṭaka* of Southern Buddhism:

What corresponds among the Northern to the Tripitaka of the Southern Buddhists are the nine Dharmas, though it is difficult to understand why those nine works should have been selected from the bulk of the Buddhist literature of Nepal, and why divine worship should have been offered to them.[10]

Thus the *Nava-Dharma* acquired an authenticity corresponding to Southern *Tripiṭaka*. But the reason why those nine scriptures were selected, as he commented here, remains unclear.

Sudan Shakya of Shuchi-in University, kyoto recently provided some background information on this question. Nava-Dharma is a set of scriptures which was used in the *Dharma Maṇḍala*, as I said above. The Dharma Mandala is also one constituent of the three maṇḍalas comprising the *Tri-Ratna Maṇḍala*. *Tri-Ratna* is a common word referring to the well-known three precious treasures for Buddhists: *Buddha*, *Dharma* and *Saṃgha*. Therefore, the offering ceremony is not for the scriptures only. But it was a part of a ceremony regrading all three of those precious treasures.

Scripture worship in the Kathmandu valley is practiced not because the Nepalese people found some mystical power to benefit people in the scriptures nor because they admit special authenticity in those nine selected scriptures. Unlike those assumption of the western scholars, the set is seemingly composed merely according to ritualistic reason.

Although we take note of the background structure of *Nava-Dharma*, the reason why those nine scriptures were selected is still vague. We need to find another scope instead of vewing the object from a doctrinal perspective. As for this purpose, I am not prepared for now to answer the question but I will venture a hint from the iconological viewpoint.

Since the *Dharma Maṇḍala* has a ritual background and is one of three equivalent maṇḍalas, the components of those three mandalas are seemingly expected to correspond to each other. From the iconological view point, the maṇḍala has Vairocana in the center, and four Buddhas are set in the four cardinal directions. The combination and arrangement of the five Buddhas are identical with the maṇḍala of *Vajradhātu* or the Diamond realm, whereas the remaining deities in the *Buddha Maṇḍala* are different from the ones in the *Vajradhātu Maṇḍala*. As to the remaining deities, the four *Buddha-mātri* or Mothers of Buddha are situated in oblique or inter-cardinal positions like in the maṇḍala of *Guhyasamāja-tantra* or the tantra of the secret community. So the *Buddha Maṇḍala* is a mixture of those two maṇḍalas, and this arrangement is identical with the central part of the mandala of *Māyājāra-tantra*.

This tantra is said to be a source of *Nāmasaṃgiti*,[11] the most popular text among Nepalese Buddhists. *Nāmasaṃgiti* is also strongly associated with *Svayambhū-prāṇa*[12] which tells the origin of Nepalese Buddhism; the *Buddha Maṇḍala* is surely rooted deep into the mythical earth of Nepalese Buddhist culture.

We can apply the same assumption about the *Buddha Maṇḍala* to the *Dharma Maṇḍala* on the grounds that the arrangement of those two maṇḍalas are considered to be corresponding each other. Thus, the arrangement of the *Dharma Maṇḍala* is to be analyzed within a ritualistic context instead of a doctrinal context. Likewise, the list of *Nava-Dharma* is to be analyzed within a ritualistic context; it is not the list of scriptures of the most doctrinal importance.

The same idea may be applied to the whole corpus of Nepal's Sanskrit manuscripts. Recent statistical research reveals that manuscripts which have a strong relationship with the unique features of Nepalese Buddhist culture are more likely to be copied and preserved.[13] In other words, the present proportion of the existing manuscripts by title is practically irrelevant to the popularity or the importance of the texts in the doctrinal sphere of Buddhism. It can only tell us how strong the relationship is between each text and the ritualistic culture of Nepalese Buddhism; we should be restraint when interpreting the situation of late Indian Buddhism based on an analysis of Nepal's Buddhist manuscripts.[14]

Reformation of *Nava-Dharma*

A knowledge of ritual background is helpful when one comes across a mystery difficult to solve only with a doctrinal view. For instance, the contents and the array of scriptures in *Nava-Dharma*, Tuladhar-Douglas said, have been reformed twice in the history of Nepalese Buddhism.[15] According to his argument, the most noticeable change was the replacement of two scriptures between the oldest set and the following two sets, which had occured along with the transformation of the ritualistic context of Newar Buddhism.[16]

The substituted original scriptures which had been in the oldest set are:

(7') *Nāmasaṃgīti*
(9') *Pañcarakṣā*

Each scripture was substituted to a new one with the corresponding number without dash(') in the Nava-Dharma list above: *Nāmasaṃgīti* and *Pañcarakṣā* are out while *Tathāgata Guhyaka* and *Suvarṇa Prabhāsottama Sūtrendra Ratnarāja* are in.

Both of the old members are very popular scriptures in Nepalese Buddhism. It is very natural that they are in the list. But in the wave of drastic reformation of Nepalese Buddhism, Tuladhar-Douglas assumed, they were eliminated because they are *Vajrayāna* scriptures. The new ones both belong to *Pāramitāyāna* and, what is more, they also have been used in another old scripture worship ritual.[17] There is no doctrinal concordance between those old substituted members and new substituting members whatsoever. So we cannot reason about this substitution from a doctrinal point of view. It must remain a mystery unless we understand the ritual background.

Emendation: A Serious Problem for Philological Research

Pāṭha/paṭhana, or recitation of specific scriptures, is very popular custom among Nepalese Buddhists for it is recommended as one of ten meritorious deeds of Buddhists (:Daśa Dharma-caryā). Although the recitation itself is performed by Vajrācāryas or the Buddhist priests in a proper ceremony, the merit is accumulated to all the participants, especially the sponsors. So the Nepalese Buddhists readily hold recitation assemblies on every special occasion.

In the Kathmandu valley, there is a custom of having the gathered recitation of *Aṣṭasahasrikā Prajñapāramitā*, the most respected scripture placed in the center of *Dharma Maṇḍala*.[18] The most famous recitation ritual of this kind is the one which is held at the *Kwa Baha* (well-known as "the Golden Temple") in Patan.

In that ritual, priests take turns to recite in a mutter the manuscripts of the scripture in public. They actually read the lines; that manner forms a clear contrast with the corresponding ritual being performed in Japan. In that Japanese ritual, called *Hannyagyo-Tendoku* and practiced only at a few prestigious Buddhist temples, priests just look over the manuscript from the beginning to the end while hastily sending pages into the air.

It is a good thing in general, and toward anthropologists especially, for the Nepalese Buddhists to actually read the manuscripts, because it represents the Buddhist culture is living and active there. But this lively culture would cause a serious problem against the philologist scholars of Sanskrit Buddhism at the same time.

On the one hand, since Nepalese Buddhists do read the lines, they can sometimes find scribal errors within the present manuscripts they are reading. On the other hand, they perform this recitation ritual so many times that the manuscripts used there can be easily damaged by the offerings or any sort of manipulation. Degradation of the manuscripts is inevitable, so continuous restoration of manuscripts, including substituting with new copies, is required to maintain this custom.

Therefore, under the lively culture of Nepalese Buddhist society, manuscripts are always subjected to continuous renovation to maintain their good condition. Every seeming error is revised and overwritten by appropriate wording according to modern authenticity; thus we will end up losing the old samples of variant readings of the text.

This includes quite a big problem in terms of the philological study. Making a critical edition is an attempt to reconstruct a more correct "original" by comparing and examining multiple manuscripts containing various different readings when the original cannot be obtained. Every critical edition will remain forever in a hypothetical reconstructed version of the original; the text which seems to be definitive at the present time always has the possibility of being corrected by a newly found variant reading. Therefore, all the information of the manuscripts should be preserved for the future higher criticism.

However, under the circumstances of Nepalese Buddhist culture, all the variant readings are most likely to be lost due to the practical reasons noted above.

A case: "vaineya vaśāt" in the *Saddharmapuṇḍarīka* Chap.15

We can see a typical example in a manuscript of *Saddharmapuṇḍarīka* Chap.15 of the *Thapa collection*[19]. Before checking how the words go in the manuscript of the *Thapa collection*, we shall see the wording of a corresponding portion in a modern critical edition of the same scripture. The target here is a sentence in the middle of Chap.15, *Tathāgatāyuṣpramāṇa parivarta*, of *Saddharmapuṇḍarīka*. The wording in a modern edition[20] is as follows;

> ...sadā sthitaḥ| aparinirvṛtas tathāgataḥ parinirvāṇam ādarśayati vaineya vaśāt| na ca tāvān me kulaputrā...(p.271.15-p.272.1)

For comparison, we quote here the corresponding part of the Kumārajīva's Chinese translation.

> ...常住不滅 諸善男子...

There are only eight characters in the Chinese translation. It is obviously insufficient if it is a translation of the sentence above; the underlined portion in the Sanskrit text is entirely wanting in the Chinese translation. In such case, two possibilities are conceivable: the translator intentionally omitted to translate the portion, or the portion did not exist in the source text of the translator from the beginning.

Most modern scholars have supported the former possibility, because the translater here, Kumārajīva, is known not to have cared about literal word-by-word translation. But would the latter possibility be also hard to dismiss if we had a manuscript without this portion?

The Institute for the Comprehensive Study of the Lotus Sutra of Rissho University published a series of books entitled *Sanskrit Manuscripts of Saddharmapuṇḍarīka,* which collected 30 manuscripts available at that time along with two critical edition and aligned them in parallel in order to compare all the texts in a single view. The portion we are now checking is on p.60 of the 8th volume of this book.

We can comfirm that although 6 of 32 texts are totally wanting of this portion, all the remaining 26 texts have the portion in question, containing some minor variant readings like the positions of danda(|) or the substitution of "vaśāt" with "vaśena" and so on.

Next, we proceed to check another manuscript in the *Thapa Collection.* The wording of the corresponding portion is as follows;

...||sadā sthita aparinirvṛtas tathāgataḥ parinirvāṇam ādarśayati | na ca tāvat me kulaputrāḥ|...(fol.178 verso.5-6)

A careful observation informs us that the underlined portion which corresponds to the untranslated part in the Chinese version is shorter than what in the first example. Two words, "vineya vaśāt", are dropped from the line. What we shall remember here is that no existing manuscript, except this one in the *Thapa Collection,* is wanting this part.

This variant reading is a small but significant sign in that it suggests the possibility that there was no such part in the "original" text. Of course this omission of two words might be the result simply of a simple scribal error. But it is no less important even if that were the case, because it would bring about a new import of the text, which leads us closer than ever to the supposed original.

A New Approach: Shifting the Focus Onto Publishing "Diplomatic Text"

Thus, from the philological point of view, ideally we should record every minor variant reading. This was practically nearly impossible until we become able to deal with massive volumes of data using electronic devices. Now, with the help of various electronic devices, we can not only store big data but also utilize and process it, and, what is more, even publish it in the form of digital data. The popularization of these new technologies can make real this long-time hoped ideal of philology.

Philologists have ever taken the method of publishing so-called "diplomatic copy" of the source manuscripts when they found a new and important copy of them. "Diplomatic" here means exactly reproducing an original version with some simple process like transcription for publishing purposes. This method was taken only when a few limited philologically important texts were to be published because of the cost-effectiveness; a diplomatic version is so bulky in general containing much noise that only a few experts could realize the value of that version.

Now we can easily deal with the bulky data by applying new technologies, in light of the philological ideal, which is to record and publish every single variant readings along with noise-like minor information, no matter how big the data becomes, so that we can shift the focus onto proactive use of diplomatic copy.

Manuscripts of philological importance, so far, often have been kept concealed behind collectors for long periods of time until they finish preparing to publish. Although it was somehow inevitable in the circumstances of yesteryear, that custom has caused a delay in the progress of study in this field. Instantly publishing a raw data in the diplomatic format is far more efficient in reaching a good text with the help of many outside experts, rather than publishing the same text after one deliberately prepared critical edition personally. So we had better shift our first priority to taking the method of diplomatic publication for the benefit of the whole.

Through this methodological shift, we can expect some good side-effects. Making private raw materials open by proactively sharing them through publication in the diplomatic format, we can attract many experts working in the same field around the material. The host institute would be served as a platform and can take the initiative of organizing a research project in the particular field.

Therefore, even though it does not look professional for a philologist to publish raw material without a critical edition, it is far more beneficial to the whole if we strategically share our own properties with outsiders as quickly as possible. An ancient Asian proverb says, "It's better to be brisk and slapdash than painstaking but slow."

About the *Thapa Collection Digital Library of Nepal Sanskrit Buddhist Manuscripts*

These last few years, the *Rissho University Nepal Academic-Research Project* (RNAP)[21] has carried out comprehensive research into Nepalese Buddhism. We are currently working on a study on Nepal's Sanskrit Buddhist Manuscripts, a collaborative research project with Prof. Shanker Thapa of Tribhuvan University, a Nepalese native scholar working in this particular field.

Prof. Thapa has been working on collecting and preserving Nepal's Sanskrit Manuscripts as a private activity without any financial support from any institute. He works independently, walking around the Kathmandu valley to visit private houses and temples which possess never-before published manuscripts.

He collects the manuscripts in digital data format, not the real objects; actually he only asks the owners to let him photograph those manuscripts. This is his strategy to access those unpublished manuscripts. Since those manuscripts are valuables for each owner for various reasons — for some owners they are practically used in rituals and for others they are cashable properties and so on — the owners will not take the risk of showing their possessions if he were asking them to hand over the actual manuscriptes. Prof. Thapa is indifferent to the value of the manuscripts as real properties. He just wants to know and record the whole picture of the present status of Nepalese Sanskrit manuscripts before their traditional contents disappear for reasons such as continuous renovation of manuscripts in the ritual culture, which I refered above, or export outside Nepal through private trade, etc. He takes color photos of all the folios of the manuscripts one by one, and has compiled a huge amount of data in CRW[22] and JPG format.

Through this activity, Prof. Thapa has collected digital data for over 1,000 titles of private unpublished Sanskrit manuscripts. In the collaborative work with Prof. Thapa, RNAP have been given access to the entire data of this collection, which is exactly the same as what Prof. Thapa stores/will store in his storage device. Cataloguing the whole collection is now underway by RNAP. It will be published in several volumes from time to time within a couple of years.[23]

Prospect of the Activity of RNAP

In the section before last, we proposed a new approach for philological study of Sanskrit Buddhism. Following our own proposal, we shall start publishing raw materials in the diplomatic format from the huge stock of manuscript data in the *Thapa Collection*.

The first issue will be the diplomatic text of the *Saddharmapuṇḍarīka* (No. 12-002), from which the portion of text we quoted above was taken. This manuscript is the very thing worth publishing in the diplomatic format because it preserves several new variant readings not found in any other versions, as we saw above.

We will also proceed with further study of *Nava-Dharma*. Although this set of scriptures is not the authentic core of Northern Buddhism, as Hodgson had wrongly assumed, it is no less important on the point that it is deeply rooted in the unique and most significant feature of Nepalese Buddhism, ritual. So, if we understand the *Nava-Dharma* well — the structural background, the history of reformation and so on, we can see the Buddhism of Nepal more systematically. Manuscripts of all the 11 scriptures associated with the *Nava-Dharma* are found in the *Thapa Collection*, including *Tathāgata Guhyaka*, a very rare scripture of which only one complete manuscript has ever been discovered.

Because the *Thapa Collection* consists of clear, full-color, high-resolution photo data, we can utilize it for bibliological study, which is difficult to undertake with the rough monochrome microfiche hard copy. Take the cover paintings for instance. The Rissho University Library possesses a Sanskrit manuscript of *Gaṇḍavyūha* that was brought from Nepal to Japan by Ven. Ekai Kawaguchi. It has beautiful cover paintings on the first folio of the manuscript. Interestingly enough, *Laṅkāvatāra* in the *Thapa Collection* also has a cover painting almost identical with the one on the *Gaṇḍavyūha* at Rissho University. Cover painting, in general, relates to the workshop which duplicated the manuscripts. Therefore, it is most probable that both of these manuscripts were the product of the same workshop. This conclusion leads us to another philological or bibliographical assumption that hints the lineages of duplicated manuscripts both remain in Nepal and scattered around the world.

Conclusion

By focusing on the practice of scripture worship in the Kathmandu valley, we have first drawn out many topics to argue for a comprehensive understanding of Nepalese Buddhism. Firstly, we are to realize that Sanskrit Buddhism which the western pioneers of modern Buddhist study try to draw out from Nepalese Buddhism was somewhat imaginary and need revision. We should not hope too much to find a medieval Indian Buddhism behind Nepalese Buddhism.

On that basis, we can proceed to study Nepalese Buddhism as it is, to gain a comprehensive understanding of it. At that level, knowledge of the *Nava-Dharma* is helpful in grasping the whole strunture of Nepalese Buddhism.

Then, we shall take up the manuscripts that are the container of the scriptures and see how they function or dysfunction in the ritualistic cultural context. Actually, the ritualistic culture is not always beneficial to Sanskrit Buddhism, especially from the philological point of view.

In those circumstances, what we should do is record as many documents as we can. This has become possible thanks to the recent development of information technology. Prof. Thapa actually has been doing this. We can make free use of the data he has collected.

Now, RNAP is preparing to publish it in various ways and is ready to lead the study in this field.

*This research was financially supported by *Rissho University Nepal Academic Research Project* (RNAP), Japan.

Notes

1. *The Company*: The East India Company (EIC), also known as the Honourable East India Company (HEIC) or the British East India Company.
2. According to Max Muller (1881), Hodgson made the list with the help of Amritananda. The list should be almost identical with the one in his essay. He elaborately collected almost all manuscripts in the list and sent it to the Asiatic Society of Bengal but no one started studying them, so they made new two sets and sent them to London and Paris. This was in 1924.
3. Max Muller (1881) p.185.

4. Hodgson insisted that he found a manuscript which had been transmitted to Kathmandu in the 2nd century of the Christian era. This information is also from Max Muller (1881). The oldest academically confirmed existing manuscript, however, is the *Suśrta Saṃhitā* in the Kaisal Libray.
5. Shanker (2018). p.3.
6. *prakāśa* is also one of the *Daśa-karma*. See Takaoka (1984) for the detail.
7. Tanaka Kimiaki & Yoshizaki, Kasumi (1998).
8. *Aṣṭamīvrata* is a fasting celemony which worships the Amogapāsa Avalokiteśvara. The Buddhist story of bringing Avalokiteśvara from Assam to Kathmandu is depicted in genealogy text. See Sasaki (2018).
9. Hodgson (1874) p.13.
10. Max Muller (1881) p.170.
11. *Mañjuśrī-jñānasattvasya-paramārtha-nāmasaṅgīti* (大正蔵1187-1190, 北京 No.2). This scripture is said to be derived from the Samādhi Chapter of *Māyājāratantra*. But the present Māyājāra doesn't contain such a portion.
12. See Shakya (2015).
13. Tanaka & Yoshizaki (1998).
14. Tuladhar-Douglas reported the Darbhanga Institute's case. This Mithila based institute "chose to publish editions of these same nine texts on the basis of Hodgson's descriptions of Sanskrit Buddhism." He continues; "This has led many student of Sanskrit Buddhism to the false assumption that the navagrantha are a category within medieval Indian Buddhism." P.67.
15. Tuladhar-Douglas (2003).
16. Regarding this transformation, see Tuladhar-Douglas (2006).
17. A ritual of *Guhya-sūtra/tantra*. Tanaka (2010), p.91.
18. *Aṣṭasāhasrikā Prajñāpāramitā* called *Bhagavatī or* the mother of the Buddha.
19. The *Thapa Collection* is introduced in a later section of this paper.
20. Here we use the edition of Wogihara and Tsuchida: *Saddharmapundarikasūtram, Romanaized and Revised Text of the Bibliotheca Buddhica Publication by Consulting a Sanskrit MS. and Tibetan and Chinese Translations,* Tokyo, 1934.
21. The office of the project is situated in the Faculty of Buddhist Studies, which is jointly directed by Fumio SHOJI and Kazunori SASAKI.
22. The RAW data format produced by Canon digital cameras.
23. RNAP has published a tentative catalogue of Prof. Thapa's first phase collection (containing 235 titles) in *the Journal of Institute for the Comprehensive Study of Lotus Sutra (Hokekyô Bunka Kenkyûjo)*, vol.44, 2018.

References

Burnouf, E. (1852). *Le Lotus de la bonne loi: traduit du sanscrit, accompagné d'un commentaire et de vingt et un mémoires relatifs au buddhisme*. Paris: Impr. nationale.

Burnouf, E; translated by Buffetrille, Katia & Lopez, Donald S. (2010). *Introduction to the History of Indian Buddhism*. Chicago: University of Chicago Press.

Emmrich, C. (2009). "Emending perfection: prescript, postscript, and practice in Newar Buddhist manuscript culture," *Buddhist Manuscript Cultures: Knowledge, Ritual, and Art*, Routledge critical studies in Buddhism, 52. London; New York: Routledge.

Hodgson, B. H. (1874). *Essays on the Languages, Literature, and Religion of Nepal and Tibet: Together with Further Papers on the Geography, Ethnology, and Commerce of Those Countries*. London: Trübner.

Institute for the Comprehensive Study of the Lotus Sutra, Rissho University (1977-1980). *Sanskrit Manuscripts of Saddharmapuṇḍarīka: Collected from Nepal, Kashmir, and Central Asia*, 1-12 vols. and Romanized text 1-2 vols. Tokyo: Publishing Association of Saddharmapundarika Manuscripts.

Max M., F. (1881). "Buddhism," *Selected Essays on Language, Mythology and Religion*. London: Longman. pp.160-223.

Sakuma, R. (2015). "A Study on the Prajñāpāramitā-sādhana," *Tokai Bukkyo*, 60, pp.(164)-(150) (in Japanese).

Sasaki, K. (2018). "Nepalese mythical explanation of the origin of the Avalokitesvara-Matsyendranath worship: An annotated translation of The King Varadeva's part from a Nepalese genealogical work," *Osaki gakuho*, 174, pp.1-24.

Sato, Y. et al. (1988). "A Study of Newari Buddhism," *SAMBHĀṢĀ*, 10, pp.1-99 (in Japanese).

Shoji F. (2013). "A Study on the Archives of Ekai Kawaguchi Kept in the Rissho University Library (1): Transliterated Sanskrit Text of the *Gaṇḍavyūha* (1)," *Journal of Institute for the Comprehensive Study of Lotus Sutra*, 39, pp.17-33 (in Japanese).

Shoji, F. (2018). "The Legacy of Tanzan Ishibashi: The Books Formerly Kept by Ekai Kawaguchi Preserved at Rissho University," *The Academic Pilgrimage to Sustainable Social Development*, Tokyo: Heibonsha, pp.9-44.

Singh, H. L. (2004). *Buddhism in Nepal: A Brief Historical Introduction*. Ratna Pustak Bhandar: Kathmandu.

Shakya, S. (2015). "Taking Refuge in Three Jewels and Triratna-maṇḍala in Nepalese Buddhism," *Journal of Esoteric Buddhism*, 51, pp.211-227 (in Japanese).

Takaoka, S. (1984). "The religious beliefs and the rituals in Nepalese Buddhism." *Ars Buddhica*, 153, pp.95-120 (in Japanese).

Tanaka, K. (1990). "On the Buddhist Sanskrit Manuscripts in Nepal and the Nepal-German Manuscript Preservation Project," *Journal of Indian and Buddhist Studies*, 39(1), pp.385-381.

Tanaka, K. (1998). "Newly Identified Buddhist Tantric Manuscripts from Nepal," *Journal of Indian and Buddhist Studies*, 46(2), pp.913-909.

Tanaka, K. & Yoshizaki, K. (1998). *Nepaaru Bukkyou (Buddhism in Nepal)*, Tokyo: Shunjusha (in Japanese).
Thapa, S. (2018). "Buddhist Sanskrit Manuscripts of Nepal: Continuity of Ancient Indian Textual Tradition in the Himalaya," *Manuscript and Indian Culture*, New Delli: Kaveri Books, pp.1-20.
Thapa, S., Shoji F. & K., Sasaki (2018). "A Succinct Catalog of Shanker Thapa's First Phase Digital Collection of Private Sanskrit Buddhist Manuscripts in Patan, Nepal," *Journal of Institute for the Comprehensive Study of Lotus Sutra*, 44, pp.1-12.
Tuladhar-Douglas, W. (2003). "The *Navagrantha*: an historical précis," *Pale-swam*, 20, pp.65-68.
Tuladhar-Douglas, W. (2006). *Remaking Buddhism for Medieval Nepal: The Fifteenth-century Reformation of Newar Buddhism*. London: Routledge.
Yoshizaki K. (2011). "Three Works on Newar Buddhism Published Recently in Japan," *Journal of Indian and Buddhist Studies*, 60(1), pp.512-506.
Yoshizaki K. (2012). *The Kathmandu Valley as a Water Pot: Abstracts of Research Papers on Newar Buddhism in Nepal*. Kathmandu: Vajra Publications.

On Academic Training in the Early Nichiren Sect: With a Focus on Cases from the Nikkō Lineage

Shumbun Homma

Abstract

It is beyond dispute that there is a level of study and training that a monk must accumulate before they can reach maturity as a monk. Within his literary works, such as *Kaimokushō* ("The Opening of the Eyes") and *Soya Nyūdō-dono gari gosho* ("Letter to Soya Nyūdō-dono"), the founder of the Nichiren Sect, Nichiren (1222–1282) gave teachings to his disciples and patrons on the place of academic education in the course of cultivating one's path in Buddhism. His position on this must also have been made clear to his followers time and again.

How, then, did the disciples who inherited Nichiren's teachings go on to handle academic training in the early sect subsequent to the founder's passing? This question is an issue of import in grasping the monks' basic endeavors and what the original circumstances of the sect were like. However, few historical materials exist such as writings by direct disciples in the early sect after Nichiren's death, and to date, no systematic investigations have been conducted on academic training at that time.

Therefore, to make a first step toward bringing to light the actual conditions of academic training in the early Nichiren sect, and having sorted out research that has already been done, this paper will look to the Nikkō lineage founded by Byakuren Ajari Nikkō (1246–1333)—of whose self-penned writings the greatest volume are extant among the six direct disciples (six senior priests) of Nichiren—in an attempt to investigate the circumstances of study within the lineage based on reliable historical materials.

Introduction

As is widely known, Nichiren (1222–1282), counted as one of the monks who brought about the rise of "Kamakura New Buddhism," studied at the Seichō-ji temple in Awa Province from a young age and spent long days in training, also making trips to study at temples in the vicinity of Kyōto, including on Mount Hiei. In the 5th year of Kenchō (1253), then proclaiming his absolute devotion to the Lotus Sūtra, he declared the foundation of his own sect and forged a new beginning as its founder.

Now, just as there exists the Threefold Training of higher virtue, higher mind and higher wisdom that all who aspire to the Buddhist path must cultivate, it is beyond dispute that there is also study and training that a monk must accumulate in order to reach maturity as a monk. With regard to this studying, Nichiren stated in *Kaimokushō* ("The Opening of the Eyes"), written in the 2nd month of Bun'ei 9 (1272), for instance: "There are three things one should study. These are what are called Confucianism, the outer [non-Buddhist paths] and the inner [Buddhist path][1]." In *Soya Nyūdō-dono gari gosho* ("Letter to Soya Nyūdō-dono") written on the 10th day of the 3rd month of Bun'ei 12 (1275) he recorded: "For the promulgation of this Great Dharma, one should be sure to keep the sacred teachings of Śākyamuni's life close at hand and study the scriptures and commentaries of the eight schools [of Mahāyāna][2]." He thus gave teachings to his disciples and patrons on the place of academic education in the course of cultivating one's path in Buddhism. Here we are afforded a glimpse of part of Nichiren's position toward study, and this position must also have been shown to his followers time and again.

The question of how it was that the disciples who inherited Nichiren's teachings then went on to handle academic training in the early sect subsequent to the founder's passing is an issue of import in grasping what the original circumstances of the sect were like. Among materials making reference to the circumstances of studying by monks in the medieval era are: Makoto Nagamura's research[3] dealing with the production and function of temples' historical materials, taking into account the organizational structure of temple society, based on literature that has been passed down at temples such as Nanto Tōdai-ji, Kōfuku-ji and Kyōto Daigo-ji; and Eichi Terao's body of research[4] dealing with studying by Gyōgakuin Nitchō (1422–1500), a scholar monk representative of the Muromachi-era Nichiren sect, and related issues. With this research, great results have been achieved through the analysis of varied and voluminous literature and historical materials. With regard to the circumstances of studying in the early Nichiren sect, however, related literature—including writings by direct disciples of Nichiren—is scarce. While research[5] has been advanced that focuses on individual works completed in the early period of the sect, such as the *Kinkōshū* ("*Vajra* [Diamond] Collection") and *Hokke mondō shōgishō* ("Judgments on Questions and Answers Concerning the Lotus [Sūtra]"), there are still many obscure points that presently remain regarding the state of academic training by early followers of Nichiren.

With this paper, then, having sorted out prior research that has been done, I will fix my perspective on the Nikkō lineage founded by Byakuren Ajari [=Acharya] Nikkō (1246–1333)—of whose self-penned writings the greatest volume are extant among the six direct disciples (six senior priests) of Nichiren—in attempting to investigate the circumstances of study within the lineage based on reliable historical materials. Through this I would like to make a first step toward bringing to light the actual conditions of academic training in the early Nichiren sect.

In advancing my discussion in this paper, I will take my definition of the "early Nichiren sect" to be the sect as it existed up until the era of the disciples of Nikkō's disciples—namely, the mid-14th century.

1. An Overview of Academic Training in the Nichiren Sect's Early Period

It is not difficult to envision Nichiren's followers striving under his watch on the dual path of study and training with he himself demonstrating strong leadership in commanding them following his foundation of the sect. As related in quotes subsequent to Nichiren's retirement to Mount Minobu in particular—"When the people are away, there are forty; when present, sixty[6];" "The sound of Lotus [Sūtra] recitations echoing into the blue skies / Voices expounding on the Single Vehicle audible amidst the mountains[7]"—suggestions come to mind of numerous disciples and patrons assembling before Nichiren, with the Lotus Sūtra being recited and debated or expounded upon. Such *dangi* (debating and expounding upon scriptures' and treatises' meanings, sects' doctrines and so on) was one method of a monks' study. An important element in the training of medieval scholar monks, it was widely practiced within various sects. As illustrated in the passages quoted above, it can be seen that in the Nichiren sect as well *dangi* was practiced from an early date as a form of study, and also that the training of followers was being advanced.

I would like to first attempt to provide an overview of how specifically Nichiren and his followers carried out their academic training in the midst of such circumstances. On the basis of that, I will then investigate the main topic of the actual conditions of academic training in the Nikkō lineage.

(1) Nichiren's Academic Training and Education of Followers

As shown in the previously mentioned *Kaimokushō* and *Soya Nyūdō-dono gari gosho*, Nichiren had taken a look at literature from a wide range of fields. It has been pointed out that, in the body of work Nichiren left behind, quotations can in places be found from not only Buddhist texts but also philosophical works, history books and old records, dictionaries and encyclopedias, anthologies of war chronicles, diaries and narratives, collections of [classical Chinese] poetry and prose, waka, and so on[8]. Also, among extant manuscripts transcribed by Nichiren are: the *Juketsu Entaragi-shū Tōketsu*, attributed to Enchin (a holding of the Shōmyō-ji temple in Kanagawa Prefecture, entrusted to the Kanazawa Bunko); Saichō's *Kenkairon engi* ("Clarification of the Precepts Origin Chronicle"); Genshin's *Ichijō yōketsu* ("Determining the Essential Points of the One Vehicle"); Kakuban's *Gorin kuji myōhimitsu-shaku* ("The Illuminating Secret Commentary on the Five *Chakras* and the Nine Syllables"); Jōdo sect book the *Jōdo-shū yōketsu* ("Determining the Essential Points of the Jōdo Sect"; the aforementioned holdings of the Nakayama Hokekyō-ji temple); and the classic of dynastic study the *Zhēnguàn zhèngyào* (Japanese reading: *Jōgan seiyō*; "Essentials of Administration in the Zhenguan Era"; a holding of the Kitayama Honmon-ji temple); and among prized works of Nichiren's that are extant: the *Tendai shikyō ryakushō* ("Synopsis of the Fourfold Teachings of Tiantai") and *Tendai jingokushō* ("Profound Secrets of Tiantai", holdings of the Nakayama Hokekyō-ji temple) . Furthermore, beyond these, it has been noted that a great number of fragmentary extracts have been passed down along with *yōmon-shū* (collections of essential passages) that extract from sūtra commentaries and interpretations such as: the *Tendai kan'yōmonshū* ("Essential

Tendai Passages"); *Shūku jisshō-shō* ("Ten Superior Doctrines Described in the Outstanding Principles of the Lotus Sūtra"); *Sōshi yōmon* (the aforementioned holdings of the Nakayama Hokekyō-ji temple); and *Chū Hokekyō* ("The Annotated Lotus Sūtra"; a holding of the Tamazawa Myōhokke-ji temple.) According to Yutaka Takagi, the excerpted transcription of *yōmon* (essential passages) from scriptures and commentaries was the basic method of study for Tendai monks; the results of their study with these essential passages would be collected together to form *yōmon-shū*, and then based on these, *yōmon-shū* of a still higher order—in other words, selections of their work—would be produced[9]. We can probably conclude that the aforementioned *yōmon* and *yōmon-shū* of Nichiren's were results of his study produced through such a process.

From even just what we can verify from extant historical materials in such ways, it can be deduced that Nichiren had read from an extremely large range of literature. This approach of Nichiren's is entirely in accordance with the passage from the *Kaimokushō*: "There are three things one should study. These are what are called Confucianism, the outer [non-Buddhist paths], and the inner [Buddhist path]." While the monks Hōnen, Shinran and Myōe who lived concurrently to him equated study with "a pursuit of truth and reality within Buddhism," it has been pointed out that Nichiren was unique in expanding his scope to include even non-Buddhist paths[10].

Through his education with this wide range of literature as well as the persistent ordeals that had befallen him subsequent to his founding of the sect, Nichiren came to place the Lotus Sūtra as the single genuine sūtra among all the scriptures, uniquely suited to the current *Mappō* period of Dharma decline. Deepening his awakening and resolve as a devotee of the Lotus Sūtra, he developed the teaching of *honge-betsuzu* based on thought regarding the *honmon* origin teachings found in the second half of the Lotus Sūtra.

The question of what sort of guidance Nichiren provided to his followers with regard to studying is again problematic. Offering partial suggestions concerning this issue are the existence of his *Ichidai goji zu* ("Diagram of the Five Periods of the Buddha's Lifetime Teachings")[11] and accounts of his sermon on the *Móhē zhǐguān* (Japanese reading: *Maka shikan;* "Principles of Śamatha and *Vipaśyanā* Meditation," from Sanskrit *"Mahāśamatha Vipaśyanā."*)

The *Ichidai goji zu* is a diagrammatical record in which Nichiren graphically represented the spread of Dharma teachings during Śākyamuni's life based on the great Tientai teacher Zhìyĭ's Five Periods evaluative framework of Buddhist teachings, expressing his conviction that the Lotus Sūtra was the vital essence of Śākyamuni's life teachings. It is thought to have been something Nichiren used when delivering lectures to his followers[12]. The *Tei-i* (an authoritative guide to the body of work Nichiren left behind) lists nine versions of the *Ichidai goji zu* authenticated as Nichiren's[13], and none of these contain the identical text, according to Eichi Terao. In light of this fact, he indicates that Nichiren had penned the same diagram anew each time the occasion arose[14]. This means, in other words, that as one instance of academic training by Nichiren, it is assumed that there were many times when he would employ the *Ichidai goji zu*—which represents an outline of his own comprehension of Buddhist principles—in lectures to directly present the history of Buddhist thought to followers as epitomized in the Lotus Sūtra.

There are also instances found in Nichiren's letters from which it can be discerned that he had been lecturing on the *Móhē zhǐguān* at the time. Examples of this are given below.

Ueno-dono haha-ama gozen gosho ("Letter to the Lay Nun, Mother of Ueno-dono,") 22nd day of the 12th month, Bun'ei 7 (1270)
"Regarding the fifth volume of the *[Móhē] zhǐguān*, we will begin reading this at the hour of the dragon [around 8 AM] on the 1st day of the 1st month. [...] Wholly looking toward the next existence we shall discuss śamatha and *vipaśyanā* until the 15th but do not have a great deal of texts. I wonder if you might use your good offices[15]."

Matsuno-dono nyōbō gohenji ("Reply to the wife of Matsuno-dono,") 20th day of the 6th month, Kōan 2 (1279)
"Reading the Lotus Sūtra day and night, discussing the *Móhē zhǐguān* morning and evening; this is akin to the Pure Land of Holy [Eagle] Peak, of no difference from Mount Tientai[16]."

As the preceding letters illustrate, we can surmise that Nichiren was delivering lectures on the *Móhē zhǐguān* to his followers. Furthermore, during Nichiren's life, it seems that his disciples and patrons held Tendai *daishi kō*[17] memorial events for Zhìyĭ on a monthly basis by turns and that lectures on the Lotus Sūtra and *Móhē zhǐguān* were delivered at these[18]. Hōyō Watanabe speculates that Nichiren's inheritance of Tendai doctrine was passed on to his followers through his lectures on the *Móhē zhǐguān* at these events and that the lectures led to the subsequent development of his unique doctrine of *kaigon [kenjitsu]* ("opening [and discarding] the provisional teachings and revealing the true teaching") sublating *śamatha* and *vipaśyanā* in Nichiren's principle work *Kanjin honzon-shō*[19] ("The Object of Devotion for Observing the Mind.")

Nichiren's followers must also have strived further in their studies on the basis of such lectures as these that Nichiren delivered, transmitting to them his ideology and doctrine.

(2) Doctrine Inheritance and Academic Training by Followers

As I have already stated, there is a paucity of historical materials with regard to just how Nichiren's disciples—and their disciples—actually strived in their academic training, and the actual details of this remain somewhat unclear still. I would like to now take a look at some of the works his followers left behind.

It is well known that so-called *"dangi-sho"* (books of discourses) were produced through the *dangi* as one form of scholar monks' endeavors in the medieval period. With regard to their methods of compiling sacred teachings in the course of their study efforts, Makoto Nagamura points out that there were works produced by reading and transcribing excerpts from departed teachers' works and those that reproduced accounts of the *dangi*[20]. The Nichiren sect is no exception with regard to such endeavors, and among written works left behind by direct disciples of Nichiren are several *kikigaki* (written notes on things heard) said to have been produced upon receiving lectures by Nichiren. The following are among principle works in the literature characterized thus; from Nisshō, one of the six senior priests: *Gashi go-hōmon kikigaki* ("A Record of Our Teacher's Dharma Gateway") and *Gohō chōmonki*[21] ("A Record of Things Heard Regarding the Dharma"); from Nikō, another of the six senior priests: the *Kinkō-shū*[22]; and from second head of Okanomiya Kōchō-ji temple, Nippō: *Go-hōmon on-kikigaki*[23] ("A Record of the Dharma Gateway") and *Shōnin no go-hōmon chōmon bunshū*[24,25]. Though the *kikigaki* from direct disciples of Nichiren's that have been passed down to the present day are few in their actual number, there must have been a variety of *dangi-sho* made at the time by the many disciples who heard the lectures of their teacher, Nichiren.

Still, other than this, there is also said to be in the possession of the Izu Jitsujō-ji temple a work called the *Chōkō kenmonroku* ("Record of Lectures Heard") made in Kenji 3 (1277) by Nichiren's direct disciple the Kyo Ajari [=Acharya] Nichimoku (1260–1333) at the age of eighteen compiling lectures of Nichiren's[26]. As yet unseen, details about it are scarcely provided in published works, but it is a valuable resource for obtaining a glimpse of the circumstances of Nichimoku's academic training. This is one work into which I look forward to future research.

Mariko Watanabe points out that various approaches to producing *dangi-sho* were taken in terms of their content: some were notes put together by *nōke* (senior lecturers) in preparation for their own *dangi*; some were written records made by *nōke* upon receiving *dangi*; some were records of lectures made by *nōke* through re-examinations of their records they had collected and edited together, and so on[27]. If we rely on this classification, although the text contained in the two aforementioned works of Nisshō's cannot be verified, others such as the *Kinkōshū, Go-hōmon on-kikigaki* and *Shōnin no go-hōmon chōmon bunshū* can probably be seen as works produced from subsequent compilation and editing of written records of Nichiren's lectures in consideration of such factors as their content, structure and volume of text.

Also around this time there were a variety of works compiled by Nichiren's followers discussing the evaluation of *gonjitsu* (teachings' provisional or genuine natures) and sects' various ideologies in order to validate the superiority of the Lotus Sūtra. Nikō's *Kinkonshū* and Nippō's *Go-hōmon on-kikigaki* and *Shōnin no go-hōmon chōmon bunshū* that I just mentioned are among these, as well as works by Kyōto Myōken-ji temple founder Nichizō: the *Hizōshū*[28] ("Secret Treasury Collection") and *Shoshū mondō kusakushū*[29]; third head of Nakayama Hokekyō-ji temple, Nichiyū: the *Mondō kan'yōshō*[30] ("Dialogue Essentials") and *Tōke hōmon meyasu*[31]; Nichizen of the Nakayama lineage: the *Hokke mondō shōgishō*[32]; and Munehide Oikawa: *Mondō yōishō*[33].

With regard to the fundamental ideology of the era of Nichiren's direct disciples, it is taken by Kankō Mochizuki and Hōyō Watanabe to have chiefly been an era focused on the concrete actions of remonstration and preaching on a national level based on the ideology characterizing Nichiren's *Risshō ankoku-ron* ("On Establishing the Correct Teaching for the Peace of the Land."). The main issue with regard to their doctrine concerned the evaluation of *gonjitsu* to express the Lotus Sūtra's rightful status as the true Mahāyāna teaching—and while the superiority of the Fundamental Aspect (*honmon*) over the Manifestation Doctrine (*shakumon*) with regard to comprehension of the Lotus Sūtra did become an issue, this amounted to nothing more than a matter of views of the Sūtra's two aspects' relation relative to one another. Direct disciples' works were largely characterized by considerable plainness, with no outstanding doctrinal works to be found among them, in their appraisal[34]. While, as Mochizuki and others point out, there are no works found in this period that provide a systematic framework of Nichiren doctrine, we can probably say that one characteristic of study by early Nichiren followers is on the point that the aforementioned works dealing with *gonjitsu* evaluation and sectarian ideologies were produced by Nichiren followers. As far as a work that presented a grouped arrangement of sects' various ideologies, as touched on previously, Nichiren's *Ichidai goji zu* does exist[35]. The relationship of aforementioned works to it can be assumed in light of their content and structures. We can deduce, in short, that Nichiren's *Ichidai goji zu* lectures were transmitted to followers who then produced new works based upon them.

As one role of these works that compiled *gonjitsu* evaluations and various sectarian ideologies such as this, they are considered to have been produced as materials for criticizing other sects in preparation for *hōron* (Dharma debates) with them to come. Nichiren's followers also vigorously expanded their efforts at remonstration and proselytization towards the government with demands of devotion to the "true Dharma" [of the Lotus Sūtra] and cessation of reliance on the "wicked" [other scriptures] subsequent to his passing[36], aiming to actualize the ideals of "establishing the correct teaching for the peace of the land" Nichiren had set out in his *Risshō ankoku-ron*. The works must have served as a useful foundation for debates and formulation of petitions to the government on such occasions. Looking at the literature that has been passed down, we can take from it that, in their expansion of propagation efforts, followers of Nichiren of the time were keenly aware of debates on the Dharma with other sects.

With the discovery of *kikigaki,* thought to have been produced by followers of Nichiren upon receiving his lectures, along with the widespread production—as a trend—of works compiling *gonjitsu* evaluations and outlines of sectarian ideologies as materials for *hōron* debates, we can conjecture that followers of the time were involved in the production of literature with an eye toward accomplishing propagation goals as one instance of academic training.

2. Academic Training in the Nikkō Lineage

Up until this point I have given an overview of aspects of academic training in the early Nichiren sect. As far as the direction the Nikkō lineage was headed around that era, following Nichiren's passing, Nikkō himself spent a certain amount of time residing at Mount Minobu before relocating to the Fuji District in Suruga Province. Then after laying the foundation for the Taiseki-ji temple in Ueno, he again relocated in Einin 6 (1298) from Ueno to Omosu where he laid the foundation for the Honmon-ji temple. Nikkō's direct disciple Nichimoku then came to administer Taiseki-ji, and subsequently plans were laid for a veritable expansion of the lineage with Taiseki-ji and Honmon-ji serving as bases.

With formation of the lineage's infrastructure being advanced like this, one can imagine the monks in the Nikkō lineage vigorously striving at their studies as well. What sort of consciousness did teachers in the lineage actually hold towards study, though, and were they transferring it into action? I would like to take a look into the specific circumstances regarding that while taking into consideration the preceding overview.

(1) Perceptions of Studying and Literature Collection in the Nikkō Lineage

Among letters written by teachers from the Nikkō lineage, some can be found that give an idea of the state of academic training in the period. Below I will list some relevant passages.

> 1. Letter of Nikkō's: *Yo Minbu-dono sho* ("Letter to Minbu-dono,") year and date unknown
> How is the state of your studies? Please apply yourself with diligence. [...] Jibu-kō is originally one whom I have not instructed. Please assent to all and study together. Also, Taifu-kō and Yakurō are on familiar terms. Please include them and apply yourself [to your studies] all together[37].

2. Letter of Nikkō's: *Yo Minbu-kō gobō sho* ("Letter to Lord Minbu,") 27th day of 7th month, year unknown
   I feel sorry to be unable to provide paper and so on to those who are studying[38].
3. Letter of Nichimoku's: *Yo Kikuta no Shirōhyōe-dono sho* ("Letter to Shirōhyōe-dono of Kikuta,") 25th day of 10th month, year unknown
   Shōni-no-kimi is applying himself with diligence to his studies as well as training. Upon having him study yet more, I shall have him go there[39].
4. Letter of Nichimoku's: *Yo Minbu ajari gobō sho* ("Letter to Ajari Minbu,") 25th day of 10th month, Shōkyō 1 (1332)
   Having thoroughly read the *gika* (Tendai sect debate books) and organized notes on them, I would like for you to spend the 2nd and 3rd months here holding *dangi* with the young monks and juveniles[40].
5. Letter of Nichimoku's: *Yo Saishō ajari gobō sho* ("Letter to Saishō Ajari,") year and date unknown
   Next year I would like you to stay here from spring until the 10th month and hold *dangi*. Please come having read the *Heihō* ("The Art of Warfare") and bring the book with you. Also, I believe you had the *Hazen yōmon* and papers on the submission of the various sects transcribed. Please bring those as well. Those books are not present here[41].
6. Letter of Nikkō's: *Minbu-kō gobō gohenji* ("Reply from Lord Minbu,") 18th day of 6th month, Shōwa 3 (1314)
   I am very pleased to have had the *Sanmon Sōjō* transcribed[42].
7. Letter of Nikkō's: *Shikan no go-shōsoku* ("Regarding Śamatha and Vipaśyanā,") year and date unknown
   I have instructed the messenger to take the *Móhē zhǐguān*, box and all[43].
8. Letter of Nikkō's: *Ryōshō gobō gohenji* ("Reply from Ryōshōgobō,") 7th day of 6th month, year unknown
   I have sent the *Kokinjo* that you desired. I also have the *Shin-Kokinjo* as well as the *Kawara-no-in-no-fu* here as well. Please return it as soon as transcription is finished[44].
9. Letter of Nikkō's: *Tsubone no go-shōsoku*, year and date unknown
   Thank you for the ten high-quality brushes. I made an offering of them before the Buddha right away to inform the departed Nichiren. I was just thinking of transcribing the *Daiji no Shōgyō*, so I was very pleased as high-quality brushes such as these cannot be obtained in the countryside[45].

To start out with, 1 and 2 are letters Nikkō addressed to a disciple of his disciple Lord Minbu Nichijō (1287–unk.). In 1, along with inquiring about the state of Nichijō's studies, Nikkō admonishes him to diligently strive in his studying together with the various teachers. In 2, Nikkō laments his current inability to send necessities such as paper to Nichijō who is in the middle of his studies. Also, 3 is a letter Nichimoku addressed to a patron called Shirōhyoe in which he expresses his intention to pay a visit, having offered encouragement to him—who he refers to as *"Shōni no kimi"*—to be diligent in their studies. These are just a few examples, but these letters offer a glimpse of the encouragement and concern shown by Nikkō and Nichimoku toward young monks who were in the course of pursuing studies.

Then in the letters shown in 4 and 5, passages can be found in which Nichimoku invites his disciples Nichijō and Saishō Ajari Nichigō (1293–1353) to come to Fuji and participate in *dangi*. In other words, we can take from this that Nichijō and Nichigō were both in positions to be involved in the education of followers at this point in time. Yet, since letters 1 and 2 refer to the state of Nichijō's (own) studying period, we can probably assume that a certain amount of time has passed between them (1 and 2) and 4 where Nichijō is inviting young monks to participate in *dangi*. I will touch on this later, but in the Nikkō lineage there was a place of study called the Omosu Seminary (Omosu-dansho) established at Honmon-ji temple following Nikkō's relocation to Omosu. The Omosu Seminary had a chief instructor *(gakutō)*, and Nikkō, as abbot *(jūji)* of Honmon-ji temple, must have been engaged in the education of followers together with this chief instructor. On the other hand, in letters 4 and 5, Nichimoku's disciples are being called to assemble by the order of Nichimoku who administered Taiseki-ji temple. Taking this fact into consideration, we can consider that these *dangi* invitations are for *dangi* held not at the Omosu Seminary but at Taiseki-ji temple. While the literature does not reveal to us whether or not a place of study such as a seminary existed at Taiseki-ji temple at this time, it does allow us to verify that in the early period of the Nikkō lineage, academic training was being advanced at both Honmon-ji temple and Taiseki-ji temple. Also with regard to the term of the *dangi*, Nichimoku was inviting Nichigō and the others to a *dangi* lasting for a fixed term as shown in the passage from 5: "Next year stay from spring until the tenth month and we should have *dangi*." On this point, I judge that Nichimoku Shōnin would strive at studies at Taiseki-ji temple every year with a term set from spring until about the tenth month and that this was something set up for the education of younger monks[46]. However, it is difficult to read from extant historical materials whether this was really set up "every year" and "for the education of younger monks," so at the current point in time it is probably not possible to make a decisive conclusion like this. We can, however, verify from letters 4 and 5 the facts that Nichimoku was central in inviting disciples to study at Taiseki-ji temple and that he had taken a role in the education of followers.

Further, Nichimoku in his later years acceded to a *Yuzuri-jō*[47] ("Document of Conveyance") in the 11th month of Karyaku 2 (1327) for his disciple Nichidō, transferring to him the Kaminiida-bō (currently Hongen-ji temple) built in Sannohazama, Mutsu Province, where he had strived himself at propagation efforts, and appointing him lecturer for the Kaminiida region. We should also be able to say that the fact that Nichimoku installed Nichidō as the lecturer who would work to lecture on the scriptures and spread the teachings to monks and laymen in the region attests in part to Nichimoku's academic consciousness.

Next I would like to take a look at relics of literature collections in the early period of the Nikkō lineage. Among letters and names of collected literature that make relevant references, the following can be verified: 5 *Heiho*[48]: *Hazen yōmon* and *Shoshū kifuku no sōshi*[49], 6 *Sanmon sōjō*, 7 *Shikan-bako* and 8 *Kokinjo* ("Preface to the *Kokin Wakashū* ['Collection of Japanese Poems of Ancient and Modern Times']"). Among those, 5 is an example of a collection by Nichimoku, 6 and 7 examples of collections by Nikkō and 8 a collection by disciple Ryōshō-bō Nichijō (unk.–1318.) 8 is distinguished by the way it reveals not only that Nikkō sent a copy of *Kokinjo* to Nichijō but that he had books like the *Shin-Kokinjo* and *Kawara-no-in-no fu* on hand and was able to loan them out. With regard to the literature given in 5 through 8, although we may not be able to immediately determine their contents through their titles alone, we can infer—with the exception of the *Kokinjo*—that their content concerned sectarian ideologies and doctrines.

With Nikkō and the others moving the base of their propagation efforts to Suruga, this was a period when they began to seriously expand the scope of the Nikkō lineage—in other words, a period of firming up the infrastructure of the lineage's framework. It goes without saying that, since having Buddhist books was indispensable in the study of Buddhism, the maintenance of an environment where a wide range of literature could be perused was a crucial matter for monks. As recorded in the *Ichigo shoshū zenkon kiroku* ("Record of Good Deeds Performed in a Lifetime") by Nichiyū of Nakayama Hokekyō-ji temple that he had traveled to the capital in Shōchū 1 (1324) for the purpose of transcribing holy scriptures[50], in this period when it is thought that a study environment had not been sufficiently set up, there must have been active efforts being made to collect literature by those around Nikkō too[51]. Does it not seem in fact that the aforementioned examples of literature collection speak to the spirit of initiative being taken toward literature collection in the lineage? Relevant examples were seen for these monks who each maintained different bases of activity: Nikkō (abbot of Honmon-ji temple), Nichimoku (abbot of Taiseki-ji temple) and Nichijō (active from a base in Kamakura.)

With regard to this, letter 9 relates how a high-quality brush was delivered to Nikkō from a certain person as he was about to transcribe "important holy scriptures." It is impossible to determine which "important holy scriptures" specifically were being referred to, but this is another account that tells of work being done in the Nikkō lineage to collect literature. There must have actually been even more literature being transcribed and collected, but as far as cases of collection efforts we can verify here, this is one that conveys such a trend.

With regard to the specific contents of study, in the aforementioned *dangi* invitation 4, Nichimoku tells Nichijō that he would like him to thoroughly read the *"gika"*—in other words the Tendai debate books—and to hold *dangi* with young monks upon organizing it or making notes on it. Also in the aforementioned *dangi* invitation 5, it seems from consideration of the context that Nichimoku was making a request for *dangi* concerning *"Heihō"* (The Art of Warfare) to Nichigō. A *gika* is one of the three topics of questioning in the Tendai sect—*gika* (debate topics), *shūyō* (essential questions regarding the sect) and *mon'yō* (supplemental questions.) Made up of basic questions on Tendai arguments validating the self-realized nature of the sect's doctrine through discussing a syllabus of scriptures and commentaries and a doctrinal comparison of the sect with others, they consisted of 16 or 22 questions.

In Nichiyū's *Honzon shōgyōroku*, a catalog of books in the collection of the early Nakayama lineage, there is a category for *"gika*, etc." that gives 22 types of *gika* titles[52] including *Sokushinjōbutsugi shiki* ("The Meaning of Becoming a Buddha in This Very Body' Personal Record"), *Sanbōmyōshū* ("Three Dharma Marvels Collection") and *Shi anrakugyō ryakushō* ("Synopsis of the Four Peaceful Practices") through which we can verify that *gika-sho* (books of debate topics)[53] such as these were in their collection at the time. Accordingly, we can infer that studying through the use of *gika-sho* was being conducted in the Nakayama lineage as well. In the *dangi* mentioned in 4, it is unclear what sort of topics were the subject of discourse but, we can presume that training was being conducted in the Nikkō lineage as in the Nakayama lineage making use of *gika* in the course of studying.

Though examples are scarce, in this way, it is possible to take a look at the specific contents of *dangi* in the Nikkō lineage at the time. Although references to intended purposes for the collection of literature other than described above do not appear in the available literature, it seems that they must have been used in a similar manner as texts for debates, lectures and personal academic training.

(2) Nikkō's Works

Next I would like to trace part of lineage founder Nikkō's academic training at the time through the works he left behind. To first of all list works thought to concern studying from among the hand-penned works of Nikkō's that have been handed down, the following eleven titles can be given:

a *Ankokuron mondō* ("'Peace of the Land' Discourse")
b *Buppō sōjō kechimyaku futō zatsuroku* ("Miscellaneous Records on Blood-Lineages of the Dharma")
c *Shiki shōroku* ("Summary of 'Shǐjì' [Records of the Grand Historian]")
d *Kōrai-Shiragi-Kudara no koto* ("Matters of Goryeo, Silla and Baekje")
e *Zen tenma yuen no koto* ("On the Grounds for Considering Zen Demonic")
f *Risshū kokuzoku no koto* ("On Risshū Traitors")
g *Honmon guzū no koto* ("On Propagation of the Fundamental Aspect")
h *Shoshū yōmon* ("Essential Passages from the Various Sects")
i *Naige kenmon sōshi* ("Inner and Outer Matters Seen and Heard")
j *Hōmon yōmon* ("Essential Passages from Buddhist Texts")
k *Gengishū yōmon* ("Essential Passages from the Profound Meaning Collection")

To give a little bibliographic information about this literature, first of all it has been pointed out that since **a** through **d** were written in the same hand and their relationship to the *Risshō ankoku-ron* has been recognized, there is a possibility that they originally formed a single work[54]. Similarly, it is possible that **e** through **g** were also from a single work, as they were also written in the same hand as well[55]. Also with regard to **k**, which forms a single work in its present form, its first and second halves are viewed as having originally made up two works. Suggesting this is the fact that the first half contains mainly quotations from *Hokke gengi*, and the second half contains passages concerning correct rules, considerations and methods of persuasion for promulgators of the Lotus Sūtra[56]. Their differences in terms of content have been thus pointed out. In such ways it seems that there has been a certain level of discrepancy that has come to be recognized between the present states and original forms of Nikkō's works.

To present an overview of the contents of listed titles, while there are no instructional works containing systematic organizations of Nichiren's teachings to be found, the category of *yōmon-shū* consisting of excerpts from scriptural commentaries make up the majority. On this point, it is just as the aforementioned Mochizuki and Watanabe have pointed out. Among these, **e** and **f** are collections of *yōmon* regarding the Zen and Ritsu sects, and **g** is a *yōmon-shū* focused on the Lotus Sūtra's *Honmon* [Fundamental Aspect] section. It is thought that these *yōmon-shū* were produced as materials for putting promulgation into practice, with the thought of criticizing other sects and spreading the teaching of the Lotus Sūtra along with deepening his own understanding of Buddhism. The possibility that **e** through **g** originally formed a single work has been pointed out, but taking into consideration the fact that Nichiren's followers at the time were frequently appealing for the cessation of reliance on "wicked" [scriptures other than the Lotus Sūtra] and devotion to the "true Dharma" [of the Lotus Sūtra] in their efforts at remonstration and proselytization towards the government authority, taking a look at them in terms of their content it does seem that **e** through **g** may have been part of a series. Also, it has some points of commonality with Nichiren's *Ichidai go-ji-zu* in terms of form, with its mixture of diagrams and *yōmon* in evaluating the various sects' founders along with their characteristics and validity. It is assumed that these were produced for the purpose of grasping the sects' ideologies and were also used as materials for criticizing them.

In **j**—which expresses the five periods occurring in Śākyamuni's life at the beginning, then presents the signification of the Nenbutsu through quotes from the *Senchakushū* ("Passages on the Selection [of the Nembutsu in the

Original Vow]") and finally expounds on the superiority of the Lotus Sūtra—and in the second half of **k** which lists *yōmon* regarding correct rules, considerations and methods of persuasion for promulgation of the Lotus Sūtra, there are many readings of characters given as well as indications of transliteration. With the characters written relatively large as well, it is probably valid to consider these to have been produced as learning materials for followers' studies[57]. As far as similar historical materials other than these, there is also Nichigen's transcription of the *Risshō ankoku-ron* with character readings and markings to indicate Japanese transliteration. However, **j** and **k** are the primary examples of works not only among Nichiren's body of work but also among works Nikkō himself left behind to be used as teaching materials. According to Kidō Daikoku, the *yōmon-shū* in **a, e, f, i, j** and **k** have no small amount of overlap in terms of content with works such as the *Kinkō-shū* from Minobu's Nikō and the *Go-hōmon on-kikigaki* from Okanomiya's Nippō—and he points out that a great deal of caution is called for with regard to the relation between Nikkō's works, the *Kinkōshū*, Nippō's *kikigaki* and so on[58].

With regard to this sort of *yōmon-shū* production by Nikkō, reproductions and full reprintings of works in the collection of the Hota Myōhon-ji temple have recently been made available: the *Gyōnin-shō*, *Hizō yōmon* ("Essential Passages from the Secret Treasury") and *Hōchi-bō jūdōjitō yōmon*[59]. The *Gyōnin-shō* is a *yōmon-shū* penned by Nichiren, Nikkō and two others; the *Hizō yōmon* is a *yōmon-shū* by Nichiren, Nichimoku and several others; and the *Hōchi-bō jūdōjitō yōmon* is a *yōmon-shū* by Nichimoku and one other. All are small-format volumes, and it is speculated that they were produced with the intention of use for Dharma discussions and sermons. The two aforementioned *yōmon-shū* for which Nichiren and followers are acknowledged to have had a hand, are of a similar type as works such as the *Hisho yōmon* and *Tendai kan'yōmonshū* (both holdings of the Nakayama Hokekyō-ji temple) and *Sanbukyō kanjin yōmon* ("Essential Passages from the Threefold Sūtra"; a holding of the Ikegami Honmon-ji temple), and may be valuable as examples of Nichiren and followers jointly producing *yōmon-shū* together under Nichiren's supervision. These works are of a similar type as those of Nikkō's mentioned above, and since all three books are speculated to have been produced in the mid-13th century, we can infer from this that the central figures of the Nikkō lineage's early period, Nikkō and Nichimoku, started producing *yōmon-shū* from an early date. From these works we can get a partial glimpse of how, as pointed out earlier by Takagi, the transcription of excerpts of *yōmon* was carried out as a basic method of study also in the Nikkō lineage to be then used as a basis for further training.

Passages concerning the transcription of the *Hazen yōmon* are found in Nichimoku's letter *Yo Saishō ajari gobō sho* (previously given as 5,) and passages concerning the transcription of the *Sanmon sōjō* in Nikkō's letter *Yo Minbu-kō gobō gohenji* (previously given as 6.) These references could possibly be related to the Yōmon-shū **e** concerning the Zen sect as well as to **e**, **i** and **h**, which contain passages concerning *Sanmon*.

(3) Training with the Body of Work Nichiren Left Behind

Like *dangi* debates, transcription of the literature is a fundamental and vital element of monks' efforts at studying and literature collecting. Here I would like to take up for consideration in particular evidence of transcription being done of the corpus of work Nichiren left behind.

The practice of followers' transcribing of Nichiren's body of work dates back to his own lifetime. Later, many works of transcription were produced by his followers, with 127 currently verifiable transcriptions of Nichiren's works produced during the Kamakura Period[60]. Transcriptions made by teachers in the Nikkō lineage that have been handed down are particularly numerous, with their number amounting to 70% of those 127. In other words, we can read from this that transcriptions of Nichiren's body of work begin from an early stage in the Nikkō lineage and the collection of his body of work was being advanced. Below I will give the number of transcribed works certain to have been transcribed in the Kamakura Period by Nikkō lineage teachers. It should be safe to state that transcriptions are historical materials that tell the tale of training with Nichiren's body of work, and that they are vital pieces of evidence through which we can conjecture about the way Nichiren's body of work was accepted by his followers.

Nikkō (Lineage founder): 32
Unknown (A holding of Taiseki-ji temple; author of the *Gohitsushū* ("A Collection of His Writings")): 31
Nitchō (Direct disciple of Nikkō): 21
Nichijun (Direct disciple of Nikkō): 3
Nichimoku (Direct disciple of Nikkō): 2

Nichidō (Direct disciple of Nikkō): 2
Nissai (Disciple of Nikkō's disciple): 1
Nichigen (Disciple of Nikkō's disciple): 1

Surveying works transcribed by early Nichiren followers, there tends to be a high proportion of works transcribing Nichiren's body of work. The reason for this is attributable to their intention in transcribing the work. In the postscript to *Kubo-ama gozen gohenji* ("Reply to the Lay Nun of Kubo"), a work of transcription by an unknown author from the Nikkō lineage produced in the Kamakura period, a passage is found relating that, in the main text, transcriptions on dogma are central, while passages concerning things like offerings are omitted[61]. As authors like Ken'ichi Kanmuri and Eichi Terao mention, that is to say, among works of Nichiren's transcribed by followers, those expressing his doctrine and ideology in detail were the main focus[62], it is thought, as followers of the time placed their emphasis on studying and receiving transmission of the doctrine and creed of Nichiren.

There is a distinctive approach to transcribing the body of work seen in the Nikkō lineage. Namely, this concerns the fact that not only Nichiren's books but even his letters were actively transcribed. The existence of a collection called the *Gohitsushū* held by Taiseki-ji temple directly reveals this. The *Gohitsushū* is an anthology that collects together 31 letters transcribed by a certain Nikkō follower in the Kamakura Period and could as well be called "The Collected Letters of Nichiren." Early Nichiren followers' transcription of his body of work suggests, as discussed above, a trend of taking his books as the holy teachings in which to pursue his dogma as the chief aim of their transcription efforts. In the *Gohitsushū*, however, his letters, too, were transcribed and collected with the intention of finding in them Nichiren's doctrine and ideology—assigned a place among targets of their transcription work. A distinguishing characteristic of the *Gohitsushū*, in other words, is the clear implication it presents that correspondence was considered to be among his holy teachings. Yet the appearance of this characteristic is not restricted to the *Gohitsushū* alone; over half the works transcribed by Nikkō—17 out of 32—were transcriptions of Nichiren's letters. This can be interpreted to mean that Nikkō shared the same discernment in engaging in his transcription of the work. We may assume that this attitude of the lineage head towards transcription efforts was passed on to his followers, with the appearance of the *Gohitsushū* being among the results.

In this way, indications are that in the early days of the Nikkō lineage transcription of Nichiren's body of work was something often engaged in. The following historical materials give a sense of how they would strive at their training on the basis of those transcribed books.

Nichimoku's letter *Yo Minbu ajari gobō sho*, 25th day of 10th month, 1332:
Having grown older, I have come to want to learn more of the Dharma. This year as well, I have conducted *dangi* on the "*gosho*[63]."
Sanuki-ko Nichigen Shahon *Risshō ankoku-ron*:
Seventh day of the nineth month, Karyaku 4 (1329), transcribed Nissai's copy, with his personal markings, at Fuji-san Honmon-ji temple. Confidential markings that must not be revealed externally, 24th day of the 2nd month of Karyaku 2 (1327)[64].

Nichimoku's letter *Yo Minbu ajari gobō sho*, first of all, contains the elderly Nichimoku's proclamation of a willingness to study as well as relating that he, who administered the Taiseki-ji temple, lectured on the *"gosho"* ("honorable writings")—in other words, Nichiren's body of work—every day for the approximately half-year from the 4th month through the 20th day of the 9th month. This is a valuable passage offering clear conveyance of the fact that early Nichiren followers were training on Nichiren's body of work. As mentioned previously, there is a passage found in a letter of Nichimoku's in which he invites his disciple Nichigō to stay at Taiseki-ji from the spring until the 10th month for *dangi* (previously given as 5), and we might speculate that Nichimoku conducted lectures on Nichiren's body of work in such a course of events as this.

Next, based on an editorial note added in Kakei 2 (1388) to a copy of the *Risshō ankoku-ron* transcribed by Nichigen, we can understand that Nichigen transcribed the work in Karyaku 4 (1329) from a transcription of the *Risshō ankoku-ron* by Nissai supplied with character readings and markings indicating Japanese transliteration. There are two extant copies of transcriptions that Nichigen made of the *Risshō ankoku-ron*—one from Kenmu 4 (1337) and another from Jōwa 5 (1349)—and checking these existing copies, it can be seen that both the Kenmu- and Jōwa-era versions contain character readings and markings indicating Japanese transliteration[65]. These are seen as being Nichigen's re-transcriptions of the Karyaku-era book[66]. Since Nichiren's

On Academic Training in the Early Nichiren Sect: With a Focus on Cases from the Nikkō Lineage

Risshō ankoku-ron, as he originally penned it contains neither character readings nor transliteration guides, it is thought that the addition of character readings and markings to indicate Japanese transliteration were done in the course of followers' training with the work. Kaoru Ōshima indicates that *kundoku* (the transliteration of classical Chinese texts into Japanese) was one fundamental approach to scriptural interpretation and was a method of comprehension meant to be acquired by monks from an early age[67]. The transliteration guides found in Nichigen's transcriptions were thought to have been produced in the course of such endeavors, it is thought, and may have been intended to facilitate beginners or for the use in subsequent self-study.

In making an examination of academic training around Nikkō, one matter that cannot be overlooked is the evidence of transcription of the *Ichidai goji keizu*. Five copies of the *Ichidai goji keizu* have currently been identified, which we can take to mean that Nikkō made repeated transcriptions of the same diagram. It has been pointed out as well that, in his transcriptions, Nikkō did not merely transcribe the same work but would also correct mistaken transcriptions of quotes by Nichiren, add related quotes and phrases for the individual items and so on[68]. As mentioned previously, Nichiren would pen copies of the *Ichidai goji zu* time and again and use them in conducting lectures to aid in the comprehension of Buddhist history in Śākyamuni's lifetime. Nikkō, as a direct disciple, must have received those lectures himself. Naturally, the reason for Nikkō's multiple transcriptions of the *Ichidai goji keizu* must have been to make use of it, with the intended purpose of use in academic training. From this evidence we can presume that Nikkō himself would have had a chance to review the contents of the diagram each time he had the occasion to transcribe it and that, like Nichiren, he would have given lectures using the *Ichidai goji keizu* on multiple occasions. In this we are given a look into one instance wherein Nichiren's lectures were passed down to followers' occasions of study.

To take a look at other lineages, and in particular the Nakayama lineage, catalogs of early-period holdings the *Jōshū-in honzon shōgyō no koto* by Nichijō and *Honzon shōgyōroku* by Nichiyū list transcribed works in substantial numbers. In the Nakayama lineage as well, that is to say, it seems that active efforts were being carried out to transcribe and collect Nichiren's body of work. The *Hokke mondō shōgishō* by Nichizen and the *Honjaku sōi* ("Differences Between the *Honmon* [Fundamental Aspect] and *Shakumon* [Manifestation Doctrine]") by Okanomiya Kōchō-ji temple's Nippō also contain many quoted passages from Nichiren's body of work, but it is probably reasonable to consider these books to have been compiled using transcribed works that had been collected. There is no question, then, that from the early period an emphasis on transcribing and training with Nichiren's body of work was seen throughout the whole Nichiren sect. Among lineages, the Nikkō lineage in particular offers points worthy of close observation: that many works transcribed at an early stage have been passed down, and that we are able to obtain a peek at actual instances of these works of Nichiren's being put into use as texts in followers' studying.

(4) Academic Training at the Omosu Seminary

By the late Kamakura Period, seminaries called *dangisho*, *dansho*, *danrin* and so on for the specialized purpose of conducting *dangi* had come to be established within various sects. One example of this from the Nichiren sect is the study center known as the "Omosu-dansho" (Omosu Seminary) installed onsite after Nikkō established his propagation base in Omosu, Fuji District, Suruga Province in Einin 6 [1298]. The earliest named educational institution in the history of the Nichiren sect that can be documented, the Omosu Seminary, is considered an early instance of such in the whole of Japan as well alongside seminaries such as the Tsugane-ji Dangisho in Shinano Province, Sanuki Dansho in Kōzuke Province and Shimōsa Province Dangisho[69]. Considered from this vantage, Nikkō's establishment of the Omosu Seminary was an occurrence of great importance as the first instance of educational facilities being set up in the Nichiren sect.

While many points regarding the Omosu Seminary have been clarified through research by Nichikō Hori[70], Tomoyoshi Tanji[71], Hōyō Sakai[72] and others, related historical materials are scarce, and at present many issues remain to be resolved regarding what actual circumstances at the seminary were like. While referring to that preceding research I would like to attempt a reconfirmation of what academic training at the Omosu Seminary may have been like.

First of all, with regard to the name "Omosu-dansho," it is thought to have first been seen in the postscript to Nikkō's transcribed work *Yorimoto chinjō* ("Letter of Petition from Yorimoto") from the 20th day of the intercalary 10th month of Shōwa 5 (1316) that I will give next.

• Nikkō's transcribed work *Yorimoto chinjō* from the 20th day of the intercalary 10th month of Shōwa 5 (1316):
Transcribed using revised copy at Omosu Seminary in Fuji Kamigata, Suruga Province, 20th day of intercalary 10th month, Shōwa 5 (1316)[73].

In consideration of the fact that the first chief instructor of the Omosu Seminary, Jakusen-bō Nitchō, passed away on the 14th day of the 3rd month of Enkyō 3 (1310), the seminary's date of establishment must have at least preceded that[74].

Nikkō was originally head priest of the Tendai sect's Shijūku-in temple in Kanbara, Suruga Province, located in the vicinity of the Tendai sect's Iwamoto Jissō-ji temple where, serving as chief instructor at the temple concurrently, was Harima Hōin (later renamed Nichigen) whose chance encounter with Nichiren—like Nikkō—had prompted him to convert to being a Nichiren follower. Nikkō then spent a certain period of time in residence at Minobu following Nichiren's passing so as to maintain and supervise Minobu where Nichiren's mausoleum was located. According to Nikkō's letter *Hara-dono go-henji* ("Reply from Hara-dono"), while Nikkō was in residence at Mount Minobu, one of the six senior priests Nikō subsequently ascended Minobu to become chief instructor[75] and served together with Nikkō at educating followers and administering the temple. This is the earliest instance of the chief instructor position known in the Nichiren sect. The establishment of the position is thought to have been a measure enacted with the recognition of its indispensability in promotion of their doctrine in the pursuit of further growth following the founder's passing when the Nichiren sect was still in its early stages.

While historical materials conveying in detail the trajectory by which Nikō came to be appointed chief instructor of Minobu have not been found, it at least seems very unlikely that Nikō would have been appointed as chief instructor without Nikkō, who administered Minobu, at least being party to it. My feeling is that, likely, Nikō's appointment as chief instructor was in no small part influenced by—or modeled on—the way Tendai sect temples had been organized as experienced by Nikkō; and this is in consideration of facts such as the following: that Nikkō had been chief priest of a Tendai sect temple; that it was located near Jissō-ji temple, which had a chief instructor in place; and that Nikō served as chief instructor concurrently with Nikkō's residence at Mount Minobu. The fact that Nikkō had promptly established the

Omosu Seminary within the sect also suggests that he was of a mind to channel his energy toward establishing training facilities to further promote the spread of their doctrine.

Let me now give historical materials related to the issue of specifically what sort of studying was being carried out at the Omosu Seminary.

- Sanmi Ajari Nichijun: *Hyōbyaku* ("Invocation,") 24th day of the 11th month of Bunpō 2 (1318)
  "Offering five devotions and lecturing on the true scripture of the One Vehicle, prepare for the joy of receiving the teachings of the Buddha. [...] Hold a discussion at the Omosu Seminary. Teacher's invocation[76]."
- Nichijun *Nichijun zasshū* ("NichijunMiscellaneous Collection"), *Kanjin honzonshō kenmon* postscript, Tenbun 14 (1545) transcribed work by Yōjun-bō
  "The book says: On 5th day of 3rd month in 5th year of Bunna [1356] at Minami-no-bō in village of Omosu at foot of Mount Fuji, [...] attending [the monk,] watching and listening with Shimoyama-no-bōzu, were the following acolytes: Saishō Ajari, Minami-no-bōzu, Shikibu-kō and Shōryu, these four[77]."

Historical materials specifying what studies were like at the Omosu Seminary are extremely scarce, and no documents from the first chief instructor Nitchō are extant. The preceding passage from second chief instructor Nichijun sheds just a little light for us.

First of all, from reading *Hyōbyaku* authored on the occasion of the Tendai daishi kō memorial event of Bunpō 2 [1318], we can infer that Nichijun served as lecturer for a discussion referred to as *ichiza no rondan*. Though the contents of this discussion are not specified, we can view it as likely having been a lecture conducted on "the true scripture of the One Vehicle"—in other words the Lotus Sūtra—in consideration of the context. This is a valuable passage that conveys the conditions of studying carried out with the Omosu Seminary as venue.

Also the *Nichijun zasshū* is a work that lists all together the *kikigaki* on the gateway to the Dharma, Nichiren's body of work and so on taught to Nichijun by his teacher Nikkō. Specifically, it is made up of items such as the *Senjishō chū kenmon* ("Things Seen and Heard in 'The Selection of the Time,'")

Kaimokushō jō shikenmon ("Things Personally Seen and Heard regarding 'The Opening of the Eyes,'") *Kanjin honzonshō kenmon* ("Things Seen and Heard in 'The True Object of Worship,'") *Jūkaisan Nichijun hōmon, Shishin gohon yōmon* ("Essential Passages from the Four Stages of Faith and the Five Stages of Practice,") *Zakkan kenmon* and *Hokke honmon kenmon* ("Things "Seen and Heard Regarding the Lotus Sūtra's *Honmon* [Fundamental Aspect] Section.") According to the postcript to the *Kanjin honzonshō kenmon* from among these, it seems that Nichijun conducted a lecture on the *Kanjin honzonshō* from Nichiren's body of work in Bunna 5 (1356), and the four monks Saishō Ajari, Minami-no-bōzu, Shikibu-kō and Shōryu were in attendance as acolytes. This lecture, however, was conducted at a venue called the "Omosu Minami-no-bō," and it is not known which building this specifically refers to. Incidentally the *Hokke honmon kenmon* also contains references to lecturing on the significance of the Lotus Sūtra's *honmon* portion by Nichijun at the beginning of Bunpō 2 [1318][78], but the venue this time is given as the Mieidō with no mention of the seminary. Further forthcoming investigation will be required with regard to questions such as whether Nichijun's lecturing described in the *Nichijun zasshū* in fact offer hints about academic training at the Omosu Seminary, what the scale of the Omosu Seminary was like and what activities conducted there were actually like in the first place.

With regard to studying at the Omosu Seminary, I must conclude, with the only real evidence for us to see being offered by Nikkō's work of transcription the *Yorimoto chinjō* and Nichijun's *Hyōbyaku*, an elucidation of the actual circumstances still lies far off. Taking into consideration the facts, however, that a study center called the Omosu Seminary had been established, a chief instructor had been installed there and the founder of the lineage Nikkō was in residence at Honmon-ji temple as well, one might at least anticipate that the academic training being carried out there was of a level equivalent to or higher than the studying by Nichimoku and others at Taiseki-ji temple.

Conclusion

I have advanced so far in this paper an examination of one aspect of academic training in the early Nichiren sect on the basis of hints from relics found in relevant literature from the Nikkō lineage. These instances from the Nikkō lineage serve as valuable pieces of evidence complementing what we know of the actual circumstances of academic training in the early Nichiren sect, as first surveyed; and they also convey something of the work carried out by scholar monks at the time. In concluding this paper, I would like to point out the following matters.

First of all, we can confirm that academic training was being actively advanced within the lineage: various efforts at the collection of literature were conducted following Nichiren's passing; there was a push to establish study environments for monks at temples serving as operational bases; and *dangi* were being conducted on a continual basis among followers. The fact of the Omosu Seminary's establishment at Honmon-ji temple in particular must truly speak to the emphasis being placed on the promotion of studying within the lineage.

Second is an example of such efforts to collect literature. Nichiren's body of work too was being actively collected in transcribed form without a distinction between his books and correspondence being made, and many transcriptions of works from his corpus were already being produced during Nikkō's lifetime. We are afforded glimpses of the way followers would employ these transcriptions in striving at their training with Nichiren's body of work as well as hints of the way Nichiren's works were given the status of textbooks for study from an early stage. Training with Nichiren's corpus can be clearly documented in the literature, and this point could be said to be one of the characteristic features regarding academic training in the Nikkō lineage.

Third, almost all of the books lineage *founder* Nikkō left behind were in the format of *yōmon-shū* excerpting from scriptural commentaries; a great deal are found that collect together *yōmon* regarding sectarian ideologies or attesting to the Lotus Sūtra's status as the true Dharma, and these are thought to have been produced with the purpose of preparation for *hōron* debates to come. Looking at Nikkō's works, one gets the sense that a considerable consciousness existed in the Nikkō lineage with regard to the issue of criticizing other sects in the course of expanding the lineage. As previously stated, teachers from other concurrent lineages too were successively compiling works grouping together determinations of teachings' statuses as provisional or genuine and sectarian ideologies in preparation for *hōron* debates. Making an analogical inference from this, we may assume that studying on subjects largely in common with the Nikkō lineage was being pursued within other lineages as well, and the emphasis was on producing literature aimed particularly at accomplishing propagation goals. It is thought that approaches to the academic training of followers at the time was greatly influenced by the widespread and firmly entrenched emphasis throughout the whole sect on criticizing other sects.

For literature produced in the course of academic training such as this, relations to Nichiren's *Ichidai goji-zu* must be assumed. The structure of the *Ichidai goji-zu* on which Nichiren delivered lectures during his lifetime—expressing sectarian ideologies and relevant *yōmon* to conclude ultimately in the Lotus Sūtra's superiority—formed the basis of their studies and is thought to have had a great influence on subsequent methods of study by followers and the compiling of books. The fact that Nikkō had transcribed the *Ichidai goji-keizu* on multiple occasions can only mean that the diagram played an important role in academic training in the Nikkō lineage as well. Through this we can verify in part the specific circumstances in which Nichiren's lectures were transmitted to followers to form the basis for further studying at which followers would strive.

While many subjects in this paper were limited to being presented as overviews, the existence of scriptural commentaries quoted in literature authored by teachers from the Nikkō lineage including Nikkō himself ought to provide beneficial hints toward investigating the circumstances of academic training in the early Nikkō lineage. On the basis of this present consideration I hope to further my investigation of these topics in the future and approach at least a bit closer to a clarification of the actual conditions of studying pursued at the time.

*This paper is reprinted from ŌSAKI GAKUHŌ The Journal of Nichiren Buddhist Studies, issue 172. (Risshō Daigaku Bukkyō Gakkai, 2016.)

Notes

1. Rissho University Institute of Nichiren Buddhist Studies, ed. *Shōwa teihon Nichiren shōnin ibun*. (Minobu-san Kuon-ji, 2000 revised and enlarged edition) pg 535. Abbreviated as *Tei-i* below.
2. *Tei-i*, pg 910.
3. Nagamura, M. *Chūsei jiin shiryōron*. (Yoshikawa Kōbunkan, 2000.)

4. Terao, E. *Gyōgakuin Nitchō kankei no shōgyō ni tsuite*. (*Journal of Indian and Buddhist Studies*, vol. 57, issue 2, The Japanese Association of Indian and Buddhist Studies, 2009.)
   Gyōgakuin Nitchō no zōsho keisei ni tsuite. (*Journal of Indian and Buddhist Studies*, vol. 58, issue 2, 2010.)
   Gyōgakuin Nitchō no Hokekyō dangi-sho ni tsuite. (*Journal of Indian and Buddhist Studies*, vol. 60, issue 1, 2011.)
5. Among principle research on the *Kinkōshū*:
   Miyazaki, E. *Nichiren shōnin ibun no bunkengaku-teki kenkyū*. (Mochizuki, K., ed. *Kindai Nihon no Hokke Bukkyō*. Heiraku-ji Shoten, 1968.)
   Asai, E. *Kinkōshū to Hokke mondō shōgishō*. (ŌSAKI GAKUHŌ The Journal of Nichiren Buddhist Studies, issue 134, Risshō Daigaku Bukkyō Gakkai, 1981.)
   Taira, M. *Nihon chūsei no shakai to Bukkyō*. (Hanawa Shobō, 1992.)
   Nakajo, G. *Nichiren-shū jōdai kyōgaku no kenkyū: Kinkōshū no kenkyū*. (Heiraku-ji Shoten, 1996.)
   Also, among principle research on the *Hokke mondō shōgishō:*
   Saito, Y. *Shōchūzan zō "Shōgishō" ni tsuite*. (*Seishin*. Issue 22, Sozangakuin Dōsōkai Bungakubu, 1937.)
   Asai, E. *Kinkōshū to Hokke mondō shōgishō*.
   Ikeda, R. *"Hokke mondō shōgishō" no Nichiren ibun o megutte*. (*Kōfū*. Issue 18, Kōfū Dansho, 2006.)
6. *Hyōe Sakan dono go-henji*. (*Tei-i*, pg 1,606.)
7. *Bōjikyō-ji*. (*Tei-i*, pg 1,151.)
8. Takamori, D. *Nichiren shōnin no gakumon-teki kankyō ni kan suru ichi-shiron*. (*Journal of Nichiren Buddhism,* issue 32, Rissho University Institute of Nichiren Buddhist Studies, 2005.)
9. Takagi, Y. *Nichiren-kō*. (Sankibō Busshorin, 2008) Ch. 3: *Chūsei Tendai sō no gakushū: Seishun no Nichiren to kasane-awasete*, pgs 66-72.
10. Sasaki, K. *Nihon chūsei shisō no kichō*. (Yoshikawa Kōbunkan, 2006.) Vol. 3, ch. 1: *Bukkyō to "gakumon."*
11. In the body of work Nichiren left behind are found titles similar to the *Ichidai goji zu* including *Ichidai goji keizu* (with two different versions of the character for *kei*) and *Shaka ichidai goji keizu,* but for convenience I will denote all of them as *Ichidai goji zu* in this paper.
12. Miyazaki, E. *Nichiren shōnin no monka kyoiku* (*Journal of Indian and Buddhist Studies*, vol. 2, issue 1, 1953) pg 176.
13. *Tei-i,* vol. 3. Registration numbers for the works: 9 - 13 - 20 - 22 - 24 - 25 - 28 - 29 - 30. Other than these, several pieces have been passed down that are thought to be fragments of the *Ichidai goji zu* in his own hand as well as the book that once existed at Minobu-san Kuon-ji temple that is introduced in the following:
    Terao, E. *Nichiren "Ichidai goji zu" no Minobu-san sozon-hon: Kyōto Honman-ji no Nichiken hitsu rinsha-hon ni tsuite*. (*Minobu Ronsō*, issue 3, Minobusan

University Association for Buddhist Studies, 1998.)
14. Terao, E. *Nichiren "Ichidai goji zu" no Minobu-san sōson-hon: Kyōto Honman-ji no Nichiken hitsu rinsha-hon ni tsuite,* pg 47.
15. *Tei-i,* pg 460.
16. *Tei-i,* pg 1,651.
17. *Toki-dono go-shōsoku.* (*Tei-i,* pg 440);
    Kingo-dono go-henji. (*Tei-i,* pg 458) etc.
18. Rissho University Institute of Nichiren Buddhist Studies, ed. *Nichiren shōnin ibun jiten: Rekishi-hen.* (Minobu-san Kuon-ji, 1985) pg 679.
    Minobusan University Tōyō Bunka Kenkyūsho, ed. *Chion hōon: Minobu-san Gakuen 450-nen shi.* (Minobusan University, 2007) pg 4.
19. Watanabe, H. *Nichiren-shū shingyōron no kenkyū.* (Heiraku-ji Shoten, 1976) pg 122.
20. Nagamura, M. *Chūsei jiin shiryōron.* Ch. 3: *Jiin shōgyōron.*
21. The two books mentioned above are given in the following work, but the main text is unseen:
    Mochizuki, K. *Nichiren-shū gakusetsu shi.* (Heiraku-ji Shoten, 1976) pg 22.
22. Rissho University Institute of Nichiren Buddhist Studies, ed. *Nichiren-shū shūgaku zensho,* vols. 13–14. (Sankibō Busshorin, 1961.) Abbreviated as *Shū-zen* below.
    Regarding the work, however, the following book contains another theory that it was a selection made by Nisshin (1271–1334), the third abbot of Minobu-san Kuon-ji temple:
    Ikeda, R. *"Hokke mondō shōgishō" no Nichiren ibun o megutte,* pgs 81-82.
23. Nippō Shōnin Goshoji-bon chōsa Iinkai, ed. *Go-hōmon on-kikigaki.* (Kōchō-ji, 1990.)
24. *Shū-zen,* vol. 1 (Sankibō Busshorin, 1959) pg 91.
25. The following passage, however, appears in the *Nichiren shōnin nenpu* by Nissei, 17th abbot of Taiseki-ji temple:
    "There was a lecture on the *Ankokuron* from the 25th day of the 9th month of the same [year, Kōan 5 (1282.)] This was because there was a person with questions or criticisms about the *Ankokuron.* Nikkō recorded this in the *Ankokuron mondō taii.*" (Shōhondō Konryu Kinen Shuppan Iinkai, ed. *Nichiren shōshū rekidai hossu zensho,* vol. 2, pg 122. Taiseki-ji, 1974.)
    Also, it has been claimed that Nikkō's *Ankokuron mondō* was a record of a lecture by Nichiren as well. (Nikkō Shōnin Zenshū Hensan Iinkai, ed. *Nikkō Shōnin Zenshū,* pg 3. Kōfū Dansho, 1996. Abbreviated as *Kō-zen* below.)
    However, Nichikō Hori presented a negative view of the theory that Nikkō's *Ankokuron mondō* was a record of a lecture by Nichiren in the following:
    Fuji Nikkō shōnin shōden. (Soka Gakkai, 1983) pg 413.
    Here I have relied on Hori and left the theory out.
26. Hori, N. *Fuji Nikkō shōnin shōden.* pg 467.

Nichimoku Shōnin Shuppan Iinkai, ed. *Nichimoku Shōnin.* (Keimyō Shinbunsha, 1998) pg 262.
27. Watanabe, M. *Chūsei ni okeru sōryo no gakumon: Dangisho to iu shiten kara.* (*Hirosaki Daigaku Kokugo Kokubungaku*, issue 28. Hirosaki Daigaku Kokugo Kokubun Gakkai, 2007) pg 32.
Tendai dangisho o meguru gakumon no kōryū. (Yasurō Abe, ed. *Chūsei bungaku to jiin shiryō-shōgyō.* Chikurinsha, 2010) pg 450.
28. Kyoto National Museum, ed. *Nichiren to hokke no meihō: Hana-hiraku Kyōto machishū bunka.* (Kyoto National Museum, 2009) pgs 108, 109, 264.
29. *Chōken-ji kaisan 700-nen kinen shoshū mondō kusaku-shū.* (Chōken-ji Kaisan 700-nen Kinen Jigyō Kensetsu Jikkō Iinkai, private printing, 2011.)
30. *Shū-zen*, vol. 1, pg 353.
31. ŌSAKI GAKUHŌ The Journal of Nichiren Buddhist Studies, issue 89. (Risshō Daigaku Shūgaku Kenkyūshitsu, 1936) pgs 115–.
32. *Kōfū Sōsho [10]–[14]: Nakayama monryū Tōgaku-in Nichizen sen "Hokke mondō shōgishō."* (Kōfū Dansho, 2006–2010.)
33. *Kōfū Sōsho [16]: Minobu Bunko zō Oikawa Munehide sen: "Mondō yōishō" / Nikkō Tenkai zō: "Shoshū mondō haryū yōmonshū"* (Kōfū Dansho, 2012.)
Another consideration of this work is the following:
Sakai, H. *Minobu Bunko zō "Mondō yōishō" no kiso-teki kōsatsu.* (*Kōfū*, issue 23, 2011.)
34. Mochizuki, K. *Nichiren-shū gakusetsu shi,* pg 98.
Watanabe, H. *Nichiren-shū shingyōron no kenkyū,* pg 120.
35. Watanabe, H. *Nichiren-shū shingyōron no kenkyū,* pg 124.
36. Author's manuscript. *Shoki Nikkō monryū ni okeru kangyō katsudō no tenkai.* (ŌSAKI GAKUHŌ The Journal of Nichiren Buddhist Studies, issue 167, 2011.)
37. *Kō-zen,* pg 184.
38. *Kō-zen,* pg 186.
39. *Nichimoku shōnin,* pg. 390.
40. *Nichimoku shōnin,* pg. 383.
41. *Nichimoku shōnin,* pg. 389.
42. *Kō-zen,* pg 183.
43. *Kō-zen,* pg 242.
44. *Kō-zen,* pg 177.
45. *Kō-zen,* pg 244.
46. *Nichimoku shōnin,* pg. 95.
47. Nichimoku. *Yuzurijō:* "I cede to the Ben Ajari the Kaminiida-bō along with the region as well. He Shall be teacher for Kaminiida as well." (*Nichimoku shōnin,* pg. 378.)
48. *Nichimoku shōnin,* pg. 212, speculates that this work may be related to *hōron* debates with other sects.
49. *Nichimoku shōnin,* pg. 213, speculates that this work may be akin to Saichō's

Ebyōshū.
50. *Shū-zen,* vol. 1, pg 447.
51. As Nichiren too was in the course of relocating between Kamakura, Sado and Minobu, one could imagine that he may have often relied on disciples and patrons to collect literature. See Daijō Takamori's *Nichiren shōnin no gakumon-teki kankyō ni kan-suru ichi-shiron.*
52. The ordering of questions and number used differs depending on the historical materials consulted, however, and is not fixed. See:
Ogami, K. *Nihon Tendai-shi no kenkyū.* (Sankibō Busshorin, 2014) section contained within: *Tendai gika no seiritsu katei.* (First published 1970.)
Tendai shūten hensan-sho, ed. *Seizoku Tendai-shū zensho mokuroku kaidai.* (Shunjūsha, 2000) pg 128.
Fujihira, K. *Tendai rongisho no shokeitai.* (*Annual of Buddhist Studies*, issue 36, Eizan Gakuin, 2014.)
53. *Shiryō shōkai (11) Honzon shōgyō-roku.* (*Nichiren Kyōgaku Kenkyū-sho Kiyō*, issue 11, 1984) pg 15.
54. Daikoku, K. "*Nikkō shōnin zenshū" seihen hensan hoi.* (*Kōfū,* issue 11, 1997) pg 299.
55. *Kō-zen,* pg 129 headnote.
56. Daikoku, K. "*Nikkō shōnin zenshū" seihen hensan hoi,* pg 304.
57. Sakai, H. *Omosu Honmon-ji to Taiseki-ji.* (*Kōfū,* issue 11) pg 141.
58. Daikoku, K. "*Nikkō shōnin zenshū" seihen hensan hoi,* pg 303.
59. *Kōfū Sōsho [18]: Chiba Myōhon-ji zō:* "*Gyōnin-shō,*" "*Hizō yōmon,*" "*Hōchi-bō jūdōjitō yōbun*" (Kōfū Dansho, 2014.)
60. Author's manuscript. *Shoki Nikkō monryū ni okeru Nichiren ibun no shosha ni tsuite.* (ŌSAKI GAKUHŌ The Journal of Nichiren Buddhist Studies, issue 171, 2015.) Regarding the number of transcribed works, some works are collections that compile many transcriptions within them, such as the *Gohitsushū* in the property of Taiseki-ji temple, but here I have individually counted each work from his body of work that is compiled in such collections on its own.
61. *Kō-zen,* pg 151.
62. Kanmuri, K. *Chūsei ni okeru Nichiren ibun no shosha ni tsuite.* (*Seishin.* Issue 65, Minobusan College Association, 1993) pg 88.
Terao, E. *Nichiren shōnin shinseki no keitai to denrai.* (Yuzankaku, 1997) pg 327. (First published 1995.)
63. *Nichimoku shōnin,* pg. 383.
64. Nichiren Shōnin no Sekai Ten Seisaku Iinkai, ed. *Zuroku Nichiren shōnin no sekai.* (Nichiren Shōnin no Sekai Ten Jikkō Iinkai, 2001) pg 108.
65. *Zuroku Nichiren shōnin no sekai,* pg 108 reproduces plates from endpapers for two of Nichigen's transcribed works.
66. *Tōgō shisutemu,* 2015 edition. (Kōfū Dansho, 2015.) *Risshō ankoku-ron* section included in *Kaidai-tō shiryō.*

67. Ōshima, K. *"Jikidan" Saikō.* (*Interdisciplinary Studies in Japanese Buddhism*, issue 3, Association for the Interdisciplinary Studies of Japanese Buddhism, 2004) pgs 66–69.
68. See:
 Sakai, H. *Nikkō shahon "Ichidai goji keizu" o megutte.* (*Kōfū*, issue 14, 2002.)
 Sato, H., and Sakai, H. [*Shiryō shōkai*] *Awa Myōhon-ji zō: Nikkō shahon "Ichidai goji keizu," bō hitsu "Ōdaiki narabi ni Hachiman bosatsu no koto."* (*Studies on Humanities and Social Sciences of Chiba University,* issue 24, Graduate School of Humanities and Social Sciences, Chiba University, 2012.)
69. Ogami, K. *Nihon Tendai-shi no kenkyū*, pg 18. (First published 1960.)
 Nakamura, H., Fukunaga, Mitsuji, et al., eds. *Iwanami Bukkyō jiten,* 2nd edition. (Iwanami Shoten, 1989) *"Dangisho"* entry.
70. Hori, N. *Fuji Nikkō shōnin shōden.* pgs 299-304.
71. Tanji, T. *Omosu dansho no kyōikushi-teki kōsatsu.* (Takagi, Yutaka, and Kanmuri, Ken'ichi, eds. *Nichiren to sono kyōdan.* Yoshikawa Kōbunkan, 1999.)
 Omosu dansho no jinmyaku to kyōsen. (*Sasaki Koken Hakase Koki Kinen Ronshū "Bukkyō-gaku Bukkyō-shi ronshū,"* Sankibō Busshorin, 2002.)
 Omosu dansho no gakutō sanmi Nichijun. (*Journal of Nichiren Buddhism,* issue 30, 2003.)
72. Sakai, H. *Omosu Honmon-ji to Taiseki-ji,* pgs 138-145.
73. *Kō-zen,* pg 148.
74. Sources such as the following give the period of Nitchō's appointment to head instructor as being from Kagen 2 (1304) to Tokuji 1 (1306):
 Shigyo, K. *Kōmon kyōgaku no kenkyū.* (Kaishūsha, 1984) pg 87.
 Kageyama, G, ed. *Shinpen Nichiren-shu nenpyō.* (Nichiren-shū Shinbunsha, 1989.)
 Fuji nenpyō. (Dainichiren Publishing Co., Ltd., 2008 expanded 2nd edition.)
75. *Kō-zen,* pg 353.
76. *Shū-zen,* vol. 2, pgs 314–317.
77. Hori, N. *Fuji shūgaku yōshū,* vol. 2. (Fuji Shūgaku Yōshū Kankōkai, 1961) pg 92.
78. *Fuji shūgaku yōshū,* vol. 2, pg 124:
 "For 8 days in the 1st month of Bunpō, began this. In the morning carried it out at the Daibō, and in the evening in the Mieidō was someone who explained of it to me. Spent the night in the Mieidō on the 27th day of the 12th month of the 1st year of Bunpō (1317) and from the 1st day of the 1st month went through the Lotus Sūtra a volume at a time for 8 days."

References

Asai, E. (1981). Kinkōshū to Hokke mondō shōgishō. ŌSAKI GAKUHŌ, *The Journal of Nichiren Buddhist Studies, issue 134*, Risshō Daigaku Bukkyō Gakkai.

Chōken-ji Kaisan 700-nen Kinen Jigyō Kensetsu Jikkō Iinkai, ed. (2011). *Chōken-ji kaisan 700-nen kinen shoshū mondō kusaku-shū.* private printing.

Daikoku, K. (1997). "*Nikkō shōnin zenshū*" seihen hensan hoi. *Kōfū, issue 11.*

Fujihira, K. (2014). Tendai rongisho no shokeitai. *Annual of Buddhist Studies, issue 36.* Eizan Gakuin.

Homma, S. (2011). Shoki Nikkō monryū ni okeru kangyō katsudō no tenkai. ŌSAKI GAKUHŌ, *The Journal of Nichiren Buddhist Studies, issue 167.*

Homma, S. (2015). Shoki Nikkō monryū ni okeru Nichiren ibun no shosha ni tsuite. ŌSAKI GAKUHŌ, *The Journal of Nichiren Buddhist Studies, issue 171.*

Hori, N. (1961). *Fuji shūgaku yōshū, vol. 2.* Fuji Shūgaku Yōshū Kankōkai.

Hori, N. (1983). *Fuji Nikkō shōnin shōden.* Soka Gakkai.

Ikeda, R.(2006). "Hokke mondō shōgishō" no Nichiren ibun o megutte. *Kōfū. Issue 18.* Kōfū Dansho.

Kageyama, G, ed. (1989).*Shinpen Nichiren-shu nenpyō.* Nichiren-shū Shinbunsha.

Kanmuri, K. (1993). Chūsei ni okeru Nichiren ibun no shosha ni tsuite. *Seishin. Issue 65.* Minobusan College Association.

Kyoto National Museum, ed. (2009). *Nichiren to hokke no meihō: Hana-hiraku Kyōto machishū bunka.* Kyoto National Museum.

Minobusan University Tōyō Bunka Kenkyūsho, ed. (2007). *Chion hōon: Minobu-san Gakuen 450-nen shi.* Minobusan University.

Miyazaki, E. (1953). Nichiren shōnin no monka kyōiku. *Journal of Indian and Buddhist Studies, vol. 2, issue 1.*

Miyazaki, E. (1968). Nichiren shōnin ibun no bunkengaku-teki kenkyū., Mochizuki, K., ed. *Kindai Nihon no Hokke Bukkyō.* Heiraku-ji Shoten.

Mochizuki, K. (1976). *Nichiren-shū gakusetsu shi.* Heiraku-ji Shoten.

Nagamura, M. (2000). *Chūsei jiin shiryōron.* Yoshikawa Kōbunkan.

Nakamura, H., Fukunaga, Mitsuji, et al., eds. (1989). *Iwanami Bukkyō jiten, 2nd edition.*

Nakajo, G. (1996). *Nichiren-shū jōdai kyōgaku no kenkyū: Kinkōshū no kenkyū.* Heiraku-ji Shoten.

Nichimoku Shōnin Shuppan Iinkai, ed. (1998). *Nichimoku Shōnin.* Keimyō Shinbunsha.

Nikkō Shōnin Zenshū Hensan Iinkai, ed. (1996). *Nikkō Shōnin Zenshū.* Kōfū Dansho.

Nippō Shōnin Goshoji-bon chōsa Iinkai, ed. (1990). *Go-hōmon on-kikigaki.* Kōchō-ji.

Ogami, K. (2014). *Nihon Tendai-shi no kenkyū.* Sankibō Busshorin. (First published 1970.)

Ōshima, K. (2004). *"Jikidan" Saikō. Interdisciplinary Studies in Japanese Buddhism, issue 3*, Association for the Interdisciplinary Studies of Japanese Buddhism.

Rissho University Institute of Nichiren Buddhist Studies, ed. (1961). *Nichiren-shū shūgaku zensho, vols. 13–14*. Sankibō Busshorin.
Rissho University Institute of Nichiren Buddhist Studies, ed. (1985). *Nichiren shōnin ibun jiten: Rekishi-hen*. Minobu-san Kuon-ji.
Rissho University Institute of Nichiren Buddhist Studies, ed. (2000). *Shōwa teihon Nichiren shōnin ibun*. Minobu-san Kuon-ji.
Sakai, H. (1997). Omosu Honmon-ji to Taiseki-ji. *Kōfū, issue 11*.
Sakai, H. (2011). Minobu Bunko zō "Mondō yōishō" no kiso-teki kōsatsu. *Kōfū, issue 23*.
Sakai, H. (2002). Nikkō shahon "Ichidai goji keizu" o megutte. *Kōfū, issue 14*.
Saito, Y. (1937). Shōchūzan zō "Shōgishō" ni tsuite. *Seishin, Issue 22*. Sozangakuin Dōsōkai Bungakubu.
Sasaki, K. (2006). *Nihon chūsei shisō no kichō*. Yoshikawa Kōbunkan.
Sato, H., and Sakai, H. (2012). Shiryō shōkai: Awa Myōhon-ji zō: Nikkō shahon "Ichidai goji keizu," bō hitsu "Ōdaiki narabi ni Hachiman bosatsu no koto." *Studies on Humanities and Social Sciences of Chiba University, issue 24*, Graduate School of Humanities and Social Sciences, Chiba University.
Shigyo, K. (1984). *Kōmon kyōgaku no kenkyū*. Kaishūsha.
Shōhondō Konryu Kinen Shuppan Iinkai, ed. (1974). *Nichiren shōshū rekidai hossu zensho, vol. 2*. Taiseki-ji.
Taira, M. (1992). *Nihon chūsei no shakai to Bukkyō*. Hanawa Shobō.
Takagi, Y. (2008). *Nichiren-kō*. Sankibō Busshorin.
Takamori, D. (2005). Nichiren shōnin no gakumon-teki kankyō ni kan suru ichi-shi-ron. *Journal of Nichiren Buddhism, issue 32*, Rissho University Institute of Nichiren Buddhist Studies.
Tanji, T. (1999). Omosu dansho no kyōikushi-teki kōsatsu. Takagi, Yutaka, and Kanmuri, Ken'ichi, eds. *Nichiren to sono kyōdan*. Yoshikawa Kōbunkan.
Tanji, T. (2002). Omosu dansho no jinmyaku to kyōsen. *Sasaki Koken Hakase Koki Kinen Ronshū "Bukkyō-gaku Bukkyō-shi ronshū"*. Sankibō Busshorin.
Tanji, T. (2003). Omosu dansho no gakutō sanmi Nichijun. *Journal of Nichiren Buddhism, issue 30*.
Tendai shūten hensan-sho, ed. (2000). *Seizoku Tendai-shū zensho mokuroku kaidai*. Shunjūsha.
Terao, E. (1997). *Nichiren shōnin shinseki no keitai to denrai*. Yuzankaku. (First published 1995.)
Terao, E. (1998). Nichiren "Ichidai goji zu" no Minobu-san sozon-hon: Kyōto Honman-ji no Nichiken hitsu rinsha-hon ni tsuite. *Minobu Ronsō, issue 3*. Minobusan University Association for Buddhist Studies.
Terao, E. (2009). Gyōgakuin Nitchō kankei no shōgyō ni tsuite., *Journal of Indian and Buddhist Studies, vol. 57, issue 2*, The Japanese Association of Indian and Buddhist Studies.
Terao, E. (2010). Gyōgakuin Nitchō no zōsho keisei ni tsuite., *Journal of Indian and*

Buddhist Studies, vol. 58, issue 2, The Japanese Association of Indian and Buddhist Studies.

Terao, E. (2011). Gyōgakuin Nitchō no Hokekyō dangi-sho ni tsuite., *Journal of Indian and Buddhist Studies*, vol. 60, issue 1, The Japanese Association of Indian and Buddhist Studies.

Watanabe, H. (1976). *Nichiren-shū shingyōron no kenkyū*. Heiraku-ji Shoten.

Watanabe, M. (2007). Chūsei ni okeru sōryo no gakumon: Dangisho to iu shiten kara. *Hirosaki Daigaku Kokugo Kokubungaku, issue 28.* Hirosaki Daigaku Kokugo Kokubun Gakkai.

Watanabe, M. (2010). Tendai dangisho o meguru gakumon no kōryū. Yasurō Abe, ed. *Chūsei bungaku to jiin shiryō-shōgyō*. Chikurinsha.

Gentrification and Spatial Polarization in Eastern Inner-City Tokyo: The Restructuring of the Kyojima Area in Sumida Ward

Fumiko Kohama

Abstract
This study focuses on the Kyojima area in Sumida Ward, Tokyo, a typical inner-city Tokyo neighborhood, which serves as an exemplar of redevelopment and gentrification in a Japanese context. It explores the attributes of gentrifiers, an urban middle-class social group new to Japan and with notable characteristics. Although previous studies on Tokyo have focused on its three central wards, few have examined its wider inner-city dynamics. This study examines a redevelopment that is changing the face of the *Shitamachi*, the working class neighborhoods located in the low land areas of Tokyo, which survived World War II bombings and where micro, small and medium-sized local manufacturing industries remain concentrated. Similar to other large cities such as London, Paris, and New York, Tokyo has experienced changes in its socio-economic structure since the 1960s, associated with population growth following the redevelopment of its inner urban areas. This study determines some of the characteristics of Japanese gentrification; it is informed by the 2015 population census, as well as interview data collected since 2012. Drawing upon empirical case study data, the general sociological discourse of the local as "defensive response to the increasing general power of globalising forces" (Savage, 2005:200) is critically evaluated in light of this particular Japanese example of gentrification.

Introduction

This article focuses on the Kyojima area in Sumida Ward, (256 thousand population whilst Tokyo Metropolitan Area of 9,273 thousand population), an exemplar of inner-city Tokyo neighborhoods,[1] to analyse the phenomenon of gentrification and establish the profile of Tokyo gentrifiers.

Inner-city redevelopment and changes in socio-economic structures were first identified in London in the 1960s, New York in the 1970s and Tokyo in the 1980s. Population growth in urban centers and neighboring inner-city areas plunged them into the so-called "re-urbanization" stage[2] described in the urban development model of Klaassen, et al., (1981). According to national censuses conducted in 2010 and 2015, Tokyo metropolitan areas experienced the country's highest population growth rates, at 4.6% and 2.7% respectively. Population growth rates in some wards for those years reached as high as 5.4% and 3.5%, respectively. This phenomenon has been called a "back-to-the-city movement", but since the focus here is on a social stratum that has never previously lived in the inner city, such a blanket term is not appropriate.

In terms of population growth and the change in socio-economic structure, if gentrification[3] is equated with a reinvestment of capital targeting urban centers and inner-city areas, it is also recognized as having a close relationship to demographics and land value. Smith, (1996) viewed gentrification as an effect produced by the return of capital, and keenly pointed out the negative aspects of private investment. He stressed that gentrification is caused when maximum profit is gained through a rent gap generated between potential land rent and capitalized land rent. At the same time, a focus on newcomers shows that potential gentrifiers, considered a new urban middle class, are notable for their new attributes and lifestyles that include being predominantly young, well-educated "DINKs" (double income no kids) or single, urban-minded professionals and technicians who focus on their private lives. It has been noted that their presence is a necessary condition of gentrification (Rose, 1984, Beauregard, 1988; Hamnett, 1991).

Recently, gentrification has become a focus of research in Japan. In particular, studies on Tokyo have tended towards an analysis of urban centers[4]. Of the three urban wards in the city core, redevelopment rapidly progressed, from the latter half of the 1980s in Tsukuda 1-chome and Tsukishima 1-chome/3-chome ('chome' is an urban block) in Chuo Ward, blazing a trail for the redevelopment of their urban centers. In Okawabata River City 21, where construction commenced in 1986, some 2,500 residences were built in a seven-building complex of high-rise apartments constructed by Tokyo

Metropolitan Government, Tokyo Metropolitan Housing Supply Corporation, the Urban Renaissance Agency and a private company, —Mitsui Fudosan. A resident population of 7,500 was planned. Later, neighborhood associations were established in high-rise apartments in the Mitsui area at the unit level. Residents in these buildings built active neighborhood relationships that came to be expressed as *tatenagaya* [a stacked, traditional, wooden-terraced house], rather than "the lifestyle akin to living in a hotel", anticipated by Mitsui Fudosan[5] in its promotional literature. Originally, not all high-rise developments in River City 21 established neighborhood associations. In most cases, high-rise households joined the neighbourhood association on an individual basis. Neighborhood associations formed within the same high-rise apartment building also fell within the purview of the Tsukuda 2-chome block council. Such high-rise households therefore belonged to two neighborhood associations at the same time, an unusual government arrangement (as normally there is a single neighborhood association in an urban block).

The hosting of the 2020 Olympic and Paralympic Games in Tokyo is driving redevelopment in the city's three central urban wards. Residential areas are being transformed into commercial districts and accomodating national urban functions in the form of "National Strategic Special Zones". But the inner-city gentrification phenomenon in Tokyo differs from what is happening in the three urban wards in terms of their historical social background. This article focuses on the Kyojima area in Sumida Ward to examine as a case study of the kind of redevelopment arising in Tokyo currently and exposes the implications for future Japanese gentrification.

1. Phases of Inner-city Change in Tokyo, and a Profile of the Targeted Districts

Starting in the late 1980s, the polarization of Tokyo as a "World City" (Freedman, 1986) was accelerated by re-urbanization. Although subject to criticisms that claim no inner-city problems existed in Tokyo, Takahashi (1992) showed, through empirical research, that overdevelopment in Tokyo simultaneously involved both urban growth and urban decline, and that the resident population continued to decrease, notably in Joto (Taito, Sumida, Arakawa wards) and Jonan communities (Shinagawa, Ota Ward). In many cases this involved the clearance and transformation of modern *shitamachi*, working class neighborhoods located in geographically lowland areas which had previously housed self-employed urbanites from rural regions seeking upward social mobility. A key factor in the success or failure of inner city regeneration in major cities has been the extent of proactive urban development endeavors by successors to these self-employed residents (business owners and family workers with no employees). It is impossible to ignore the existence of self-employed workers as the agents of urban development in these wards, as research undertaken by the present author since 2012 shows.[6]

In contrast to the transformation of commercial and business districts that garnered attention as a growth strategy in Tokyo, and even as structural change was evident in the decline of local manufacturing in inner city areas, a significant time lag arose between policy-making and project delivery. In 1982, the Multi-Core City Initiative that appeared in the 1st Tokyo Long-Term Plan specified the seven sub-centers of Shinjuku, Ikebukuro, Shibuya, Ueno/Asakusa, Kinshicho/Kameido and Osaki, and even named the inner-city Joto area in the Tokyo growth strategy. Later, the Metropolitan Government promoted urban development in the Ueno/Asakusa vicinity of Tokyo as an area to attract tourists. However, after the economic bubble collapsed in the early 1990s, the country's Economic Strategy Council advocated "mobilization/effective utilization of real estate", "redevelopment projects to promote redevelopment business" and "facilitation/expedition of bidding procedures". Urban policies became a means to escape the lengthy recession. Indeed, the *Special Measures Concerning Urban Reconstruction Act* enacted in 2002 and the *Designated Urban Areas Requiring Urgent Reconstruction Act* enacted in 2011 were implemented in the context of loan defaults, and financial deregulation. The 1994 Metropolitan Government switched from the Multi-Core City Initiative previously advocated to the Ringed Megalopolis Initiative. The new policy aimed to focus investment in the inner area of the Central Circular Route, considered the central core, and the nucleus of Japanese government, economics, and culture (Tokyo Metropolitan Government, 2000). Thus, the stimulation of housing demand in commercial and business districts through urban redevelopment was promoted as "a policy in which a city that survives global competition brings in people viewed as 'desirable' actors for that purpose". Meanwhile, "residuary housing for people who are 'undesirable,' such as the economically weak and needy", was not provided for the households displaced by the redevelopment process (Takagi, 2015:58–68). According to the Tokyo Basic Ordinance on Housing, the objective is "securing housing sufficient for all city residents to receive ample manner of housing".[7] In actuality, "in the urban vision pointing to success in economic competition, housing policies based on urban reconstruction policies promote a course of housing development to discriminatingly gather suitable residents to these urban centers on the one hand, while decreasing housing for 'unsuitable people,' such as those who possess the qualifications to live in municipal housing" (Takagi, 2016:71–72). The aforementioned displacement obviously differs from the situation in which residents of Kasumigaoka Municipal Apartments had to be displaced to rebuild the National Stadium in Meiji Jingu Gaien (Inaba, 2015), but it seems social policy has contributed to the negative costs of gentrification in inner city areas that have a relatively large amount of municipal housing.

There was also the impact of the Urban Renaissance initiative by the vitality of private sector that was incorporated into 1983 comprehensive economic measures. In Sumida Ward, under Multi-Core New Urban Development program presented in the My Town Tokyo Concept, the Kinshicho Station North Exit Area Redevelopment Project was promoted from 1997 within the Tokyo Long-Term Plan. In 1980, the Kinshicho Vicinity Basic Plan, which depicted a future vision of the sub-center, was publicized in the Sumida Ward Basic Concept, and the establishment of a large base for commercial facilities was realized. Elements that promoted redevelopment were identified; in the northern area of Kinshicho there was neighboring private land, municipal land, ward land, and approximately 3.5 ha of land once utilized for, among other things, housing exhibitions and storage for the former Japanese National Railways. Around 4.0 ha of land were established by a three-party council of the former Japanese National Railways, Tokyo Metropolitan Government and Sumida Ward. However, there was pushback from residents over environmental consequences due to redevelopment, such as the blockage of sunlight in homes, wind damage, disaster prevention, and transportation. This is because residents were afraid that redevelopments could break neighborhood ties, mutual aid and local knowledge, which had developed over the years. In addition, rocketing land prices brought on by an economic bubble led to greater twists and turns in consensus-building among local residents. A gap existed between appraised land value and actual market value in the ward. That is, major corporations purchased and subdivided private land within the development area.[8] The sale price significantly exceeded the ward's appraised land value, and landowners were understandbly dissatisfied with this mismatch. The transfer of ownership did not go smoothly. Many of the landowners were self-employed businesses that handled convenience goods, such as sweets and soft drinks, and wholesalers and sellers of millet, and they were very concerned about whether their businesses could endure redevelopment after moving into high-rise buildings. Moreover, redevelopment was in danger of being halted in the aftermath of the Great Hanshin-Awaji Earthquake due to factors ranging from the withdrawal of major department stores and insurance companies which were the biggest investors in the project. Notwithstanding these challenges, by 1997 project completion was in sight.

Meanwhile, in the northern area, urban infrastructure was not yet well-developed and, rather than the aforementioned kind of site development project, issues such as disaster prevention, vitalization of local industry, and improving the housing environment were viewed as problematic. As a result, the redevelopment policies, plans and delivery programs of the Tokyo Metropolitan Government and Sumida Ward were not aligned. Full-scale redevelopment in the area began in the 2000s as manufacturing industry shrank and urban corporatization progressed due to investment in real estate and land, namely the "built environment".[9] According to Machimura, who analyzed the Tokyo Metropolitan Government's *Annual Report of Building Statistics*, the "total floor space of buildings under construction in the 2000s indicates the phenomenon of decline". The gap between the considerable changes to the city and superficial impressions was explained as follows. "Since the latter half of the 1990s, the degree of urban corporatization in Tokyo has rapidly increased in terms of urban space production. In construction, changes in the balance between individual landowners, corporations and local government, especially the prominence of the corporate sector, have led to conspicuousness of numerical figures and spatial transformations".[10] A situation unfolded in which space that could survive under the strategy of "selection and concentration" was being replaced by space built according to the very same strategy.

Sumida Ward is generally considered as a southern area where roads were constructed that fall under the former Honjo ward, where alleys that were once narrow farm roads included in the former Mukojima ward, or as an area that can trace its history back to being a *sangyochi* entertainment district (licensed only for restaurants, tea houses, places for couples to meet secretly, and *geisha* houses). The district began being used as a residential

Photo 1 A neighborhood exuding nostalgia
Taken by the author on 19 May 2012

Photo 2 A streetscape retaining *shitamachi* alleys
Taken by the author on 10 September 2016

area after the Kanto earthquake of 1923. Disaster victims from the northern area of the district built lots and settled in this marshy area—site of a key transportation canal for food supply in old Edo (former capital of Tokyo)—however the associated urban infrastructure was not developed at the same pace. Having been lucky enough to escape aerial attacks during World War II, the area became crowded with displaced people from elsewhere (the population density exceeded 500 people per hectare). The media characterised the streetscape of homes built between the late Taisho era and early Showa era as creating a unique *shitamachi* kind of nostalgia. (See photos 1, 2.)

Meanwhile, the Basic Plan announced by the Tokyo Metropolitan Government Bureau of Housing in 1971 proposed to "demolish and rebuid", providing high-rise housing to replace neighborhoods lacking in disaster prevention and amenities, rather than preserving the heritage of the Showa-era construction and the *shitamachi* social relations.

The Kyojima area in Sumida Ward (Kyojima 1-chome to 3-chome) was identified as being at extremely high risk of natural disaster in the 1993 Tokyo Metropolitan Government *Report on Risk Assessment Survey*. Even with a boost from the *Act on Promotion of Improvement of Disaster Control Districts in Populated Urban Districts* (Ministry of Land, Infrastructure, Transport and Tourism, 1997), the development program has not proceeded as planned. The district in question is a densely built-up area of deteriorating wooden homes

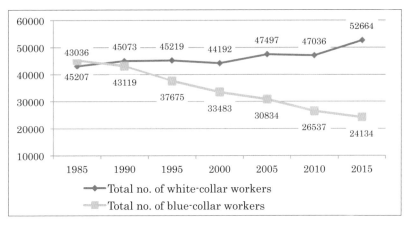

Fig.1 Shifts in the composition of Sumida Ward by occupation 1985–2015

extending over an area of approximately 25 hectares. Furthermore, rather than simply accomodating a single "work status" category (self-employed workers and family workers), self-employed residents that lead neighborhood associations like those in other inner-city areas constitute "a social stratum possessing a distinctive cohesiveness and presence self-formed through participation in neighborhood associations " (Takenaka, et al., 1988:47). From the perspective of social mobility, the transformation of the local economy made surviving in self-employment an extremely difficult challenge. Figure 1 shows that up until 1985, blue-collar workers exceeded white-collar workers, but declined considerably in the 1990s and beyond.

In 2008, Sumida Ward accomodated six community areas in the Basic Plan (based on guidelines for urban development in which local residents take a role), and established area divisions for area-specific initiatives. Of the six areas, the Mukojima, Kyojima, and Oshiage areas identified the following as major area issues: (1) improving safety in densely built-up areas of wooden homes; (2) creating a living environment enabling continued residence through appropriate guidance for high-rise apartments ; (3) improving convenience of parks and waterfronts; (4) forming landscapes that utilize landscape resources with scenic focal points and area characteristics; and (5) urban development that takes coexistence with local industry into account

(Sumida Ward, 2008: 108–109).

Moreover, in 1978 the Urban Renaissance Agency (an independent administrative corporation) introduced the 'Living Environment Development Model' project as a community-based disaster preparedness planning scheme in the Kyojima area, and accordingly the Kyojima Urban Development Council was established in 1980 to foster resident participation. Densely populated areas of traditional one-storey single-unit dwellings were reprovided in the from of low-rise, multiple-dwelling complexes. New "community residences" became permanent homes for residents who lost their homes when land and buildings were sold to the ward, and for residents of dilapidated homes and those that were displaced by road-widening projects.

As for the communicative aspects of urban development, since 1986 the Kyojima Urban Development Council has issued the *Kyojima Area Urban Development News,* and the Kyojima Cultural Festival has been held since 1988. Community-based disaster preparedness planning in the same area garnered attention from the viewpoints of public administration, urban sociology, urban planning and architecture as a new trend in urban planning featuring participation by residents. However, from 1990 the budget for these activities was scaled back, and subsidies for urban development projects from the national government dropped from around 1.45 billion yen in 1993 to 3.9 million yen in 2001. As a result, continuing disaster preparedness programs based on collaboration between national government, Tokyo Metropolitan Government and Sumida Ward became impossible, and the strength of the urban development initiatives waned. In 1988, the Kyojima Urban Development Council, members of the Hitokotokai Group in the Ichiderakototoi area, residents, professional groups and others explored the possibility for new urban development and, in 2002, established the Association of Mukojima Studies, a non-profit organization (NPO).

To elaborate, the revitalization of groups in *shitamachi*-type local communities sought new opportunities through collaborative initiatives for urban development bringing together professional groups specialized in public administration, urban planning, small and medium-sized business policy, and self-employed residents. The Kyojima Urban Development Council was formed in 1981, and in the following year the objectives of the Kyojima Area General Urban Planning Framework were announced: (a) creating a good residential environment; (b) maintaining close proximity between work and home that integrates dwellings, commerce and industry; (c) improving safety to withstand earthquakes/fires; and (d) establishing a population over 10,000. The General Framework covered a number of topics: (1) community road planning; (2) building and development delivery planning (public/private division of roles); and (3) community facilities planning. The framework was oriented toward refurbishment and improvement rather than clearance and reconstruction. It was valued for its cooperative urban development approach featuring resident participation and public-private partnerships. After drawing up the General Framework, the activities of the Council stalled, and it is now regarded as primarily communicating government intentions rather than delivering them (Sumida Ward, 1996). While efforts were made to encourage fireproofing in densely built-up wooden housing areas over the 30 years since 1981, there was a questionable level of stakeholder engagement stakeholders with the Urban Development Council and city development projects. Whilst the public sector should in principle with residents, consult on the course of urban development, and involve them in the detailed design of specific proposals, in actuality urban development easily defaults to leadership by the government or the public-private sector without obtaining consensus among residents, due to factors such as the complexity of land ownership and public apprehensions regarding redevelopment. Ultimately, urban planning endeavors became tied to informal activities attempted by NPOs (non-profit organizations).

2. The Path towards Gentrification in Kyojima 1-chome

Strategic-level plans have been formulated by the Tokyo Metropolitan Government and Sumida Ward for the vicinity of Hikifune Station (Higashi-Mukojima 2-chome, Oshiage 2-chome, and Kyojima 1-chome) in Sumida Ward.[11] In the Kyojima area, there is a high percentage of both low-rise residential buildings of one- to three-storeys and land for industrial use, in addition to land in mixed use. However, in terms of population, Kyojima 1-chome shows distinctive characteristics. In Sumida Ward population growth soared in the year 2000 (Fig. 2). But in Kyojima 1-chome a rapid and sustained increase occurred in 2005 (Fig. 3), with a rise in white-collar workers[12] the same year (Fig. 4), indicating a time lag with respect to overall population growth in the ward corresponding to the knock-on effect of redevelopment in areas around major stations. Urban development projects in this part of the city had initially been focussed on large-scale redevelopment in and around the station in 1-chome subsequently a small-scale maintenance/expansion project was planned in 2-chome and 3-chome. In the same period work also commenced on a crossover project and numerous railroad crossings were phased out in order to promote the integration of urban areas, such as Keisei Oshiage Line as an urban development project by Tokyo Metropolitan Government.

The 'rent gap' theory helps explain the rise of gentrification. 'Rent gap' refers to the disparity between actual land rent prior to redevelopment and potential land rent after redevelopment. The question of whether an increase occurred in the relevant areas due to potential land rent is answered by looking at shifts in publicly assessed land values in Sumida Ward as a whole, the Tokyo Skytree vicinity, the Hikifune vicinity (including the Kyojima area), and the Oshiage vicinity (see Fig.5). Results indicate that, in general, rising prices peaked in 2008 and have levelled off since 2010. Remarkably, the only area that can be judged to have experienced a rise in land prices is the vicinity around Tokyo Skytree. Then again, in the Hikifune vicinity, the 2008 peak is low compared to other areas and cannot be said to reflect the potential land rent. In 2016, a downward trend is evident compared to 10 years earlier. It can be surmised that the high-rise multiple-dwelling complexes in the Hikifune area, which did not fully experience the economic mechanism involving real estate, were a response to the popularity of high-rise tower apartments when regulations were eased following the *2002 Act on Special Measures Concerning Urban Reconstruction*. These apartments were comparatively easy for young families and professional singles to afford. Though the development of business districts is not regulated in the same way as residential areas in accordance with the *Building Standards Act*, residential high-rise buildings can be constructed in business districts. Therefore, if land rent for housing created by high-rise apartments as a whole exceeds commercial land rent, it easily leads to the development of residential high-rises.

The fact that gentrification is usually accompanied by the displacement of former residents is considered a problem. Housing maps and interview data were used to determine whether displacement had taken place. Table 1 shows the extent of displacement caused by building renovations prior to and after redevelopment.[13] In lot numbers 1 and 2 of Kyojima 1-chome, there were medium-and-large size manufacturers, restaurants, retailers, and residential areas in 2000, but in 2015 the lots had become large high-rise housing and large retail stores. It is methodologically difficult to determine where the former residents relocated. In cases where continuing a family business in a small shop is difficult or there is no choice but to move, conflicting interests in the change of freeholds, leasehold and tenancy rights can tear human relationships apart and residents are reluctant to talk about it.[14]

The richness of life histories embedded in place prior to redevelopment, where several rightful claimants maintained and used a building in a unified manner, exceeds any reductive categorization as 'cooperation'. Population continued to relocate form that area through the 1990s, and abandoned homes and vacant lots became noticeable. Meanwhile, in 2006 the decision was made to construct Tokyo Skytree as an attraction. Turning the area into a series of tourist attractions is one of the ward's key strategies, and the redevelopment of Oshiage Station and Hikifune Station vicinity gained momentum. Private developers acquired dilapidated homes and land, and the construction of ready-built housing, parking lots, studio and family apartments accelerated. Redevelopment and infrastructure projects intensified in 2003. Furthermore, shifts in land usage—namely, changes in urban functions, retail, manufacturing and residential areas, brought with it high-rise multiple-dwelling complexes and large supermarkets. This is confirmed by superimposing housing maps from 2015 on housing maps from 2000. In Table 1, the existence of super high-rise apartments (buildings of 20 stories or higher) in 2015 is conspicuous. For instance, East Core Hikifune Niban-kan, which was completed in 2008, has 41 aboveground stories and 557 dwellings. All but one are skyscrapers. From the perspective of local people and longtime residents, the neighborhood landscape has been totally transformed. The split in attitudes over redevelopment between those who approve and those with negative sentiments is correlated with the aforementioned issues such as land interests, involvement in one's own business and the location of one's home. Self-employed workers native to the area, who now run businesses in the vicinity of Hikifune Station commented on rapid redevelopment in major station areas.

"Redevelopment was inevitable. The neighborhood has become brighter and interaction among people has blossomed, so I've never felt that the arrival of high-rise apartments is bad".[15]

"In the Mukojima area, the small single-unit dwellings are deteriorating. So I'd like for redevelopment to move forward in that area, too".[16]

On the other hand, the self-employed natives to the area that run businesses

Gentrification and Spatial Polarization in Eastern Inner-City Tokyo: The Restructuring of the Kyojima Area in Sumida Ward

Photo 3 A tower similar to the Panopticon
Taken by the author on 20 May 2012

Photo 4 Redevelopment area in Kyojima 1-chome
Taken by the author on 10 September 2016

in places distant from a station reported negative effects: "The sunshine is blocked and the wind has changed".[17] "There are fewer people I recognize and whose names I know. Neighborhood relations and the flow of people have changed".[18]

There are aspects of administrative and government power that are hidden in urban development. Also, there are likely incontrovertible counterpoints that could be cited in response to residents' desire for "brightness", including the new look that contrasts negative aspects, such as deterioration, high density, and vulnerability to disaster. It has been pointed out that awareness of urban development enables the broad classification of residents into three types: (1) the traditional "commerce and industry/humanity" type; (2) the "housing/humanity" type (majority) in which only the ideology of *"shitamachi* humanity" is separated from the foundation of commerce and industry/society; and (3) the "housing/individuality" type that is the polar opposite to the long-established pattern. A response that is in line with residents' social strata is also considered necessary to the orientation of urban development (Takenaka, & Takahashi, 1990: 111–112).

The next section clarifies elements such as newcomer attributes, social relationships and attitudes toward permanent residents concerning redevelopment in Kyojima 1-chome, an area where redevelopment is furthest progressed. Thereafter, profiles are drawn of Japanese gentrifiers based on interviews with participants from the new middle urban class that moved to the northern area (broadly classified as "housing/humanity" types or "housing/individuality" types).

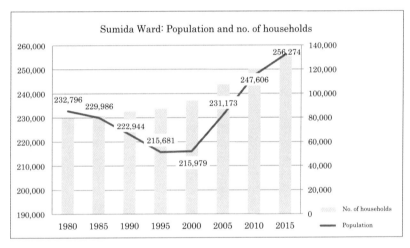

Fig.2 Shifts in population and no. of households in Sumida Ward
Source: created by author based on the national census in each year

Gentrification and Spatial Polarization in Eastern Inner-City Tokyo: The Restructuring of the Kyojima Area in Sumida Ward

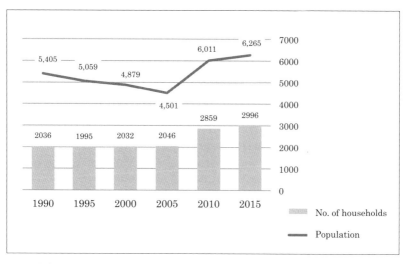

Fig.3 Shifts in population and no. of households in Kyojima 1-chome
Source: created by author based on the national census in each year

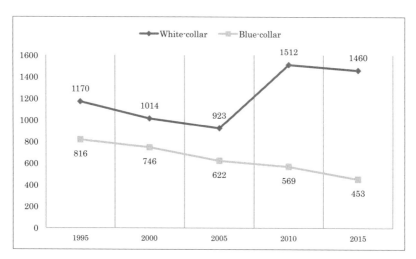

Fig.4 Shifts in white-collar and blue-collar workers in Kyojima 1-chome
Source: created by author based on the national census in each year

Table 1—Changes in urban functions in residential area maps

Targeted areas	2000 housing map	2015 housing map
Kyojima 1-chome 1	Nagayanagi Co, Ltd. Tahara Koyu Co., Ltd. Tahara Koyu Co., Ltd. Residences	East Core Hikifune Ichiban-kan/ Niban-kan
Kyojima 1-chome 2	Restaurants Retail Shiseido Co., Ltd.	East Core Hikifune Sanban-kan/ Ito-Yokado Hikifune
Kyojima 1-chome 36	Manufacturing Residences	Mark Front Tower Hikifune/ Mark Zero One Hikifune Tower
Kyojima 1-chome 8	Residential area	Atlas Tower Hikifune
Kyojima 1-chome 27	Parking Rora Kyoshima Kanekubo Amimono Co., Ltd.	Mark Zero One Hikifune Residence HORIZON

(Source: created by the author based on *Tokyo Housing Series: Hai Map Sumida Ward Housing Map*, 2000, Seiko-sha; *Zenrin Housing Maps Sumida Ward, Tokyo*, 2015, Zenrin)

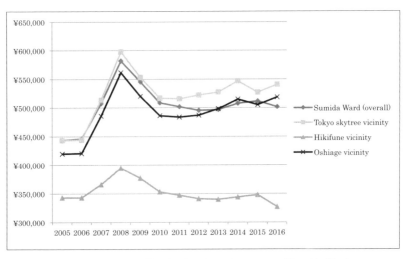

Fig.5 Shifts in publicly assessed land values in various areas of Sumida Ward
(Source: created based on the Ministry of Land, Infrastructure, Transport and Tourism "Land General Information System" for each year.)

3. Gentrifiers in Kyojima 1-chome and Higashi-Mukojima 2-chome, Sumida Ward

Generally, gentrifiers in Japan are referred to as *tawaman jumin* (residents of high-rise apartments) and have been shown to have distinctive characteristics. "Tower mansion" high-rise apartments are tower-type super high-rise apartments exceeding 60 meters (approximately 20 stories), as defined by the *Building Standards Act*. Analysis has shown that tower residents are characterized by transportation convenience (location), enhanced common facilities, and large household numbers, but a lack of desire for community ties or residential relationships. High-rise apartments in the Tsukishima area of Chuo Ward in Tokyo and the Musashi-Kosugi area in Nakahara Ward in Kawasaki have been noted as typical examples (*AERA*, 2013: 61–65).

This article presents results of interviews and a survey in 2012 to first clarify the attributes, social relationships and attitudes toward permanent residence of the "new urban middle class" tower residents who fall under the aforementioned "housing/individuality" type.

(1) Attributes of gentrifiers

As shown in Table 2[19], gentrifiers are primarily in their 30s and notable for being highly educated, with 67% having graduated from university or graduate school. In many cases their birthplace was not Sumida Ward. Instead, 93% hail from other wards or prefectures, hence they can be overwhelmingly considered as newcomers. The data shows that they lived elsewhere in the 23 wards of metropolitan Tokyo prior to moving to Sumida Ward. It was thought that providing the residents with precise occupational classifications would be confusing. Therefore, only their employment status is shown. Results indicate that 75% are full-time managers and employees, while 25% are unemployed or retired. The fact that there were no self-employed or family workers confirms the presence of newcomers. Family composition includes married couples, residents who live alone, and nuclear families, in that order. There were no three-generation households. As for household income, rent is typically around 30%, and income is estimated to be between 6 million and 10 million yen for residents living alone, and 10 million yen or more for dual-income households.

The main reasons for choosing these apartments were good access to transportation (convenient access to both Narita and Haneda airports), good scenery (rooms with a view of Tokyo Skytree, fireworks) and well-equipped facilities (including security). Other reasons included reasonable rent and finding Hikifune appealing.

(2) Social relationships

In the same high-rise apartment the 2011 Great East Japan Earthquake prompted the formation of neighborhood associations that did not exist at the time construction was completed. Leaseholders who established the neighborhood associations stated "Even if for a short time, we want to create connections among residents in the same apartment building" (Yoshihara, & Chikamori, 2013: 104). In 2012, the participation rate was 25%. However a website was also created by a private organization consisting of residents of neighboring apartment buildings and employees of large retail shops, somewhat differently neighborhood associations whose participation is semi-compulsory.

In a 2012 survey, for 86% of residents, neighborhood relations remain at the level of "exchanging greetings" and "bowing to an acquaintance". The website of East Core Hikifune Neighborhood Association sets out the difference between the homeowners' association and neighborhood associations: "It is safe to say that the homeowners' association is a group that considers the building in terms of unit owners, while neighborhood associations are groups that considers services for and communication between people (on a voluntary basis)". Those residents have difficulty finding common interests in an organization that hinges on community ties, but some 60% of residents are interested in information on neighborhood associations shared via electronic community notices. It cannot be simply said that residents seek superficial neighborhood relations.

(3) Attitudes towards permanent residents

According to the questionnaire in a survey 2012

- 37% answered "I'd like to continue living in the apartment building" ;
- 22% stated, "I'd like to continue living in Sumida Ward" ; and
- 41% stated, "I don't know". .

Given that "don't know" was the most common answer, it can be remarked that this reflects a characteristic of rental tenants, but if commuting access or the view were to change, or they were to feel anxious about security, it is conceivable that the possibility of moving home would arise. Eighty percent of residents rated redevelopment in the Hikifune Station vicinity as desirable. It can be surmised that some of them also responded "don't know", considering the possibilities of decline in the property value and landscape change caused by further redevelopment. It is presumed that people who responded "don't know" would be likely to move out of the area depending on the circumstances around them.

Residents who participated in the interview were predominately highly educated, occupied professional/management positions and lived in either single or dual income households (for instance, an international married DINKs couple with jobs in civil service management and IT technology). If employed full time in a job with frequent business travel, rather than use traditional shopping areas that carry convenience goods, they conventionally prefer to use *Solamachi* and a large supermarket connected to the apartment site, home delivery from a co-op, online shopping, and urban department stores. Gentrifiers create their own social networks through personal communication, and are not reliant on local relationships. Their lifestyles can be constructed from points that go beyond locality. However, they cannot be defined as completely disinterested in community relationships. There are possibilities for loose ties—through the website for example—if common interests are identified, and their motivations correspond most closely to the "housing/individuality" type.

Though somewhat distant from the high-rise apartments in front of Hikifune Station, a married couple living in an apartment located five minutes walking distance from Hikifune Station was interviewed. The 13-story high-rise apartment completed in 2000 has 47 units, and there are alleys and gardens planted with shrubbery in the vicinity. It is clearly different than other redeveloped, orderly areas. Based on this interview[20] a gentrifier profile distinct from the above type became clear—the "housing/humanity" type.

Prior to moving into the apartment the couple lived for three years in a somewhat small rented unit near Hikifune Station, which had two rooms and a dining/kitchen area. They then purchased their current three-room apartment unit with a living room and dining/kitchen (75 m^2), and intend to continue living there. Residents of this apartment building are primarily aged in their 40s and comprise a relatively large number of young married couples.

The family of four consists of a wife and husband in their mid-30s, a daughter (aged 6) and a son (aged 3) who both go to nursery school. Both wife and husband work full-time at the same company in the city center. The 30-minute commute made the apartment attractive. The husband grew up in Kokubunji, Tokyo, and the wife in Shibamata in Katsushika Ward, Tokyo. The wife's lifestyle desires were strongly reflected in the choice of neighborhood and the purchase of the apartment. After some consideration they preferred to relocate near Hikifune Station, rather than to a secluded environment where the sound of trains at Oshiage Station cannot be heard, or Yahiro with its tanneries. They also looked at a high-rise apartment near Hikifune Station, but were put off by what they viewed as excessive layers of security.

In the interview, the wife stated:

"My parents' place is in Shibamata, so my younger brother and father went to Sumidagawa High School. We'd go and watch plays at Hikifune Culture Center, and spend our days in the area around Hikifune Station". "…I chose Hikifune Station because it's good, but the above-ground station is busier than Oshiage Station on the subway. If you go one stop further to Yahiro, there are lots of factories including those that tan old animal hides. I was told the smell drifts as far as the station. Oshiage doesn't have anything, there aren't any train sounds, and the atmosphere of the streets at night isn't very good, so we decided against it."

Wife: "The high-rise apartment security was too heavy. We went to a viewing, but there were two security procedures to push even one elevator button. The elevator only goes up to the floor you select. It seemed like there'd be even less and less interaction with other people, plus the unit was small, so I didn't think it was quite right. I appreciate having automatic locks, but I don't need the elevator to be locked. New apartments have such heavy security—it feels so impersonal. I thought getting packages delivered would also be a hassle. You'd have to take the elevator down and look for it. I don't think it's necessary to go that far".

The above comments make it apparent that there is an overlap between the area they live in and the *shitamachi* environment in which she grew up, and that she felt homes with heavy security were impersonal and would easily lead to limited interaction with others. Furthermore, she provided several points of commonality with the community of Shibamata where she grew up, that contributed to the appeal of Sumida Ward.

> Wife: "I like *shitamachi*. In summer, you can hear festival music there. I want to take my kids to festivals or other events like that. That was a positive for moving here". "…Every year I take the kids to around three events—festivals, rice cake pounding events and disaster prevention drills."

According to her husband:

> "This neighborhood doesn't have a tense feel. It's calm. When I walk with the kids I'm not on alert. It's the kind of place you can walk along without thinking about anything. Minato Ward, where I work, has a tense feeling. It's an area of offices, but *shitamachi* is slow-paced and you can relax. It's got a pleasant atmosphere".

When it comes to parks for children, there are unspoken rules about what ages should play at what time. "Local knowledge" about letting children play is also typical of *shitamachi* and learned by residents.
The wife said:

> "In the mornings, kids about my son's age play, but in the mid-afternoon, kids around my daughter's age are there. After 4:00 pm., elementary and junior high school kids play tag aggressively, so I don't take them then. If I take them, I think morning is best for kids about this age."

The couple has social relationships centering on acquaintances of the same generation they have come to know through nursery school, company colleagues and friends from their school days. The apartment residents' association is restricted to discussing maintenance and repairs. As for *chonaikai* (neighborhood association), there are no invitations to apartment residents to participate in events, but invitations are extended to the apartment next door. Interaction differs by neighborhood association Since the couple has registered with Sumida Ward to obtain the necessary information, they feel no particular need to join the neighborhood association.

A characteristic distinct from the aforementioned "housing/individuality" type, embedded in the bedrock of their lifestyle is compatibility with *shitamachi*-type human relations. These are expressed as "environmental development in residential areas and an 'unpretentious, warmhearted neighborhood' where advice can be sought out" (Takenaka, & Takahashi, 1990: 113). In other words, perhaps it can be called the "*shitamachi*/humanity" type.

Finally, this article will consider socio-cultural contexts of the residential area's history and how this may impact on how both types of gentrifiers choose where to live.

A twenty-something woman responsible for art project activities[21] in the same area said; "In terms of local character, it's not a rich neighborhood. Art is enjoyed by people with some time and money, so the question is how to fill the gap. When asked what art can do for the elderly, homeless and poor, I have to have some kind of answer. That's the problem".[22]

Through an interview held with a pawnbroker that has been in business for three generations, it was learned that even when residents know about each other's setbacks in life, hardships of living and difficulties of work, they have learned the art of being indifferent and not getting involved.[23] The films S*hitamachi no Taiyo* (The Sunshine Girl, 1963) and *Sumida-ku Kyojima 3-chome* (Kyojima 3rd Street, Sumida City, 2011) depict a neighborhood of factories that people want to escape but are unable to, along with remnants of the stigma of a *sangyochi* with a history as a red-light district. The former *Tamanoi* area was a place of employment for women from the Tohoku region pre-war, and from the Kanto region post-war (Hibi, 2010: 242–246).

Since housing/individuality- type residents give primary attention to their own living areas, past history means little. In contrast, the housing/humanity-type conducted some research before purchasing an apartment.

"I saw on TV that there are lots of older homes. There are factories, and it's sandwiched between rivers, so it also had a negative image. But after living here I find it's not true" (Husband).

There was no awareness of the past red-light district or that young artists were living there carrying out renovations. The interpretation can be made that the young married couple had a positive image of *shitamachi* and no hang-ups about its earlier history.

Conclusion

This article first addressed the gentrification of Tokyo's city center that began in the 1980s. It also pointed to the spatial polarization that emerged in the 1990s due to redevelopment that followed wider urban policy trends in Tokyo. Aspects of social policy were considered in the context of urban redevelopment in inner city areas and the negative cost of gentrification.

An examination of the Kyojima area in Sumida Ward confirmed the following points:

1. During the redevelopment of densely populated urban districts in the 1980s, in anticipation of voluntary compliance with municipal guidelines, reconstruction-type urban development produced the Kyojima Urban Development Council, and for over 30 years the Council made efforts to promote fireproofing. After establishing the General Framework for Urban Development, a consensus between the residents' interests and other stakeholders could not be reached. Activities stagnated and urban planning came to be led by government or through public-private partnerships.

2. Though decline in the industrial economy was one likely factor in the appearance of the macro-FIRE (finance, insurance, real estate) stratum, on a micro level, infrastructure development and redevelopment were congruous with the housing preferences of the new urban middle class. In an environment where many high-rise apartments were built even in social strata classified as traditional commerce and industry/humanity-type or *shitamachi*/humanity-type, when it comes for a desire for "brightness", there are two factions: one with a tendency to positively assess gentrification, and one that only passively approves.

3. In Kyojima 1-chome where infrastructure development and redevelopment projects were rapidly advanced from 2000, there was a remarkable increase in white-collar residents from 2005 and onwards. A comparison of housing maps clearly shows that residents were displaced. In addition, the area where the rent gap theory is applicable was limited to the Tokyo Skytree vicinity.

4. Gentrifiers are generally divided into the housing/individuality-type, who have come to be called "mansion dwellers" and the housing/humanity-type. The former are newcomers from parts of Tokyo outside Sumida Ward and can be described as having moved around the city, rather than falling under the heading of the so-called "back-to-the-city" "movement.

The latter at their core, have a *shitamachi*-type identity which fits with their current lifestyle,[24] and they choose to live in apartments. They can reasonably be considered to fall into the category of a back-to-the-city movement.

5. In the micro area of Kyojima, particularly in Kyojima 1-chome, spatial polarization arose together with socio-economic polarization, starting in 2005. In the area, newcomer gentrifiers on the whole felt positive about further reconstruction. Attention should be paid to the fact that the desire to seek an even better living environment sometimes tends to eliminate heterogeneity. When the intentions of the housing supplier and the residents match, the presence of gated communities becomes more prominent. They employ gated enclosures, surveillance cameras and 24-hour security guard patrols to ensure residents' safety and security. As a result, relationships of mutual trust weaken.

6. In a context where gentrifiers do not express "an attitude of revanchism" of the kind identified in Europe and the United States, there is also an element of publicly excluding people considered undesirable. This is pointed out in enforcement regulations by the Government and *chonaikai* (neighborhood associations) prohibiting the collection of aluminum tins and old paper, which are a source of subsistence for the poor and homeless. As an unintended outcome, recycling activities by Sumida Ward Office and neighborhood associations in the area drove the homeless away to the margins of society. Though indirect, this policy inevitably took away a source of subsistence. Moreover, it should be pointed out that art projects with a retro- aesthetic appreciation for the dilapidated former red-light districts and cafés led to raising of area standards and the advanced the interests of gentrifiers.

7. An additional analysis of the background showed that gentrifiers do not demonstrate a particular devotion to their residential areas. To date, in the field of sociology, locality has been considered a defensive response to the increasing general power of globalizing forces (Bauman, 1998; Beck, 2000; Castells, 1998). Thus it "reinstates the authenticity of the local as a means of challenging the claims of global to bypass place". However, "most residents talk about their local belonging in terms of connections which it allows with other places and its convenience for their everyday life". (Savage, et al., 2005: 204). Naturally, there are variations depending on whether culture in the relevant area is rooted in a part of the residents'

identities.

This study has shed light on the characteristics of Japanese gentrification and gentrifiers in the micro example of the Kyojima area in Sumida Ward, a place deemed an inner-city area of Tokyo's Joto district.

Notes

1. This article revises the discussion published in *Bulleting of the Graduate School of Humanities and Sociology, Rissho University* (2017, No. 33, 15–42) and draws on fiscal 2015 national census data.
2. In the model, the urban development stage is regulated by economic structure, but within the city there is a division between the central city (urban core and inner-city) and the vicinity (suburbs). As an indicator of population decline in the two areas and city as a whole, the model is established as: (1) urbanization (2) suburbanization; (3) desurburbanization; and (4) reurbanization. Many aspects are thought to conform to the development stages in large cities in the Europe, the United States, and Japan (Van den Berg, L., Klaassen, L. H., et al., 1982, p. 25–45).
3. For information on the concept of gentrification and historic aspects of London that set the stage for gentrification, refer to 2012 and 2015 manuscripts by the present author.
4. Research includes Ajisaka (2014, 2015), Fujitsuka (2014, 2017) and Yabe (2003).
5. Refer to Takagi (2012: 125–137) for an analysis of neighborhood relationships in River City 21.
6. Parts of the survey appeared in a record by Kohama (Department of Sociology, Faculty of Letters, Rissho University), the 2012 *Report on Social Research* and 2013 *Report on Social Research*.
7. This is according to the objective of housing policies in the Tokyo Basic Ordinance on Housing (2006, revised) (see website of the Bureau of Urban Development, Tokyo Metropolitan Government).
8. Behind land purchases by developers was the aim of receiving a construction order for a large-scale development project thought to be worth 100 billion yen. Obtaining the land and becoming the landowner would enable participation in the redevelopment preparation association, and there was an expectation that it would be easier to participate in the construction (Sumida Ward, 2006: 121–122).
9. Harvey, 2012.
10. Takashi Machimura identified three peaks in Tokyo's built environment

production. The first was around 1970, the second around 1990, and the third around 2005. Since the 2000s, over 60% of the built environment developments have been done by companies and/or organization. At times, developments by large companies and/or organizations have accounted for up to two-thirds of the total developments (Machimura, 2015: 63–64).
11. The urban development objectives of the Tokyo Metropolitan Government's urban redevelopment policy, Redevelopment Promotion Districts, the disaster prevention urban planning promotion scheme, Priority Development Areas, the Sumida Ward Basic Plan and Sumida Ward Urban Planning Master Plan include large area hubs (concentration of commerce/business, functions etc.), composite hub regions (development of safe, comfortable residential environments that are disaster- resistant), inducing a ripple effect from the new tower, and improving densely populated urban districts (reassessing projects to promote fireproofing).
12. The term "white-collar workers" in this article refers to the narrow definition of specialized/technical professionals occupations, managerial occupations and clerical occupations. "Blue-collar workers" refers to skilled craftsmen, production processing/laborers, transportation/machinery operators, construction/mining workers and transport/cleaning/packaging workers. All are based on numerical values recounted from national censuses in each year.
13. This is considered an instance when the home's exchange value is considered superior to the utility value. The definition of displacement is cited as, "displacement from a supportive, long-term environment to an alien area where substantially higher costs are involved for a more crowded, inferior dwelling" (Hartman, 1980: 196).
14. This is based on interviews with residents native to the area living in large multiple-dwelling complexes due to an exchange of rights (September 10, 2014), and self-employed workers living in the area who are familiar with the circumstances of former residents whose shops were moved (September 10, 2014). Displacement research has "often suffered from a lack of information about where people end up. For some, it was a case of wherever was cheapest, often renting with others or going to family and friends if they live in London" (Atkinson, 2000: 319).
15. Interview with native resident "A," male, aged over 80, Kyojima 1-chome, self-employed, neighborhood association officer, 10 August 2012.
16. Interview with native resident "B," male, aged over 70, Higashi-Mukojima 2-chome, self-employed, neighborhood association officer, 10 August 2012.
17. Interview with native resident "C," male, aged over 70, Higashi-Mukojima 2-chome, self-employed, 14 August 2013.
18. Interview with native resident "D," male, aged over 70, Oshiage 1-chome, self-employed, 14 August 2013.
19. In 2012, a questionnaire was posted to residents of East Core Hikifune Niban-kan rental units on floors 6–38 (41 aboveground stories, 1 underground floor,

557 units, 31 landowner units, 490 UR rental units, 36 Sumida Ward municipal housing units). The sample size was approximately 100 households (rentals), and the response rate was 28%. The sample size was determined by talking with the neighborhood association president about a number feasible to implement. To increase reliability about residents' attributes, the presidents of neighborhood associations and residents' associations were interviewed. The questionnaire also asked whether respondents were willing to be interviewed, and two single residents and two couples were interviewed in November 2012.

Table 2—Attributes of gentrifiers living in high-rise apartments

Age	aged over 30s 39%	aged over 40s 14%	aged over 50s 11%	aged over 60s 25%		
Highest level of education	University 53%	Graduate school 14%	Junior college/ technical college 14%	High school 18%	Junior high school 4%	
Birthplace	Sumida Ward 7%	Other ward/ prefecture 93%				
Previous place of residence	Within the 23 wards 63%	Within Tokyo 15%	Kanagawa/ Chiba/ Saitama 15%	Other 7%		
Occupational status	Owner-manager 7%	Full-time employee 64%	Full-time civil servant 4%	Self-employed(no employees) Family worker/ temporary employee, etc. 0%	Unemployed and retired 25%	
Household composition	Husband and wife 44%	Nuclear family 22%	One-person household 30%	Single parent and unmarried child 4%	3-generation household/ other 0%	
Neighborhood relations with residents of the same apartment	Exchange greetings 47%	Bowing to an acquaintance 39%	Chatting over tea 7%	None 7%		
Neighborhood relations with area residents	None 71%	Chatting over tea 14%	Exchange greetings 11%	Chatting without sitting down 4%	Bowing to an acquaintance 0%	

20. An interview was held with a married couple residing in an apartment in Higashi-Mukojima 2-chome on 10 September 2016.
21. For research on the art project in Sumida Ward, refer to Kim (2012).
22. The interviewee was a female resident of the Kyojima area involved in the art project as a volunteer. The interview was held on 6 September 2012 and 30

October 2012.
23. Topics that are purposely ignored and not discussed include families that have returned after living apart due to divorce, disappearance, etc., and stealing shrine offerings to help with living expenses. For information on the pawnbroker, see Kohama (2000).
24. The facts called current lifestyle in this article are as follows. The married couple met at the workplace and both work full time (household income is around 10 million yen). Their children go to a nursery school near the station; they utilize convenient transportation for their 30-minute work commute. In their leisure time, they use the neighborhood library and community center, and enjoy shopping. Seasonally, they enjoy barbecues, snowboarding and hot spring trips, making the most of their time off. They get necessary information online, and their social relationships stem from university ties, company ties and nursery school relationships.

References

AERA (2013). A new class: High-rise-apartment residents-the impact and reality of the sudden rise in urban areas, 5.20:61-65, Tokyo, Japan; Asahi Shimbun Publications, Inc.,

Ajisaka, M. (2014). High-rise apartment residents and their local lives in the era of urban core revival: A survey in Chuo Ward of Tokyo metropolitan area, *Social Science Review*, 111: 1–112.

Ajisaka, M. (2015). "Upper-middle class high-rise apartment residents and their local lives in the era of urban core revival: The Cases of Chuo Ward in Tokyo and Kita Ward in Osaka, *The Annals of Japan Association for Urban Sociology*, 33: 21–38.

Atkinson, R. (2000). The hidden costs of gentrification: Displacement in central London. *Journal of Housing and the Built Environment*, 15 (4), 307–326.

Bauman, Z. (1998). *Globalisation: The human consequences*. Oxford, UK: Blackwell.

Beauregard, R. A. (1988). The chaos and complexity of gentrification. In N. Smith & P. Williams (Eds.), *Gentrification of the city* (pp. 35–55). Boston, MA: Allen & Unwin.

Beck, U. (2000). *What is globalization?* Cambridge, UK: Polity Press.

Bridge, G., Butler, T., & Lees, L. (Eds.). (2012). *Mixed Communities: Gentrification by stealth?* Bristol, UK: The Policy Press.

Butler, T., & Lees, L. (2006). Super-gentrification in Barnsbury, London: Globalization and gentrifying global elites at the neighborhood level. *Transactions of the Institute of British Geographers New Series*, *31* (4), 467–487.

Butler, T., & Savage, M. (1995). *Social change and the middle classes*. London, UK: Routledge.

Castells, M. (1998). *The end of millennium*, Oxford, UK: Blackwell.

Davidson, M., & Lees, L. (2009). New-build gentrification: Its histories, trajectories, and critical geographies. *Population, Space and Place, 16*, 395–411.

Doucet, B. (2014). A process of change and a changing process: Introduction to the special issue on contemporary gentrification. *Tijdschrift voor Economische en Sociale Geografie, 105* (2), 125–139.

Friedmann, J. (1986). The world city hypothesis. *Development and Change*, 17 (1), 69–83.

Fujitsuka, Y. (2014). Gentrification in London, New York and Tokyo, *Japan Society for Urban Studies Journal*, 47, 277–282.

Fujitsuka, Y. (2016) The Frontiers of Gentrification Studies—The Case of London in the 2000s, *The Annals of Japan Association for Urban Sociology*, 34, 44–58.

Fujitsukai, Y. (2017) *Gentrification*, Kokon Shoin.

Harvey, D. (2012). *Rebel Cities: From the right to the city to the urban revolution*, Verso Books (=2013; translated by Seiya Morita et al. *Hanran suru Toshi—Shihon no Abanaizeshon to Toshi no Saisozo*, in Japanese, Sakuhinsha).

Hibi, T. (2010). *Tamanoi—Society and Living in the Red-light District*, Jiyukokuminsha.

Hirai, T. (2002). "A 'Bright' Rhetoric: Towards 'understanding' of urban redevelopment." *Komaba Studies in Society*, 12, 52–68.

Inaba, N. (2015). Tokyo Olympics & Kasumigaoka municipal apartments, *Yoseba: Japan Association for the Study of Yoseba Annual*, 27, 61–75.

Ishii, Y. (2005). Beyond the illusion of homogeneity: Inward-looking 'Japanese' in the age of globalization. *Social Science Japan Journal*, 8 (2), 267–271.

Jackson, E., & Butler, T. (2015). Revisiting 'social tectonics': The middle classes and social mix in gentrifying neighborhoods. *Urban Studies, 52* (13), 2349–2365.

Kim, S. (2012). The role of art in Revitalizing Tokyo's inner-city: Between gentrification and diversification of local culture, *The Annals of Japan Association for Urban Sociology*, 30, 43–58.

Klaassen, L. H., Bourdez, J. A., & Volmuller, J. (1981). *Transport and reurbanisation*. Surrey, UK: Gower.

Kohama, F. (2000). *Pawnbroking in Japan: A Social History* (Aichi University Faculty of Business Administration Publication 20), Institute of Managerial Research, Aichi University

Kohama, F. (2012) The Restructuring of Urban Space: The Wave of Gentrification, *Journal of the Faculty of Letters, Rissho University*, 35, 1–29.

Kohama, F. (2014) Regeneration of Urban Space: Histories and Trajectories, *Annual Bulletin of the Institute of Humanistic Sciences, Rissho University*, 52, 37–52.

Lees, L. (2008). Gentrification and social mixing: Towards an inclusive urban renaissance? *Urban Studies, 45* (12), 2449–2470.

Lees, L., & Shin, B, H. (Eds.). (2015). *Global gentrification: Uneven development and displacement*. Bristol, UK: The Policy Press.

Machimura, T. (2015). Who owns urban spaces? Based on the perspective of the

Tokyo landscape reaching a turning point. *Urban Issues*, 106 (11): 62–70.
Pham, C. (2015). *Tokyo smart city development in perspective of 2020 Olympics opportunities for EU-Japan cooperation and business development* [PDF document]. Retrieved from https://www.eu-japan.eu/sites/default/files/publications/docs/smart2020tokyo_final.pdf
Rose, D. (1984), Rethinking gentrification: Beyond the uneven development of Marxist urban theory. *Environment and Planning D: Society and Space*, 2: 47–74. London Routledge.
Savage, M., & Bagnall, G. (Eds.). (2005). *Globalization & belonging*. London, UK: Sage Publications.
Slater, T. (2008). 'A literal necessity to be re-placed': A rejoinder to the gentrification debate," *International Journal of Urban and Regional Research*, 32 (1), 212–223.
Smith, N. (1996). *The urban frontier: gentrification and the revanchist city*. London, UK: Routledge. (=2014; translated by Haraguchi, T. *Gentorifikeshon to Hofukutoshi—Aratana Toshi no Furontia*, Minerva Shobo).
Sumida Ward (Public Relations Project, Management Office) (Ed.) (1996). *Sumida Ward Overview*, Sumida Ward.
Sumida Ward (Public Relation, Project Management Office) (Ed.). (2006) *Sumida City Overview*, Sumida Ward.
Sumida Ward (City Planning Division, City Planning Department) (Ed.). (2008). *Sumida Ward Urban Planning Master Plan*, Sumida Ward.
Sumida Ward (Ed.) (2010). *Sumida Ward History: Overview*, Sumida Ward.
Takagi, K. (2015). The housing problem in urban policy: The transformation of the Tokyo Metropolitan Government's housing policy," *iichiko Quarterly*, 126, 58–68.
Takagi, K. (2016). Gentrification and the urban policy: A case study of the transformation of the socio-spatial structure of Tokyo Metropolitan Area. *The Annals of Japan Association for Urban Sociology*, 34, 59–73.
Takahashi, Y. (Ed.) (1992). *Restructuring a large city—Tokyo innercity issues*, Tokyo Metropolitan University Publishing.
Takenaka, H., & Takahashi, Y. (1988). Social mobility & regional formation in large city inner areas: Based on research on 'K' area in Sumida City, Tokyo (1987), *Comprehensive Urban Studies*, 34, 35–49.
Takenaka, H., & Takahashi, Y. (1990). Citizens' attitude on the changing social structure of inner Tokyo: 1989 sample survey of Sumida Ward. *Comprehensive Urban Studies*, 40, 99–115.
Policy Information Office, Tokyo Metropolitan Government. (2000) *Tokyo Vision 2000—Aiming to be a global city hosting crowds of visitor.* n
Tokyo Metrropolitan Government. (2011). *Asian Headquarters Special Concept*, Tokyo Metropolitan Government
Van den Berg, L., Drewett, R., Klaassen, L.H., Rossi, A. & Vijverberg, C.H.T. (1982). *Urban Europe: A study of growth and decline* (1st ed.). Oxford, UK: Pergamon Press.

Yabe, N. (2003). Population recovery in inner Tokyo in the late 1990s," *Japanese Journal of Human Geography*, 55 (3): 277–292.

Yoshihara, N., & Chikamori, T. (Eds.) (2013). *Understanding the Contemporary Urban Reality*, Yuhikaku Publishing Co., Ltd.

Zukin, S., & Kasinitz, P. (Eds.). (2015). *Global cities, local streets: Everyday diversity from New York to Shanghai*. New York, NY: Routledge.

Internet sources

Association of Mukojima Studies (NPO), http:www.mukojima.org/ [accessed May 27, 2012].

Bureau of Urban Development, Tokyo Metropolitan Government http:www.toshiseibi.metro.tokyo.jp/bosai/mokumitu/ [accessed October 17, 2016].

East Core Hikifune Neighborhood Association website http://greens.st.wakwak.ne.jp/home/bbs.cgi?id=905932 [accessed October 30, 2016].

A Study on the Prosperity and Decline of Buddhist Sites in Northern Bactria: Kara Tepe and Zurmala

Atsushi Iwamoto

Abstract

This paper presents research on the Buddhist sites of Kara Tepe located in Termez, Republic of Uzbekistan conducted by Rissho University in partnership with Uzbekistan research institutions. It also offers an organized arrangement of previous research concerning the Buddhist sites of Zurmala in the same region undertaken beginning in the fiscal year of 2016, along with research findings and an indication of issues facing the future. Both sites are thought to have been constructed in the 2nd Century by Kanishka I of the Kushan Empire. Preceding this in the 4th Century B.C., Alexander the Great, ruler of Macedonia, had made an expedition there with a great number of Grecians to bring the region under his command. The region later came to be governed by the Kushan Empire following the Greco-Bactrian Kingdom, the Tocharians and the Greater Yuezhi. There then, through the amalgamation of Indic and Grecian cultures, appeared Buddhist images, which are thought to have contributed to the spread of Buddhist culture. And just what were those actual images like? The sites of Kara Tepe and Zurmala provide keys to deduce this.

Introduction

In 2014, Rissho University Uzbekistan Academic Research Group (hereafter, Rissho Group) entered into a five-year research agreement with the Fine Arts Institute of the Uzbekistan Academy of Sciences (hereafter, Fine Arts Institute) and began excavations on the Buddhist sites of Kara Tepe located outside of Termez in the Surkhandarya Region of the Republic of Uzbekistan.

The excavations took place every September from 2014 to 2017 (four times in total). Based on previous research, this paper presents a summary of the study and issues stemming from it. The author was engaged in these activities on each occasion, starting from a preliminary research.[1] First is a simple introduction of the region and topics covered in this paper.

This article targeted several Buddhist sites believed to have been constructed by King Kanishka who ruled the region during the Kushan Empire in the 2nd century. Going back to the 4th century BCE, Alexander the Great, ruler of Macedonia in northern Greece, invaded the region with many Greeks and brought it under his control. The Greek culture continued under the Greco-Bactrian Kingdom that subsequently controlled the region. However, later the Tocharians, a different ethnic group, came under the rule of the Yuezhi, and thereafter the Kushan Empire took control. During the Kushan Empire, the Indian and Greek cultures Hellenistically fused and saw the emergence of Gandhara Buddhism, which is regarded as having contributed to the spread of the Buddhist culture from the time of King Kanishka.

What kind of groups were these ruling powers and how did they rule? How did Buddhism spread? Furthermore, how did Gandhara art develop, and did it influence China and Japan? There are still many unknowns, and it is the answers to these unknowns that numerous academics have pursued for many years as research themes.[2]

The following first presents an overview of the historic and geographic positioning of the Surkhandarya Region. Thereafter, previous studies, our Research Group's focal points, and issues are presented for Kara Tepe and then Zurmala.

1. Historical Geography and Archaeological Research to Date in Northern Bactria

This section gives an explanation of the historical geography of Termez, which is viewed as having been a principal city in Northern Bactria, particularly in ancient times (Fig. 1).

Termez is located on the southern edge of the Surkhandarya Region in Uzbekistan. The Surkhandarya Region is separated from its environs by high mountains and large rivers. The Amu Darya (Darya means river) flows east to west in the south, and in the east is the Babatag mountain range. Running

A Study on the Prosperity and Decline of Buddhist Sites in Northern Bactria: Kara Tepe and Zurmala

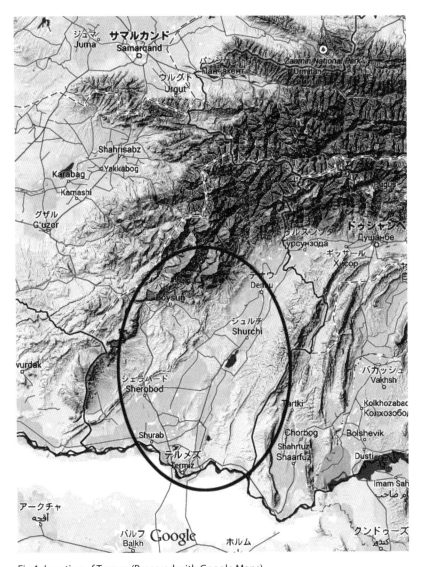

Fig.1 Location of Termez (Prepared with Google Maps)

alongside this range is the Surkhandarya (river), a tributary of the Amu Darya that flows north to south. In the far north is the Hissar mountain range stretching to the Pamir mountains, and extending to that are the Boysuntau mountains and Kugitangtau mountains in the west (Fig. 2). In addition, on the opposite side of the Amu Darya, that is, on the Afghanistan side, the land looks out on the Hindu Kush range far to the south. In the center of this region, straddled by major rivers sat Bactra, the Greco-Bactria capital (present-day

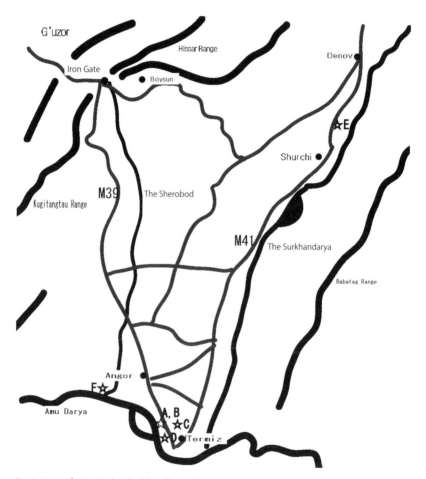

Fig.2 Map of sites in the Surkhandarya Region

Balkh on the southern bank of the Amu Darya Fig. 1). However, according to one theory, Greco-Bactria was destroyed by the invading Tocharians, and in connection with this, the entire area, including the Surkhandarya Region up to southern Tajikistan, is also called Northern Bactria or Tokharistan.

Currently, Termez is the capital of the Surkhandarya Region with a population of approximately 150,000. Before being destroyed by a Mongolian invasion, ancient Termez was located around 7km. from the center of present-day Termez along the right bank of the Amu Darya (♦D, Fig. 2; hereafter ♦denotes a position on Fig. 2). A different theory of the city's history will be introduced based primarily on the explanation presented by Sh. Pidaev (2002) (2007).

According to the opinion presented by Pidaev, in the middle of 1,000 BCE, residents living at the skirts of the Boysuntau and Kugitangtau mountains began moving to the Amu Darya river basin due to a depletion of resources. This coincided with people who conversely moved to the southern bank of the Amu Darya from the skirts of the Hindu Kush range, bringing people to the Termez settlement, which was the site for crossing the large river.

Around 329 BCE, the Macedonian army, commanded by Alexander the Great, crossed the Amu Darya in the north in pursuit of Bessus, a general in the Achaemenid Empire. At that time, the Macedonian army passed through the Iron Gate (Fig. 2, slightly north of Derbent) and exited Sogdiana. It gained control of Sogdiana and Fergana, then once again went south through the Iron Gate and crossed the Amu Darya to begin a conquest of India. From around this time, Termez was called Tarmita.

In a short while, Tarmita was temporarily destroyed by invading nomads when Alexander the Great died, but was restored during the Seleucid Empire. In the subsequent Greco-Bactrian Kingdom it developed into an important city of commerce. E. V. Rtveladze (2006) (2007) identified Alexander the Great's crossing point as the Shor Tepe sites neighboring the west side of Kampyr Tepe (♦F) in regard to the origin of Termez and its transition into a crossing site. Termez was considered an important city from the time of the Greco-Bactrian Kingdom. The aforementioned different interpretation is based on discrepancies in geographical observations and chronological views on artifacts unearthed from ancient Termez.

Later, the economic importance of Termez grew during the Yuezhi's occupation of the land. According to the Chinese historical source, Si-ma-Chen's *Records of the Grand Historian* (part of the history of Dayuan), the Yuezhi lived north of the Amu Darya. Archaeological research during the time of the Soviet Union assumed Dalverzine Tepe (♦E) and Khalchayan (Fig. 2, northern Denov) were two of their bases and that Tarmita came under the Yuezhi's power. Around the 1st century, when feudal lords under the Yuezhi are thought to have established the Kushan Empire, heavy construction was carried out in ancient Termez, particularly within the citadel. A strong defensive wall was constructed, and the town developed more and more into a commercial city.[3]

Also, Buddhist sites located next to ancient Termez, such as Fayaz Tepe (♦A), Kara Tepe (♦B), and Zurmala (♦C), are thought to have appeared in this period.[4] However, there were diverse and complex beliefs in the Kushan era, comprising Zoroastrianism, Grecian gods, and local gods. It required time for a single religion to possess significant power. Buddhism gained ground around the reign of Kanishka I, the 4th emperor of the Kushan Empire. Given that, Pidaev estimates that while contact between Tarmita and Buddhism occurred in the 1st century BCE, the formation of these kinds of temples occurred from the 2nd–4th centuries. On the other hand, Rtveladze (2007) believes Tarmita was under control of either the Yuezhi or the Tochara in the era (around the mid to late 1st century) of Vima Takto (also known as Soter Megas), the second ruler of the Kushan Empire, but that in the era of Kanishka I in the 2nd century, it came under the rule of the Kushan Empire and played a central role in Buddhism in Central Asia.

A confirmation of the Chinese historical source, the *Memoirs of Eminent Monks* shows that around the reign of Emperor Ling of the Later Han (reigned from 168–189), a Yuezhi traveled to China in this era; that is, Lokaksema, a Buddhist monk that may have been from the Surkhandarya basin, visited Luoyang. In addition to translating sutra, one of his disciple's disciples, Zhi Qian learned a variety of disciplines through six languages of the western regions. He visited Jiankang in the Wu and translated sutra. Also, Dharmaraksa (239–316) was a monk born in Dunhuang County whose secular family name was Zhi, a name used by Yuezhi descendants. He traveled the Western Regions and learned different languages and Buddhism. He is thought to have visited Chang'an and Luoyang and engaged in translating sutra up until the reign of Emperor Hui di in the Western Jin. However, it is unlikely that Zhi Qian was born in the Surkhandarya basin, and a relationship with the Surkhandarya basin cannot be called definite simply because Dharmaraksa's ancestors were Yuezhi.

In the 240s (Western calendar), Tarmita came under the rule of the Sassanid Empire through territorial expansion by Shapur I. This period was subsequently called the Kushano-Sasanian era. Pottery fragments unearthed at Kara Tepe bear writings related to this period. It next came under the control of groups such as the Kidarite and Hephthalite from the 4th century. Much of previous research purports that Buddhism under the Hephthalites was not always protected, but that its existence was not rejected.[5]

When the Hephthalites were defeated by the Western Turkic Khaganate, Tarmita came under the rule of the Sassanid Empire for a time, but there were several battles between the Western Turkic Khaganate and Sassanid Empire, and in 603, Tarmita fell under control of the Western Turkic Khaganate. At this time, Tardu Shad, the son of Khagan the khan of the Western Turkic Khaganate, established a base near Kunduz on the southern bank of the Amu Darya. During this period, the Western Turkic Khaganate held enormous power in Central Asia, and Tardu Shad took the younger sister of Yan Wenta, the king of Gaochang, as his wife. This is recorded in writings by Xuanzang, who was under the patronage of Khagan of Western Turkic Khaganate.[6]

During the Tang Dynasty, many passed through Tokharistan. For example, Xuanzhao, a monk who went to Tang China and is discussed in *Da Tang Xi Yu Qiu fa Gao Seng Zhuan* (The Life of the Monks of the Tang Dynasty who Travelled to the West (Adachi 1942), traveled south through Sogdiana and Tokharistan to the Tibetan Empire (Kuwayama [1990: 128–130] indicated he traveled by way of the Wakhan road) for an audience with Princess Wencheng, who married into the Tibetan Empire. Huilun, a monk from Silla who accompanied Xuanzhao, is said to have later lived in a "wealthy and abundant" Tokharistan temple named Gandhara that was built for a Tokharistan who had visited India. Around the 7th century, there were a certain number of Buddhist believers in Tokharistan, and active exchange with Tang China is conceivable. Recently, as research on the Sogds based in Sogdiana, located next to Tokharistan, is growing, the focus is being placed on a relationship with people from Tokharistan and Bactria. There is also research regarding commerce and religious activities by Sogds that refers to a relationship with Tokharistan (Yoshida 2011, Fukushima 2010).

Yoshida (2010) has discussed monks who visited China from Central Asia and their home city. A monk surnamed in the memoirs as Kang—that is, viewed as being from Samarkand—visited China and translated sutra, but numerous questions remain unanswered, such as Buddhist sites from that time not being found in Sogdiana and Chinese writings/Buddhist scriptures thought to have been translated by them that exist today, having been translated from the 8th century. Thus, the state of Buddhism in Central Asia at this time holds important keys to clarifying the process of Buddhism's spread to the East.

In the 6–7th centuries, Termez maintained a certain degree of political independence, but in 689 was seized by an Arabian general who provoked a rebellion, and in 704 the city became a caliphate. Later, it was controlled by the Samanid Empire, Kara-Khanid Khanate, Ghaznavid Dynasty, Seljuq Dynasty, and Khwarezm. Today, the Al Hakim At-Termizi Mausoleum located in ancient Termez (adjacent to ♦D) is said to originate from a facility from around this time.

During the Mongolian invasion of 1220, Termez demonstrated strong resistance and in the end was destroyed. Later, the city was moved to its current location some distance from old Termez and closer to the Surkhandarya (river). As the above shows, in typical research, the history of Termez has been interpreted from the geographical environment of the Surkhandarya Region and chronological views of excavated artifacts from sites in the area, but there are many uninvestigated sites and shortcomings in rationalizations.

Rtveladze (1974, 1982) provides a general comprehensive overview of ancient medieval sites in Surkhandarya (around the 2nd–7th centuries BCE). In addition, while focused solely on Buddhist sites, Stavisky (1977), Litvinskiy (1996), and Kato (1997) provide information on Central Asia as a whole, including this region. Furthermore, recently Iwai (2006) (2013) and Abdullaev (2015) can be said to have provided a sizeable overview of Buddhist sites in Northern Bactria. There is also a long history of archaeological studies on Afghanistan and Pakistan, which are located south of the Amu Darya, conducted in particular by the French (MAFOUZ). A considerable number of reports have been published, as well as several reports from Kyoto University. These are essential to considering the historical and geographical environment of Termez in Bactria and Tokharistan.[7]

It can be said that the prosperity and decline of Kara Tepe, temple sites outside of Termez that are discussed below, are inseparable from that of these sites found in the region and the historical understanding derived from them.

2. Excavation and Research of Kara Tepe

The next section introduces previous research on Kara Tepe, which was the main subject of excavations by the Research Group from 2014 to 2017, and a summary of those excavations.

Kara Tepe is situated outside of present-day Termez, 8km to the northwest and approximately 400m north of ancient Termez (citadel sites). It is a complex of Buddhist buildings atop a sandstone hill on the northern riverbanks of the Amu Darya. The Amu Darya sandbank (Aral-Paygambar Island, Uzbekistan) and the opposite bank are clearly visible. Around 70km from there is Balkh, where the capital of the Greco-Bactrian Kingdom is believed to have once stood. The location and sites sit within a training area managed by the Uzbekistan army. Entry requires application months in advance.

(1) Previous research and issues

According to previous research, Kara Tepe was a Buddhist temple built in the rule of Kanishka of the Kushan Empire. A cave temple complex has been studied off and on since its existence was confirmed by a study done in the 1920s soon after the Soviet Union was established. Earnest excavations began from 1961 by a research group centering on B. J. Stavisky, resulting in the discovery of several complexes that included a small stupa, a courtyard, and caves on the southern hill. The same research group conducted excavations on a part of the sites on the northern hill, but in 1994 the research group accomplished a great deal and determined these sites were from around the 2nd–5th centuries, after which it ceased activities. During that time, six reports were published. The final report (Stavisky 1996) is particularly important (Grek, et al. 1964; Imperatorsky Ermitazh, et al. 1969; Institut vostokovedenya 1972; Stavisky 1975, 1982, 1996; a portion of these were translated into English: Stavisky 1980, 1984; Livshits et al. 1996; a portion of the final report was translated into Japanese: Stavisky translated by Kato 2002; Zeimal translated by Kato (2007); Stavisky translated by Kato 2007).

With the collapse of the Soviet Union in 1991, the Republic of Uzbekistan became an independent nation, and excavations by Sh. Pidaev and Kyuzo Kato resumed. In addition to progress being made on the study of the western hill, sites were found on the northern hill comprised of a large stupa and rectangular monastery. The caves on the southern hill were carved out of sandstone hills, and while religious installations made of sun-dried brick were included in the cave entrances, on the northern hill several buildings were established constructed only of sun-dried bricks.

There are numerous unsolved issues regarding the sites of Kara Tepe, but the period in which the temple was abandoned garners particular attention. As has been noted, a research group centering on archeologists from the Soviet era such as Stavisky believed this temple was no longer used from around the late 4th century. That was based on the determination that many of the caves that had been used for purposes such as monks' cells were converted into burial places before the late 4th century. Also, the period the rooms were used could be derived based on excavated currency found on the floors of monks' cells (Stavisky translated by Kato 2002, 2007).

However, objections have been raised on the identified period of abandonment based on excavation results from the northern hill. The observations made according to the discovered currency are valid for estimating the upper limit of building utilization, but cannot be said to be conclusive for estimating the lower limit. In addition, it was already understood that the monastery on the northern hill could not have existed when Kara Tepe was originally built, based on the architectural style of the large stupa and monastery. The famous French scholar, Fussman (2011) examined the sites in detail and pointed out that different size sun-dried bricks were intermixed and used in the monastery and large stupa on the northern hill, and that some parts of the construction appear as if they were added later. In addition, numerous plinth stones have been discovered at highly unnatural positions inside the monastery on the northern hill. Based on these findings, a process of original appearance, destruction, and repeated reconstruction of the monastery on the northern hill can be surmised. Furthermore, Fussman organized a collection of earthenware fragments that contained ink writing unearthed at the Kara Tepe sites and at Fayaz Tepe, sites of a somewhat older Buddhist temple situated several hundred meters away. Furthermore, Fussman organized a collection of earthenware fragments containing ink writing unearthed at the Kara Tepe sites and at Fayaz Tepe, sites of a somewhat older Buddhist temple situated several hundred meters away.

Moreover, based on that, Iwai (2013) suggested the possibility that even during that period when the southern hill was being used as a burial site, the sites on the northern hill were being repeatedly reconstructed and functioned as a temple (Fig. 3).

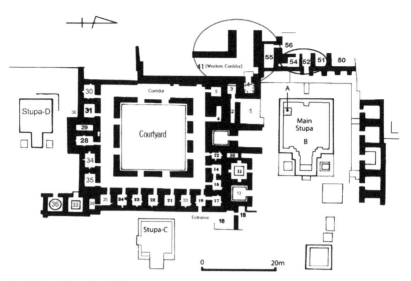

Fig.3 Plan of northern hill at Kara Tepe (Produced based on Rissho University (2016). Area inside oval excavated by Rissho University team.)

Actually, an historical record that perfectly dovetails with this interpretation has been known for some time. This historical record is the *The Great Tang Dynasty Record of the Western Regions*, thought to be based on writings made when Xuanzang was traveling to India. That record says the following about Termez.

"Termez is more than 600 *li* from east to west and over 400 *li* from south to north, its capital city being more than 20 *li* in circuit, long from east to west and narrow from south to north. There are more than ten monasteries with over 1,000 monks. Many stupas and the venerated images of the Buddha are mostly miraculous and cause spiritual manifestations. To the east of this country is the country of Chaganiyan" (Mizutani 1971).

It is known that Xuanzang did not travel to all the place names written in the *Great Tang Records of the Western Regions*, but it is widely agreed that the characters, "呾蜜国" indicate Termez and that Xuanzang passed through it. Since he departed Chang'an around 629, in the first half of the 7th century there were more than ten temples and over 1,000 monks, as well as stupa and Buddhist statues. If so, it is possible that Xuanzang saw the stupa on the northern hill of Kara Tepe, which had the largest stylobates of those presently known located outside of Termez.

According to conventional interpretation, it was abandoned prior to the late 4th century, but it is hard to believe that if Xuanzang saw the stupa on the northern hill of Kara Tepe it was already in sites. Also, Buddhist temples and stupa sites have been excavated in Termez in places other than Kara Tepe. There is no need to focus solely on the condition of the northern hill of Kara Tepe when Xuanzang passed through Termez. Meanwhile, according to Fussman's interpretation, there is the possibility that only the northern hill still functioned as a temple. Could it be that the rise of Buddhism in Termez recorded in the *Great Tang Records of the Western Regions* that is noted above was written without actual observation of the abandoned temple?

The question of whether temples constructed in Termez during the Kushan Empire existed until the 5th or 7th century is important for understanding the state of the political powers of the Kidarite, the Hephthalites, and the Western Turkic Khaganate that ruled there from the 4th century. In addition, as has already been noted, for an historical look at Buddhism it is also important to understand how Buddhism spread from here to the Sogds (including whether it really was disseminated) and the territories of the Chinese dynasties. Though the routes spreading Buddhism to the east were not limited to those passing through this area, there were those from this region who engaged in propagating Buddhism in Chinese dynasties and monks from the Chinese dynasty who visited Tokharistan. Also, it is unlikely that the existence of temples is unrelated to the economic benefactors supporting those religious facilities and groups. The matter of how and until when Kara Tepe was maintained is extremely important information and is essential for explaining the role this region played.

(2) The progress of the Rissho Group's excavation

In 2014, the Rissho Group began studying the unexcavated areas on the western side (the Amu Darya side) of the monastery on the northern hill (Fig. 3, room no. 41 north side). According to Fussman (2011), construction of monasteries around the 5th century in surrounding regions such as Afghanistan were generally designed so that the center axis runs through the center of the stupa in the neighboring temple tower area and the hall where the principal image is placed (Fussman believes this to be room no. 28, no. 29). In addition, at the sites of Guldara in Afghanistan, which Fussman indicated similarity with Kara Tepe, the monastery was constructed symmetrically to the center axis. However, prior to the 2015 excavation, the monastery on the northern hill of Kara Tepe was only viewed as a construction asymmetrical to the center axis. Fussman found that inexplicable and believed the western side of the monastery required research.

Prior to the excavation, it did not appear as if structures were buried on the western side of the monastery on the northern hill, but it was a location that promised new discoveries in consideration of the above points. However, excavations outside of the western side of the monastery corridor on the northern hill conducted in FY2014 showed there is a wall that follows the exterior of the corridor within the monastery and that it was painted red (room no. 3, no. 5 exterior western wall), but the excavation finished without being able to confirm whether a structure exists on the western side. Later, the existence of a wall on the western side was clarified, and the area the Research Group excavated was revealed to be a path between structures. At the time of the 2014 excavation, it was understood that a large amount of soil had been cast onto that area. A confirmation of the horizon made some facts clear, including that a large quantity of soil was deposited by strong winds that sometimes blow from the direction of Afghanistan and the Amu Darya (called Afghanetz); that during a certain period earthenware fragments and a portion of clay figures from the Kushan Empire were deliberately thrown into the corridor; and that when the monastery had been buried to a certain degree, there were people who used fire in the depression that formed on the nearly buried path. In addition, earthenware fragments and a portion of limestone figures discovered together with the soil were of the same material and style as already known artifacts from Kara Tepe. It was determined that the majority belonged to the Kushan Empire. However, very few new discoveries were connected to the monastery, stupa structure, or clarification of dates.

In spring 2015, a little excavation work was conducted on the Uzbek side, which led to the understanding that a wall also existed on the side opposite of the corridor's western wall (Fig. 3: west of room no. 3, no. 5, the wall appearing on the very top of the figure; sun-dried bricks). In other words, the site excavated by the Research Group in 2014 was a passageway or path on the monastery's outside corridor, which had already been discovered. In the fall, the Research Group made good progress on the dig and confirmed that the western outer wall wound even further to the west and the passageway faced the direction of the Amu Darya (Fig. 3: room no. 6 towards the west).

On the western side of the monastery, it is possible there is a buried structure that is slightly smaller than the already known monastery.

In addition, more relics were unearthed in 2015 than in 2014. Human bones were found in the excavated corridor and in room no. 55 near the floor surface on the western side of the temple tower area, which was simultaneously excavated. They were identified through radiocarbon dating as being from the 6th–early 7th centuries (Yoneda, et al. 2016). Typically, most human bones discovered at Kara Tepe were judged as dating from the 4th–5th centuries, but the fact that human bones from a different period had been found from monks' cells on the northern hill became a clue for determining when the monastery on the northern hill stopped functioning as a temple. That is to say, it is reasonable that when Xuanzang passed through Termez, the stupa and monastery on the northern hill of Kara Tepe (the areas already discovered) were being used by monks, but were abandoned soon thereafter. If so, conceivably the Buddhist faith was maintained in this place for a long period stretching from the Kushan Empire to the Western Turkic Khaganate. Though a hasty conclusion cannot be made, it is one focal point for excavations and research going forward.

Excavations in 2015 also yielded limestone figures from the Kushan Empire including fragments from which the shape of figures could be recognized, such as the heads of human figures and the head and feet of Garuda, as well as small plinths decorated with lotus flowers (Fig. 4). Furthermore, four earthenware fragments with ink writing were excavated (one with Bactrian writing was unearthed from room no. 55). Two of the fragments had only partial character strokes and identifying the type of writing was difficult (thought to be Kharosthi script), but the remaining two were inscribed with numeric characters similar to the cursive script of Greek letters. Yutaka Yoshida (2016) from Kyoto University identified them both as being written in Bactrian. In 2017, there were also two earthenware fragments discovered from room no. 41 inscribed with Kharosthi script.

Until the first half of the 1990s, the only major materials featuring Bactrian were just a few inscriptions (stele) and cursive script in ink on earthenware fragments discovered from northern Afghanistan and southern Uzbekistan/Tajikistan (pieces discovered from Kara Tepe and the neighboring Fayaz Tepe were particularly numerous). However, later analysis by N. Sims-Williams at School of Oriental and African Studies (SOAS), University of London, progressed on the Khalili Collection (cursive script) whose archaeological site

Fig.4 A portion of artifacts excavated in the fiscal year 2015 (Left: Head of limestone human figure; Right: Head of Garuda, Limestone)

is unknown, and the grammar and vocabulary was generally clarified (Sims-Williams 2012, Yoshida 2013, Miyamoto 2015). Bactrian is thought to have been used when creating official documents in the Kushan Empire, and it is worth considering why a comparatively large amount of the examples have been excavated from Kara Tepe. Many fragments have been discovered from Kara Tepe and the neighboring Fayaz Tepe that are inscribed not only with Bactrian, but also Kharosthi and Brahmi scripts. Based on these, it has been demonstrated that in the Kushan Empire Kara Tepe was called the emperor's monastery, and Fayaz Tepe was called the horse's monastery (Fussman 2011).

Kharosthi script was originally used to write the Gandhari language and was also widely used during the Kushan Empire. After the Later Han Dynasty withdrew from the Western Regions, it is believed that the power of the Kushan Empire extended to the Western Regions, and relics with identical script have been found in present-day Niya and Loulan in the Xinjiang Uyghur Autonomous Region. The Research Group contributed to discovering some of those kinds of materials.

In 2016, a few days before the excavation began, Kyuzo Kato was to have been traveling around the Uzbekistan-Kazakhstan area actively collecting data, but tragically passed away suddenly. However, the excavation began soon after his body was sent back to Japan.

Excavation continued on room no. 41; that is, the archaeological dig continued on the corridor area. Discoveries were made near the floor's surface of several sheep bones and fragments of a wall painting that appears to be a part of a human face. At the same time, ongoing excavation of room no. 52 yielded wall painting fragments depicting some kind of design, while the nearly complete excavation of room no. 55 yielded several candle stands. A wall painting was also detected near the exit of room no. 55, which foreshadowed a wall painting that was later discovered.

As in every year, the Research Group finished the excavation at the end of September, but the Fine Arts Institute Group continued independently working from October to November. They dug in the room next to room no. 55 (room no. 56) and made a new discovery of a wall painting. Some of the photos published by the Fine Arts Institute Group in an academic magazine are reprinted here (Fig. 5, Pidaev 2016). At a glance, they seem similar to wall paintings at Fayaz Tepe and Miran in the Xinjiang Uyghur Autonomous Region, and are without a doubt a groundbreaking finding in terms of both the history of Asian art and the historical study of the Kushan Empire. Yasuda (2018) has presented a very interesting discussion about them.

In 2017, the last year of the archaeological digs, excavation continued in locations including room no. 41 (corridor area), room no. 52, no. 54, and no. 55. A relic was unearthed from the vicinity of room no. 54 and no. 55 that is almost identical to the small pillar in front of the well-known Buddha triad unearthed at Fayaz Tepe. The aforementioned wall painting and the small

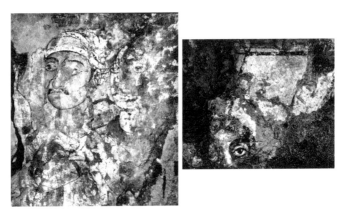

Fig.5 Portions of wall paintings excavated in the fiscal year 2016 by the Uzbek team

pillar in front of the Buddha triad can truly be said to evoke images of the hall enshrining the principal image at Fayaz Tepe.

Furthermore, the Research Group found several bone fragments in multiple sun-dried bricks used in structures on the northern hill of Kara Tepe, as well as animal bones on the floor's surface exposed by excavation. The group requested they be radiocarbon dated by The University Museum, The University of Tokyo. Results confirmed that room no. 41 (corridor area) was already being buried around the end of the late 3rd century, and there were bone fragments that could be identified as dating from around the 7th century in the sun-dried bricks from the western wall of room no. 5. Although radiocarbon dating cannot be said to definitively determine time periods, this further reinforced the possibility that vestiges of additions to structures exist on the northern hill. Ikegami (2016) presents a comprehensive discussion of these.

Based on the above, structures and unearthed relics from rooms no. 41, 52, 54, 55, and 56 prompt fundamental rethinking of the establishment and extension/reconstruction process of the monastery on the northern hill that were surmised by previous research.

A formal report on the full image and preservation of wall paintings from the Fine Arts Institute Group is anticipated. In any case, the archaeological four-year study by the Research Group unquestionably was an important first step in elucidating a full picture of Kara Tepe and the state of Buddhism in Tokharistan.

3. Research of the Zurmala and Preservation Activities

Zurmala (♦C) can be seen from Kara Tepe at a distance of approximately 4km and is regarded as remnants of a Buddhist stupa. A large quantity of sun-dried bricks is stacked in an orderly fashion to form a tower 13 meters high. Its existence is uncommon in Central Asia. However, a large fissure has opened up in the past decades, and preservation measures are deemed urgently needed. Around 90 years ago when research began, the issue was whether this was a Buddhist stupa, but the current issue is what kind of status this should be given in the historical transition of the style of Buddhist stupa from India to Central Asia. Figure 6 is a photo of Zurmala, and Figure 7 is a diagram by Pugachenkova, who will be noted later.

Fig.6 Zurmala (Photographed in 2015)

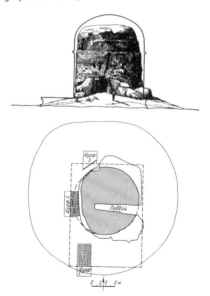

Fig.7 Plan of Zurmala (Pugachenkova 1967)

(1) Previous research and issues

The oldest records already known to exist related to Zurmala are the previously introduced writings on Termez by Xuanzang. Xuanzang left Chang'an (Xi'an) in 629, and it is highly likely that he crossed the Amu Darya in the vicinity of Termez. In the *Great Tang Records of the Western Regions*, he wrote, "Termez…(omitted) the stupas and the venerated images of the Buddha are mostly miraculous and cause spiritual manifestations. To the east of this country is the country of Chaganiyan" (Mizutani 1971).

Zurmala is very likely one of many stupas that existed in Termez at the start of the 7th century. However, only the "possibility" of what Xuanzang saw can be indicated.

A reliable source is a report (1928–1929) by A. S. Strelkov who actually researched and wrote about Zurmala. He was involved in a study by a Termez research group that was conducted 1926–1928 and led by B. P. Denike of the State Museum of Oriental Art.

Strelkov points out the following: the fact that locally it was called Zurmala or Katta Tepe, the aforementioned records by Xuanzang, the size of the sun-dried bricks that were used, and the height, which is similar to stupa in places such as Afghanistan and Gandhara in northern India. Also, structurally there is a passageway that used a pit in the middle of the floor and a pit near the floor's surface; it can be imagined to have had a corridor. Zurmala is viewed as a part of a temple, and each of the two large pits is thought to connect to the corridor. However, after being unnaturally destroyed by something (illegal digging) the two pits have further disintegrated through natural degradation. Though the points made by Strelkov are not believed valid, he greatly helped later research with other accurate indications.

After the research group led by Denike, M. E. Masson formed the Termez Pluridisciplinary Archaeological Expedition (TAKE) and studied sites in the vicinity of Termez from 1936–1938. At that time, he conducted a simple study of Zurmala, and in his report he published just a few photos. He also found two drawings on stupa at "Cave no. 1" (surmised to have been in the southern hill) of Kara Tepe, which had yet to have been earnestly excavated (TAKE 1941).

Furthermore, Pugachenkova researched Zurmala in 1964. There are two points in his research (Pugachenkova 1967, translated by Imamura 2017; Fig. 7). First, he attempted to confirm the stylobate of Zurmala by digging a trenches in the southwest and northwest sections. Second, he carried out surface collection within a 500-meter radius of Zurmala.

Zurmala was conceivably constructed in the Bactria period or thereabouts since its sun-dried bricks measure 32cm–33cm × 32cm–33cm square, are 11cm–12 cm thick, and also in light of their size and shape. In addition, establishing trenches in those two locations led to the conclusion there was a stylobate measuring 22m × 16m, and since there was a cylindrical part sitting on top made of sun-dried brick that measured 14.5m in diameter and 13m in height, it was estimated that a restoration taking into account the collapse of the upper portion would utilize 1.2 million sun-dried bricks at a height of 16m. Plus, the surface collection gathered cornice fragments and limestone blocks that fell in the vicinity of the tower, and it was initially surmised that an exterior finish existed. These deductions by Pugachenkova are oriented to a restoration of the entire image based on exploratory digging in the Zurmala vicinity and even today can be called important views on Zurmala.

Based on this work, Kato (1997) believed these sites to be a stupa built in the 2nd century around the rule of Kanishka I, and thought its existence merits attention in the study of Buddhism's spread north. Based on the findings of Turgunov and others, he also referenced a circular structure (stupa) called the Tumboy of Airtam at sites outside of Termez. In addition, there is a stupa in a field near Denov that is shaped remarkably like the Zurmala stupa. Kato introduced characteristics such as the fact that it is split in two lengthwise, and that Al'baum, who comprehensively researched sites in this area, wrote that he thought it is a structure related to the religion of Zoroastrianism.

Furthermore, Kato (2002) attempted to assign status to stupa in Surkhandarya based on previous research on the expansion of stupa from North India to Central Asia/East Turkistan by researchers such as Marshall, Franz, and Kuwayama. In research conducted prior to that, it was thought that stupa changed from the inverted bowl shape (circular design) in India to the square platform in Gandhara during the Kushan Empire. At the same time, it was thought that shapes were passed down that placed an enclosure called harmika on top of a dome, and on top of that a five to seven-tiered parasol-like canopy (chatras). However, opinions were divided on the origin of the change from circular to square designs. In particular, the square design thought to be the oldest was theorized to stem from either Zoroastrianism or temples during the Achaemenid Empire, or to have been influenced by Hellenism or Rome. Kato supported the theory of influence by Hellenism based on comparisons with structures such as Ai-Khanoum temples. Kato also focused on the relationship between unique stupa discovered at Kara Tepe and Airtam—that is, structures with small, embedded stupa in places that were not central—and the three-tiered stylobate of the Kuṇala stupa in Taxila believed to date from the 3rd–4th centuries.

In the future, it is indispensable to closely compare stupa located in Pakistan and Afghanistan with those in southern Uzbekistan.

On 20 April 2012, relics were discovered that may be related to the Zurmala sites. Found 400m south of the stupa and reservoir near Zurmala (Abdullaev, K., Annaev, T. 2012), they include the bodies of two figures, stuck together, that seem to the configuration of a scene from *Illustrated Biographies of the Buddha*. Another relic is a portion of limestone relief that appears to be the exterior of a stupa. Together with the limestone blocks and cornice fragments mentioned in Pugachenkova's paper, they are important clues to surmising the state of the surrounding vicinity and exterior of the stupa.

(2) Recent research and studies/preservation activities by the Rissho Group

Thus, over 90 years have passed since research on Zurmala began. Restoration and preservation work has already finished on Fayaz Tepe, which has been the focus of attention since early on as a relic in this area. Excavations have also progressed on Kara Tepe and Chingiz Tepe, and the existence and transformations of Buddhist facilities are being clarified. As this is occurring, interest in Zurmala, which has yet to be thoroughly explored, is certain to grow going forward while preserving the only stupa form in the vicinity.

Recently, when Fussman mentioned the location of the large stupa in Balkh he compared it to Zurmala in Termez; like the latter, it is in a location visible from a distance, and was situated at an edge or an entrance of the city (Fussman 2015: 186). He also purports that Zurmala is perhaps a part of a monastery that presently is not visible from the ground (Fussman 2015: 192). In other words, when considering the Buddhist sites in Tokharistan (within Afghan territory), which are difficult to excavate, Zurmala in Termez can become criteria that itself includes unexplained issues.

Based on the above examinations, several issues emerge.

It is necessary to confirm the form of the stylobate based on the conclusions rendered by Pugachenkova. It is also necessary to carefully examine

Zurmala's exterior and the environment encompassing the stupa. Doing so requires examinations of the architectural history based on archaeological research on Pakistan and Afghanistan conducted by groups such as the French and Kyoto University research groups. This includes, for example, Kato, Yatani, and Masui (2009).

In addition, a comparison of present-day photos of Zurmala to photos taken in the 1970s kept by Termez Archaeological Museum shows a large fissure has emerged that did not exist in photos taken 40 years earlier. The fissure is already splitting the stupa in half. Details are given by Iwamoto (2017b). Naturally, rain enters the fissure, so it can be surmised there is increasing risk of the stupa collapsing. Urgent preservation measures are required.

Based on the above, the Research Group will expand research on the transformation of Buddhist stupa in Zurmala and the vicinity. At the same time, under the supervision of Toshiya Matsui (professor at the University of Tsukuba) whose area of expertise is the preservation of sites, the Research Group is setting up meteorological observatory equipment in the vicinity of Zurmala to research the impact that the area's climate has on the sun-dried bricks and sites (Matsui 2017), and is implementing preparations for appropriate preservation.

Conclusion

The following is a summary of the above.

(1) The history of Termez prior to the 13th century and the entire Tokharistan region is indivisible and has a strong relationship with the orientation and progress of research on ancient sites in present-day Afghanistan, Pakistan, and Southern Tajikistan. The same is true for Buddhist sites.
(2) Kara Tepe, archaeological remains of a Buddhist monastery thought to have been built during the Kushan Empire under the rule of Kanishka, has been studied since the 1920s. The southern and western hills have been excavated, and today excavation is underway primarily on the northern hill. When the southern and western hills were excavated, the sites were thought to have functioned as a monastery until the 4th century, but analysis of the results of excavation on the northern hill pointed to the possibility that a part of the monastery functioned after the 5th century while

being extended and reconstructed. Excavations by the Rissho Group from 2014 clarified the function and structure of the western side of the northern hill, which had been unexplained, and corroborated that the monastery functioned after the 5th century. At the same time, there were several discoveries that forced reconsideration of the transformation of the northern hill as a whole. The discovery of a wall painting has led to considering a relationship with Buddhist sites in the Xinjiang Uyghur Autonomous Region.

(3) Study of the sites of the Buddhist stupa, Zurmala that is believed to have been built during the Kushan Empire under the rule of Kanishka began in the 1920s. In the 1960s, exploratory digging and surface collection took place and generally clarified that it is a Buddhist stupa. However, at some point from the 1970s a large fissure opened up in the stupa, placing it in imminent danger of being destroyed. In the future, a comparison of architectural history with stupa in present-day Afghanistan, Pakistan, and the Xinjiang Uyghur Autonomous Region is necessary, as well as scientific examination targeting preservation and measures based on them.

The author of this paper has already reported on the current state of research on sites in the vicinity and the ongoing status of Kara Tepe excavations in Iwamoto (2015, 2016a, 2016b, 2016c, and 2017a). Iwamoto (2017b) presents an overview of Zurmala research. This paper adds new information to Iwamoto (2018), which extracted information from the aforementioned papers with slight additions and corrections.

*This paper is a part of the results of the "Rissho University Academic Interchange Project with Uzbekistan," a Private University Research Branding Project by the Ministry of Education, Culture, Sports, Science and Technology

Notes

1. The Uzbekistan Academic Research Group was launched around teachers from the Faculty of Buddhist Studies and Faculty of Letters Department of History. Under the then university president, Yamazaki, research on sites in the region related to Buddhism's spread to the north, a topic proposed by Haruki Yasuda (Faculty of Buddhist Studies) and Satoru Ikegami (Faculty of Letters), was

recognized as befitting the spirit of the foundation of a Buddhism-based university and the promotion of the globalization of academic learning. Research began on Kara Tepe because of advice received from the late Kyuzo Kato (professor emeritus of the National Museum of Ethology; professor emeritus of Soka University; special staff to the Institute for the Comprehensive Study of Lotus Sutra) who was involved for a long time with the excavations. The endeavor's immediate realization was due to support from Hiroaki Furusho (previously special staff to the Institute for the Comprehensive Study of Lotus Sutra of Rissho University) who had a wealth of local experience. In addition, initially the Zurmala was only subject to observation, but later developed into earnest research after partnering with the Termez Archaeological Museum. When Prime Minister Abe made a round of visits to Central Asia, it was mentioned in a joint statement with the president of Uzbekistan.
2. For example, recent publications include Harry Falk (2015), Yu (2015), Miyaji (2016), and Wang (2017). In addition, Odani (2010) published a Chinese translation in 2017.
3. Pugachenkova, Rtveladze, and Kato (1991) (1997), among others, have written about Dalverzin Tepe. For example, Kuwayama (1987: 137) raised doubts about Pugachenkova's theory.
4. This paper discusses Kara Tepe and Zurmala later, but in regard to Fayaz Tepe, in addition to Fussman (2011), Mkrtychev translated by Kawasaki (2016) is garnering attention for suggesting a new view on dating based on criticism of the opinions of Al'baum.
5. The paper compiled by Kazuo Enoki (1992) is useful for grasping the basic relevant historical materials concerning research on the Kidarite and Hephthalites. Also, recently several relevant papers have been compiled on the Hephthalites, including papers by Yu (2012), Naito (1975), and Alram, M., et al. (2010).
6. Regarding this topic, Mizutani (1971), Kuwayama (1995), and Nagasawa (1998) are translations with annotations or research that are easily obtainable in Japan.
7. Leriche P., Pidaev Ch. (2008) and Leriche, P. (2013) are examples of discussions on sites in Termez based on historical research by France and Russia.

References

Western languages
Research Group Reports
Rissho University (2015): Compiled by Rissho University Uzbekistan Academic Research Group, "The Kara Tepe Sites in the Surkhandarya Region of the Republic of Uzbekistan—FY2014 Research Overview—," Tokyo, Rissho University.
Rissho University (2016): Compiled by Rissho University Uzbekistan Academic

Research Group, "The Kara Tepe Sites in the Surkhandarya Region of the Republic of Uzbekistan—FY2015 Research Overview—," Tokyo, Rissho University.

Rissho University (2017a): Compiled by Rissho University Uzbekistan Academic Research Group, "The Kara Tepe Sites in the Surkhandarya Region of the Republic of Uzbekistan—FY2016 Research Overview—," Tokyo, Rissho University.

Rissho University (2017b): Compiled by Rissho University Uzbekistan Academic Research Group, "Zurmala: A Stupa in Termez—Basic Research Report—," Tokyo, Rissho University.

Rissho University (2018): Compiled by Rissho University Uzbekistan Academic Research Group, "The Kara Tepe Sites in the Surkhandarya Region of the Republic of Uzbekistan—FY2017 Research Overview—," Tokyo, Rissho University.

Japanese

Adachi, K. (Yi Jing Compilation) (1942). *Da Tang Xi Yu Qiu fa Gao Seng Zhuan* (The Life of the Monks of the Tang Dynasty who Travelled to the West), Tokyo, Iwanami Shoten.

Ikegami, S. (2018). "The Age of the Kara Tepe Sites," previously cited, Rissho University (2018).

Pugachenkova, G. A. (Eiichi, I. trans.). "Two Buddhist Stupa in Southern Uzbekistan," previous cited, Rissho University (2017b), pp. 13–22.

Iwai, S. (2006). "Transformations in Buddhist Monasteries in Afghanistan and the Surrounding Area," *Bukkyo Geijutsu* (Buddhist Art) No. 289, pp. 100–112.

Iwai, S. (2013). "The Temporary Decline of Buddhist Monasteries in Bactria," *Journal of Oriental Studies* Vol. 88, pp. 422–403.

Iwamoto, A. (2015) ."Buddhist Sites in the Amu Darya Middle Basin & the State of Research," previously cited, Rissho University (2015).

Iwamoto, A. (2016a) ."An Overview of Ancient Sites in Northern Bactria: Based on a Rationalization of Research History in the Surkhandarya Region," previously cited, Rissho University (2016), pp. 44–62.

Iwamoto, A. (2016b). "Kara Tepe Newly Discovered Written Materials & Sites in the Vicinity: Centering on the Termez/Angor Region," *The Historical Reports of Rissho University* No. 119, pp. 1–18.

Iwamoto, A. (2016c). "Buddhist Sites in Tokharistan & Xuanzang: Based on Research by the Research Group" *The Journal of Tang Historical Studies* No. 19, pp. 256–264.

Iwamoto, A. (2017a) ."Ancient Sites in Southern Uzbekistan: A Focus on Buddhist Sites" *Eurasian Studies* No. 56, pp. 5–9.

Iwamoto, A. (2017b). "Looking Back on and at the Future of Zurmala Research: Stupa in Southern Uzbekistan and the Kushan Empire" previously cited, Rissho University (2017b), pp. 3–12.

Enoki, K. (1992). *Kazuo Enoki Collection: Central Asia I*, Tokyo, Kyuko Shoin.

Odani, N. (2010). *Yuezhi—Investigating the Mysterious People of Central Asia (2nd*

Ed.), Tokyo, Toho Shoten.

Rtveladze, E.V. (Ch., Obiya trans.) (2006). *Delving into the Eastern Expedition of Alexander the Great: Unknown Achievements & Truths*, Tokyo, NHK Publishing.

Kato, K. (1979a). "Bactria in the Kushan Era-5- Historical & Cultural Issues," *The Toyo Gakujitsu Kenkyu* 18 (3), pp. 154–164.

Kato, K. (1979b)."Bactria in the Kushan Era-6—Historical & Cultural Issues," *The Toyo Gakujitsu Kenkyu* 18 (4), pp. 177–187.

Kato, K. (1997). *Studies on Buddhist Sites of Northern Central Asia* (Silk Roadology: Bulletin of the Research Center for Silk Roadology, Vol. 4), Nara, Research Center for Silk Roadology.

Pidaev, Sh. (K., Kato trans.) (2002). *New Finds of Uzbek Archeology*, Osaka, Toho Shuppan.

Kato, K. (2002). "The Origins and Characteristics of Kara Tepe Stupa: The Development of Stupa in the Spread of Buddhism to the North," previously cited, *New Finds of Uzbek Archeology*, pp. 109–126.

Stavisky, B. J. (K., Kato trans.) (2002). "A New Discussion on Kara Tepe: A Short Summary of 1978–1989 Excavations," *Ay Khanum, ed. and compiled by Kyuzo Kato*, Hadano, Tokai University Press.

Pidaev, Sh. (K., Kato trans.) (2007a). "The History of Termez (Prior to the Arabs): The Origins and Development of the City," *Ay Khanum, ed. and compiled by Kyuzo Kato*, Hadano, Tokai University Press, pp. 7–20.

Pidaev, Sh. (K. Kato trans.) (2007b). "Excavations of the Northern Hill & Western (Middle) Hill of Kara Tepe (1998–2007)," previously cited, *Ay Khanum 2007*, pp. 59–130.

Zeimal', T. (K. Kato trans.) (2007c). "Excavations of the Northern Hill of Kara Tepe (1985–1989)," previously cited, *Ay Khanum 2007*, pp. 53–58.

Stavisky, B. J. (K. Kato trans.) (2007d). "Discoveries and Simple History of Research on Buddhist Sites in Central Asia," previously cited, *Ay Khanum 2007*, pp. 25–40.

Rtveladze, E. V. (K. Kato trans.) (2011). *The History of the Silk Road Told by Archeology: Civilization, States, and Culture in Central Asia*, Tokyo, Heibonsha.

Kato, N.; Yatani, S.; Masui, M. (2009). "The Shape and Transformations of Buddhist Stupa Platforms at Buddhist Monasteries in Central Gandhara: Research on Buddhist Stupa in Gandhara Buddhist Architecture 1, *Journal of Architecture, Planning and Environmental Engineering* 71 (637), pp. 703–710.

Mkrtychev, T. K. (K. Kawasaki trans.) (2016). "Fayaz Tepe, Sites of a Buddhist Monastery in Northern Bactria According to the Latest Research," *Silk Road Studies* No. 9, pp. 15–25.

Kuwayama, Sh. trans. (1987). *Mahayana Buddhism Scriptures (China & Japan) Vol. 9 (Great Tang Records on the Western Regions)*, Tokyo, Chuokoronsha.

Kuwayama, Sh. (1990). *From Gandhara to Kapisi*, Kyoto, Institute for Research in Humanities, Kyoto University.

Kuwayama, Sh. (1995). *Records on the Western Regions: The Travels of Xuanzang*,

Tokyo, Shogakukan.
Kuwayama, Sh. (1998). *Huichao's Wang Wu-Tianzhuguo Zhuan Record of Travels in Five Indic Regions Translation and Commentary (2nd ed.)*, Kyoto, Institute for Research in Humanities, Kyoto University.
Miyaji, A. (2016). *Deciphering Buddhist Images: Buddhist Art on the Silk Road*, Tokyo, Shunjusha, pp. 43–66.
Tanabe, K.; K., Maeda, ed. (1999). *A Complete Collection of Global Art: The Orient Vol. 15 Central Asia*, Tokyo, Shogakukan.
Naito, M. (1975). "The Hephthalite People & Their Development," Ed. in Commemoration of the 70th Anniversary of Dr. Hisao Matsuda, *Cultural Interrelations Between the East and West*, Tokyo, Yuzankaku.
Nakazawa, K. (1998). *The Travel Journal of Xuanzang: Western Regions & India* (Abridged Translation of the Biography of Master Xuanzang Daci'en Temple), Tokyo, Kodansha.
Fukushima, M. (2010). "The Li Clan of Jibin: A Study of Bactrian Merchants on the Silk Road," *Journal of Historical Science* Vol. 119 No. 2; same author *The Sogdians in Eastern Eurasia*, Tokyo, Kyuko Shoin, 2016, pp. 225–259.
Matsui, T. (2017). "Views on the Restoration & Preservation of the Zurmala Stupa: Based on Analysis of the Bricks Used," previously cited, Rissho University (2017b), pp. 23–27.
Mizutani, Sh. (1971). *Great Tang Records of the Western Regions*, Tokyo, Heibonsha.
Miyamoto, R. (2015). "An Introduction to Geographical Research on the Administration of Tokharistan," *Journal of Oriental Studies*, Kyoto No. 90, pp. 320–277.
Yasuda, H. (2018). "Newly Discovered Wall Paintings in Kara Tepe: Based on a Comparison with Examples of Relics from East Turkistan," previously cited, Rissho University (2018).
Yoshida, Y. (2010). "Religious Culture Related by Excavated Objects: A Focus on Buddhism in Iranian-speaking Countries," Yasuaki Nara; Kosei Ishii ed. *A New History of Buddhism in Asia Vol. 5 Central Asia: The Crossroads of Civilizations and Culture*, Tokyo, Kosei Publishing Co., Ltd.
Yoshida, Y. (2011). "The History of Sogdians and Sogd," Hiroshi Sohukawa; Yutaka Yoshida ed. *The Art and Language of the Sogdians*, Kyoto, Rinsen Books Co., pp. 7–78.
Yoshida, Y. (2013). "The Current State & Issues in Research on Written Bactrian Documents," *Studies on the Inner Asian Languages*, XXVIII, pp. 39–65.
Yoshida, Y. (2016). "Bactrian Inscriptions on Pottery Fragments," previously cited, Rissho University (2016), pp. 39–43.
Yoneda, M.; Ozaki, H.; Omori, T. (2016). "Radiocarbon Dating of Human Bones Unearthed from the Kara Tepe Sites," previously cited, Rissho University (2016), pp. 72–74.
Pugachenkova, G. A. chief ed.; E.V. Rtveladze, K., Kato ed. (1991). *Antiquities of*

Southern Uzbekistan, Tokyo, Soka University Publishing.

Chinese

Jiang B. 〔1996〕 Dunhuang Research Academy(ed.) *Essays for the 50th Anniversary of Duan Wenjie's Career as Dunhuang Expert,* World Publishing Corporation, pp.29–45.

Yu T. 〔2012〕 *Study of Ephtalites History,* Peking, The Commercial Press.

Yu T. 〔2015〕 *Study of Kushan Dynasties History,* Peking, The Commercial Press.

Wang Xi. 〔2017〕 *Study of Tocharistan History,* Peking, The Commercial Press.

The Influence of *The Sketch Book* on Longfellow's *Outre-Mer*

Mika Takiguchi

Abstract

Henry Wadsworth Longfellow is not just a well-known 19th century American poet, but also a critically acclaimed prose writer. His best-known work of prose, *Outre-Mer: A Pilgrimage Beyond the Sea* (1835), features numerous and interspersed literary references to the works of one of America's most famous writers of the early 19th century, Washington Irving.

This paper examines *Outre-Mer* and one of Irving's best-known works, *The Sketch Book of Geoffrey Crayon* (1819–1820), placing the focus on the similarities between the two works, and the fact that they were both travelogues written with the objective of introducing the sights and culture of various European countries to the American people, who in that period were still a developing nation in terms of culture. This paper also re-evaluates Longfellow's and Irving's efforts to depict, from the perspective of foreigners, the European culture and the emphasis it places on traditions.

Introduction

Here lies the gentle humorist, who died
In the bright Indian Summer of his fame!
How sweet a life was his; how sweet a death!
Living, to wing with mirth the weary hours,
Or with romantic tales the heart to cheer;
Dying, to leave a memory like the breath
Of summers full of sunshine and of showers
A grief and gladness in the atmosphere. [1]

In 1876, the famous 19th-century American poet Henry Wadsworth Longfellow (1807–1882) secretly visited the Sleepy Hollow Cemetery located in the suburbs of New York, and read an homage to Washington Irving, a writer Longfellow had respected since childhood, who had passed away in 1859.

Among Longfellow's best-known works are such masterpieces as the poems "Paul Revere's Ride," which commemorates the hero of the American War of Independence, and "A Psalm of Life," as well as "The Song of Hiawatha," a poem about the native American mythological warrior. Apart from the fame he has earned for himself as a poet, Longfellow was also known as a writer of prose. His major prose works include the travelogues *Outre-Mer: A Pilgrimage Beyond the Sea* and *Hyperion, a Romance* (1839), as well as *Kavanagh: A Tale*, which was published in 1849. *Outre-Mer* was based on journals Longfellow kept during his journey around Europe in 1826, which he undertook for the purpose of linguistic research in preparation for the professorship he was about to assume at Bowdoin College.[2] The book features numerous literary references to the works of Washington Irving, who was the object of Longfellow's adoration and respect.

This paper explains the background to the writing of *Outre-Mer*, and compares the characteristics of the book with Irving's literary style in order to identify similarities and clarify the literary features of both authors.

1. Longfellow's Boston Period

Longfellow was born on February 27, 1807, in Portland, Maine.[3] His father, Stephen Longfellow (1776–1849), was a lawyer, and initially had hopes that his son, Henry, would follow in his steps. Yet, once he learned about Henry's passion for literature, he began to support him and is said to have helped him secure teaching positions at Bowdoin College and Harvard University. His mother, Zilpah Wadsworth Longfellow (1778–1851), had extensive knowledge about religion and books. She is believed to have had significant influence on Henry. Henry was the second of eight children in the Longfellow household. At age six, he was enrolled in the private Portland Academy, and in 1820, at the age of merely thirteen, he published the poem "The Battle of Lovell's Pond" in *The United States Literary Gazette*.[4] The poem was modeled after "The Destruction of Sennacherib" by George Gordon Byron

(1788–1824). The following year, Longfellow enrolled in Bowdoin College, which back then was an academic institution with a relatively short history that emulated Harvard University's public lectures. The first year, he stayed at his family home, and from 1822, he moved to Brunswick together with his older brother Stephen Longfellow (1805–1850), and began studying at the college. The Longfellow family had an extremely close relationship with the college. The poet's grandfather, Stephen Longfellow (1750–1824) was one of the founders of the college, and his father served as a trustee. At the college, Longfellow met Nathaniel Hawthorne (1804–1864), who would become his lifelong friend, and joined the Peucinian Society.[5] Overall, it appears that he made the most of his student life. In the meantime, he continued to write poetry, and published nearly forty poems before his graduation. Most of these appeared in the literary periodical *The United States Literary Gazette*. Also, for a short period, Longfellow studied law at his father's law office in Portland. His academic achievements during his student years were noticed by Bowdoin College, and when Longfellow graduated in 1825, he was offered a professorship at a newly-established department of modern languages. A story claims that one of the college trustees, Benjamin Orr (1772–1828), had been impressed by Longfellow's translation of Quintus Horatius Flaccus (BC65-BC8), and so a decision was made to offer him a professorship. Longfellow accepted the offer, and in order to prepare for his job, on May 15, 1826, he departed for Europe from the Port of New York to engage in research activities on the Old Continent.

Between 1826 and 1829, the year he returned to the United States, Longfellow spent time in France, Spain, Italy, and Germany, and also traveled to Austria, Bohemia, Moravia, and Slovakia, and other European countries. During his journeys, he apparently studied hard at French, Spanish, and German. His work *Outre-Mer*, which will be examined in more detail in this paper, is a travelogue based on his journals from that period. In 1827, during his stay in Madrid, Spain, Longfellow had the opportunity to meet with one of America's greatest novelists, Washington Irving. At that time, Irving was already a cultural figure of international fame, and was residing in Spain as Secretary to the American Legation there. Entries in his journal and letters testify to the extreme excitement Longfellow experienced upon meeting the great writer, whom Longfellow had idolized since childhood. This paper will examine in greater detail the encounter and the literary dialogue between Longfellow and Irving.

2. Background to the Writing of *Outre-Mer*

Longfellow is known primarily for his accomplishments as a poet, but he undertook the challenge of writing prose about three times throughout his lifetime. As mentioned above, *Outre-Mer* was his first work of prose. It was written based on the journals Longfellow kept during his first visit to Europe from 1826 through 1829.

After returning from Europe, despite the fact that the professorship at Bowdoin College kept him busy, Longfellow began anonymously publishing his work *The Schoolmaster* in a serialized form in *The New England Magazine*. *The Schoolmaster* was written in six installments upon a request from the then editor-in-chief of *The New England Magazine*, Joseph Tinker Buckingham (1779–1861). Written in the first-person format, it told the story of a teacher living in New England who shared the experience of his journeys in Europe. The series appeared in the magazine through 1833, when Longfellow suddenly terminated the publication for some unknown reason, and then began publishing the story as a booklet, again anonymously and with the title *Outre-Mer*. The completed edition of *Outre-Mer* was published in 1835 by Harpers, a New York publishing company. The book was published in two volumes. During his stay in London, Longfellow arranged for the publishing of an English edition of the book. As for the author's name, while the American version was published anonymously, the English version was published under the pseudonym "An American."

Longfellow had published several textbooks and translations even prior to 1835, but *Outre-Mer* was his first original literary work. Perhaps for this reason, he appeared to be extremely concerned over the way it was accepted by critics. It is easy to notice that Longfellow based the book on the early works of Irving. The similarities can be found in the mixture of descriptive sketches, local stories, and keen observations about people and places. Despite the fact that Longfellow's name was not on the cover, it was not difficult for his friends to surmise that he was the author of the book, mainly because the journey of the protagonist in the story—from his departure for France in 1826 to him leaving Germany in 1829—perfectly matched the travels of Longfellow himself.

For six years after Longfellow returned from Europe, *Outre-Mer* was not published in its full form, but the style of this book written by the young author gave an extremely stiff and formal impression. Until then, Longfellow had written mainly long and short poems, and had translated textbooks and foreign poems. One of the events that inspired him to write his first work of prose was undoubtedly the encounter in Madrid, Spain, during Longfellow's journey in Europe, with Washington Irving, the author of *The Sketch Book* and the first American cultural figure to achieve international fame, and the time they spent together there.

It was a well-known fact that Longfellow admired Irving from a very young age. Longfellow himself publicly spoke about this in a speech to commemorate Irving at an event of the Massachusetts Historical Society in Boston, held on December 15, 1859.[6]

> Rejoice in the completeness of his life and labors, which, closing together, have left behind them so sweet a fame, and a memory so precious. ... We feel a just pride in his renown as an author, not forgetting that, to his other claims upon our gratitude, he adds also that of having been the first to win for our country an honourable name an position in the History of Letters. [7]

Longfellow writes in a letter to his mother that, in order to prepare for his meeting with Irving, he had dinner with George Ticknor (1791–1871)[8] in New York on May 2, 1826, the day prior to his departure for Europe, and received from him advice about the journey, as well as a letter of introduction to Irving.

> I dined today with Mr Ticknor. He is a little Spanish-looking man, but exceedingly kind and affable. He has supplied me with letters to Washington Irving—Prof. Eichorn in Germany—and Robert Southey. He strongly recommends a year's residence in Germany—and is very decidedly and strongly in favor of commencing literary studies there. [9]

Longfellow actually met with his idol Irving in March 1827, after completing his journey in France and arriving in Madrid. Approximately 10 months prior to this encounter, during his stay in Paris, Longfellow met with Irving's nephew, Pierre Irving (1806–1878). In addition to the letter of introduction from Ticknor, Longfellow also received a letter of introduction from Pierre, and the high praise bestowed upon the 21-year-old Longfellow in these letters convinced Irving to give him a warm welcome. At that time, Irving was in the final stages of writing *Life and Voyages of Christopher Columbus* (1828), and was residing in the spacious and opulent mansion of the US Consul in Madrid, Obadiah Rich (1777–1850).

Longfellow was apparently extremely impressed to witness Irving's industriousness, of which he had heard so much. This is what Longfellow writes about Irving's everyday writing habits and the one time he witnessed the writer deep in work in his study at 6 a.m.: "He seemed to be always at work. One summer morning, passing his house at the early hour of six, I saw his study window already open." [10] Despite Irving's busy writing schedule in the final stages of completing his story about Columbus, he made time to socialize with Longfellow during the several months that the young writer spent in Madrid, and encouraged him to further develop his talent in the literary profession. This delighted Longfellow, and this is what he enthusiastically wrote about Irving in a letter to his father dated March 20, 1827:

> The society of the American is very limited here. Mr Everett and family—Mr. Smith his secretary—Mr. Rich the consul—Washington Irving and his brother,—Liuet. Slidell of the Navy—and myself, compose the whole. … Mr. Rich's family circle is also a very *agréable* one—and Washington Irving—who resides in the same house—always makes one there in the evening. This is altogether delightful—for he is one of those men who put you at ease with them in a moment. He makes no ceremony whatever with one—and of course is a very fine man in society—all mirth and good humor. He has a most beautiful countenance—and at the same time a very intellectual one—but he has some halting and hesitating in his conversation—and says very pleasant, *agréable* things in a husky—weak—peculiar voice. He has a dark complexion—dark hair:—whiskers already a little grey. This is a very off-hand portrait of so illustrious a man: but after writing through three sheets of paper at a sitting, I do not feel much in the spirit of minute descriptions of any kind. [11]

After leaving Madrid, Longfellow sent the following letter dated September 29 to Irving to express his gratitude:

> It was my intention to have written you from Seville, but I was there so short a time, and that short time was so fully occupied, that I found it impossible to fulfill that intention. I can assure you, that that day which saw me safely entering the gates of Seville was a jubilee for me. I have been

fortunate enough thus far to have escaped robbery and "bloody murder": —and no wooden cross by the way side designates my burial place, nor melancholy pile of stones cries aloud of Spanish blood-guiltiness. I hope you will be as fortunate as I have been. [12]

Later, Longfellow wrote the following as he reminisced about the days he spent with Irving:

> I found the author, whom I had loved, repeated in the same poetic atmosphere; and what I admired still more, still more, the entire absence of all literary jealously. He seemed to be always to be always at work ... "Sit down, I will talk with you in a moment, but I must first finish this sentence. [13]

The enormous literary impact the communication with Irving had on Longfellow's work can be inferred from the similarities between *Outre-Mer*, the first travelogue written by Longfellow apart from his translations, and one of Irving's most popular works, *The Sketch Book*.

As previously mentioned, it is a well-known fact that *Outre-Mer* is based on the journals Longfellow kept during the time he spent in Europe from 1826 through 1829, and other documents. Furthermore, as its author, Longfellow himself revealed to family and friends that the book was modeled on Irving's *Sketchbook* as an expression of the young writer's admiration. It is estimated that Irving started writing the essays that later became the archetype for *Outre-Mer* around May 1829. This becomes clear from a letter Longfellow sent to his father from Göttingen, Germany, the fourth European country he visited after France, Spain, and Italy.

> I have employed [a part of] the College vacation to make a journey through the Country of the Rhine—and visit London. I thought it best to do this at a time when there were no lectures here—in order to enable me to pursue them to the end of the course this summer, which I could not have done, had I postponed visiting England. ... I am also writing a book—a kind of Sketch Book of scenes in France, Spain, and Italy—one volume of which I hope to get finished this Summer. I hope by it to prove that I have not wasted my time: though I have no longer a very high opinion of my own prudence nor my own talents. [14]

Longfellow also conveyed information about his work on *Outre-Mer* (although at that time this was not the title of the book yet) in a letter to his friend George Washington Greene (1811–1883) in March 1833, when he was already teaching at Bowdoin College.

> And shall I tell you what I am engaged in now? Well, I am writing a book—a kind of Sketch Book of France, Spain, Germany, and Italy; —composed of descriptions—sketches of character—tales, illustrating manners and customs, and tales illustrating nothing in particular. Whether the book will ever see the light is yet uncertain. If I finally conclude to publish it, I think I shall put it out in Nos. or parts: —and shall of course send you a copy as soon as it peeps. However, it is very possible that the book will remain for aye in manuscript. I find that it requires but little courage to publish grammars and school-books—but in the department of fine-writing, or attempts at fine writing, —it requires vastly more courage.[15]

3. *Outre-Mer* and the Influence of *The Sketch Book*

Next, we discuss the similarities between these two works. One of the merits of both works is that they introduced foreign cultures to the American people, which in that period was still a developing nation in terms of culture.

The Sketch Book is focused on the culture of the United Kingdom, while *Outre-Mer* describes the cultures of France, Germany, and Italy. Also, *The Sketch Book* features two stories that are set in America: "Rip Van Winkle and "The Legend of Sleepy Hollow." One of the purposes of including them in *The Sketch Book* apparently was to make America known to the people of the United Kingdom. *The Sketch Book* also features two Native American-themed stories: "Philip of Pokanoket" and "Traits of Indian Character." It is a well-known fact that the aforementioned story "Rip Van Winkle" was inspired by an old German folk tale, which Irving Americanized and rewrote. Also, when Irving visited Walter Scott (1771–1832) in 1817, he was advised by Scott that the treasure in which America should take the greatest pride is its pristine nature. Perhaps this advice is in the historical background of the creation of the two Native American-themed stories.

I had been so accustomed to hills crowned with forests and streams breaking their way through a wilderness of trees, that all my ideas of romantic landscape were apt to be well wooded. "Aye, and that's the great charm of your country," cried Scott. "You love the forest as I do the heather—but I would not have you think I do not feel the glory of a great woodland prospect. There is nothing I should like more than to be in the midst of one of your grand wild original forests: with the idea of hundreds of miles of untrodden forest around me. ... and, in fact, these vast aboriginal trees, that have sheltered the Indians before the intrusion of the white men are the monuments and antiquities of your country."[16]

Let us go back to Longfellow, and discuss the short stories in *Outre-Mer*. It appears that from the very beginning, Longfellow approached his task with the intention of creating a work similar to *The Sketch Book*. Consider the story "The Village of Auteuil," in which the narrator spends a summer in Auteuil, a village in the suburbs of Paris. The story describes the pleasant time he spent in observation of the people he met during his stay, the lovely and well-cared for garden of the neighbors visible from his second-floor window, the dances of the village people. One day, the narrator witnessed a gorgeous village wedding. This is how the author describes the scene of the wedding, the joyful groom dressed in a blue suit, and the blushing bride beautiful in her snow-white wedding dress, with a white rose in her hair:

> I gazed on the procession till it was out of sight; and when the last wheeze of the clarinet died upon my year, I could not help thinking how happy were they who were thus to dwell together in the peaceful bosom of their native village, far from the glided misery and the pestilential vices of the town.[17]

The same evening, he witnessed a sad funeral procession. The deceased appeared to be an unmarried young woman. The quote below features expressions that made him reach this conclusion:

> The coffin was covered with a velvet pall, and a chaplet of white flowers lay upon it, indicating that the deceased was unmarried. A few of the villagers came behind, clad in mourning robes and bearing lighted tapers. ...

> The joys and sorrows of this world are so strikingly mingled! Our mirth and grief are brought so mournfully in contact! We laugh while others weep, —and others rejoice when we are sad! The light heart and the heavy walk side by side and go about together! Beneath the same roof are spread the wedding-feast and the burial-pall! The bridal-song mingles with the funeral hymn! One goes to the marriage-bed, another to the grave; and all is mutable, uncertain, and transitory.[18]

Expressions similar to this quotation can be found in the story "The Pride of the Village" in *The Sketch Book*. In that story, the narrator, Geoffrey Crayon, describes sights and scenes he witnessed on his short trip to a far-away village in the English countryside.

> Presently I saw a funeral train moving across the village green; it wound slowly along a lane; was lost, and reappeared through the breaks of the hedges, until it passed the place where I was sitting. The pall was supported by young girls, dressed in white; and another, about the age of seventeen, walked before, bearing a chaplet of white flowers; a token that the deceased was a young and unmarried female. The corpse was followed by the parents. They were a venerable couple of the better order of peasantry.[19]

A comparison between these two quotations shows several similarities. Both narrators happen to witness a funeral procession in the countryside, and the deceased in both funerals happens to be a young unwed woman. Furthermore, the opening of "The Village of Auteuil" contains numerous words and expressions that appear in the story "Rural Life in England" from *The Sketch Book*. It seems clear that Longfellow consciously used the short stories of *The Sketch Book*, which he had been reading since childhood, as a model for his work.

In the story "The Trouveres" in *Outre-Mer*, Longfellow gives his opinion on poems and other French literary works from the Middle Ages, and lavishes praise on writers and poets. Specifically, he provides a brief account of the life of the poet Charles d'Orleans (1391–1465), and brings up King James I of Scotland (1394–1437) as a poet who shares numerous similarities with Charles d'Orleans:

Charles, Duke of Orleans, the father of Louis the Twelfth, and uncle of Francis the First, was born in 1391. In general tenor of his life, the peculiar character of his mind, and his talent for poetry, there is a striking resemblance between this noble poet and James the First of Scotland, his contemporary. Both were remarkable for learning and refinement; both passed a great portion of their lives in sorrow and imprisonment; and both cheered the solitude of their prison-walls with the charms of poetry. Charles d'Orleans was taken prisoner at the battle of Agincourt, in 1415, and carried into England, where he remained twenty-five years in captivity. It was there that he composed the greater part of his poetry.[20]

Both Charles and James I lived a life of hardship in captivity, and a story about James I also appears in *The Sketch Book*. The story, called "Royal Poet," shows the narrator Crayon take a trip to the Windsor Castle and share his views on the Middle Ages and the history of English literature as he strolls through the castle. He specifically refers to the life of James I who lived in the Windsor Castle as a hostage from age 11 to 18, and praises him as a talented poet. Also, by quoting his poems, Irving expresses his admiration and yearning for history and the Middle Ages. This is what he writes in "Royal Poet":

> James belongs to one of the most brilliant eras of our literary history, and establishes the claims of his country to a participation in its primitive honors. Whilst a small cluster of English writers are constantly cited as the fathers of our verse, the name of their great Scottish compeer is apt to be passed over in silence; but he is evidently never-failing luminaries, who shine in the highest firmament of literature, and who, like morning star, sang together at the bright dawning of British poesy.[21]

Irving's father was an immigrant from a Scottish descent, and as he believed that his own roots were in Scotland, Irving apparently felt even stronger sympathy for James I.

> We sympathize with James, a romantic, active, and accomplished prince, cut off in the lustihood of youth from all the enterprise, the noble uses, and vigorous delights of life; as we do with Milton, alive to all the beauties of nature and glories of art, when he breaths forth brief, but deep-toned lamentations over his perpetual blindness.[22]

It is obvious that there are numerous similarities in the aforementioned two short stories, "The Trouveres" and "Royal Poet," including the explanations of the French poetical circles and English poetical circles in the Middle Ages, the depictions of the biographies and work of poets who led eventful lives as prisoners and hostages, and the mentions of James I.

Outre-Mer also contains a poetically-themed essay called "The Devotional Poetry of Spain." This essay, however, only focuses on three poets who wrote numerous poems in praise of Christianity, a popular genre in the Spanish poetical circles, and there is no obvious connection between this essay and "Royal Poet." This is an example of the existence of short stories in *Outre-Mer* and in *The Sketch Book*, which, despite their extremely similar titles, show no solid relevance in terms of contents. One such example is the pair of stories "The Golden Lion Inn" in *Outre-Mer* and "The Boar's Head Tavern, Eastcheap" in *The Sketch Book*. There are animals in the titles of both stories, and words that refer to lodging ("Inn" and "Tavern"). In "The Golden Lion Inn," the narrator takes a trip to Saint-Ouen in the suburbs of Paris and enjoys lone strolls through its streets. This is how he describes Saint-Ouen: "There was an air of antiquity about the whole city that breathed of the Middle Ages." In "The Boar's Head Tavern, Eastcheap,"[23] on the other hand, the narrator describes his visit to a tavern that was famous as a place frequented by Sir John Falstaff and his friends in *Henry IV* by William Shakespeare (1564–1616).

Based on the above, it can be determined that it is factually correct that Longfellow wrote *Outre-Mer* using Irving's *The Sketch Book* as a model, but it is not clear what Irving thought about having his literary style imitated in such a way. Yet, a dozen years or so after these events, in October 1852, Charles Sumner (1811–1874), a common friend of both authors, wrote in a letter to Longfellow: "Of all your works, Irving likes the best *Hyperion*. It impressed him with its profoundly American content and style." This reveals that, if nothing else, Irving demonstrated interest in Longfellow works and read them.

Readers showed great interest in the first work of prose of the famous American poet Longfellow, and for 20 years after its publication, *Outre-Mer* sold approximately 7,500 copies. Moreover, reviews of *Outre-Mer* went up in the 1860s, more than 20 years after its publication, and these reviews gradually grew more positive. One of the reasons for this seems to be the demise, in 1859, of Irving, the author of *The Sketch Book*, after which *Outre-Mer* was modeled. This perhaps made it easier to discuss the book. For instance, this is a review of *Outre-Mer* written by George William Curtis (1824–1892) and published in the December 1863 edition of *Atlantic Monthly*:

> It is the romance of the Continent, and not that of England, which inspires him. It is the ruddy light upon the vines, and the scraps of old chansons, which enliven and decorate his pilgrimage; and through all his literary life they have not lost their fascination. [24]

The Eastern Argus published in Portland also praised *Outre-Mer*, stating, "It is a book which may be read in the domestic circle without creating a false excitement in young minds, or reconciling them to crime by gilding it with splendor."[25] George Washington Greene wrote the following in The Literary Journal published in Providence, Rhode Island: "It has none of the mysticism that disfigures so large a portion of the works of the day... whose indistinct expression show that they have not their source in the heart." [26]

As seen from the above, *Outre-Mer* received critical acclaim. On the other hand, it also received the following reviews that examined it in comparison with Longfellow's second work of prose *Hyperion*:

> Longfellow's prose works are, with one exception, of minor importance. *Outre-Mer* contains vivid descriptions of Western Europe in the 1820s, and reflects Longfellow's romantic sensibility in a charming manner... Only in *Hyperion*: *A Romance* did Longfellow succeed in extended prose fiction. [27]

If, however, we take into consideration the fact that *Outre-Mer* was Longfellow's first work of prose, there is no place left for doubt that his skills and talent, as a writer, to edit literary materials are exceptional. Also, sufficient recognition should be given to his accomplishment in depicting travel in Europe, an experience that was not yet common among Americans in that age, in fascinating and nostalgic colors. Although the travel described in this work was not a religious journey as may be surmised from the full title of the book, *Outre-Mer: A Pilgrimage Beyond the Sea*, it was a true journey of self-discovery abundant with intellectual revelations. This was perhaps the greatest yield of this book both for Longfellow and for his readers.

Conclusion

This paper presented a detailed discussion of the creation process and characteristics of *Outre-Mer*, a work by Henry Wadsworth Longfellow, who was widely-popular in the nineteenth century poetical circles in the United States. It also examined the similarities in terms of literary style between him and Washington Irving, a writer who is said to have had an impact on Longfellow. An analysis of expressions used in their representative works *Outre-Mer* and *The Sketch Book* indicated numerous instances of obvious imitation. It is clear that this imitation is largely the result of the admiration and respect Longfellow had for Irving since childhood, and the time they spent together when Longfellow visited Irving in Madrid. Also, in both books there were stories written on similar topics, but these stories created different impressions. Overall, if Longfellow can be best described as a scholarly poet, then Irving can be described with the single word "humorist." The geographical location of their two works also differs. While *The Sketch Book* is set in England, *Outre-Mer* describes European countries other than England. Yet, both contain numerous stories about travel. It can be surmised that their objective, as explained in this paper, was to introduce the culture of various foreign countries to the American people, who in that period were still a developing nation in terms of culture. In that sense, the works of these two authors represent an enormous achievement, and it would not be an exaggeration to claim that they set a course for the generations of American authors to follow.

>*This is a revised and enlarged version of the paper presented at the Conference of The Chubu American Literature Society at Chubu University on September, 2012.

Notes

1. *Poems and Other Writings*, 39.
2. A private liberal arts college in Brunswick, Maine, established in 1794. Longfellow, Franklin Pierce (1804-1869), and Hawthorne are among its most famous alumni. The 2012 Best National Liberal Arts Colleges Ranking conducted by the U.S. News Report ranks Bowdoin College sixth in the United States.

3. At that time, Maine was still part of the State of Massachusetts. It became the 23rd state of the US on March 15, 1820, following the Missouri Compromise, which also admitted Missouri as a state.
4. A semimonthly literary magazine. First edited by James G. Garter, the magazine published book reviews and literary news. Longfellow and Bryant contributed poems to the magazine.
5. A literary club in Bowdoin College that was established in 1805 and exists to this day. Its members hold gatherings to discuss literary works and critical reviews.
6. Longfellow was known for his dislike of public speaking, so this speech is one of the very few precious occasions in which Longfellow engaged in public speaking.
7. *The Works of Henry Wadsworth Longfellow, with Bibliographical and Critical Notes and His Life, with Extracts from His Journals and Correspondence.* Vol. 7, p. 403–405.
8. In return for this letter of introduction, Longfellow sent Tickner a copy of the first edition of *Outre-Mer* and several translations of Spanish poems. An indication of their relationship is the fact that eventually, when Ticknor was about to retire from Harvard University in 1835, he recommended Longfellow as his replacement.
9. *The Complete Works of Washington Irving,* Vol. 1, p. 152.
10. *Poems and Other Writings*, p. 801.
11. *The Letters of Henry Wadsworth Longfellow,* Vol. 1, p. 222.
12. *Ibid.* p. 242.
13. *The Life and Letters of Washington Irving,* Vol. 2, p. 265–266.
14. *The Letters of Henry Wadsworth Longfellow,* Vol. 1, p. 310.
15. *Ibid.* p. 408.
16. *The Complete Works of Washington Irving,* Vol. 22, p. 217.
17. *The Works of Henry Wadsworth Longfellow, with Bibliographical and Critical Notes and His Life, with Extracts from His Journals and Correspondence,* Vol.7, p. 23.
18. *Ibid.* p. 23.
19. *The Sketch Book of Geoffrey Crayon, Gent.* p. 276.
20. *The Works of Henry Wadsworth Longfellow, with Bibliographical and Critical Notes and His Life, with Extracts from His Journals and Correspondence,* Vol.7, p. 42.
21. *The Sketch Book of Geoffrey Crayon, Gent.* p. 84.
22. *Ibid.* p. 79.
23. In addition to Irving, Oliver Goldsmith (1730–1774) also wrote a story set in this location.
24. *Henry W. Longfellow.* p. 34.
25. *A Small College in Maine: Two Hundred Years of Bowdoin.* p. 87.
26. *Ibid.* p. 87.

27. *Henry Wadsworth Longfellow. Pamphlets on America Writers, 35*. p. 14–15.

References

Aaron, D. The Legacy of Henry Wadsworth Longfellow. *Maine Historical Society Quarterly, 27*, 42–66.

Aderman, R. M. (1990). *Critical Essays on Washington Irving.* Boston: G. K. Hall & Co..

Anthony, D. 'Gone Distracted': 'Sleepy Hollow,' Gothic Masculinity, and the Panic of 1819. *Early American Literature, 40*, 111–144.

Arvin, N. (1962). *Longfellow: His Life and Work.* Boston: Atlantic Monthly Press.

Butler, J. The Longfellows : Another Portland Family. *Maine Historical Society Quarterly, 27*, 20–41.

Bradley, P. L. "Rip Van Winkle" and "Shiloh" : Why Resisting Readers Still Resist. *Studies in Contemporary Fiction, 48*, 137–148.

Calhoun, C., C. (1993). *A Small College in Maine: Two Hundred Years of Bowdoin.* Brunswick: Bowdoin College.

Calhoun, C., C. (2004). *Longfellow : A Rediscovered Life.* Boston: Beacon Press.

Cody, S. (2007). *Four famous American Writers: Washington Irving, Edgar Allan Poe, James Russel Lowell, Bayard Taylor: A Book for Young Americans 1899.* Middlesex: Echo Library.

Gartner, M. Becoming Longfellow: Works, Manhood, and Poetry. *American Literature, 72*, 59–85.

Giles, P. (2011). *The Global Remapping of American Literature.* Princeton: Princeton UP.

Higginson, T., W. (1902). *Henry Wadsworth Longfellow.* Boston: Houghton Mifflin. Co..

Hilen, A. (1967). *The Letters of Henry Wadsworth Longfellow. 2 Vols.* London: Oxford UP.

Hirsh, E., L. (1963). *Henry Wadsworth Longfellow. Pamphlets on America Writers, 35.* Minneapolis: University of Minnesota.

Irving, W. (1978). *The Complete Works of Washington Irving.* Edited by Richard, Rust. Boston: Twayne Publishers.

Irving, W. (2009). *The Sketch Book of Geoffrey Crayon, Gent.* Edited by Susan Manning. New York: Oxford UP.

Jones, J., B. (2007). *Washington Irving: An American Original.* New York: Arcade Publishing.

Kennedy, W., S. (1882). *Henry W. Longfellow.* Boston: Flanklin Press, 1882.

Longfellow, H., W. (2000). *Poems and Other Writings.* Edited by J. D. McClathcy. New York : Literary Classics of the United States.

Longfellow, H., W. (1966). *The Works of Henry Wadsworth Longfellow, with Bibliographical and Critical Notes and His Life, with Extracts from His Journals and Correspondence. 14 Vols.* Edited by Samuel, Longfellow. New York: AMS Press.

McFarland, P. (1979). *Sojourners*. New York: Atheneum.

McLamore, R., V. The Dutchman in the Attic: Claiming an Inheritance in *The Sketch Book of Geoffrey Crayon, Gent.. American Literature 72,* 31–57.

Pauly, Thomas H. *Outre-Mer* and Longfellow's Quest for a Career. *The New England Quarterly, 50,* 30–52.

Pethers, M., J. Transatlantic Migration and the Politics of the Picturesque in Washington Irving's *Sketch Book. Symbiosis 9,* 135–158.

Trent, W., P., Hellman, G., S. (1921). *The Journals of Washington Irving. 3vols.* Boston: Bibliophile Society.

Tuttleton, J., W. (1993). *Washington Irving: The Critical Reaction.* New York: AMS Press.

Willis, L. Henry Wadsworth Longfellow, United States National Literature, and the Canonical Erasure of Material Nature. *The American Transcendental Quarterly: A journal of New England Writers, 20,* 629–639.

Penal Reform for Drug Offenses in Japan[1]

Yasuhiro Maruyama

Abstract

The "Report of the study group on the state of criminal law regarding young persons" was released in December of 2016. The focus of this report concerns the criminal law system regarding young people, particularly matters such as the qualifying age at which the Juvenile Act applies and policy measures. The report primarily considers measures that would enable making correctional treatment programs mandatory for prisoners, These programs would be implemented, after integrating prison terms and imprisonment. The report also proposes an examination of the "unification of punishment," addressing prison terms particular to Japan, as they relate to the international standards of imprisonment.

In contrast to the above views, and amid discussions of the Prison Law Amendment, which is based on the perspective of respecting the independence of the inmate, many researchers have pointed to the necessity of discretion regarding the relationship between the principle of the treatment of the sentenced person and the "obligation" for correctional treatment. In addition, even in the United Nations Standard Minimum Rules for the Treatment of Prisoners (the Mandela Rules), the state of treatment ensuring inmate independence is clearly expressed, and the above mentioned report may contradict this.

Against this backdrop, this paper aims to clarify the issues in Japan's attempt to reform punishment, via restricted freedom, for drug offenses in which "recovery" is enforced.

Introduction

The "Report of the study group on the state of criminal law regarding young persons" (hereafter, Report) was released in December 2016. As the title suggests, the Report focuses on the criminal law system regarding young people, particularly focusing on their qualifying age for application of the Juvenile Act and policy measures, etc. The discussion on lowering the qualifying age considered that there are cases involving people over the age of 20 that contribute to improved reformation and rehabilitation and prevent recidivism in young persons. Based on this enriching disposition and assessment, the following issues were examined: (1) "criminal policy measures for enriching the institutional treatment of sentenced persons"; (2) "criminal policy measures for strengthening the link between institutional treatment and community-based treatment"; (3) "criminal policy measures for enriching community-based treatment"; and (4) "criminal policy measures for preventing the recidivism of persons subject to a fine or a suspended prosecution."[2]

In relation to (1) "criminal policy measures for enriching the institutional treatment of sentenced persons" in this discussion, the Report states, "(in short) with regard to 'imprisonment with work' within the punishment terms of the existing law, work is considered the substance of the criminal sentence. Work fulfills an important role in the improvement of a sentenced person's reformation and rehabilitation; a specific period must be set aside for work in cases where other correctional treatment is also suitable, considering the characteristics of the sentenced person. In short, correctional treatment should be limited to better suit the individual, such as by devoting a large part of the prison term to reform guidance and course instruction, etc., suited to the inmate's characteristics. Furthermore, in relation to 'imprisonment without work', the carrying out of work can be made uniformly obligatory, and there are cases, depending on the characteristics of the sentenced person, wherein work is useful for the improved reformation and rehabilitation of a person. Accordingly, legal and institutional measures that make work obligatory for a sentenced person, including all kinds of correctional treatment, are considered based on integrating imprisonment with work/imprisonment without work." The unification of the two modes of imprisonment (with/without) was considered a significant point to be examined.[3]

Hayashi, Director-General of the Criminal Affairs Bureau in the Ministry of Justice, raised the matter of prosecutorial activities focused on the recent "entry support" efforts for prevention of recidivism and called this a "lively period for criminal policy."[4] Furthermore, Hayashi noted that a similarly vivacious stage for criminal policy was also seen for several years after 1955. During this period, the "Yokohama method" was introduced through cooperation on probation, centering on the Yokohama District Public Prosecutor's Office. Hayashi stated that there was also "lively" debate about the conditions of punishment during the aforementioned period. In other words, he pointed to the debate that took place during the Penal Code Amendment Preparation Draft Bill (1956), the Amendment of the Penal Code Draft Bill (1971), which was considered and determined by the Special Committee on Criminal Law of the Legislative Council of the Ministry of Justice, and the Amendment of the Penal Code Draft Bill (1979). Hayashi pointed out that within these debates, the issues of the unification of punishment had already been raised, but it was not realized although the basis for actively carrying out correctional treatment not limited to prison work was stated explicitly.[5] Furthermore, Hayashi indicated that work on the amendment of the Penal Code was not realized due to the strong criticism against the Amendment of the Penal Code Draft Bill; however, he felt that there is a need to reconsider, from a contemporary viewpoint, the system for prevention of recidivism, including a debate on punishment unification in the context of the amendment work.[6]

In the debate concerning the Prison Law Amendment, Ishizuka, on the other hand, expressed the need for care with respect to the relationship between the principle of the sentenced person regarding treatment and the "obligation" for correctional treatment from the viewpoint of respecting the independence of the inmate.[7] In particular, concerning the treatment principle, in the outline that became the substance of the Prison Law Amendment of 1980, the treatment of sentenced persons was to "develop their awareness," but in the 1982 Bill, the expression "develop their awareness" was deleted, and then re-inserted in the 1987 Bill, and finally retained in the 1991 Bill. Furthermore, the term "develop their awareness" also remains in the Act on Treatment of Inmates. Examining the text from this perspective gives the impression that great importance is given to the independence of the inmate. However, Ishizuka points out that the aim of the treatment in the outline was "correction" and "re-integration into society," and furthermore, that there was conflict on whether the phrase "appeal to self-awareness" was driven from a functional perspective to carry out effective treatment or was from a perspective based on the autonomy/independence of the inmate.[8] There is arguably a need to reconsider the discussion concerning the recent "unification of punishment" from the perspective of the "independence of the inmate" in the changes in the debate surrounding these Prison Law amendments as well.

There has been discussion on the relationship and harmonization of the active education improvement principle in the administration of punishment and passivism in the administration of punishment. This struggle has been reflected particularly in the debates around drug offenses, which are indeed the subject of this article. This is the "Drug dependency withdrawal guidance" is included as special reform guidance in the Act on the Treatment of Inmates, which has been enforced since 2006 resulting from the above Prison Law Amendment. Also, in the Recidivism Prevention Promotion Plan, it is clearly expressed as a separate specific type of crime alongside the state of support for elderly people and people with disabilities. Furthermore, "dependence" on medical care is a problem for a person's independence and way of life, and whether to protect this for social security reasons or to continue to perceive it as a criminal justice problem is also becoming an issue increasingly present at international levels.[9] Accordingly, this article will survey the law reforms and lawmaking surrounding people who commit drug offenses, and in particular, people who have committed the offense of simple self-use and the offense of simple possession with the intention for self-use, which make up the 90% of the violations of the Stimulants Control Act. This article examines how the merits and demerits of special reform guidance and "developing their awareness" in the treatment principle of the Act on the Treatment of Inmates should be perceived and the various issues in implementing a "recovery program" in criminal justice.[10]

I. Law Reform Surrounding Drug Offenses

1. Law reform and lawmaking to date

Thorough regulation of simple self-users and simple possessors was central to the response in Japan's criminal justice to drug offenders. A high likelihood of a suspended sentence in the case of a first offense was the norm.[11] However, cases of a subsequent offense during a suspended sentence (re-use or possession for that purpose) led to a jail sentence. The assessment of culpability pronounced becomes heavier for each person and there is evidence of increasingly severe punishment.[12] However, the solution to this fundamental problem did not see a reduction in the rate of recidivism. Therefore, change has been slow through collaboration with and support of private institutions and through recovery support and administration for users. It is not true that strict regulation exists only for terminal users as per the Five-Year Drug Abuse Prevention Plan and the Ministry of Justice Ministerial Meeting Concerning Measures against Crime, etc.

It is on this background that law reform and law making in criminal justice have taken place. These cover items such as implementing policy that includes cognitive-behavioral interventions and counseling to divert people from criminal justice at the earliest possible period, enriching drug dependency withdrawal guidance within penal institutions, etc., and carrying out drug tests on probationers and counseling them while on conditional release. For example, a summary trial procedure commenced based on the "Law for Partial Amendment to the Code of Criminal Procedure and Other Related Laws" (Act No. 62 of 2004), a summary trial procedure commenced, and in the case of drug offenses where there are few cases of denials, disposal through courts became quick. By implementing this, suspended sentences with probation are handed down and community-based treatment is carried out in which drug improvement programs and urine testing are performed under the administration of probation officers. The law reform responsible for this was the "Act for Partial Amendment of the Probationary Supervision of Persons Under Suspension of Execution of Sentence Law" (Act No. 15 of 2006). As a result of this law reform, the special compliance rules, which until then could only be attached to item (iii) surveillance, etc., for persons on parole, could also be attached to persons on a suspended sentence, an item (iv) subject that is probation. Furthermore, the "Offenders Rehabilitation Act" (Act No. 88 of 2007) led to the rearrangement and consolidation of the Offenders Prevention and Rehabilitation Act and the Act for Partial Amendment of the Probationary Supervision of Persons Under Suspension of Execution of Sentence Act. In other words, with the introduction of the above legal reforms, it became possible to create a program, based on cognitive-behavioral therapy, making drug testing obligatory as a special compliance rule for a person on a suspended sentence.

Furthermore, the object of the discussion in the 2016 Report and the Justice Ministry's Legislative Council Juvenile Act / Penal Code (Related to the Age of Juveniles / Treatment of Criminals) Subcommittee was recidivism prevention measures that were aimed at suspension of prosecution and deferred sentences. Furthermore, as a result of the "Act to Partially Amend the Penal Code and Related Laws" (Act No. 49 of 2013) and the "Act Concerning Partial Suspension of Execution for Persons Committing the Offence of Drug

Possession and Related Offences" (Act No. 50 of 2013), it became possible to partially administer a prison sentence or a suspended sentence entirely, such that part of it would be a prison sentence, and the remainder of the prison term would be a suspended sentence, while until then sentencing necessarily resulted in either a prison sentence or a suspended sentence.[13] Indeed, while this law is not only targeted at drug offenders, an analysis of the implementation of the law one year after it came into force showed that a partial suspension was handed down to 1,596 defendants, of which 93% were for drug offenses (including not only stimulant drugs but also others covered under the Cannabis Control Act, etc.).

I will next survey the law surrounding drug offenders in criminal institutions. In particular, special reform guidance became possible as a result of the "Act on Detention Facilities and Treatment of Inmates" (Act No. 50 of 2005) (strictly speaking, it came into being one year earlier through Article 82 of the Law on the Detention Facilities and the Treatment of Sentenced Persons). The special reform guidance led to the eventual participation of the staff of private recovery support institutions, such as the Drug Addiction Rehabilitation Center (DARC), in the program, something that was previously part of Blocker education. Programs using cognitive-behavioral therapy centered on SMARPP were then established.[14] In other words, treatment shifted from education (which consisted in communicating the harm of initial use) to a more systematic program of dependence recovery. In the next section I will examine the debate surrounding these reforms, that many regard as natural outcome of the Act on the Treatment of Inmates.

2. The debate on the unification of punishment

Using the opportunity of the reduction in the voting age from 20 years to 18 years, the reduction of the applicable age for the Juvenile Act was also debated. The first meeting of the Liberal Democratic Policy Research Council "Special Committee on Age of Adulthood" took place in April 2015, while in September 2015, the "Recommendation concerning the Age of Adulthood" was submitted to the Minister for Justice.[15] Furthermore, in November 2015, the Ministry of Justice "Study Group on the State of Criminal Law Regarding Young People" commenced, and 10 hearings, etc., were conducted. In December 2016, the Ministry of Justice Study Group on the State of Criminal Law Regarding Young people released its "Report." The discussion in the

Report was primarily the state of "criminal policy measures regarding young people" and not the issue concerning age, which was the main theme. However, a few points from the criminal law reform debate were evident. This would be a repeat of the "introduction," but it was considered that there are cases that contribute to improved rehabilitation and prevention of recidivism in young people even above the age of 20 years, and not necessarily only among those below the age of 20. On the basis of enriching disposition and assessment, the following issues were examined: (1) "criminal policy measures for enriching the institutional treatment of sentenced persons"; (2) "criminal policy measures for strengthening the link between institutional treatment and community-based treatment"; (3) "criminal policy measures for enriching community-based treatment"; and (4) "criminal policy measures for preventing recidivism of persons subject to a fine or a suspended prosecution."[16]

In (1) "criminal policy measures to enrich the institutional treatment of sentenced persons," in this discussion, the Report states, "(in short) in respect of imprisonment with work within imprisonment in the existing law, work is considered the substance of the criminal sentence. Work fulfills an important role in the improvement of the sentenced person's reformation and rehabilitation; a specified period must be set aside for work in cases where other correctional treatment is also suitable, considering the characteristics of the sentenced person. In short, correctional treatment should be limited to better suit the individual, such as by devoting a large part of the prison term to reform guidance and course instruction, etc., suited to the inmate's characteristics. Furthermore, in relation to imprisonment without work, the carrying out of work can be made uniformly obligatory, and there are cases, depending on the sentenced person, in which work is useful for a person's improved reformation and rehabilitation. Accordingly, legal and institutional measures that make work obligatory are considered for integrating imprisonment with work / imprisonment without work, including all kinds of correctional treatment, for a sentenced person." "The unification of punishment," centered on imprisonment with work and not on imprisonment without work, was raised as an item for examination.[17]

Kawaide, one of the members of the Ministry of Justice "Study Group on the State of Criminal Law Regarding Young People" stated that "having lowered the applicable age, there was also a proposal to make it possible to apply protective measures when necessary to young adults including 18-and

19-year-olds as well. If this was to be applied in the correctional context, measures corresponding to juvenile institution referral would be implemented for young adults, and correctional education would be conducted." Kawaide raised the fact that in former correctional operations, persons under the age of 26 years had been detained in juvenile prison and given special treatment, etc. However, from a theoretical viewpoint, the state of treatment of young adults, elderly people, disabled people, and so on- in other words, not limited to juveniles, should be actively evaluated from the perspective of seeking the sentenced persons' improved reformation and rehabilitation, which is considered an issue. Kawaide is explicit in saying that it merits examination.[18] Indeed, by doing away with the difference between imprisonment in which prescribed work is obligatory pursuant to Article 12 of the Criminal Code and imprisonment in which it is not, and by integrating the punishment, it might be possible to carry out effective treatment from the perspective of "preventing recidivism" by taking legal and institutional measures that can make work, including all kinds of corrective treatment, obligatory for a sentenced person. However, as Matsumiya states, this appears to be an integration into an "expanded punishment with work" as well by the abolishment of imprisonment without work.[19]

I wish to also consider the discussion that even if the applicable age is reduced, protective measures in correctional facilities, etc., can be put in place so that they can also be implemented for people over the age of 20 years. Indeed, raising the applicable age and carrying out protective measures for young adults, who are the subject of punishment, and reducing the applicable age and carrying out protective measures for young adults, who are the subject of criminal punishment, are close but different, in other words, the protective measures of juvenile institutions determined by domestic courts, provided for in Article 23 of the Juvenile Act, and the protective measures of penal institutions carrying out the punishment of imprisonment with work, provided for in Article 12 of the Penal Code, greatly differ. Hamai, based on his experience in attending court as an expert witness in lay-judge trials in criminal cases involving juveniles, points out that it is difficult to clearly understand the difference between a juvenile institution and a juvenile prison only from institution pamphlets and explanations provided by staff members.[20] With respect to the treatment in juvenile institutions, Hamai states that, from the prescription that the warden of the juvenile institution must not assign inmates work unrelated to correctional education, all treatment in a juvenile institution must be education for the purpose of the juvenile's re-integration into society. He goes on to state that, on the other hand, juvenile prison is a place where punishment, not education, is carried out, and that even the same "work" and occupational training have a greatly different meaning.[21] Hence, even though a juvenile sentenced person (character "J"; this is an index of Japanese corrections) receives treatment in a juvenile prison and an adult sentenced person (character "Y") will receive treatment in a juvenile prison until the age of 26 years, it can never be considered that an educational (treatment) environment is in place, such as that in juvenile institutions. Particularly, in contrast to the duration and frequency of face-to-face meetings with juveniles in a small-scale juvenile institution, in a large-scale prison, the focus is on managing the treatment of the many sentenced persons. Hence, Hamai argues that while there has been progress in the specialization of staff members and personnel and in the efficient management of the prison, the response to those in need of re-upbringing has not been sufficient.[22]

As outlined above, in the first place, the reason for the existence of juvenile institutions (achieving the aims of the Juvenile Act to strive for education to provide for the healthy development of juveniles) and prisons (a place to carry out punishment) largely differ. Many issues remain no matter how "protective measures" are sought within this context.

II. Is Special Reform Guidance an Obligation?

According to Kawaide, correctional education with an emphasis on education arose from the need to attach importance to educative measures at the place where punishment is executed for juvenile inmates under 16 years. The decoupling of imprisonment with work and without prison work, and the fact that both persons sentenced to imprisonment with or without work also undergo correctional education, like persons sentenced to imprisonment with work, is regarded as ground breaking. Furthermore, this way of thinking is deemed to have become embodied in a general form in the later Act on Penal Detention Facilities and Treatment of Inmates. In other words, Kawaide points out that, in addition to prison work, a legal foundation is provided so that reform guidance and course guidance can be carried out, and it becomes possible to make these obligatory.[23] According to commentary opinion, etc., inmates have a legal obligation to accept special reform guidance carried out on the basis of treatment guidelines decided by investigation results pursuant to paragraph (3) of Article 84 of the Act on Penal Detention Facilities and the Treatment of Inmates. If guidance is refused without just cause, it would result in a violation of the compliance rule in subparagraph (ix), paragraph (2) of Article 74 of that Act, and disciplinary punishment would be imposed on the basis of paragraph (1) of Article 150. There is a strong view that reform guidance has been made obligatory based on this. However, in relation to this, there are still those who consider that "while it is obligatory, care should be taken in its implementation" and also those who argue that "it was not obligatory in the first place, and that penal provisions also cannot be imposed."[24] However, the debate on whether special reform guidance can be made obligatory continues to be lively.

Yoshioka offers the following reasons for not considering reform guidance obligatory. That is, the perception that reform guidance is compelled by being obligatory is unjustifiable from the perspective of regarding it as treatment of a "criminal." Yoshioka firmly considers that from the perspective of the possibility of acquittal on retrial, the word "criminal" treatment itself is not appropriate; rather, it is the treatment of a "sentenced person."[25] Therefore, he regards as inconsistent the act of the state carrying out treatment to forcibly reform and rehabilitate such persons. Furthermore, Yoshioka considers it natural to think of the "treatment principles" in Article 30 of the Act on Penal Detention Facilities and the Treatment of Inmates as including not only a person who has been sentenced to imprisonment with work but also a person who has been sentenced to imprisonment without work, and the treatment principles cited for detainees awaiting a judicial decision and inmates sentenced to death. In other words, he regards this treatment principle as being close in meaning to the general treatment in the institution and that the rationale underlying this treatment is to make persons sentenced to imprisonment with work and persons sentenced to imprisonment without work to work as well as carry out reform guidance and course guidance in parallel. That is, Yoshioka states "from the point of view that, at the least, correctional treatment (paragraph (1) of Article 84) does not distinguish between inmates sentenced to imprisonment with work and those sentenced to imprisonment without work and treats them equally, so that the obligation as correctional treatment does not mean "mandatory" in the sense of the content of the punishment. This has significance because rules in the institution that inmates, including sentenced persons, should comply with are only to that extent, even if indirect compulsion through disciplinary punishment, etc., is possible, and there is no mistake that the level is substantially different from that under the old Prison Act.[26]

Furthermore, according to Toyama, Director-General of the Correction Bureau in the Ministry of Justice, "it is not an obligation arising from the Penal Code, but an obligation arising from the administration of punishment."[27] However, an examination of the view that something that is not an obligation arising from the Penal Code can be undertaken through the administration of punishment is probably necessary. For example, there are cases where there are reasons from the point of view of the administration of punishment, such as not permitting acts being committed, that impair the appropriate correctional institution operations for the institution management. Article 74 of the Act on Penal Detention Facilities and the Treatment of Inmates prescribes acts that correspond to compliance rules. Paragraph (1) provides that "wardens of penal institutions are to determine the rules to be observed by inmates," and the following specific compliance rules are set by paragraph (2). That is, that paragraph prescribes (i) "prohibition against criminal acts," (ii) "prohibition against any behavior or statement made in a rude or outrageous manner, or any act causing trouble to others," (iii) "prohibition against self-harm," (iv) "prohibition against obstructing staff members of the penal institution from performing their duties," (v) "prohibition against acts likely to hamper the secure custody of themselves or other inmates," (vi) "prohibition against acts which may disrupt the security of the penal institution," (vii) "prohibition against acts detrimental to hygiene or public morals inside the penal institution," (viii) "prohibition against the wrongful use, possession, transfer, etc., of cash and other articles," (ix) "prohibition against evading work prescribed in Article 92 or 93, or refusal of the guidance prescribed in the items of Article 85, paragraph (1), Article 103, or 104 without just cause," (x) "beyond what is set forth in the preceding items, matters necessary for maintaining discipline and order in the penal institution" and (xi) "prohibition against any attempt to conduct, incitement, inducement, or aid of acts against either the compliance rules, which stipulate the matters set forth in the preceding items, or the special compliance rules prescribed in Article 96, paragraph (4)." Furthermore, paragraph (3) provides "beyond what is provided for in the preceding two paragraphs, wardens of penal institutions or staff members designated by them may, if necessary for maintaining discipline and order in the penal institution, give instructions to inmates with regard to their life and behavior." In this way, the compliance rules prescribed in paragraph (2) of Article 74 are all set for the purpose of safe administration, for the safety of inmates, and for the safety of staff members. Even from the perspective of administrative law, it is probably difficult to say that, despite this, compliance rules unilaterally infringe on the rights of inmates. If this were the case, then it could not be considered that only (ix) applies as a unilateral right violation. In other words, the setting for an obligation arising from the administration of punishment is limited to situations where there is a possibility of risk in the context of the operation of institution administration, such as safety of the institution, safety of inmates, safety of staff members, etc. It is reasonable to consider that a person not wanting to receive reform guidance is a "just cause," insofar as there is no possibility that the danger will extend to the institution, such as an outbreak of riots, etc.

Furthermore, also from the aspect of the effect, a problem also arises when it does not involve developing the person's self-control. Nowadays, evidence-based decision-making is cited, but this does not fit with things such as guidance for drug dependence relapse prevention and guidance for organized crime group disassociation. For example, unlike guidance for prevention of sex offenses, which is a program based on the results from Canada, guidance for drug dependence relapse prevention, for organized crime group disassociation, etc., and particularly for enhancing a person's willpower, is considered based on one decisive factor. In particular, in group meetings of recovery programs for a certain drug in the context of special reform guidance for drug-related offenders, the AA and NA method, called the 12-steps program, is often used. The first part of the 12-steps program is that treatment starts from acknowledging that one is powerless with respect to drugs and dependence. This is not to say that all people who do not undertake the 12-steps program will not recover, but unmistakably, at least recognizing one's drug problem and in some way aspiring to recover from it is an important factor. Therefore, it is important to carry out a motivational interview with a person who has ambivalent feelings toward drug use, such as "I want to change my behavior, but I don't really care."[28] The method, based on the premise of contradictory emotions, such as "I want to stop, but do not seem able to," continues to change the feelings of a negative person to the rejection of criminality, without allowing the person to confront these emotions. In other words, it works by not denying the feelings at both extremes, but by clarifying the contradiction through empathy and supporting the feeling of self-affirmation. In this way, "developing their awareness" is sought to the extent possible, and efforts are repeatedly made so that people enroll in a drug dependency recovery program themselves.

III. What Does "Developing Their Awareness" Mean?

1. Changes in the Amendment of the Prison Law

The issue of the legal status of inmates has developed together with debate concerning reform of the Penal Code and the Prison Act. Ishihara argues that, there needs to be harmony between the active education improvement principle in the administration of punishment, from the perspective of human rights protection for sentenced persons, and passivism in the administration of punishment, which refrains from intervention. Ishihara states that "while pre-suppositionally endorsing the move from retribution to reform education, the modern (1970s) idea of administration of punishment in imprisonment led to a suspicion that emphasizing reform education under an administration of punishment structure, such as that of today (1970s), would lead to the strengthening of interventions with regard to sentenced persons, an expansion of obligations, and cause the sentenced persons to be dealt with as objects of treatment. Based on this, expansion of independent freedom and security of human rights of sentenced persons were emphasized. Self-restraint in the administration of punishment and deterrence in the administration of punishment, which is the power function of the state, were asserted as a human rights protection model for the administration of punishment. However, on the other hand, if this is excessively emphasized and if it denies the meaning of treatment that a penal institution carries out, there is probably a risk of it sliding into the nihilism of administration of punishment. Considering the administration of punishment going forward and also the debate concerning amendment of the administration of punishment legislation, neither side should be pressured, and a pathway that harmonizes and sublates both needs to be sought" (notation of (1970s) in above quote is by the author).[29] Ishihara points out that there is a huge gap in content regarding the necessary legal status of sentenced inmates in the reform of the administration of punishment and in the administration of punishment legislation.

It may be said that this was also a central point in the debate on the legal status of inmates, in particular, debates on the treatment principle, and independence and individualization. In relation to the treatment principle, Kamoshita states that "while there was no clear provision relating to the treatment principle in the old law, paragraphs (1) and (2) of Article 24 of that law were interpreted to imply that the aim of treatment was to provide sentenced persons with reformation and rehabilitation and help them re-integrate into society."[30] In fact, the need for sentenced persons to "develop their awareness" has been stipulated in the law since Article 30 of the Act on Penal Detention Facilities and the Treatment of Inmates (strictly speaking the Act on the Treatment of Sentenced Persons of the previous year), which provides that "sentenced persons are to be treated with the aim of stimulating motivation for reformation and rehabilitation and developing adaptability to life in society by developing their awareness while taking into consideration their personality and circumstances." However, in the debate on the reform of the Prison Law, there were changes surrounding the wording "developing their awareness" before it was given statutory form. Ishizuka points out that there was contention surrounding the treatment principles as follows.[31] That is, the "General Plan for the Outline of the Prison Law Amendment" (report of the Legislative Council of the Ministry of Justice, November 25, 1980) provided that "the treatment of sentenced persons is to be carried out considering their personality and circumstances, developing their awareness, stimulating their motivation for reformation and rehabilitation, and developing adaptability to life in society in order to provide their re-integration into society." The Penal Institution Bill (April 28, 1982, submitted to the 96th session of the Diet) provided that "sentenced persons are to be treated with the aim of stimulating motivation for reformation and rehabilitation and developing adaptability to life in society while taking into consideration their personality and circumstances and continuing to ensure their detention." The words "developing their awareness" were deleted, and the words "ensure their detention" were added in their place. Also, after this, the words "encouraging their awareness" were added in the "Penal Institution Bill" (1985), which provided that "sentenced persons are to be treated with the aim of stimulating motivation for reformation and rehabilitation and developing adaptability to life in society by encouraging their awareness while taking into consideration their personality and circumstances and continuing to ensure their detention." The words "encouraging their awareness" were once again amended to "developing their awareness" in the subsequent "Penal Institutions Bill" (1987, submitted to the 108th session of the Diet), which provided that "sentenced persons are to be treated with the aim of stimulating motivation for reformation and rehabilitation and developing adaptability to life in society by developing their awareness, while taking into consideration their personality and circumstances and continuing to ensure their detention." Furthermore, "developing their awareness" also remained in the "Prison Institution Bill" (1990, submitted to the 117th session of the Diet). Also, the treatment principle in the new laws of 2005 and 2006 became "sentenced persons are to be treated with the aim of stimulating motivation for reformation and rehabilitation and developing adaptability to life in society by developing their awareness while taking into consideration their personality and circumstances." In the end, the words "continuing to ensure their detention" were left out, and the words "developing their awareness" remained.

An examination of the form of these provisions reveals that, apparently, the independence of inmates is regarded as important; however, Ishizuka points out that there is an issue in its substance.[32] This is because he considers it ambiguous as to whether "developing their awareness" is wording for something based on inmates' independence/autonomy, or whether it is only sought as a necessary factor from the functional point of view of carrying out effective treatment. Fujii criticizes this point saying that "from the development of international human rights, the subjects of treatment are inmates, and institutions are something that focus on support persons for inmates. Despite this, the wishes of inmates are no more than 'considered' and not only is the institution not bound by the inmates' wishes, but it is able to enforce treatment contrary to their will."[33]

2. The independence of inmates according to international standards

In the 1955 "Standard Minimum Rules," attention was not given to the subjectivity of inmates; rather, the effect of the treatment was prioritized. However, in the 1973 "European Standard Minimum Rules for the Treatment of Prisoners," the active participation of inmates in the preparation of treatment plans and communication between inmates and personnel are the guiding principles. Further, the 1987 "European Prison Rules" provides for respect for people, and that following a discussion between an inmate and a staff member(s), an individual treatment plan should be prepared. This led to a promotion of inmates independently participating in the treatment. The subject is the inmate, and the institution has an obligation to offer the inmate opportunities to participate in its various activities. This probably means that it is necessary to provide for a comprehensive educational program that allows the inmate to achieve his or her needs. Furthermore, the United Nations Standard Minimum Rules for the Treatment of Prisoners (Mandela Rules) also refines imprisonment with Rule 3, which provides that "imprisonment and other measures that result in cutting off persons from the outside world are afflictive by the very fact of taking from these persons the right of self-determination by depriving them of their liberty. Therefore, the prison system shall not, except as incidental to justifiable separation or the maintenance of discipline, aggravate the suffering inherent in such a situation."[34]

Furthermore, an examination of the image of an inmate assumed by the Act on Penal Detention Facilities and the Treatment of Inmates is necessary. For example, the commentary of the Act provides that "inmates, largely, lack normal consciousness; their mind and body are unhealthy and they do not possess the necessary knowledge of and attitude toward life to adapt to society."[35] The tendency is to view inmates as the object of treatment. Therefore, this became law in which institutions emphasize giving instructions such as, "wake up," "grow," and "learn" to people who become the object of reform guidance.[36]

IV. Implementing "Drug Dependence Recovery Programs" in Criminal Justice

1. Contemporary issues

Based on endorsing the assumption that presently there continues to be a move again in the administration of the punishment principle of imprisonment from punitiveness to reform education, a path probably needs to be sought that balances and sublates the active and passive models of the administration of punishment. In particular, the point on intervention for active re-integration into society has become frequent in the debates surrounding forensic social services, and there are modern methods to evaluate this. As noted in Section I of this article, there seems to be a change in the intervention regarding drug offenders together with the actual state of affairs.

Special reform guidance is implemented as per Article 103 of the Act on

Penal Detention Facilities and Treatment of Inmates, and from merely educating offenders of the evils of drug use until now, it has become possible for people from external private support institutions to carry out recovery programs, with recovery programs using cognitive behavioral therapy. In the debate concerning the unification of imprisonment for drug offenses in Japan, an active administration of punishment is being sought, rather than a refinement of imprisonment, such as the Mandela Rules, etc. In other words, the focus of the debate is increasingly becoming about integration into an expanded imprisonment with work and not imprisonment without work. Accordingly, in the final section, I consider the implementation of drug dependency recovery programs in criminal justice in the current situation of unification of imprisonment.

As referred to in the "Introduction," the Report states, "(in short) in respect of imprisonment with work within imprisonment in existing law, work is considered the substance of the criminal sentence. Work fulfills an important role in the improvement of the sentenced person's reformation and rehabilitation, and a specific period must be set aside for work in cases where other correctional treatment is also suitable, considering the characteristics of the sentenced person. In short, correctional treatment should be limited to better suit the individual, such as by devoting a large part of the prison term to reform guidance and course instruction, etc., suited to the inmate's characteristics. Furthermore, in relation to imprisonment without work, the carrying out of work can be made uniformly obligatory, and there are cases, depending on the characteristics of the sentenced person, wherein work is useful for the improved reformation and rehabilitation of a person. Accordingly, legal and institutional measures that make work obligatory for a sentenced person, including all kinds of correctional treatment, are considered based on integrating imprisonment with work/imprisonment without work." "The unification of imprisonment," centered on imprisonment with work and imprisonment without work, was raised as an item for examination.[37] Furthermore, the "Recidivism Prevention Promotion Plan" (below, the Plan) was submitted on December 15, 2017, as a result of the Recidivism Prevention Promotion Act, which was approved in December 2016.[38] There are 115 measures included in the Plan. In addition to work of former inmates, securing residences, and promotion of medical and welfare services, the Plan focuses on the recidivism rate of drug offenders and refers to carrying out treatment/support. As outlined above, while implementation of law reform and system for recovery support continues to come together, there is continuing evidence that "drug offenders" should be dealt with punishment.

2. "Therapy" and "welfare"

Internationally, drug addiction is originally considered not a problem of will, but a problem associated with the state of the recovery programs. There is debate on whether this has to be dealt with by criminal law, and if it is, how to eliminate the element of force, how to treat "consent," and whether to deal with it as social security without relying on criminal law.[39] However, in Japan, there is a tendency to regard drug dependence withdrawal guidance as obligatory and enforceable as a necessary treatment for reformation and rehabilitation. Indeed, by creating an awareness about it as a "sickness" and the person as needing treatment, criticism of the act of deviation is alleviated. However, while regarding it as a sickness, people who become the object of this problem are pressurized into "receiving treatment."[40] However, mandatory treatment that restricts freedom through criminal law procedures cannot happen only because the treatment for the sickness is considered beneficial for the person. This is because mandatory treatment for social security and crime prevention becomes a problem that is also linked to measures aimed at preserving public peace.

However, Gostin points out that treatment compulsorily carried out is justified if it is acceptable to the person involved.[41] In particular, he considers it possible if the treatment is readily accepted and it does not contravene procedural due process to the extent possible. However, the problem that this "choice" is based on criminal punishment continues to remain. However much it is termed as "treatment" and "welfare," "the element of punishment" underlies the treatment program. One cannot forget that this is taking place in the context of criminal law procedures. Regardless of the extent of the treatment intervention, the state must not be granted the authority to restrict freedom for social security. Even when the treatment is beneficial "for the person," the problem remains that the implementation is based on criminal punishment.

Conclusion

This article focused on the debate concerning the unification of punishment in correctional institutions for drug offenses. The discussion by the Justice Ministry's Legislative Council Juvenile Act / Penal Code (Related to the Age of Juveniles / Treatment of Criminals) Subcommittee includes in its agenda new items for community-based treatment, such as "the state of the suspended sentence system for all sentences," "the state of recidivism prevention measures accompanying suspension of prosecution, etc.," "deferred sentences," etc. The meaning of imprisonment, not limited to drug offenses, is being re-questioned from its origin.

Arguably, in recent years, room to debate on what is "punishment" seems to be disappearing in the university law faculty as well. Even in criminal law classes, opportunities to spend a large amount of time to study the theory of punishment are also on the verge of disappearing. Probably in the present state of affairs in the context of fewer and fewer law faculties conducting courses on criminal policy, the opportunities to reconsider society surrounding "crime" and "re-integration into society" from a criminological view will continue to further decrease. Here, I wish to introduce the view of criminology.

In *The Exclusive Society*, Jock Young stated that "with structural unemployment arising and crimes taking place, exclusion occurs in response to these anti-social acts."[42] It appears as if the social structure, called "the exclusive society," is contrasted with "the inclusive society," in which thoughts on re-integration into society are mainstream. However, this is not simply exclusion from society only for being strict with regard to crime. Rather, Martin Fisher and Helen Beckett point out that since neoliberalism, in a society in which fluid personalization is advancing, the cause also leads to the use of treatment programs in drug offenses in the criminal justice system because of its cost-effectiveness.[43] Labeling theory gave rise to the viewpoint of using selective sanction and labels to give rise to further deviation. In the setting of re-integration into society, this also becomes a label. In other words, a treatment program meant for "re-integration into society" is pressed upon the object and carried out. Therefore, people who do not receive the so-called effective treatment are considered a risk factor. It is considered that a drug offender views receiving treatment as a rational choice.[44] Jock Young, who defined the "exclusive society," later points out that an "excessively inclusive" society will also be a problem.[45] "Exclusive inclusion," such as the debate on the unification of imprisonment, which regards treatment for improved reformation and rehabilitation to be obligatory, is not giving rise to an age of thought on re-integration into society. It only demonstrates the making of a person who has a drug dependency into a stranger and the creation of an existence that lacks rational judgment and turns a rational and normal person into a "sick person."[46]

Notes

1. This article is a revised and amended version of the author's article "Jiyūkei no tanitsuka to yakubutsujihan [Unification of imprisonment and drug offences]," Keihōdokushokai "Hanzai to Keibatsu [Crime and Punishment]," Seibundoh, 2018, No. 27, pp. 51–72.
2. "Report of the study group on the state of criminal law regarding young persons" http://www.moj.go.jp/content/001210649.pdf (last accessed on June 30, 2018) pp. 4–16.
3. (Report: footnote 2) pp. 9–10.
4. Makoto Hayashi "Keijisesaku to rippō [Criminal policy and lawmaking]" "Tsumi to batsu [Crime and Punishment]" Vol 53, No 4 (2016) p. 2.
5. (Hayashi: footnote 4) pp. 2–4. Hayashi also points out that items other than those discussed in the "Report of the study group on the state of criminal law regarding young people" and the "Conference for the Recidivism Prevention Promotion Plan" (such as the state of the second suspended sentences and the state of the deferred sentence system) had already been debated regarding the Penal Code amendment and that in order to enrich the current criminal policy, it is our duty to continue to advance the discussion from a modern viewpoint.
6. (Hayashi: footnote 4) p. 4.
7. Shinichi Ishizuka "Sengokangokuhōkaiseishi to hishūyōshashogūhō – kaikaku no tōtatsuten toshite no jukeisha no shutaisei – [History of post-war Prison Law amendments and Inmate Treatment Law – The autonomy of sentenced persons as the goal of reform" "Hōritsujihō" Vol 80, No 9 (2008) pp. 53–57.
8. (Ishizuka: footnote 7) pp. 54–55.
9. Debate has begun in the United Nations Office on Drugs and Crime (UNODC) as to whether the punishment of drug users through criminal justice itself is a "human rights violation." "Treatment and Care of People with Drug Use Disorders in Contact with the Criminal Justice System: Alternatives to Conviction or Punishment." http://www.unodc.org/unodc/en/drug-prevention-and-treatment/

treatment-and-care-of-people-with-drug-use-disorders-in-contact-with-the-criminal-justice-system_-alternatives-to-conviction-or-punishment.html (last accessed on June 30, 2018).

10. "Imprisonment," the theme of this article, should also properly examine community-based treatment. However, because this article focuses on examining the special theme "unification of punishment" and for reasons of article length, community-based treatment is omitted. Further, in relation to community-based treatment issues surrounding drug offenses, please refer to the author's article "Shanaishogū no aratana hōkōsei – yakubutsujihansha o chūshin ni – [A new direction for community based treatment – a focus on drug offenders]" Ryukokuhōgaku, Vol. 43, No. 1 (2010) pp. 176–208.
11. According to the annual report of judicial statistics, the punishment delivered for violations of the Stimulants Control Act in the District Court in 2015 was suspended sentences for 3,701 of the total 9,520 cases.
12. (article by author: footnote 10) pp. 193–196.
13. Since a partial suspended sentence is rather a partial prison term, it could be suggested that I should have included it in the "unification of imprisonment" issue, which is the subject of this paper. However, for details regarding the issues in the partial suspended sentence system, refer to the author's article "Yakubutsushiyōsha ni taisuru kei no ichibu no shikōyūyoseido – kei no kobetsuka to ichibuyūyo [The suspended sentence system of partial imprisonment for drug users – the individualization of imprisonment and partial suspension] Rissho Law Review, Vol. 46, No. 1–2 (2013) pp. 87–199.
14. Matsumoto Toshihiko and Fumi Imamura "SMARPP-24 - busshitsūshiyōshōgai-chiryō puroguramu – [SMARPP-24- substance use disorder treatment program" (Kongoshuppan, 2015).
15. Liberal Democratic Policy Research Council "Recommendation concerning the Age of Adulthood" http://jimin.ncss.nifty.com/pdf/news/policy/130566_1.pdf (last accessed on June 30, 2018).
16. (Report: footnote 2) http://www.moj.go.jp/content/001210649.pdf (last accessed on June 30, 2018) pp. 4–16.
17. (Report: footnote 2) pp. 9–10.
18. Toshihiro Kawaide "Jiyūkei ni okeru kyōseishori no hōtekiichizukeni tsuite [On the legal status of correctional treatment in imprisonment]" Keisei, Vo. 127, No. 4 (2016) pp. 14–15.
19. Takaaki Matsumiya "'Jiyūkei no tanitsuka' to keibatsumokuteki / gyōkeimo-kuteki ['Unification of imprisonment' and aim of punishment / aim of administration of punishment]" Hōritsujiho Vol. 89, No. 4 (2017) p. 79.
20. Koichi Hamai "Shōnenjiken no saibaninsaiban de gironsarerubekikoto – shōnenin to shōnenkeimusho no chigai o chūshin – [What should be debated at lay judge trails in juvenile cases – focusing on the difference between juvenile institutions and juvenile prisons]" Quarterly Keiji Bengo, No.78 (2014) pp.

125–126.
21. (Koichi: footnote 20) p. 126.
22. (Koichi: footnote 20) p. 126.
23. (Kawaide: footnote 18) pp. 16–17. According to Kawaide, the reason for it to be obligatory is "in the Act on Penal Detention Facilities and the Treatment of Inmates, where correctional treatment takes place on the basis of the understanding that the aim of imprisonment with work and imprisonment without work includes re-integration into society by the person's reformation and rehabilitation. In this case, the rights of sentenced persons can be limited to a necessary scope (for instance, limitations with respect to access to books and visits) for achieving the aim of correctional treatment."
24. In terms of sources that consider that it cannot be made obligatory, see Masakazu Doi 'Shakaifukki no tame no shogū [Treatment for the purposes of re-integration into society] in "Keimusho shisutemu saikōchiku e no sishin [A guide for the re-building of the prison system]" edited by Kōichi Kikuta and Yūichi Kaido (Nippon Hyoron Sha, 2007) p. 81, (Ishizuka: footnote 7) pp. 55–56 etc. Also, the author's article "Keijishihō ni okeru yakubutsuizonchiryō puroguramu no igi – kaifuku suru kenri to gimu – [The significance of drug dependency treatment programs in criminal justice – the right and obligation to recover]" Keihō Zasshi, Vol 57, No. 2 (2018) pp. 229–247.
25. Kazuo Yoshioka 'Kangokuhō no kaisei to keijishūyōshisetsu no tenbō [The amendment of the Prison Act and the outlook for penal detention facilities] edited by the publication committee for the compilation of essays in celebration of Professor Maeno Ikuzō's 70th birthday "Keijiseisakugaku no taikei [Outline of criminal policy studies]" (Gendaijinbunsha, 2008) pp. 3–17.
26. (Yoshioka: footnote 25) pp. 3–17.
27. Satoshi Tomiyama 'Keijishisetsu ni okeru jiyūkei no shikkō to kyōseishogū no ichizuke [The execution of imprisonment in penal institutions and the status of correctional treatment] Tsumi to batsu [Crime and Punishment], Vol. 54, No. 2 (2017) pp. 2–4.
28. Akira Satomi '*Dōkizuke* mensetsuhō (mae) – kihontekina kangaekata [Motivational interview methods (first part) – the fundamental way of thinking]' ("Keisei", Vol. 120, No. 6, 2009) pp. 98-104, Emi Togawa 'Dōkizuke mensetsuhō (gō) – kōseijitsumu ni okeru jissen – [Motivational interview methods (second part) – implementation in correctional practice]' ("Keisei", Vol. 120, No. 7, 2009) pp. 114–119.
29. Akira Ishihawa 'Jukeisha no hōtekichiikōsatsu no hōhōron – shōraino gyōkei no tame ni – [Methodology in the consideration in the legal status of sentenced persons – for future administration of punishment]' Keihōzasshi, Vol. 21, No 1 (1976) p. 2.
30. Moritaka Kamoshita "Zenteishingyōkeihōyōron [complete guide to the newly revised law administration of punishment law]" (Tokyo Horei Publishing, 2006)

p. 370.
31. (Ishizuka: footnote 7) pp. 54–55.
32. (Ishizuka: footnote 7) p. 55.
33. Gō Fujii 'Kobetsutekishogūkeikaku no jishi – "shogū no kobetsuka" kara "kobetsukasareta enjo" e [Implementation of individual treatment plans – "from individualized treatment" to "individualized support"]', edited by Keijiripōkenkyūkai "21 seiki no keishisetsu – gurōbaru standādo to shiminsanka – [Penal facilities in the 21st century – global standards and citizen participation]" (Nippon Hyoron Sha, 2003) p. 139.
34. 'United Nations Standard Minimum Rules for the Treatment of Prisoners (Mandela Rules)' (translation by Prison Human Rights Centre) https://www.penalreform.org/wp-content/uploads/2016/12/Nelson-Mandela-Rules_Japanese_final.pdf (last accessed June 30, 2018). In terms of material raising the issue of the independence of the "treatment principle" based on international standards, see Doi Masakazu 'Ikkanshita shakaitekienjo [Constant social support]' Keisei, Vol. 108, No. 4 (1997) p. 55, (Fujii; footnote 33) p. 140 etc. For the debate on the relationship between treatment principle and the "unification of imprisonment," see: (Matsumiya: footnote 19) pp. 80–82.
35. Makoto Hayashi, Atsushi Kitamu and Toshiya Natori "Chikujōkaisetsu keijshūyōshisetsuhō [Annotated commentary Penal Detention Institution Law] (3rd edition)" (Yuhikaku Publishing, 2017: 1st edition published 2010) pp. 499–502.
36. (article by author: footnote 24) pp. 235–236.
37. (Report: footnote 2) pp. 9–10.
38. Ministry of Justice Conference for the Recidivism Prevention Promotion Plan 'Recidivism Prevention Promotion Plan (December 15, 2017)' http://www.moj.go.jp/content/001242753.pdf (last accessed June 30, 2018).
39. For material that examines the question of how to respect the "consent" of a person who is in criminal justice, please refer to the author's article "Keijishihō ni okeru yakubutsuizonchiryō puroguramu – 'kaifuku' o meguru kenri to gimu – [Drug dependency treatment programs in criminal justice – Rights and obligations surrounding 'recovery']" (Nippon Hyoron Sha, 2015). Further, for material that examines the implementation of social security without reliance on criminal punishment, refer to the author's article 'Porutogaru no yakubatsu seisaku chōsa hōkoku / 2014–2015 [Investigative report of drug policy in Portugal / 2014–2015]' Rissho Law Review, Vol. 49, No. 2, pp. 196–234.
40. Talcott Parsons Social structure and personality, New York Free Press, 1964, [Translation: Ryōzō Takeda, translation supervisor "Shakaikōzō to pāsonaritei" (Shinsensha, 1973, special edition published in 1985)].
41. Lawrence O. Gostin "Compulsory Treatment for Drug-dependent Persons: Justifications for a Public Health Approach to Drug Dependency," The Milbank Quarterly, 69 (4), 1991. pp 573–587.
42. Jock Young The Exclusive Society: Social Exclusion, Crime and Difference in

Late Modernity, SAGE Publications, 1999 [Translation: Hideo Aoki, Tairō Itō, Masahiko Kishi and Mahoro Murasawa "Haijogatashakai: Kōkikindai ni okeru hanzai / koyō / sai" (Rakuhoku Publications, 2007)] pp. 28–30.
43. Martin Frisher and Helen Beckett "Drug Use Desistance," Criminology and Criminal Justice, Vol. 6, No. 1, pp 127–145.
44. Pat O' Malley and Mariana Valverde "Pleasure, Freedom and Drugs: of 'Pleasure' in Liberal Governance of Drug and Alcohol Consumption," Sociology, Vol. 38. No. 1, pp. 25–42.
45. Jock Young The Vertigo of late modernity, SAGE Publication, 2007. [Translation: Chigaya Kinoshita, Yoshitaka Nakamura and Masao Maruyama "Kōkikindai no memai" Seidosha, 2008].
46. (Jock Young: footnote 45) p. 380.

References

Aoki, H., Itō, T., et al. (2007). *Haijogatashakai: Kōkikindai ni okeru hanzai / koyō / sai.* Kyoto: Rakuhoku Publications. 28-30.

Doi, M. (1997). Ikkanshita shakaitekienjo [Constant social support]. *Keisei, Vol. 108*, No. 4, 55.

Doi, M. (2007). Shakaifukki no tame no shogū [Treatment for the purposes of re-integration into society]. *Keimusho Shisutemu Saikōchiku e no Shishin* [A Guide for the Re-Building of the Prison System]. Tokyo: Nippon Hyoron Sha, 81.

Frisher, M. & Beckett, H. (2006). Drug Use Desistance. *Criminology and Criminal Justice, Vol. 6*, No. 1, 27–145.

Fujii, G. (2003). Kobetsutekishogūkeikaku no jishi–Shogū no Kobetsuka kara *Kobetsukasareta Enjo* e [Implementation of individual treatment plans–*From Individualized Treatment* to *Individualized Support*], *21 seiki no Keishisetsu– Gurōbaru Sutandādo to Shiminsanka–*[Penal Facilities in the 21st Century–Global Standards and Citizen Participation]. Tokyo: Nippon Hyoron Sha. 139.

Ishihara, A. (1976). Jukeisha no hōtekichiikōsatsu no hōhōron–shōraino gyōkei no tame ni–[Methodology in the consideration in the legal status of sentenced persons – for future administration of punishment]. *Keihōzasshi, Vol. 21, No* 1, 2.

Kamoshita, M. (2006). *Zenteishingyōkeihōyōron [Complete Guide to the Newly Revised Law Administration of Punishment Law].* Tokyo: Tokyo Horei Publishing. 370.

Gostin, L. O. (1991). Compulsory Treatment for Drug-dependent Persons: Justifications for a Public Health Approach to Drug Dependency. *The Milbank Quarterly, 69(4)*, 573–587.

Hamai, K. (2014). Shōnenjiken no saibaninsaiban de gironsarerubekikoto–shōnenin to shōnenkeimusho no chigai o chūshin–[What should be debated at lay judge trails in juvenile cases–focusing on the difference between juvenile institutions and juvenile prisons]. *Quarterly Keiji Bengo, No.78.* 125–126.

Hayashi, M. (2016). Keijisesaku to rippō [Criminal policy and lawmaking]. *Tsumi to Batsu* [Crime and Punishment] *Vol 53*, No 4.

Hayashi, M., Kitamu, A. and Natori, T. (2017). *Chikujōkaisetsu Keijshūyōshisetsuhō [Annotated Commentary Penal Detention Institution Law]* (3rd edition). Tokyo: Yuhikaku Publishing. 499–502. (1st edition published in 2010).

Ishizuka, S. (2008). Sengokangokuhōkaiseishi to hishūyōshashogūhō–kaikaku no tōtatsuten toshite no jukeisha no shutaisei–[History of post-war Prison Law amendments and Inmate Treatment Law–The autonomy of sentenced persons as the goal of reform. *Hōritsujihō Vol 80*, No 9, 53–57.

Kawaide, T. (2016). Jiyūkei ni okeru kyōseishori no hōtekiichizukeni tsuite [On the legal status of correctional treatment in imprisonment]. *Keisei, Vo. 127*, No. 4, 14–15.

Matsumiya, T. (2017). *Jiyūkei no Tanitsuka* to keibatsumokuteki/gyōkeimokuteki ['Unification of Imprisonment' and aim of punishment/aim of administration of punishment]. *Hōritsujiho Vol. 89*, No. 4, 79.

Matsumoto, T. & Imamura, F. (2015). *SMARPP-24 - Busshitsūshiyōshōgaichiryō Puroguramu* [SMARPP-24- Substance Use Disorder Treatment Program. Tokyo: Kongoshuppan.

Maruyama, Y. (2010). Shanaishogū no aratana hōkōsei–yakubutsujihansha o chūshin ni–[A new direction for community based treatment–a focus on drug offenders]. *Ryukokuhōgaku*, Vol. 43, No. 1, 176–208.

Maruyama, Y. (2013). Yakubutsushiyōsha ni taisuru kei no ichibu no shikōyūyose-ido–kei no kobetsuka to ichibuyūyo [The suspended sentence system of partial imprisonment for drug users–the individualization of imprisonment and partial suspension]. *Rissho Law Review, Vol. 46*, No. 1–2, 87–199.

Maruyama, Y. (2015). *Keijishihō ni okeru Yakubutsuizonchiryō Puroguramu– 'Kaifuku' o meguru Kenri to Gimu–[Drug Dependency Treatment Programs in Criminal Justice–Rights and Obligations Surrounding 'Recovery']*. Tokyo: Nippon Hyoron Sha.

Maruyama, Y. (2015). 'Porutogaru no yakubatsu seisaku chōsa hōkoku/2014–2015 [Investigative report of drug policy in Portugal/2014–2015]. Rissho Law Review, Vol. 49*, No. 2, 196–234.

Maruyama, Y. (2018). Keijishihō ni okeru yakubutsuizonchiryō puroguramu no igi–kaifuku suru kenri to gimu–[The significance of drug dependency treatment programs in criminal justice–the right and obligation to recover]. *Keihō Zasshi*, Vol 57, No. 2, 229–247.

Ministry of Justice Conference for the Recidivism Prevention Promotion Plan 'Recidivism Prevention Promotion Plan (December 15, 2017)' http://www.moj.go.jp/content/001242753.pdf (last accessed June 30, 2018).

O' Malley, P. &nd Valverde, M. (2004). Pleasure, Freedom and Drugs: of 'Pleasure'

in Liberal Governance of Drug and Alcohol Consumption. *Sociology, Vol. 38*. No. 1, 25–42.
Parsons, T. (1964). *Social Structure and Personality*. New York: New York Free Press, 1964. 〔*Takeda*, R., et al. (1973). (trans). *Shakaikōzō to Pāsonaritei*. Tokyo: Shinsensha. (Special edition published in 1985)〕.
Satomi, A. (2009). Dōkizuke mensetsuhō (mae)–kihontekina kangaekata [Motivational interview methods (first part)–the fundamental way of thinking]. *Keisei, Vol. 120*, No. 6, 98–104.
Togawa, E. (2009). Dōkizuke mensetsuhō (gō)–kōseijitsumu ni okeru jissen– [Motivational interview methods (second part)–implementation in correctional practice]. *Keisei, Vol. 120*, No. 7, 114–119.
Tomiyama, T. (2017). Keijishisetsu ni okeru jiyūkei no shikkō to kyōseishogū no ichizuke [The execution of imprisonment in penal institutions and the status of correctional treatment]. *Tsumi to Batsu* [Crime and Punishment], *Vol. 54*, No. 2, 2–4.
Yoshioka, K. (2008). Kangokuhō no kaisei to keijishūyōshisetsu no tenbō [The amendment of the Prison Act and the outlook for penal detention facilities]. *Keijiseisakugaku no Taikei* [Outline of Criminal Policy Studies]. Tokyo: Gendaijinbunsha. 3–17.
Young, J. (1999). *The Exclusive Society: Social Exclusion, Crime and Difference in Late Modernity*. London: SAGE Publications.
Young, J. (2007). *The Vertigo of Late Modernity*. London: SAGE Publications. [Kinoshita, C., Nakamura, Y., & Maruyama, M. (trans.) (2008). *Kōkikindai no Memai*. Seidosha].
Report of the study group on the state of criminal law regarding young persons. (n. d.). Retrieved June 30, 2018, from http://www.moj.go.jp/content/001210649.pdf, 4–16.
Treatment and Care of People with Drug Use Disorders in Contact with the Criminal Justice System: Alternatives to Conviction or Punishment. Retrieved June 30, 2018, from http://www.unodc.org/unodc/en/drug-prevention-and-treatment/treatment-and-care-of-people-with-drug-use-disorders-in-contact-with-the-criminal-justice-system_-alternatives-to-conviction-or-punishment.html.
Liberal Democratic Policy Research Council (n. d.). *Recommendation concerning the Age of Adulthood*. Retrieved June 30, 2018, from http://jimin.ncss.nifty.com/pdf/news/policy/130566_1.pdf.
http://www.moj.go.jp/content/001210649.pdf.
United Nations Standard Minimum Rules for the Treatment of Prisoners (Mandela Rules). (trans. by Prison Human Rights Centre). Retrieved June 30, 2018, from https://www.penalreform.org/wp-content/uploads/2016/12/Nelson-Mandela-Rules_Japanese_final.pdf.

Is Social Security Reform Really Willing to Deal with Poverty?

Ju Kaneko

Abstract

In Japan, the growing issue of poverty has been in the spotlight since 2000. Due to the government's Social Security Reform, the state of anti-poverty policy, including the public assistance system, has come into question, and new structures (philosophies and systems) for supporting poor and needy persons have started to be introduced. This movement is not unrelated to ideological discussions and trends occurring in social security policy in the West and East Asia.

While presenting trends in poverty research and social security policy (specifically, anti-poverty policies) in Japan and abroad, this paper first confirms the kinds of restructuring of social security systems recently taking place in various countries in light of conceptual/ideological discussion and political/economic background. Second, this paper presents and assesses movements in specific social security policies in Japan and abroad, while referencing frameworks for ideological discussion such as basic income theory. Third, the challenges that remain in Japan's anti-poverty policy are examined based on the above discussion by contrasting them with social security policies abroad, particularly focusing on problems regarding minimum subsistence and income redistribution.

Introduction: Awareness of Issues and Research Objectives

Japanese anti-poverty policy was developed with a focus on a public assistance system (Public Assistance Act [1946]) which combined minimum subsistence (economic benefits) with support (social work to provide support with living and employment). This public assistance system was designed as comprehensive social assistance and was operated as a social security safety net for coping comprehensively with the diverse forms of poverty. However, this form of public assistance, which was effectively weighted toward economic assistance, came under question. New anti-poverty policies began to be developed through government social security reforms against the background of increasing poverty, particularly in the mid-1990s and beyond, and neo-liberalism. These policies were strikingly apparent in the strengthening of a workfare program called "jobseeker support" and the introduction of "the self-reliance support system for needy persons" (Act for Supporting the Self-reliance of Needy Persons [2015]), which partially replaced and supplemented public assistance.

These changes are thought to have been implemented with significant impact from anti-poverty policy trends and ideological discourse in Europe and North America, including the movement toward strengthening the guarantee of services (or "intervention") for the poor, unemployed and low income earners, who are regarded as requiring livelihood support, which is also referred to as workfare and activation, in addition to monetary benefits for economic poverty. This trend emphasizes not only monetary benefits, but also services (the term "support" is used in Japan). Such service-focused initiatives were also being developed in Japan under the names of "jobseeker support" and "social inclusion" in the 2000s and beyond. It can be said that the self-reliance support system for needy persons truly embodies the ideology and incorporates its substance. Also having impact was the trend toward introducing more universal and rational income guarantee systems (jobseeker's allowance, tax credits and tax benefits, minimum guaranteed pension, etc.) rather than the highly selective public assistance, which is associated with stigma and the related ideological discussions (basic income theory, negative income tax theory, etc.). Although it has been stated that economic benefits and "support" were implemented in combination in Japan, some researchers have pointed out the need for them to be separated, making income security into a more rational system.

It can be said that the development of such anti-poverty policies was generally evaluated positively in Japan as an effort to build new mechanisms for guaranteeing minimum subsistence to replace conventional public assistance, which was high selective. However, any evaluation of the outcomes of such new anti-poverty policies amid the promotion of reform to the social security system based on neo-liberalism, which champions the "marketization" of welfare, needs to be carefully discussed.

In this paper, I will first examine the characteristics seen in the emergence of the poverty problem in Japan and the nature of the social security policy (in particular, the anti-poverty policy) that was developed based on social structure and ideology. Secondly, taking the perspective of "marketization" as the characteristic of the anti-poverty policies implemented in 2010 and beyond in particular, I will show that these policies were developed against a background of neo-liberalism, leading to operation with an emphasis on cost-effectiveness and reduced costs. Thirdly, based on the above, I will examine a converse strengthening of "selectivity" and "managerialism" in social assistance and the loss of the minimum subsistence guarantee perspective in the development of Japan's new anti-poverty policy.

1. Poverty and Social Security Policy in Japan in the 1990s and Beyond

1.1 Rapid Development of "Poverty" in Japan

"Poverty" rapidly came to be recognized as a social problem in Japan in the second half of the 1990s. As Japan concentrated on expanding and maintaining its industrial economy from the 1950s through the first part of the 1990s, it had managed to avoid confronting the problems of poverty, unemployment and low incomes despite experiencing the oil crisis. Problems such as workers in irregular employment, the working poor, and single mothers were overlooked as Japan long maintained full-time full employment premised on an industrial economy and families based on gender norms.

Subsequently, Japan entered a prolonged recession accompanying changes in its industrial structure, and the aging of its population entered the severe stage at the same time (the aging rate rose sharply from 14% in 1994 to 23% in 2010). In the early 2000s, unemployment and irregular employment became social problems due to an increase in redundancies and flexible employment, and the issues of a sharp expansion in homelessness ("rough sleepers") in urban areas and youth poverty (NEET: "not in employment, education or training") were discussed. In addition, as social welfare philosophy turned to deinstitutionalization, disabled people and the elderly were removed from social hospitalization and came to live alone or with family support in the community. With inadequate welfare services for such vulnerable people, families were expected to be responsible for their care. As a result, poverty involving families increased, and the problems of family abuse and violence and those of young carers emerged. This "new poverty," featuring abuse, violence, isolation and exclusion of long-term unemployed people, homeless people, and elderly people, suddenly appeared at the center of Japan's social problems.

Due to the sharp increase in "new poverty," research questioning the concept and semantic content of poverty drew attention starting in the 2000s. Much of this research was strongly influenced by British and French social exclusion theory, and it was argued that a shift from economic poverty to "relational poverty" had also occurred in Japan (Spicker, 2007; Bhalla and Lapeyre, 2004; Iwata, 2008). In addition, the significance of "inclusion" as opposed to exclusion was discussed as a part of the problem with calls for guaranteed participation and entry (Miyamoto, 2004).

The concept of social exclusion has come to be used favorably to direct the policy known as workfare in the EU and individual countries since the 2000s (Bhalla and Lapeyre, 2004). However, it is also a concept that justifies passive policy on economic benefits for the poor, and has a tendency to be used in conservative politics to reduce the problem of income redistribution to an issue of inequality in employment opportunities, thus portraying poverty as merely personal (Lister, 2004; Byrne, 1999).

Thus, the argument that initiatives focused on "employment" and not only on economic benefits are essential to address poverty attracted attention in Japan as well. As a policy to address social exclusion, more emphasis has come to be placed on the guarantee of "recognition," that is initiatives that secure a place of residence and encourage social participation, than on the redistribution of income.

1.2 Inability of Social Security Structure to Deal with Poverty

One of the reasons for the focus on social exclusion theory is related to a multi-disciplinary discussion of the fact that Japan's social security system contains "structural issues" that were created historically. Social security in Japan was completed in the early 1960s as a system with a two-fold structure of social insurance for all citizens and public assistance (the framework for that had been established in the 1930s). It was considered that universal social insurance primarily supported independence for full-time workers and their families, while selective public assistance was mainly a residual assistance system for those without the ability to work and those without relatives. Moreover, these policies assumed labor norms that stress independence through full employment and working, gender roles based on the male breadwinner household model, and a nation state with no immigration.

Social insurance is stratified with a two-fold structure involving pension, health and unemployment insurance proportional to remuneration for employees, and pension and health insurance for farmers, the self-employed, and "other citizens."

Despite the term employees, it basically assumes coverage for full-time workers (male breadwinners) and their families, while part-time workers and people in irregular employment are treated as "other citizens." It is stressed that the pension system based on the insurance principle, as well as the increase in the number of people in irregular employment, have meant an increase in the number of people at risk of having no pension. In addition, with no "unemployment benefits" for farmers, the self-employed, and people in irregular employment, public assistance also made no attempt to cover the unemployed and the working poor (Kaneko, 2017).

Social assistance was operated in an extremely residual manner based on the package of benefits under the public assistance system. The recipient rate of the system operated on the principle of selectivism stood at 0.7% at its lowest in 1995 and finally exceeded 1.0% in 2003 (and 1.6% even in 2017). The public assistance system also includes publicly funded health care and housing benefits (rent subsidies). However, it is practically impossible for these special benefits to be provided by themselves (single payments), and only the "limited poor" who pass all the asset requirements and family support requirements can receive the public assistance package in exchange for the stigma.

The media has frequently reported on "incidents" in which public assistance is operated excessively only for people with no capacity for work and assistance has been terminated when there was some capacity for work, resulting in deaths at home as people were unable to get food or medicine or in which applications from the homeless have been rejected due to the lack of a residence. If "people with work capacity" fall into poverty, they are called the working poor. These people cannot easily access public assistance, and there is no system for guaranteeing their income in Japan.

This public assistance system, which could be termed the only social assistance, was characterized by selectivity and a residual nature through its rigid operation. In particular, many of the workers in irregular employment and working poor who fall through the net of social insurance but have some savings or family considered able to support them are unable to pass the requirements and are thus ineligible for public assistance. The unemployed, people in irregular employment, and those referred to as the working poor are effectively not included in the scope of public assistance, and with no other system for them, poverty is becoming more severe without any relief.

1.3 Various Problems of the Rigid Social Assistance System

The inability of the social assistance system to respond to diverse forms of poverty is a problem that has long been debated in Japan. It has been argued that while the basis of the problem is the system structure related to the requirements for receipt and the means test, operational issues in the administrative agencies that actually implement the system form a "dark area" that further exacerbates the structural issue (Kaneko, 2017). At the heart of the operational issues lies the tactic adopted by the administrative agencies, termed the "*mizugiwa* (waterfront) strategy," by which they refuse to accept applications for public assistance at welfare offices without conducting screening. This involves inappropriate actions such as conducting interviews with the needy who consult welfare offices that deter them from applying for assistance or sending them home without giving them the application forms. In some cases, intimidating interviewers are assigned to welfare offices to make applicants reluctant to apply by encouraging them to seek employment and providing ambiguous (or untrue) representations about family support and assets requirements.

Although public assistance operates in such a rigid manner, the number of recipients has continued to rise since the 2000s. The reasons for this are the increasing severity described previously, particularly the sharp increase in such problems as long-term unemployment, the increase in the number of people in irregular employment, the aging society, and the increase in homelessness.

The Democratic Party of Japan coalition government, which took office in 2009, attempted to improve operations to implement appropriate public assistance for the homeless and working poor. As a result, the number of recipients increased sharply. However, since the Liberal Democratic Party coalition government returned in 2012, curbs on social security expenses (like the UK austerity policy) and operation that restrains public assistance have been implemented once again. The recipient rate for public assistance exceeded 1.7% in 2015, but subsequently fell for the first time in 20 years in 2017, standing at around 1.6% again (Figure 1).

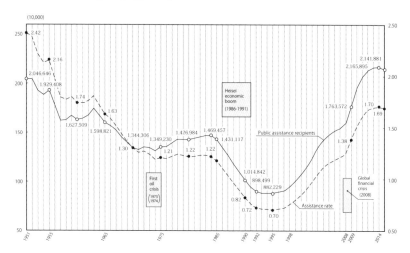

Fig.1 Changes in the number of public assistance recipients and recipient rates (Source: Ministry of Health, Labour and Welfare)

In 2010, the Ministry of Health, Labour and Welfare announced estimates for the take-up rate. Where the take-up rate is defined as "the percentage of households receiving public assistance out of the number of low income households (considering income and assets)," the take-up rate for public assistance was determined to be 32.1% (Ministry of Health, Labour and Welfare, 2010). However, according to research by Kensaku Tomuro, making an estimate based on materials such as the Employment Status Survey and Survey on Public Assistance Recipients, the take-up rate was calculated at 15.5% (2012). According to this research, Toyama Prefecture has the lowest take-up rate at 6.5%, while Osaka Prefecture has the highest take-up rate at 34.2%. Toyama Prefecture is the prefecture with the lowest recipient rate for public assistance while Osaka Prefecture is the prefecture in the highest category. In other words, there was found to be a positive correlation between the take-up rate and the public assistance recipient rate by region (Tomuro, 2016).

In general, a low recipient rate for public assistance has been accepted as a demonstration that poverty is not a serious problem. However, this research clearly showed the problem that recipient rates are lower in regions where public assistance is operated in a rigid manner.

2. Anti-Poverty Policy Reform and Its Political Objectives

2.1 A New Development in Anti-Poverty Policy: Strengthening "Support for Independence"

The period since the 2000s has not been without opportunities for "improvement" of Japan's problem-riddled anti-poverty policy. One of these opportunities is the reform of the public assistance system, and another opportunity is the creation of anti-poverty policies outside of the public assistance system.

The 2004 report delivered by the Expert Committee on the Future of the Public Assistance System, which had been established by the Ministry of Health, Labour and Welfare, formed the key impetus that initiated the reform of the public assistance system. This report presented a reform plan to reconstruct public assistance into a system that makes it "easier to enter and exit," and recommended further strengthening "support for self-reliance" of recipients. Strengthening of "support for self-reliance" here marked an intention to enhance various programs such as workfare and activation to promote reform with a focus on "services" in the name of support for self-reliance rather than purely economic benefits.

As a result of this discussion, the services (support for self-reliance) provided in the form of the public assistance system have been changing since the second half of the 2000s. The Support Service Programs for Self-Reliance was introduced in fiscal 2005, social workers with more expertise than in the past were hired, and the outsourcing of services was promoted. Employment support was emphasized in particular, and welfare offices (public assistance benefit service centers) and public employment security office (employment service centers) were partially integrated, with the assignment of experts.

Under the Support Service Programs for Self-Reliance, local governments were encouraged to actively use private-sector service providers. Private-sector service providers have gradually come to be used not only in employment support but also in areas such as employment preparation support, education and vocational training, financial management support, and social participation support for mentally disabled people. The Personal Support Service implemented since 2009 is also a model project that utilizes private-sector service providers while offering one-stop support that matches the needs of people in poverty. Model projects have been implemented in 27 regions nationwide with the support of NPOs and NGOs (Okuda, et. al., 2014).

2.2 The Introduction of the Self-reliance Support System for Needy Persons

As the second reform, new anti-poverty policies were introduced to replace and supplement the public assistance system. One of these policies is the self-reliance support system for needy persons implemented in 2015. This system aims to promote independence of needy persons through the provision of various programs such as independence counselling and support and employment preparation assistance as well as paying housing benefits to needy persons. The eligible "needy persons" are defined as "persons at risk" of falling into poverty (receipt of public assistance payments), effectively including people in poverty while also assuming the low income group just above those in poverty.

In addition, the self-reliance support system for needy persons made it possible for the government to provide financial backup for a range of private support for the poor provided in the community (support for the homeless, housing assistance, children's cafeterias, meals-on-wheels, learning support). Local governments were able to provide independence advice and support programs and subcontract them to private-sector service providers (NPOs, NGOs and for-profit companies, etc.), including "employment preparation support" and other optional programs.

Among the various programs, the independence advice and support program was stipulated as mandatory for local governments. Local governments have to implement an independence advice and support program based on advice and support for employment and other types of independence and the creation of plans for the utilization of the program. Previously in Japan, the application and welfare center for public assistance of each local government dealt with intake consultations from people in poverty, and they tended to deploy the negative tactics described previously. Under the independence advice and support program, intake consultations can be outsourced to private-sector service providers. In the statistics for 2017, 61.0% of local governments have outsourced the independence advice and support program to a private-sector service provider (Ministry of Health, Labour and Welfare, 2017).

Another mandatory program for local governments under the same law is a mechanism for providing housing benefits to needy people of working age who have lost their home due to losing their job. This is a system for the payment of the cash equivalent of rent (public assistance criteria), and can be described as the first systematic public housing benefit in Japan outside of public assistance. However, actual use was only 6,631 new payments in fiscal 2015 (Ministry of Health, Labour and Welfare, 2017).

On the other hand, four programs stipulated as optional were employment preparation support, temporary livelihood support, household finance advice and support, and learning support, and there is a range of programs for each depending on the local government. For example, the household finance advice and support programs provide support for the management of household finances and support related to rent and tax delinquency, debt consolidation and loan facilitation. Many local governments also provide integrated loan and financial management services called the livelihood and welfare loan program, which can also be said to be a program that involves many social work functions. Many local governments organize learning sessions for low income households as learning support programs to address childhood poverty and the "reproduction of poverty."

Thus, in comparison with the public assistance system, the self-reliance support system for needy persons is based on a group of systems that focus more on services (support) than economic benefits, and its potential has been discussed (Goishi, et. al., 2017). However, I would like to evaluate the system below, taking into account how it is actually forced to operate.

2.3 Reform of the Social Security System Focused on Cost Effectiveness

Anti-poverty policies to strengthen "support for self-reliance," developed as described above, exist, but what position are they considered to occupy within the government's overall social security policy? In considering this, I would like to give some attention to the Social Security System Reform Bill (2012) and the Report of the National Council on Social Security System Reform (2013). Both of these set out "building a sustainable social security system that maintains the balance between benefits and burden" as the philosophy for social security in the future. Based on this philosophy of sustainability, the government stressed that curbing benefits and increasing the burden on citizens will be essential in order to maintain the existing system. In addition, it clearly showed that social policy is a part of an economic policy aimed at stimulating the market economy.

This philosophy has also been guiding anti-poverty policies. For example, the strengthening of "appropriate implementation" of public assistance (tightening of application procedures and strengthening of employment support), revision (lowering) of the public assistance threshold, and the reforms that include greater use of private-sector service providers in anti-poverty policies have aspects of being implemented in conjunction with the curbing of benefits and marketization in anti-poverty policies.

Among these, the idea that revision was equal to the lowering of the public assistance threshold caused controversy. The public assistance threshold, which is also the poverty line, has been progressively lowered since the mid-2010s. The government has downwardly revised the public assistance threshold, thereby reducing the number of public assistance recipients, and poverty has once again been made invisible. Some see the reduction in recipients while lowering the public assistance threshold as a "political achievement," but it is natural that the number of recipients will decrease if the threshold is lowered.

This lowering of the public assistance threshold was driven by the Ministry of Finance and the Cabinet. The grounds for lowering it were the populist ones of considering the motivation of the working poor to work and ensuring that working people do not "lose out," with the approach taken to consider the balance between the consumption of households in receipt of public assistance in comparison with that of low income earners not in receipt of public assistance. In other words, households in receipt of public assistance were regarded as having a higher standard of living than low income earners not in receipt of public assistance, and the government concluded that the public assistance threshold should be lowered based on the concept of so-called less-eligibility (Kaneko, 2017). Again, this confirms that public assistance has failed in democratic operation and implementation.

Another trend of the reforms is the focus on cost effectiveness through the marketization of social assistance. For example, the Plan to Advance Economic and Fiscal Revitalization included in the government's Basic Policies decided by the Cabinet in June 2016 set out curbing social security benefits and the "industrialization" of social security as key pillars. In addition, in order to achieve this, the plan aimed to incorporate a number of management techniques into the service provision system for public assistance. By doing this, the aim to control the total costs related to each field of social security in addition to pursuing the implementation of benefits and services with a focus on measurement of results through cost effectiveness were set out as important objectives (Kawakami, 2015). As shown in these government objectives, it can be said that social security policy became incorporated into the trend of neo-liberalism aimed at curbing benefits and "marketization."

The Economic and Fiscal Revitalization Action Program compiled by the Council on Economic and Fiscal Policy in December 2015 added further momentum to this trend. The "visualization" in the program referred to making both "amount of public money spent" (inputs) and the results (outputs) visible to demonstrate more effective policy implementation. In addition, the program emphasized a "focus on necessary expenditures with high policy effects," drawing a distinction between expenditure that should be prioritized and expenditure that should be curbed.

The Action Program broke down each of the reforms set out in the Plan to Advance Economic and Fiscal Revitalization, their targets and time schedules in a reform schedule in an attempt to implement the policies effectively. A trend had been observed toward the introduction of private-sector management techniques such as New Public Management (NPM) and Private Finance Initiative (PFI) into social security policy since the 1980s. However, the Action Plan has now adopted the key performance indicators (KPIs) management technique in the reform schedule.

For example, the Council on Economic and Fiscal Policy's Reform Schedule 2016 Revised Edition set out concrete policy objectives and the KPIs for each one. The use of KPIs is considered to be a management technique that clearly states policy targets and fiscal cost effectiveness as numerical values in order to "visualize" policy challenges and to confirm achievement levels in detail (Kawakami, 2016). For example, the Reform Schedule set out a total of 18 KPIs for the "Public Assistance, etc." category. Specifically, there were numerical targets that included "60% participation rate in employment support programs by fiscal 2018" and "100% formulation of generic drug use promotion plans by local governments aimed at rationalization of healthcare assistance."

Satoshi Kawakami has organized the characteristics of KPIs as a management technique into the following three points (Kawakami, 2016).

(1) Areas that cannot be quantifiably identified are excluded and not indexed.
(2) Since the indicator is for the purpose of achieving and improving management targets, corporate headquarters basically manage and operate it in an integrated manner.
(3) A major precondition is use of ICT, which promotes big data management, monitoring, and use of analysis results.

The fact that areas that cannot be quantified are excluded produces the problem that support with outcomes that are difficult to identify in a simple quantification of outcomes is disregarded. For example, no matter how much a private-sector service provider offers courteous, face-to-face support and provides comfortable, secure places to live, it may only be evaluated on "employment rate" under the KPIs.

In addition, the Action Program made local governments the unit of reform and employed a method of encouraging greater efficiency through autonomous reform by stirring up competition between local governments while conducting comparative analysis of policy effects between them. For example, the items that contribute to "lowering costs" such as "the percentage of people who were able to find employment through employment support" are evaluated in a one-dimensional manner without taking account of circumstances such as the population distribution and employment situation in the region as well as social resources. This manner of policy development that is excessively focused on cost-effectiveness gives rise to the issue that will be considered next.

3. The Challenge of Anti-Poverty Policy in the Face of Fiscal Austerity and Managerialism

3.1 Client-Focused, Business-Like Anti-Poverty Policy?

Based on policy development to date, I will now consider risks regarding the challenges arising in Japan's anti-poverty policies (the public assistance system and the self-reliance support system for needy persons), particularly the marketization of anti-poverty policies leading to operations with a priority on cost-effectiveness and reduced costs.

As a trend in social policy in each country since the 1980s, Sarah Banks has discussed the observation of policy development with a focus on measurement of cost-effectiveness in service provision, including New Public Management (NPM) and value for money. This approach features the following five points (Banks, 2012, pp. 186–7).

(1) Marketization: a concern to offer 'customer choice', alongside increasing efficiency and competitiveness in service delivery.
(2) Consumerism: a concern to offer a consistent standard of service, linked to service users' rights and quality assurance.
(3) Managerialism: which seeks greater control over the work of employees.
(4) Authoritarianism: which emphasize the social control function of practitioners.
(5) Deprofessionalization: a process that entails characterizing social workers as officials carrying out agency policy and/or as sales brokers.

This discussion indicates that the reform of service provision in social security also has a significant impact on social work setting. According to Banks, rationalistic management techniques such as "the production of quality standards, procedural manuals and assessment schedules" have been introduced into the support setting through the development of modern social security policy in addition to establishment of goals for service and support and measurement of the performance of social workers (ibid., p. 186). In other words, it is becoming possible to extend mechanisms for the control and management of users into every corner of social work and support settings for fiscal and resource purposes.

Banks offers the critique that through this promotion of enhanced management, a "client-focused, business-like model" has become entrenched in social work settings, giving rise to cost containment (cost-saving) measures and a "target culture" (a culture involving the setting of targets and pursuit of their quickest achievement). Moreover, she points out that "management by results" symbolized by cost-effectiveness takes the approach of depersonalizing and privatizing welfare services in addition to being linked to imperative demands for cost reductions (ibid., p. 189).

Thus, amid the implementation of economic and fiscal policies that give cost containment the greatest value in accordance with the "cost reduction imperative," social policy and social work that produces the maximum performance at low cost is sought. This means that management and control-oriented reforms that value fiscal rationalization will be developed. It leaves major challenges when seen from the perspective of ensuring satisfaction of the needs and protection of the rights of users as well as improving quality of life. As discussed in this paper, Japan's anti-poverty policies, and the self-reliance support system for needy persons in particular, are at risk of approaching this "client-focused, business-like model."

3.2 Further "Targeting" of the Poor and Managerialism

Moreover, the fact that social security system reforms have been carried out in combination with "marketization" has further increased this risk. While controlling both the inputs (finance) and outputs (results) of private-sector service providers, the government is also extending its authority across the community. For example, a private-sector service provider that needs to consider organizational and business survival is forced to target and guide users. Consequently, service providers might positively coordinate employment support services for a person with high potential for employment, but a person with low potential for employment may be "passed around" from service provider to service provider. In other words, it yields targeting of the parties eligible for services. Targeting is conducted so that clients who are likely to produce results from the outset are accepted as eligible for support while those who seem unlikely to produce results are excluded from eligibility for support ("cream skimming").

Can private-sector service providers guarantee independence while receiving government funding? Can they listen to participants without being trapped by paternalism amid the demand for results? The more outsourcing is increased and the more organizations take on large paid staffs, substantial assets and social responsibilities, the more they will be unable to escape from this loop.

Although the development of social security policies focused on cost effectiveness appear to have achieved strong performance through the visualization of the "business-like" results (fiscal rationalization) of the policies, because they are introduced in combination with lowering costs, they serve to leverage power over service users and social workers, giving rise to management and control as distinct from meeting needs (Kaneko, 2017). Introducing business management methods into social security will not be the best way to carry out an anti-poverty policy without paternalism.

3.3 Minimum Subsistence Guarantee Missing from Discussion

Finally, I will consider whether the development of Japan's anti-poverty policies against the background of fiscal austerity and managerialism can meet the needs of the poor.

Japan's public assistance system uses an old style of social assistance that integrates economic benefits with services. By contrast, the self-reliance support system for needy persons is a system centered on the "support" of workfare and activation, which is considered as achieving differentiation from public assistance. In other words, through the introduction of the system, the path of symbolic separation of "benefits" from "support" was selected for Japan's anti-poverty policy. Most of the "benefits" are limited and concentrated in public assistance, while "support" has been enriched in the form of the self-reliance support system for needy persons.

There is discussion in Japan about several advantages and disadvantages of an anti-poverty policy that separates "benefits" and "support." However, the policy of "separation" should be implemented as a part of rationalization in order to meet the "needs" of the poor. In other words, there is a need to reaffirm that rationalization is not for fiscal, management and control purposes (Kaneko, 2017). With regard to the "benefit," the need for creating a universal social security system beyond the constraints of public assistance has been discussed. For example, the basic income theory has been debated with a certain reality, rather than idealistic thought, in recent discussion in

Japan. Basic income here is not limited to a system that provides a minimum subsistence guarantee (or the so-called full basic income), but rather a discussion of reconfiguring income redistribution mechanisms, including the tax system and allowances. In recent debate, such concepts as a universal benefit for people deprived of work through the threat from artificial intelligence (AI), and the concepts of tax deductions for the working poor and a minimum guaranteed pension for elderly people who do not have a pension have been discussed as similar to that of the basic income. This concept of an income guarantee has been under focus as being more rational and economically efficient than social assistance. It must be observed that the perspective of a minimum subsistence guarantee is missing.

With regards to the "support," as seen in this paper, outsourcing to the community and the private sector accompanied by lowering cost should be avoided, and there should not be excessive reliance on evaluation based on the perspectives of cost effectiveness and value for money. The government and private-sector service providers should build trusting relationships to provide for the needs of parties receiving support as a right rather than based on paternalism.

Today when the discussion of social security policy has increased opportunities to speak in the logic and terms of the "market" and "finance," I would like to once again affirm the need for a comprehensive discussion of the future of anti-poverty policy from the perspective of a minimum subsistence as a right and support as a right.

References

Banks, S. (2012). *Ethics and Values in Social Work*, Macmillan.
Byrne, D. (1999). *Social Exclusion*, Open University Press.
Bhalla, A. S. and Lapeyre, F. (2004). *Poverty and Exclusion in a Global World*, 2nd edition, Macmillan.
Ferguson, I. (2008). *Radical Social Work: Challenging Neo-Liberalism and Promoting Social Justice,* Sage.
Goishi, N., Iwama, N., Nishioka, M., and Arita, A. (eds.) (2017). *Seikatsu Konkyusha Shien de Shakai wo Kaeru* (Transforming Society through Support for the Needy), Horitsu Bunka Sha.
Iwata, M. (2008). *Shakaiteki Haijo – Sanka no Ketsujo Fukakuna Kizoku* (Social

Exclusion – Lack of Participation, Uncertain Belongingness), Yuhikaku Publishing Co., Ltd.

Kaneko, J. (2017). *Nyumon Hinkonron – Sasaeau/Tasukeau Shakai wo Tsukuru Tameni* (Poverty Studies: An Introduction), Akashi Shoten.

Kawakami, S. (2015). "*Keizai Zaisei Unei to Kaikaku no Kihon Hoshin (Honebuto no Hoshin) 2015 Kara Yomitoku Kozo Kaikaku no Gendankai*" (The Current Stage of Structural Reform Based on *Analysis of Basic Policy on Economic and Fiscal Management and Reform (Basic Policy) 2015)* in *Chingin to Shakaihosho No. 1643*.

Kawakami, S. (2016). "*Keizai Zaisei Saisei Akushon Puroguramu to KPI Kaikaku*" (Economic and Fiscal Revitalization Action Program and KPI Reform) in *Chingin to Shakaihosho No. 1659*.

Ministry of Health, Labour and Welfare (2010). *Seikatsuhogo Kijunmiman no Teishotoku Setaisu no Suikei ni Tsuite* (April 9, 2010) (On Estimates of the Number of Low Income Households below the Social Assistance Threshold) https://www.mhlw.go.jp/stf/houdou/2r98520000005olm-img/2r98520000005oof. pdf (accessed June 24, 2018).

Ministry of Health, Labour and Welfare (2017). *Seikatsu Konkusha Jiristsu Shienho no Shiko Jokyo* (May 11, 2017) (Implementation Status of Act for Supporting the Self-reliance of Needy Persons) https://www.mhlw.go.jp/file/05-Shingikai-12601000-Seisakutoukatsukan-Sanjikanshitsu_Shakaihoshoutantou/0000164562.pdf (accessed June 28, 2018).

Lavalette, M. (ed.) (2011). *Radical Social Work Today: Social Work at the Crossroads*, Policy Press.

Lister, R. (2004). *Poverty*, Polity Press.

Miyamoto, T. (2004). "*Shuro Fukushi Wakufea*" (Work, Welfare and Workfare) in Shionoya, Y., Suzumura, K., and Goto, R., (eds.) *Fukushi no Kokyo Tetsugaku* (Public Philosophy of Welfare), University of Tokyo Press.

Miyamoto, T. (ed.) (2014). *Chiiki Hokatsu Kea to Seikatsu Hosho no Saihen* (Integrated Community Care and Restructuring of Social Assistance), Akashi Shoten.

Nakagawa, K. (1991). "*Kiteyokatta Fukushi Jimushoni*" (Welcome to the Welfare Office) in Bitou, H., Kinoshita, H., and Nakagawa, K., (eds.). *Dare mo Kakanakatta Seikatsu Hogoho* (The Public Assistance Act that Nobody Wrote), Horitsu Bunka Sha.

Okuda, T., Inazuki, T., Kakita, Y., and Tsutsumi, K. (2014). *Seikatsu Konkyusha e no Banso-gata Shien* (Accompanying-Style Support for Needy Persons), Akashi Shoten.

Spicker, P. (2007). *The Idea of Poverty*, Policy Press.

Tomuro, K. (2016). "*Todofukenbetsu no Hinkonritsu, Wakingupuaritsu, Kodomono Hinkonritsu, Hosokuritsu no Kento*" (Study into Poverty Rates, Rates of Working Poor, and Capture Rate by Prefecture), *Faculty of Literature & Social Sciences,*

Yamagata University Annual Research Report, No. 13.

Yoshinaga, A. (2015). *Sekikatsu Hogo 'Kaikaku' to Seizonken no Hosho* (Public Assistance 'Reform' and Guarantee of the Right to Existence), Akashi Shoten.

How Do Parents Communicate with Their Infants?
: The Function of Parental Proxy Talk in Pre-Verbal Communication

Yoriko Okamoto[1]
Yukie Sugano[2]
Reika Shouji[3]
Chie Takahashi[4]
Akiko Yagishita-Kawata[5]
Yayoi Aoki[6]
Ayuchi Ishikawa[7]
Miyako Kamei[8]
Manabu Kawata[9]
Osamu Suda[10]

Abstract

How do parents communicate with their infants before the infants learn to talk? It has been observed that the parents use Parental Proxy Talk (PPT) as if the speech came from the infants' own voice. In other words, PPT reflects their expectations of what the infants were thinking and feeling. The present study of PPT explored how PPT functions from birth to 15 months of age, and how PPT contributes to communication with pre-verbal infants. The results showed that there are three periods in the development of the use of PPT; (1) a gradual increase between 0 and 3 months, (2) a peak period from 6-9 months, and (3) a period of decreasing use of PPT from 12-15 months. The study also showed that PPT functions to support not only the pre-verbal infants but also parents themselves, e.g., in parents' emotion regulation.

Issue

To what extent can we communicate with infants who cannot yet talk? This research paper on the proxy talk used by parents examines how communication between pre-verbal infants and parents is constructed and how this communication develops.

When adults communicate with most other people, they use language and culturally-specific non-verbal means—in other words, expressions and gestures. But what do they use when talking to a pre-verbal infant? Communication between pre-verbal infants and parents is also built on asymmetrical relationships in terms of verbal and other communication skills, and in terms of cultural development on a non-verbal level (Adamson, Bakeman, Smith, & Walters, 1987). Miscommunication is an everyday occurrence even between adults, which demonstrates the complexity of exchanging thoughts and feelings. In a clearly asymmetrical relationship such as that between parent and infant, it seems communication would be nearly impossible. How do parents communicate with a pre-verbal infant? If we reexamine parent-infant communication from this perspective, we find that not only does the parent talk to the infant from the parent's perspective, but also articulates what the infant seems to be saying—in other words, the parent speaks from the infant's perspective as the infant's proxy.

Through this proxy talk, the parent verbalizes the thoughts and feelings of the infant, for example, saying "Yummy! ("*oishii*" in Japanese)" to the infant when he/she is eating or "Aah, clean and fresh!" when changing the baby's diaper. In this situation, even when the same word "yummy" is being used, the parent can confirm with the baby by asking "Is it yummy?" or stating "I bet it's yummy," and also speak from the infant's perspective with "mmm, yummy! ("oishii" in Japanese)" and even say "(We think it's) yummy, don't we ("*oishii-ne*" in Japanese)" from both the baby and the parent's own perspective (in other words, "our perspective")[11]. In this research, "proxy talk" refers to a method of utterances that includes the infant's perspective. Okamoto (2001) focuses on the parent's speech in communication with pre-verbal infants, and attempts to analyze their communication in terms of who the subject of the utterance is in the talk. The results showed that the parent's utterances are not a dichotomy between speech from the parent's perspective and speech from the child's perspective. Instead, it was found that the parent's utterances include four types of proxy talk: utterances from (only) the child's perspective (proxy talk from child's position), utterances from the perspective of both the child and the parent (proxy talk from parent-child position), utterances in which the perspective is vague (proxy talk from ambiguous position), and utterances in which the perspective shifts midway from parent to child or from child to parent (proxy talk from transitional position). Utterances that do not include the infant's perspective are not deemed proxy talk. So how does proxy talk function in communication between parent and child? This research delves into parent-child communication methods from the parent's perspective through proxy.

The research on communication in asymmetrical relationships during the pre-verbal stage is too numerous to list comprehensively. Research on interactional synchrony (Condon & Sander, 1974), imitation during the neonatal stage (Meltzoff & Moore, 1977; Field, Woodson, Greenberg, & Cohen, 1982), the infants' preference for facial stimulation (Fantz, 1961; Simon, Macchi, Turati, & Valenza, 2003), and intersubjectivity (Trevarthen, 1979; Newson, 1977) found that infants focus on the stimulation provided by the adult facing them and are then able to respond. This research describes the orientation of infants toward people. In research on infant-directed speech (IDS) (Jacobson, Boersma, Fields, & Olson,1983; Fernald et.al., 1989; Kitamura & Burnham, 2003; Bryant & Barrett, 2007), infants show a preference for IDS itself and the emotional tone of IDS (Fernald, 1985; Kitamura & Lam, 2009), indicating the role that IDS plays in regulating emotion (Trainor, Austin, & Desjardins, 2000) and directing attention (Kaplan, Goldstein, Huckeby, Owren, & Cooper, 1995). In other words, before infants understand the linguistic meaning of the speech directed at them, they react to IDS in their own way.

In this way, research on communication in the pre-verbal stage and IDS research shows that even in asymmetrical relationships, infants express directionality to people and the speech directed at themselves and can participate in communication.

However, the infants' actions that make this kind of communication are very undeveloped and undifferentiated. Communication is not taking place because of the contributions from the infant alone, but rather the adult is attaching meaning to the immature actions of the infant (for example, Kato, Kurebayashi, Yuki, 1992; Adamson et al., 1987; Kaye, 1979; Marcos, Ryckebusch, & Rabain-Jamin, 2003; Masuyama, 1991). Parents respond even to infant behavior that does not have any particular significance as if the infant is trying to convey something, and this helps the infant's consciousness emerge (Masuyama, 1991), while the parents' interpretation encourages developmental changes in the infant (Adamson et al., 1987). Valsiner (2007) calls this the "as-if" structure. Interpretations prompt the "as-if" nature. i.e., leaps in inference and organization of particular situations.

The proxy talk that we attempt to address in this research is formed on the back of this as-if structure. Parents act as proxies by speaking in the infant's stead, as if the infant is thinking and feeling what the parent voices. Given the asymmetrical relationship between parent and child, the thoughts and feelings of the infant given expression via proxy talk do not necessarily accurately reflect those of the infant, but are instead the result of the parent's leaps in inference and organization of the situation. In the sense that this leap compensates for the part that cannot be fully interpreted, it is similar to the semi-interpretation described by Okamoto (2001; 2008b), who studied proxy talk.

Moreover, proxy talk is the parent articulating the infant's voice. "Voice" is a concept derived from Mikhail Bakhtin and does not refer to the actual physical voice, but voice as a sociocultural personality (Wertsch, 1991; Holquist & Emerson, 1982). This kind of voice is initially borrowed from society, and the individual spiritual function expressed via the voice has its origins in the social communication process (Wertsch, 1991). The voice has an address directed toward it, and when people borrowed the voice accepts the cultural meaning accompanied by the emotions directed toward this address. Moreover, Hermans and his colleagues (Hermans, 2001; Hermans & Hermans-Jansen, 2003) mention that the "I-position," from the multiple different perspectives associated with this voice, forms the dialogical self through repeated dialogue. This concept provides a significant suggestion and also raises questions when considering the parent's proxy talk. Proxy talk certainly makes it easier for the voice as a sociocultural personality to be internalized during the infant's development while forming his/her dialogical self, and dialogue with these internalized voices forms the foundation for the infant's dialogical self. Given this, proxy talk has a major impact on cultural development, including the infant's emotional attitude. At the same time, whose is the voice spoken as a proxy for the infant's voice? Parents have not heard the infants' voices yet, so how are the infant's voices conceived? This brings to mind the leap in the "as-if" structure mentioned above (Valsiner, 2007). A parent cannot guess at the cultural voices of the infant, which they have not yet heard, without excesses and deficiencies, but the parent likely compensates for the infant's' immature behavior in creating a voice based on the parent's own lived experiences in that culture.

Children are born into particular regions, households, and historical times, and are guided by adults and elders (such as parents) who are accustomed to that community. While acquiring cultural voices, they are able to participate in the community. This process is not one in which children passively internalize culture in the community, but rather a process in which children appropriate cultural tools such as speech. At the same time, from the parent's perspective, this implies a process in which they use the cultural tools they have already acquired and have the chance to mold the existing culture anew, while adding their own interpretation of the infant's actions. Proxy talk is an internalized process of a child's cultural development, and at the same time, an externalized process of the parent's cultural experience. In other words, proxy talk is a cultural intermediation through which culture is transferred between parent and child. This research attempts to reexamine development as a process by which the infant participates in the cultural community (Rogoff, 2003) and a process that includes cultural transfer, not simply the infant's own personal history. Needless to say, it is difficult to approach cultural transfer between generations in this research. However, by examining the parent's proxy talk in detail, we can grasp the threads of the argument behind the externalization of the parent's cultural experience.

Given the above, this study aims to take another look at the functions that proxy talk play from the parent's perspective in communication between parents and pre-verbal infants between the ages of 0–15 months. We will discuss the externalization of the parent's cultural experience, which supports the process by which infants participate in the cultural community, and the possibility of internalization from the infant's perspective.

Method

Study participants

The study analyzes 12 pairs of mothers and infants living in the Tokyo suburbs who participated in a longitudinal study from pregnancy. Observational data from 0–15 months after birth is used. The average age of the mothers at birth was 29.2 (from 24–36years of age) and all of the children were firstborns (six boys and six girls). When the longitudinal study began from pregnancy, participants were recruited from the mother's class or both parents' class held by local cities and towns, and the study was explained in writing and at a panel that explained the observation. After the parents gave their informed consent, they were included in this study.

Study period

July 1997 to January 1999

Procedures

The authors visited the participants' homes for observation. The data was analyzed a total of six times, when the child was 0, 3, 6, 9, 12, and 15 months of age. The observation lasted 15–20 minutes, and the parent was instructed to play with the infant as usual, and there were no restrictions on toys other than those that make a loud noise and could affect the analysis. All of the processes were recorded on video with the parent's permission. The observers tried not to be involved in the parent-child interaction, but when the infant and parent seemed to be nervous and the observer was approached, the observer responded enough to keep the atmosphere natural (for details, refer to Okamoto, 2008a). The parts in which the observer responded were excluded from the analysis.

Analysis

The utterances and vocalizations between the parent and child and the contexts in the recorded scenes were transcribed. All of the utterances from the mother that could be discerned were given an ID number, and 50 utterances from the start of the observation were analyzed in each observation setting. The observation began after the recording started and the attention directed to the observer up until that point shifted to the play between parent and child. The starting part of the observation was included in the analysis because it is difficult for very young infants in particular to maintain a good mood as the observation time passes, and the observation began when the infant was calm. Fifty utterances were analyzed for each observation at the six time periods for the 12 pairs. In order to ensure that differences in the number of utterances by parents did not affect the overall analysis, the number of utterances was standardized in each case. Utterance units were identified by syntactic cut-off points or one second or more of silence.

First, we determined the perspective of the mother's utterances and identified the proxy talk in terms of who was the subject of the utterance. Based on Okamoto (2001; 2008b), each of the utterances was coded according to the four types of proxy talk and non-proxy talk. The specific categories were 1) proxy talk from child's position, 2) proxy talk from parent-child position, 3) proxy talk from ambiguous position, 4) proxy talk from transitional position, and 5) non-proxy talk. Non-proxy talk refers to utterances that do not include the infant's perspective, and the subject of these non-proxy utterances is not necessarily the parent (in subsequent analysis, it was found that the subject of the speech was occasionally a toy). A dichotomized category of proxy talk and non-proxy talk was not used because the utterances could include a vague and context-dependent perspective by nature (specifically, proxy talk from parent-child position, proxy talk from ambiguous position, and proxy talk from transitional position) in order to consider the utterances that broadly included the different infant's perspectives as proxy talk. The category definitions and examples are shown in Table 1. After the first author and third author discussed the category definitions beforehand, the coding work was divided up. The concordance rate for the two authors was considered for 10% of all of the data, showing that the concordance for the five categories was .90 and the non-proxy talk concordance was .92. In the case of disagreement, the author in charge of coding made the decision.

Table 1—Definitions of four types of proxy talk and non-proxy talk

Categories		Definitions	Examples
Proxy talk	Proxy talk from child's position	Proxy talk by the parent, who is speaking from the child's position with the child as the subject of the utterance	【Zero-month old baby girl and mother】When the mother stops breastfeeding, the mother asks the child if she wants to drink more. Asking "is your stomach full?," she brings her breast close to the child, but the child does not put it in her mouth. Seeing this, the mother uses proxy talk from the child's position, stating "*no more.*" Confirming by asking, "you don't need anymore?," she decides that they are done breastfeeding. 【Three-month old baby boy and mother】Hitting the baby's two hands together, the mother says "*clap clap clap*" several times.
	Proxy talk from the parent-child position	This is proxy talk by the parent uttered from the parent-child position with "us" as the subject of the utterance and the parent and child being "us."	【Three-month old baby boy and mother】When the child burps after breastfeeding, the mother responds with "Ohh, the burp came up up up!" After this proxy talk from the child's position, she said "*that was good, wasn't it,*" speaking proxy talk from the parent-child position as she rubbed the baby's back. 【Zero-month old baby girl and mother】After breastfeeding, the mother held the baby up to get her to burp, saying "*let's lift you up a little,*" explaining her own action using proxy talk from the parent-child position.
	Proxy talk from an ambiguous position	Proxy talk from an ambiguous position refers to utterances for which it is clear whether child or parent-child are the subject of the utterance or just the parent. It is not clear whether such utterances are proxy talk or non-proxy talk.	【Six-month old baby girl and mother】The child is staring at the observer. The mother looks back and forth between the child and the observer and, keeping her voice low, says "It's strange, isn't it," expressing the child's internal state from the parent-child position with proxy talk. When the child shifts her gaze to the mother, the mother says "*What is that?*" and "*what, what?*" and then answers her own question by saying "*video, video.*" In this question-and-response format, one is proxy talk and one is non-proxy talk, but we cannot clearly classify them.
	Proxy talk from transitional position	These are utterances in which the subject of the utterance shifts from the child to the parent or from the parent to the child in mid utterance. The sentences end in "say" or a question.	【Three-month old baby boy and mother】Holding the baby, the mother turns to the observer and says "See, we have a guest," using non-proxy talk, and then continues with "hello," using proxy talk from the child's position. Then she uses transitional proxy talk by adding "*say hello.*" She shifts from the proxy talk of "hello" to non-proxy talk by adding "say."
Non-proxy talk		This is the parent's utterance that does not include the child's perspective, and includes proxy talk by toys and third parties.	【Three-month old baby boy and mother】When the child begins to fuss, the mother says, "*you're still tired, aren't you.*" If this had been proxy talk, she would said "still tired" or "sleepy."

Note: The text in italic indicates the relevant category of proxy talk.

Before the analysis, we carried out a preliminary analysis to get a broad overview of the proxy talk and confirm shifts in ages overall. The preliminary analysis determined shifts in the frequency of proxy talk in the 50 utterances in each case observed and the percentages for each of the four types of proxy talk, and used this as a rough standard for qualitative analysis in Analyses 1 and 2.

In Analysis 1, a qualitative analysis based on episode interpretation was carried out to determine the repertory of functions for proxy talk, that would be possible in interaction between parent and child, and to find relations between forms and functions of proxy talk.

Specifically, the changes in ages in the proxy talk from the 12 pairs of parents and children were confirmed, and two pairs of mothers and male infants and two pairs of mothers and female infants were chosen from the pairs, ensuring that there was no excessive distribution, and the observations were analyzed with a descriptive approach up to the 50 utterances used in the preliminary analysis. Referring to the transcripts in which the types of the proxy talk had already been coded and the videos of the observations, the scenes including proxy talk that could be interpreted functionally were written out as proxy talk episodes. At this point, to ensure that context was considered, continuous speech comprising a series of utterances was analyzed as a single episode. In addition, the KJ method (Kawakita, 1967) was carried out, based on the similarities in the proxy talk functions, rather than similarities in context and utterance forms.

In Analysis 1, we examined the functions of proxy talk. On the other hand, how is communication between parents and children formed when proxy talk is not used? By considering the situations in which proxy talk was not used, we can obtain complementary data in order to show development changes in proxy talk. In Analysis 2, we treated the non-proxy talk situations and explored why proxy talk was not used and also whether or not it could have been used. We reviewed the videos of the same observations as in Analysis 1, and wrote down the non-proxy talk episodes while exploring the possibility of alternatives to proxy talk. As with Analysis 1, we used the KJ method (Kawakita, 1967) for non-proxy talk episodes.

Results and considerations

Preliminary analysis

We determined the frequency of proxy talk out of the 50 utterances in each case for infants from 0–15 months of age, and calculated and graphed the average (Figure 1). These utterances are not categorized by the type of proxy talk. Next, in Analysis 1, in order to consider whether proxy talk needed to be categorized by type, the percentage of each of the four types of proxy talk in the total number of proxy talk incidences was organized by the age of the infant observed (Figure 2).

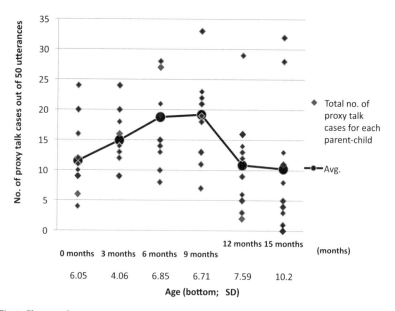

Fig.1 Changes by age in parental proxy talk
Note: Data shown using a line graph is the shift in the average proxy talk cases out of 50 utterances by mothers. Each plot is proxy talk from observation of each parent.

Proxy talk gradually increased from the age of 0 months (average of 11.5 proxy talk utterances) to the ages of three months (14.9) and six months (18.8), and reached a peak at the ages of six months and nine months (19.1). Proxy talk rapidly decreased from the age of one year (10.8 at 12 months and

10.2 at 15 months). This indicates that the quantitative changes in proxy talk can be categorized by 1) a period of gradual increases (0 and three months), 2) a peak period (six and nine months), and 3) a period of decline (12 and 15 months). Given that the distribution from one year shows that there was only one case of high values at the 12-month point and two cases at the 15-month point (when excluding these cases, the average was 9.2 at 12 months and 6.3 at 15 months), we can surmise that proxy talk has specific functions. This is considered as an important perspective in Analysis 1.

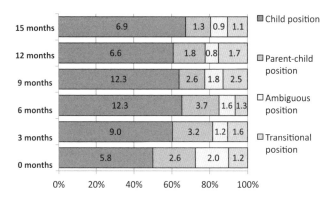

Fig.2 Percentage of each of the four types of proxy talk in the total number of proxy talk cases by age
Note: In the graph the average frequency (out of 50 utterances including non-proxy talk) is shown for each group.

Next, as shown in Figure 2, there are no major discrepancies in the frequency of the four types of proxy talk by age, and at every age, proxy talk from the child's position was the most common. The four types of proxy talk and the relation to functions will have to be considered in the future, but in Analysis 1 we looked at the four types separately so as to avoid affecting fluctuations in the function of proxy talk with changes in age.

Analysis 1

We attempted to analyze the function of proxy talk in the episodes from a qualitative perspective. There were 62 proxy talk episodes in the interactions

Table 2—Function of proxy talk in parent-child communication

Proxy talk tailored to child	Encouragement
This is proxy talk that accepts the child's condition and intention and responds accordingly. It compensates for the child's lack of linguistic development in various situations.	Encouragement of child's semi-intentions
	Proxy talk to express child's clear intention
	Proxy talk from child to observer
Proxy talk directing the child	Guidance
When the parent wants the child to do something, the parent uses proxy talk as a tool.	Inactive direction
	Situation-dependent verbalizatic

Proxy talk to address situations	Filling time
Proxy talk to fill time and preserve a situation.	
	Request to share the parent's internal state
	Emergency
Proxy talk as parent's interpretation aid	Parent's acknowledgement of situation
Proxy talk in which the parent tries to voice the child's fragmentary intentions and actions; directed at oneself or observers.	Apologies to observer

	Age	0	3	6	9	12	15	
				No. of Episodes				
xy talk intended to keep the child engaged he current activity for longer and further ourage the child.		0	1	4	2	2	0	
s kind of proxy talk is used when the d's intention is not clear, but the mother s it to encourage the child's intentions he has interpreted them, taking the ditions into account.		0	0	1	2	3	2	
sive proxy talk that simply verbalizes the d's clear intentions as conveyed to the ent via gestures and utterances clearly cted at the parent.		0	0	0	1	2	4	Proxy talk for the child Verbalization of the child's actions and thoughts at present or desired in the future.
and the child's world to include a third y.		0	0	0	1	1	1	
s is an attempt to lead the child away n a negative state by giving meaning to rances that are completely opposite.		0	1	0	0	0	0	
xy talk that changes the activity while ching the child's response. This includes xy talk intended to re-focus the child.		4	1	1	1	0	1	
xy talk in which the parent is telling the d that he/she must do this or say this given situation would be included in category. When eating, the parent says nmy," and when playing house, the parent "I'm leaving now."		0	0	2	1	2	0	
ing time, play-by-play feeling; proxy used when the parent cannot focus on the d while taking care of the child, but must erve the child's mood.		4	1	0	1	0	0	Proxy talk for the parent's sake This proxy talk can be interpreted as a way for the parent to regulate his/her feelings and fill time, including the time needed to adjust feelings.
y talk for the parent's internal state; y talk situation, but the parent comes to orefront.		0	0	0	1	0	0	
ing time in emergences; proxy talk to ent the child from becoming bored.		0	0	0	0	2	1	
alization of conditions using proxy talk ok for a remedy and accept conditions.		7	2	1	0	0	0	
y talk about the child's condition that s like excuses and apologies made to the rver.		0	1	0	0	0	0	

Table 3—Examples of proxy talk episodes and non-proxy talk episodes (summary)

【Episode 1】 Six-month old baby girl and mother (Utterance ID 300625~300646)
A child sitting and held by her mother reaches out her hand and leans forward. The mother says, "Where do you want to go?" (300629/non) and "you want to try going?" (300631/non), which indicated that the mother had interpreted her child's movements as a desire to crawl (although she couldn't crawl yet). The mother put the baby down on her stomach, supporting her, and as the baby moved, she used proxy talk such as "upsy-daisy" (300633/ch) and "flop" as well as non-proxy talk such as "you can do it" (300638/non). This proxy talk, tailored to the child's actions, actualizes the child's desire to crawl, and sustains and encourages the action the child has started. Although the mother was probably unconscious of it, she used proxy talk when she supported the child's body, and used non-proxy talk when she took her hands away and looked into the child's face.
【Episode 2】 12-month old boy and mother (Utterance ID 601212~601221)
The child is walking around pushing a toy car. When the toy car gets caught up in electrical cords or bumps into the bookcase, the mother says "Ah!" (601212/ch) and "Oh!" (601219/ch) as proxy talk that expresses the child's surprise and other internal states. The child continues playing with a calm expression, and the tone of the mother's proxy talk is not particularly exaggerated. The mother did not respond to these small events during play (the truck tangling in the cord and hitting a bookcase) by going to the child's side herself or offering specific help. However, using proxy talk in an understated way to voice and thus assimilate any negative emotions the child may feel at these times preserves the child's stable playtime alone. The proxy talk simply consisted of "Ah!" and "Oh!" and did not have a specific subject, and can be said to reflect the child's semi-intentions.
【Episode 3】15-month old boy and mother (UtteranceID 601513~601514)
The child carries a large case of blocks and hands it to his mother. While looking straight at his mother, he says "ooh." The mother responds with proxy talk, saying "Oh, it's heavy, isn't it" (601514/pa), to which the child responds by making a fist with both hands and putting strength into the pose, essentially epitomizing the mother's proxy talk of "heavy" in his own gestures. The mother used proxy talk ("heavy") to express the child's clear intention, and the child seemed to understand the condition himself due to the assistance from the proxy talk.
【Episode 4】 Three-month old baby girl and mother (Utterance ID 300313-300321)
While the baby's diaper is being changed, she becomes grumpy and the mother tries to restore her good temper by rubbing her feet and saying "beat [the bad feelings], beat" (300318,300319,300320/ch), repeating this proxy talk three times. Just before this incidence, the mother had said "it's not the right time for this" (300314/ch), voicing the child's state as is and understanding that the child's mood is beginning to worsen. However, the mother did not directly confront the baby's bad mood, but tried to bring her around to a better mood with proxy talk with the exact opposite meaning as the child's condition as the mother had interpreted it. The child's fussing gradually grew louder and louder, as if to cover the mother's voice when she said "beat, beat" for the third time. At that point, the mother responded to the child's fussing with "yes yes, yes yes" (300321/non) and gave up trying to improve the baby's mood, immediately shifting to an acceptance of the baby's bad mood.

[Episode 5] Zero-month old baby girl and mother (Utterance ID 300036)
The mother used the proxy talk "let's try opening your eyes" (300036/pa) to the sleepy baby. Although the mother did not want the baby to sleep because it was in the middle of observation and she didn't want it to be interrupted, she also didn't want to use clear directions using non-proxy talk, such as "open your eyes." Not only did she use "try" to indicate an attempt, but also used "let's try," using proxy talk from the parent-child position that added the implication that the mother and child will do this together. Proxy talk functions as a gentle direction when encouraging the baby to do something.

[Episode 6] Six-month old baby boy and mother (Utterance ID 600612-600618)
While the mother is feeding the boy baby food, the noise of a vacuum cleaner comes from another room. The child turns his head in that direction. The mother acknowledges the child's distraction with proxy talk, saying "the vacuum cleaner is making a noise," but while carrying the spoon to the child's mouth, she says in a louder voice (somewhat forcefully), "Aaahh" (600614/ch) and tries to draw the distracted child's attention back to the food.

[Episode 7] Zero-month old baby boy and mother (Utterance ID 340003-340015)
While changing the baby's diaper, the mother continues to use both non-proxy talk and proxy talk as if she is almost offering a play-by-play, saying "upsy-daisy" (340003/non) and "now you're all fresh" (340010/ch). It leaves an impression of rapid-fire events. She is not observing the baby and using proxy talk—in fact, she has no time to look at the baby's expression because she is changing his diaper, but it looks like she is continuing to talk to the baby just enough to prevent him from becoming bad-tempered.

[Episode 8] 12-month old baby girl and mother (Utterance ID 301206-301213)
The child points to a ball that has rolled behind her back. The mother says "go get it" (301206/non), but the child does not immediately go and retrieve it. The mother claps her hands and encourages her, saying "Get set, go!" (301209, 301210/non), but does not use proxy talk. She calls her by name several times and repeats "go get it" until finally the baby crawls over to get the ball.

between the four pairs of parents and children at 0, 3, 6, 9, 12 and 15 months of age. In all of these episodes, a description of the function is added, so 62 kinds of functions are is available data. The KJ method was used with a focus on these functions. As a result, the proxy talk functions were divided into 12 categories and then into the top four categories (Table 2). Looking at the number of episodes in Table 2, we find that the overall number of the episodes is high at the younger ages. This might look like it contradicts the result of the preliminary analysis showing that the number of proxy talk utterances was minimal at the younger ages, but when defining an episode as a series of speech utterances in the same context, we found that the context was shorter the younger the infant, and the number of utterances (including proxy talk) included in a single episode increased the older the infant. Table 3 provides examples of proxy talk episodes. The utterance ID and type of proxy talk or non-proxy talk is noted by the speech used in Table 3 and the text are appended [12].

Proxy talk function (1)—Proxy talk tailored to child

"Proxy talk tailored to child" includes "encouragement," "encouragement of child's semi-intentions," "proxy talk to express child's clear intention," and "proxy talk from child to observer," included in the lower-ranked category. "Encouragement" refers to proxy talk used to ensure that the child continues with the action they are already engaged in, or to encourage further action of the same sort. For example, in Episode 1 (Table 3), the parent used proxy talk to encourage the infant's action. "Encouragement" was observed at three to 12 months, and primarily at six months.

"Encouragement of child's semi-intentions" refers to situations in which the mother used proxy talk to encourage what she interpreted as the child's intention to be in situations in which the child's intention was not clear, but the mother found clues in the situation and the infant's expression. For example, in Episode 2 (Table 3), the child was pushing a push-along car and walking around the room, but when the push-along car got stuck on electric cords or other similar events occurred, the mother would express the child's internal emotions of surprise with sounds such as "Ah" or "Oh." The child continued to play with a calm expression and did not exhibit any obviously negative emotions, but the mother, knowing the child's everyday life, likely understood that such events could trigger a negative emotion in the child. The voice in which the parent delivered her proxy talk was not particularly exaggerated, and she did not stand up and go to help the child, but simply responded carefully to small events and used proxy talk each time, voicing the negative emotions the child may have felt and letting them evaporate. Moreover, the proxy talk itself consisted of "Ah" and "Oh," without any specific target for these references, which reflected the child's semi-intention. "Encouragement of child's semi-intentions" was observed at 6–15 months. At this age, this reflected the development of the infant's intentions.

In contrast, "proxy talk to express child's clear intentions" refers to proxy talk in response to the child's clear demonstration of intention. This was used in situations in which children were clearly trying to convey their intentions, such as through body movement and vocalization directed at the parent. This proxy talk faithfully voices these intentions. For example, in Episode 3 (Table 3), the infant says "u—" while looking straight ahead at the mother, but it seemed to be difficult for the infant to convey intention independently using physical movement or verbalization. The mother responded to the "u—" by saying "Oh, that's heavy isn't it," and then the child but seemed to have grasped the situation and, even though the block case was already on the floor, grasped both hands and gestured with strength. The infant seemed to understand the meaning of the situation through the proxy talk. "Proxy talk to express child's clear intentions" was seen from nine months, and increased up until 15 months of age.

As regards "proxy talk from child to observer," the child expresses clear intentions, and if this is directed at the observer, the parent talks as the child's proxy and conveys this to the observer.

As such, "proxy talk tailored to the child" is proxy talk that fits the infant's conditions and intentions, and have the function to compensate the linguistic immaturity of the child.

Proxy talk function (2)—"Proxy talk directing the child"

"Proxy talk directing the child" includes "guidance," "inactive direction," and "situation-dependent verbalization." "Guidance" refers to directing children to other situations by using proxy talk with the opposite meaning in order to resolve the children's negative situation. Episode 4 (Table 3) is an episode in which the child begins to grizzle, and the parent tried to guide the infant's mood by not confirming the child's poor mood and leaving aside the cause to try and guide the child's mood with the opposite proxy talk. They did not use non-proxy talk to confirm by saying "you don't like that" when the child becomes ill-tempered, or oppose the child's poor temper using non-proxy talk. In order to divert the infant's mood, the parent used proxy talk. However, the infant's grizzling grew even louder, drowning out the third time the parent said "you can win, you can win." The parent seemed to decide that it would be difficult to distract the child. The parent said, "yes, yes," and gave up on trying to guide the child with proxy talk. The parent instantly switched to accepting the infant's poor mood.

"Inactive direction" refers to proxy talk that directs a switch in action while watching the child's reaction. For example, in Episode 5 (Table 3), when the child began to look sleepy during the observation, the parent said, "let's try to open our eyes!" If this were an exchange between adults, "let's try to" is an invitation to do something together, and can be seen as proxy talk from the parent and child's perspective from an "our" standpoint. In other words, the parent did not want the observation to be interrupted, but also did not want to use a direct instruction to this infant she was not yet used to, such as using non-proxy talk and saying "open your eyes." She used the encouragement of "let's try to open our eyes!" to make her speech more gentle. Moreover, as in Episode 6 (Table 3), this includes proxy talk to re-focus the infant's attention. "Inactive direction" is observed during a broad observation period, but primarily at 0 months.

"Situation-dependent verbalization" refers to proxy talk in which, even though the child has not clearly indicated intention, the parent uses words closely related to situations in which the parent felt that situation-dependent and cultural perspective required that it should be voiced in this way. For example, there is an episode in which, although the infant (a six-month old boy) did not express "yummy" when eating," the parent uses proxy talk from the parent-child perspective such as "so yummy, right?" (600625/pa), and an example of proxy talk from child's position in which, when playing house, even though the infant (a six-month old boy) did had not waved his hand, the parent waved her hand and said "bye-bye (600127/ch)." In these proxy talk situations, in contrast to situations in which the infant has no vocalization or physical movement along with the situation, the parent uses expressions to indicate "yummy" and waves her hand, and by adding actions to proxy talk, the cultural context is verbalized, and direction based on the situation is given. "Situation-dependent verbalization" is observed at 6–12 months.

As such, "proxy talk directing the infant" is proxy talk used to make the child do something or feel something, and functions to direct the child.

Function of proxy talk (3)—Proxy talk as address to situations

The "proxy talk as address to situations" includes "time filling," "parent's desire for shared internal states," and "emergency." "Time filling" includes proxy talk to fill in time with the child. For example, in Episode 7 (Table 3), while changing the infant's diaper, the mother explained her own actions in non-proxy talk and gave the infant a play-by-play rundown of her infant's actions as a proxy talk. When changing diapers or caring for the baby in other ways, the mother does not have the leeway to closely watch the baby and respond with proxy talk tailored to the infant's conditions. In fact, the parent did not turn her glance to the infant during this episode. The parent uses proxy talk to stall for time without the infant becoming grumpy. This kind of proxy talk serves to fill time. This "time filling" was observed through nine months, particularly at zero months.

"Parent's desire for shared internal states" refers to proxy talk of internal conditions (such as stress) of the parent herself. Proxy talk is the parent's effort to vocalize in the child's voice, so it can be seen as the parent's de-visualization, but in episodes falling into this category, the parent becomes visible by voicing her internal condition to share it. Moreover, "emergency" refers to proxy talk in which the parent expresses emergency situations, for example, the spitting out of a sweet that the infant was eating. While responding to the situation (picking up the sweet that was spit out, for example), the parent uses proxy talk somewhat quickly to try and keep the baby in a good mood. "Emergency" was observed at 12 months and 15 months.

As such, "proxy talk to encourage situations" is proxy talk used to fill time and proxy talk used to maintain conditions, and plays a role in acting on the parent and child's stalled condition.

Function of proxy talk (4)—Proxy talk as parent's interpretation aid

Proxy talk as the parent's interpretation aid includes "parent's acknowledgement of situation" and "apologies to observer." The "parent's acknowledgement of situation" is a type of proxy talk in which the parent verbalizes the assumption she creates in an attempt to understand the child's unclear and undifferentiated situation and give it meaning. While giving a voice to this, the mother looks for an opening in the unchanging situation and attempts to accept the situation. For example, in an exchange with an infant aged zero months, when the infant interrupts the breastfeeding, the mother says, "I don't want any more" (300016/ch) and "you don't want any more?" (300017/non) in a combination of proxy talk from child's position followed by non-proxy talk. The mother spoke quietly, and seemed to lack confidence in her own interpretation, so that after the proxy talk, she asked questions to confirm. Voicing this as proxy talk likely plays the function of aiding the mother's interpretation. This "parent's acknowledgement of situation" is seen most often at zero months and was observed through six months.

"Apologies to observer" refers to proxy talk that serves as excuses and apologies to the observer for the child's situation. For example, to an infant (boy aged zero months) who began to look sleepy during the observation, the mother used proxy talk from parent-child position, saying "getting tired, aren't we, the eyelids (are getting heavy)" (600303/pa). This was a way of asking the nearby observer to be understanding of the infant's sleepiness.

In this way, proxy talk as the parent's interpretation aid is a sign of the parent's efforts to understand a child's undifferentiated intentions and actions by voicing her own assumption, and are directed at the parent herself and, on occasion, the observer.

Significance of the role that proxy talk plays in pre-verbal communication

Proxy talk seems to function as a means of compensating for the infant's lack of linguistic development as the mother verbalizes for the infant, but is this really the case? When we sort the utterances in the top four functional categories of proxy talk in terms of who the proxy talk serves, we find that there are roughly two types. The first is the top category "proxy talk tailored to the child" and "proxy talk directing the child." Proxy talk fitting these categories can verbalize the infant's current actions and thoughts or the parent's desired future actions and thoughts, and in this sense, this proxy talk can be thought of as "proxy talk for the child's sake." The second category, "proxy talk as encouragement" and "proxy talk as parent's interpretation aid," are typically used in situations in which it is difficult for the parent to understand and predict the infant's intention, and the parent voices her interpretation to settle her own feelings or to give herself time in which to settle her feelings. These kinds of proxy talk can be considered "proxy talk for the parent's sake," and even if it is proxy talk that verbalizes the infant's voice, we can observe that it does not reflect the parent's intentions and feelings, and proxy talk is used for the parent's sake as well. In other words, proxy talk is not used for just the parent or the child, but is directed toward both and supports pre-verbal communication.

Analysis 2

Thus far, we have examined the function of proxy talk, but in situations in which proxy talk is not used, why is not used? In particular, proxy talk declines from 12 months, and we wanted to look at what replaced the function that proxy talk served up until that point. The KJ method was used with non-proxy talk episodes in which proxy talk was not used in situations when it could have been used with different parent-child pairs and different observation points. The results are organized as "un-proxy talk," "response," "non-voicing of proxy talk," "proxy talk for toy" and "proxy talk for parent's utterance" (Table 4).

Table 4—Functions of non-proxy talk

		0	3	6	9	12	15
	Age			No. of episodes			
Un-proxy talk	Though using proxy talk would not be unusual in this situation, it was not used.	1	1	1	0	0	0
Response	The proxy talk for children was non-voiced; a response to the infant's unvoiced plea or question	0	0	0	1	0	0
Non-voicing of proxy talk	Non-voiced proxy talk seen as silence in situations in which proxy talk would have been voice up until this point	0	1	0	0	2	3
Proxy talk for toy	Proxy talk for the toy so that the child can understand the toy's actions and intentions	0	0	0	0	1	1
Proxy talk for parent's utterances	Parent's utterances the child may use as proxy talk	0	0	0	0	0	1

"Un-proxy talk" includes episodes in which proxy talk would likely have been used in different but similar situations. This was seen in episodes with the younger infants, and overall there was a sense of the parent's tension (about being observed) and hesitancy with the infant. These situations suggested that the parent was not accustomed to engaging with the infant.

"Response" includes episodes in which responses are given in situations in which the parent's verbal question did not take precedence. In other words, the infant's proxy talk is not voiced, and this is the parent's response to the infant's unvoiced plea or question. For example, in an interaction with a nine month-old boy, the parent said "yes" (600904/non) when the infant stretched out his leg. The parent is not using proxy talk to specifically give meaning to the act of stretching out his leg, but by replying "yes," the infant can know their own act must bring "some kind of" meaning and thus gives the exchange form. "Unvoiced proxy talk" is seen as pause in situations in which proxy talk would have been voice up until this point, and compared to the "response" situation, the child's intention was clear. For example, in

Episode 8 (Table 3), the parent is directing the infant to get a ball, repeating the non-proxy talk direct instruction of "go get it" (3012016/non). The parent encourages the infant, who did not immediately go get the ball, by pointing her finger and shaking the baby's body, but does not use proxy talk such as "oh, there's the ball!" and "the ball is gone." The mother's repetition of "go get it" shows that she knows that the child understands these words. In these cases, the mother probably curbed her use of proxy talk to respect the infant's understanding.

"Proxy talk for toy" is proxy talk for the toy in order that the child can understand the toy's actions and intentions. In this research, since utterances including the child's perspective are considered proxy talk, "proxy talk for toys" and "proxy talk for parent's utterances," discussed below, are included in non-proxy talk. "Proxy talk for parent's utterances" refers to utterances that express what the parent surmises that the child expects her to say—it is essentially proxy talk for the parent's proxy talk by the child. For example, the mother said to her 15 month-old daughter who was eating a Bolo snack, "Give one to Mama!" and when the child put one in her mother's mouth, the mother said "Aahh-n" (301521/non) as she ate it. "Aahh-n" is an utterance attached to the mother's action, so this would not be proxy talk for the child. However, when someone wants another person to eat something, the person trying to encourage this action usually says "Aahh-n" as proxy talk for the person doing the eating. In the data for infants up to 15 months of age, there were no cases in which the infant clearly used proxy talk for the parent, but if this "proxy talk for parent's utterances" is internalized, the infant herself would use proxy talk.

As such, when we examine episodes related to proxy talk, we find that the infant's utterances do not substitute for proxy talk (none of the infants spoke much during the observations), and proxy talk gradually becomes unvoiced. This shows that the mother leaves open a development pause to wait for the infant's own voice.

General arguments

In this research, after the preliminary analysis in which we examined quantitative changes in the proxy talk used in parent-child communication during the pre-verbal stage, in Analysis 1 we considered the qualitative aspects of proxy talk functions, and in Analysis 2, we looked at the substitutes for proxy talk in situations in which it was not used. Below, we examine the qualitative changes in proxy talk obtained from the preliminary analysis—in other words, we looked at the proxy talk episodes after classifying by function according to the infant's age during 1) the period in which proxy talk gradually increases (0–3 months), 2) the period in which proxy talk reaches a peak (6–9 months) and 3) the period in which proxy talk declines (12–15 months).

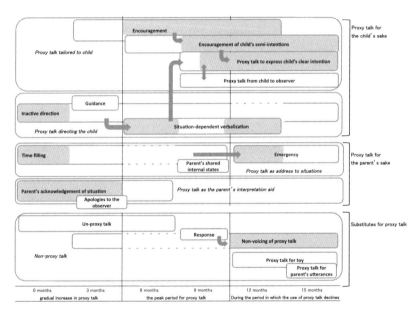

Fig.3 Proxy talk functions as the child ages
Note: ⬜ indicates the scope of incidence, and ▨ indicates 2 or more episodes for age. In addition, even within the scope of incidence, instances of 0 episodes are shown using a dotted line.

The functional categories that define the period in which proxy talk gradually increases (0 to 3 months) are "inactive direction," "parent's acknowledgement of situation," and "time filling." The participant children in this research were first-born children, so this was their first experience for the parents to engage with infants. It was difficult to interpret the undifferentiated intentions of infants, and how to talk to and how to engage with the infant was a matter of trial and error. According to the analysis of interviews with the same participants as this research (Sugano, 2008; Sugano et. al. 2009), the parents who felt negative emotions about their infants of zero months of age gave their inability to understand them as the reason. In these conditions, verbalizing voices about the infant as proxy talk would help the parent understand the infant and the conditions. The utterances the parent spoke as the infant's voice were likely what the parent herself heard the most. The parent recognizes the situation by using "parent's acknowledgement of situation" proxy talk and is also ready for the next steps of "inactive direction" and "time filling" as necessary. As regards "time filling," a young infant cannot express clear intentions, and it is also difficult for the parent to actively encourage expression at this age. "Time filling" proxy talk does not have any meaning itself, but is essentially background music for the time the parent and child spends together, which tends to be silent, and this proxy talk is also a way for the parent to regulate her feelings. As Valsiner (2007) also says, semiotic mediation using speech can put the subject outside of the context and distance herself psychologically from her emotions. In other words, verbalization allows objectification and emotional regulation. Emotions are not originally meant to be suppressed, but are instead regulator that allows a person to adapt to other people and the environment and build relationships with other people (Suda, 1999). In other words, "parent's acknowledgement of situation" and "time filling" proxy talk also plays a role in helping the mother adjust her emotions as she adapts to this new "other" represented by her infant. Moreover, the "un-proxy talk" in our analysis of non-proxy talk episodes in Analysis 2 suggests that this inexperienced mother is not yet used to the strategy of filling time with proxy talk.

During the proxy talk peak (6–9 months), there are episodes in which the parent uses proxy talk to "encourage" while interpreting the infant's actions and intentions, followed by "encouragement of the child's semi-intentions." These episodes are unique for the speaking function in place of the original significance of proxy talk. Infants from about six months of age become more active and begin to show curiosity about the outside world. The parent aligns herself to the infant's activities and interests and uses proxy talk to encourage the child to continue with those activities. In "encouragement," much of the proxy talk consists of onomatopoeic expressions, and the proxy talk is tailored to the visible actions rather than the infant's intentions. However, once there are signs of the infant's intentions, the function of proxy talk shifts to "encouragement of child's semi-intentions." Ahead of the next period of a decline in proxy talk, the infant's expression of intentions becomes clearer and the parent shifts to "proxy talk for infant's clear intentions." Moreover, during this period, when specific utterances are attached such as eating and playing house, the parent begins to use proxy talk that adds utterances that is typical for these conditions ("situation-dependent verbalization"). Through these exchanges that include this kind of situation-dependent verbalization proxy talk, the infant gradually has opportunities to learn exchanges using words for specific situations. These are drawn out from the particular situation as the child's interpretation, and succeed to the "proxy talk for infant's clear intentions" in the next stage.

During the period in which the use of proxy talk declines (12–15 months), proxy talk is used less as long as the parent and child can sustain peaceful exchanges. Compared to the proxy talk used to actively attach meaning to the infant's undifferentiated actions, as in the period when the infant was very young, the child's intentions on which this proxy talk is premised becomes clear, but "verbalization of the child's intentions" is used as a passive proxy talk to compensate for the infant's immature linguistic skills. "Proxy talk from the infant to the observer" is a case in which the infant's actions are directed at the observer, and tis proxy talk is premised on the infant's clear intentions. Moreover, this period is particularly distinct in that proxy talk decreases for many parents, but increases temporarily among some parents and children. Looking at the data for parents and children with a high number of proxy talk cases, we find "emergency" episodes. The number of proxy talk cases was high because in the "emergency" episodes, proxy talk is delivered in a continuous stream. In other words, originally in this period, non-proxy talk episodes would have been most common as a means of preserving the situation in which proxy talk would have been unvoiced (not said) and the mother offers a pause so that the infant can intervene with conversation of his/her own. However, in situations in which candy is dropped or other emergencies, the parent uses proxy talk to temporarily create an integrated status with the infant and respond while preventing the situation from collapsing significantly (such as picking up the dropped candy). In the period from 12 months, while preparing for communication, including proxy talk, the parent primarily communicates by using various kinds of non-proxy talk ("unvoiced," "proxy talk for toys," "proxy talk for parent's utterances"), and the communication between parent and child becomes multi-layered.

The above suggests that the development changes in the function of proxy talk are 1) gradual increase in proxy talk (0–3 months), when the parent uses proxy talk in her exchanges with the infant for trial and error; 2) the peak period for proxy talk (6–9 months), when proxy talk is used for limited functions tailored to the development of the infant's intentions; and 3) the period in which proxy talk use declines (12–15 months), when it is used in specific situations and for specific functions.

However, in this research, development is seen as the process by which an infant begins to participate in the cultural community (Rogoff, 2003), with proxy talk seen as cultural intermediation. How does a close other such as the parent represent the community and guide the infant in appropriating the necessary cultural voice through proxy talk?

For example, in Episode 1, when the infant stretched out his hands and leaned forward, the parent interpreted this as an indication that the baby wanted to crawl, and used proxy talk encouraging crawling. The parent did not interpret the infant's undifferentiated action of stretching out his hands and leaning forward as the infant's wish to separate from the parent. In Episode 4, when the parent is trying to respond to the infant's fussing, the parent does not say "I don't like that," but rather "you can win, you can win" in proxy talk. In other words, proxy talk is selected as the voice that best fits the culture through the parent's interpretation. An image of an infant who is actively taking up the challenge of crawling, rather than separating from his parent (Episode 1) and an infant who is trying to adjust his own negative feelings rather than displaying them (Episode 4) are cultural images that the parent has constructed in her personal history. As we have already noted, the "as-if" structure of interpretation (Valsiner, 2007) can be seen as leaps in inference and organization of particular situations, but this leap is not in a random direction, but is a cultural and historical product of the parent herself. In other words, we can view proxy talk as the process by which the parent externalizes her cultural voice, as discussed below.

When we examine changes in proxy talk by age, we find that proxy talk shifts from "encouragement" to "encouragement of child's semi-intentions" to "proxy talk to express child's clear intention" (Figure 3). The parent gradually changes from using proxy talk in response to undifferentiated actions that are difficult to interpret to proxy talk that reflects the infant's intentions to the extent that she can interpret them. We must wait for more detailed analysis, but we believe that these changes are due to developments in communication skills as the infant learns how to convey his/her intentions. In an example of "encouragement" in Episode 1, a six-month-old infant did not look at the parent to convey anything unless the parent was looking into his/her face. In an example of "encouragement of child's semi-intentions" in Episode 2, a 12 month-old child did not voice any meaningful words when observed, but there were situations in which we observed that children had acquired several understandable words. However, these were situations in which the child was playing calmly by his self and not situations in which the infant was trying to engage with the parent. The parent knows that the child can become ill-tempered when unable to skillfully manipulate a toy, but in the prior situation, it was likely unclear as to whether the child would become ill-tempered. Symbolic proxy talk such as "aa—" and "oo—" reflects the infant's intention to the extent that it can be interpreted. In other words, the parent respects the infant's vague intentions and avoids over interpretation the situation (excessive leaps). In the Episode 3 example of "proxy talk to express child's clear intention," the infant clearly directs his glance at the parent and all, so that it is clear that he intends to convey something to the parent, so only verbalization was necessary. In this way, the leap in the "as-if" structure was revised as necessary as the infant's response and the parent's experience with child-rearing accumulated.

At the same time, from the infant's perspective, even in the case of occasional actions, the parent's choice of when to use proxy talk and when not to means that she is choosing which actions and conditions to encourage or direct, and which to ignore and let go by. These will be accumulated as the child's own voices, and embodied as the child's intention in each situation. From the infant's perspective, proxy talk is the entry to the process of internalizing culture. For example, if we consider the developmental change from "situation-dependent verbalization" to "proxy talk to express child's clear intention," this comes across even more clearly. With "situation-dependent verbalization," before the child identifies meaning in the relevant situation him/herself, proxy talk was carried out automatically with the mother making utterances for the specific condition. The infant gradually begins to link the situation to the corresponding words and this is internalized as the infant's own voice so that the infant's intentions are constructed. When the parent uses proxy talk to express the child's intentions ("proxy talk to express child's clear intention"), the cultural voice is being reproduced as it passes from the parent to the child. As the infant develops, the accumulated voices begin to function as voices that forms the infant's own dialogical self (Hermans, 2001; Hermans & Hermans-Jansen, 2003), not just as the infant's intentions in that particular situation.

Of course, the cultural voices that the parent externalizes as proxy talk is not taken in as is by the infant. The "refining" process, including coincidence and the development of the infant's own understanding of proxy talk (for example, verbally), can intervene. In other words, initially conditions are vaguely positive or negative, but subsequently, as the infant understands words clearly, the infant her/himself can determine whether the proxy talk is right. For example, in Episode 3, discussed above, the parent interprets the infant's noise as meaning that the object is heavy and says, "Oh, that's heavy isn't it." And then, in response, the infant did not repeat the mother's utterance, "that's heavy" but returned the gesture, "heavy" with his satisfied expression that his intention had been conveyed. The process to appropriate the cultural voices is a process of internalization, including a kind of refinement, as the infant's subjective activity. In sum, externalization and internalization occur interchangeably, but this does not mean that the same thing is received, as if it were reflected in a mirror. Rather, the instantaneous exchanges take place with microgenetic mutual changes (for example, the way that the infant responds with gestures rather than words). Cultural development refers not only to simple internalization, but a process to appropriate the infant's own voices through the use of cultural tools. The use of proxy talk does not necessarily become the infant's internal voice without modification. Rather, it is built up over the accumulation of exchanges.

We have discussed the externalization and internalization of culture in terms of developmental changes in proxy talk, but this research also identified the function that proxy talk such as "parent's acknowledgement of situation" and "time filling" plays in helping the parent adjust her emotions. Before even looking at the infant's long-term development, the question of how parents address conditions that are inconvenient or confusing is an important issue for parents with children in their infancy. By using proxy talk, the parent at the very least avoids silence and arrives at her own interpretation through a series of self-directed questions using proxy talk and tries to settle her emotions through emotional distancing. Proxy talk is not used for the benefit of the parent or the child, but works on both levels and supports communication in the pre-verbal stage. This is also interesting in terms of the shift to the parent (for example, see Mitnick, Heyman, & Smith Slep,

2009; Katz-Wise, Priess, & Hyde, 2010, Okamoto, Sugano, and Negayama, 2003, etc.). In communication with pre-verbal infants, if the observer focuses only on the parent's use of proxy talk, it appears as if the parent and child are communicating. However, when we closely scrutinize each episode in which proxy talk is used, as we already noted, it does not necessarily reflect the intentions of the infant. Particularly when the infant is very young, the infant's condition is verbalized through proxy talk, some kind of meaning is assigned, and this allows the interpretation to be examined. In other words, proxy talk is possible not because the parent and child are communicating, but rather, proxy talk is motivated by the desire to communicate and is a kind of trial-and-error process.

Going forward, we hope to examine the relationship between the four types of proxy talk and their functions, the relationship to the development of the infant's communication skills, which are likely the trigger for changes in the proxy talk, and how communication between the parent and child develops from 15 months, when proxy talk decreases dramatically.

*This paper is the English Translation of "How Do Parents Communicate with their Infants? The Function of Parental Proxy Talk in Pre-Verbal Communication" by Yoriko Okamoto, published in *Developmental Psychology Research*, 25, 23–37, under permission of reprint by Japan Society of Developmental Psychology.

We are sincerely grateful to the families who cooperated with this research. This research received aid from the Grants-in-Aid for Scientific Research, Foundational Research (C) (Issue Number 23530884, research representative: Yoriko Okamoto). Part of this research was presented at the 17th Japan Society of Developmental Psychology (2006) and was introduced in part of Part II, Chapter 11 of *Development Psychology for Parents and Children: Essence of Vertical Research Methods* (Shinyosha), edited by Yoriko Okamoto and Yukie Sugano, and was revised and added to for this paper.

Notes

1. Rissho University
2. Aoyama Gakuin Women's Junior College
3. University of Yamanashi, Graduate School of Education
4. Tohoku Gakuin University

5. Japan Organization for Employment of the Elderly, Persons with Disabilities and Job Seekers
6. Hosen College of Childhood Education
7. Chita Welfare Consultation Center
8. Shohoku College
9. Hokkaido University, Graduate School of Education
10. Tokyo Metropolitan University
11. This Japanese word, "*oishii*" means yummy and delicious, and "*oishii-ne*" that "*oishii*" is added "*ne*" has almost the same meaning. But the two words have different presuppositions in which "*oishii*" has only one speaker who think it is and "*oishii-ne*" has the speaker and a listener(s) both (all) of whom think it is.
12. An utterance ID used in the analysis is given to the examples of proxy talk presented in this report and the tables. Utterance ID consist of a two-digit number for the cooperator, a two-digit number for the age, and a two-digit number for the utterance. After the six-digit vocalization number, "ch" is added for proxy talk from the child's position, "pa" is added for proxy talk from the parent-child position, "am" is added for ambiguous proxy talk, "tr" is added for transitional proxy talk, and "non" is added for non-proxy talk.

References

Adamson, L.B., Bakeman, R., Smith, C.B., & Walters, A.S. (1987). Adults' Interpretation of Infants' Acts. *Developmental Psychology*, **23**, 383–387

Bryant, G.A. & Barrett, H.C. (2007). Recognizing Intentions in Infant-Directed Speech: Evidence for Universals. *Psychological Science*, **18**. 746–751.

Condon, W. & Sander, L. (1974). Synchrony demonstrated between movements of the neonate and adults speech. *Child Development*, **45**, 456–462.

Fantz, R. L. (1961). The origin of form perception. *Scientific American*, **204**, 66–72.

Fernald, A. (1985). Four-month-old infants prefer to listen to motherese. *Infant Behavior and development*, **8**, 181–195.

Fernald, A., Taeschner, T., Dunn, J., Papousek, M., de Boysson-Bardies, B., & Fukui, I. (1989). A cross-language study of prosodic modifications in mothers' and fathers' speech to preverbal infants. *Journal of Child Language*, **16**, 477–501.

Field, T. M., Woodson, R., Greenberg, R., & Cohen, D. (1982). Discrimination and imitation of facial expressions by neonates. *Science*, **218**, 179–181.

Hermans, H.J.M (2001). The Dialogical Self: Toward a Theory of Personal and Cultural Positioning. *Cultural Psychology*, **7**. 243–281.

Hermans, H.J. & Hermans-Jansen, E. (2003). Dialogical Processes and Development of the Self. In J. Valsiner & K.J. Connolly (Eds.), *Handbook of Developmental Psychology* (pp.534–559). London: Sage.

Holquist, M. & Emerson, C. (1982). Glossary. In M. Bakhtin, & M. Holquist (Eds. and Trans.), Emerson, C. (Trans.) *The dialogic imagination: Four essays by M. M. Bakhtin* (pp. 423–434). Austin: University of Texas Press.

Jacobson, J., Boersma, D., Fields, R., & Olson, K. (1983). Paralinguistic Features of Adult Speech to Infants and Small Children. *Child Development*, **54**,436–42.

Kaplan, P.S., Goldstein, M.H., Huckeby, E.R., Owren, M.J., & Cooper, R.P. (1995). Dishabituation of visual attention by infant- versus adult-directed speech: Effects of frequency modulation and spectral composition. *Infant Behavior and Development*, **18**, 209–223.

Kato, T., Kurebayashi, N., Yuuki, M. (1992). *Issaiji to Yoikusha no Sogosayoniyoru Shakaitekikoi no Kozo: Yoji no "Hankoi" to Seijin niyoru "Kajo Kaishaku"* The structure of social actions in the reciprocal actions of one-year old children and their caretaker: the infant's 'half-action' and 'over-interpretation' of adults.) In *Katei Kyoiku Kenkyu Kiyo (The Journal of Family Education Research Center)*, **14**, 96–103. (In Japanese)

Kawakita, J. (1967). *Conceptualization method: for creative development*. Tokyo: Chuokoronsha (In Japanese)

Kaye, K. (1979). Thickening thin data: The maternal role in developing communication and language. In M. Bulkwa (Ed.), *Before speech: The beginning of interpersonal communication* (pp. 191–206). Cambridge, England: Cambridge University Press.

Katz-Wise, S.L., Priess, H.A., & Hyde, J.S. (2010). Gender-Role Attitudes and Behavior Across the Transition to Parenthood. *Developmental Psychology*, **46**, 18–28."

Kitamura, C. & Burnham, D. (2003). Pitch and communicative intent in mother's speech: Adjustments for age and sex in the first year. *Infancy*, **4**. 85–110.

Kitamura, C. & Lam, C. (2009). Age-Specific Preferences for Infant-Directed Affective Intent. *Infancy*, **14**, 77–100.

Marcos, H., Rychebusch, C., & Rabain-Jamin, J. (2003). Adult responses to young children's communicative gestures: joint achievement of speech acts. *First Language*, **23**, 213–237.

Mashiyama, M. (1991). *Children becoming psychological humans*. Gendai Shiso, **19**, 104–115. Tokyo: Seidosha (In Japanese)

Meltzoff, A. N. & Moore, M. K. (1977). Imitation of facial and manual gestures by human neonates. *Science*, **198**, 75–78.

Mitnick, D.M., Heyman, R.E., & Smith Slep, A.M. (2009). Changes in Relationship Satisfaction Across the Transition to Parenthood: A Meta-Analysis. *Journal of Family Psychology*, **23**, 848–852.

Newson, J. (1977). An intersubjective approach to the Systematic description of mother-child interaction. In H.R. Schaffer (ed.) *Studies in Mother-Child Interaction.* (Pp.47–61). New York : Academic Press.

Okamoto, Y. (2001). *Interaction between mother and child*. Yamada, Yoko, Sato,

Tatuya, Hirofumi, Minami (Eds.) Catalog of Field Psychology (pp. 12–19). Tokyo: Kanekoshobo. (In Japanese)

Okamato, Y. (2008a). *How to observe parent-infant interaction.* Okamoto, Yoriko, Sugano, Yukie (Eds.) Developmental Psychology of Parents and Children: Essences of a Longitudinal Investigation. (pp. 41–50). Tokyo: Shinyosha. (In Japanese)

Okamoto, Y. (2008b). *Maternal proxy talk.* Okamoto, Yoriko, Sugano, Yukie (Eds.) Developmental Psychology of Parents and Children: Essences of a Longitudinal Investigation. (pp. 134–146). Tokyo: Shinyosha. (In Japanese)

Okamoto, Y, Sugano, Y, Negayama, K. (2003). Mother *fetus interaction from the viewpoint of the pregnant women's diaries about fetal movements. The Japanese Journal of Developmental Psychology*,14, 64–76.

Rogoff, B. (2003). *The cultural nature of human development.* New York: Oxford university press.

Simon, F., Macchi, C.V., Turati, C., & Valenza, E. (2003). Non-specific perceptual biases at the origins of face processing. In O. Pascalis & A. Slater (Eds.), *The development of face processing in infancy and early childhood: Current perspectives* (pp.13–26). New York: Nova Science Publishers

Suda, O. (1999). *Development to create emotion.* Tokyo: Shinyosha. (In Japanese)

Sugano, Y. (2008). Mother's Negative Feelings Toward Her Child. Okamoto, Yoriko, Sugano, Yukie (Eds.) Developmental Psychology of Parents and Children: Essences of a Longitudinal Investigation. (pp. 147–158). Tokyo: Shinyosha. (In Japanese)

Sugano, Y, Okamoto, Y, Aoki, Y, Ishikawa, A, Kamei, M, Kawata, M, Shoji, R, Takahashi, C, Yagishita (Kawata), A. (2009). Maternal *Accounts of Negative Feelings toward Their Children: A Longitudinal Study.* Japanese Journal of Developmental Psychology 20, 74–85. (In Japanese)

Trainor, L.J., Austin, C.M., & Desjardins, R.N. (2000). Is Infant-Directed Speech Prosody a Result of the Vocal Expression of Emotion? *Psychological Science*, 11. 188–195.

Trevarthen, C. (1979). Communication and cooperation in early infancy: A description of primary intersubjectivity. In M. Bullowa (Ed.). *Before Speech: The beginning of interpersonal communication* (pp.321–347). London: Cambridge University Press.

Valsiner, J. (2007). Semiotic fields in action: Affective guidance of the internalization/ externalization process. In J. Valsiner. *Culture in Minds and Societies: Foundations of Cultural Psychology* (pp.300–357). Los Angeles: Sage Publications.

Wertsch, J. (1991). *Voices of the Mind—A Sociocultural Approach to Mediated Action.* Cambridge, Mass: Harvard University Press.

The *abc* Conjecture of the Derived Logarithmic Functions of Euler's Function and Its Computer Verification

Michinori Yamashita
Daisuke Miyata
Natsumi Fujita

Abstract
Regarding Euler's (totient) function, for an arbitrary number $n > 1$, there exists a k that possesses the characteristic where $\varphi^k(n) = 1$. In this case, if k is expressed as $L(n)$ for n, then L possesses the characteristic of being perfectly logarithmic. For this L, we (Yamashita, Miyata) have provided the following L version *abc* conjecture.

Conjecture: When a, b, and c are relatively prime, numbers are natural, and $a + b = c$, then
$$\max\{L(a), L(b), L(c)\} < 2 \cdot L(rad\,(abc))$$
is feasible.

This paper describes the properties of L and presents verification that this conjecture is correct up to 10^9 using a computer experiment. We also note that the *abc* conjecture recently considered solved by Prof. Mochizuki at Kyoto University is different from the conjecture presented here.

Introduction

Considering $\varphi^k(x) = \varphi(\varphi^{k-1}(x))$ $(k > 1)$ as $\varphi^1(x) = \varphi(x)$ with respect to Euler's function φ, when $x > 1$ then $\varphi(x) < x$. Therefore, there always exists a minimum k such that $\varphi^k(x) = 1$ for all $x > 1$. Heretofore, in regard to the properties of this k, Pilali ([1],[2]), Shapiro ([3],[9]), Murányi ([4]), et al have shown that k possesses (imperfect) logarithmic characteristics. Since then, a great deal of research on this has been conducted. Currently, it is known that by modifying this k (hereinafter, this k shall be indicated as $L(x)$), that the same becomes perfectly logarithmic.[*1]

In this paper, we describe the properties and the extensions of the logarithmic function $L(x)$ derived of Euler's function and note that the abc conjecture pertaining to $L(x)$ we provide holds even under appropriate conditions other than primitive φ-triple, and also cite ours proof of this conjecture.

1. Various Properties of $L(x)$

1.1 Perfect logarithms of $L(x)$ and the evaluation thereof

Definition. 1. (Yamashita, [5]) L *is defined for the natural number n as follows and is called* a derived logarithmic function *of Euler's function.*

$$L(n) = \begin{cases} 0 & (n = 1) \\ L(\varphi(n)) & (n: \text{odd number} > 1) \\ L(\varphi(n)) + 1 & (n: \text{even number}). \end{cases}$$

At this time,

Proposition. 2. *L is perfectly logarithmic for any natural number x, y, i.e.*,
$$L(xy) = L(x) + L(y).$$
Therefore, the following simple evaluation can be obtained for L.

Proposition. 3. *If $L(x) = n$, then*
$$2^n \leq x \leq 3^n.$$
Then, immediately from there:

Corollary. 4. (E1) *If $x \leq 2^n$ then $L(x) \leq n$.*
(E2) *If $x \geq 3^n$ then $L(x) \geq n$.*

Corollary. 5. *Let $x = 2^t \cdot x_0$ (x_0 : odd). If $L(x) = n$, then*
$$x \leq 2^t \cdot 3^{n-t}.$$

Corollary. 6. *Let $x = 2^t \cdot x_0$ (x_0 : odd). If $x > 2^t \cdot 3^{n-t}$, then*

$L(x) > n$.

etc. can be obtained, and the following evaluation formula can also be obtained.

Proposition. 7.

(E3) $\log_3 2 \left(\min\left(L(x), L(y)\right) + 1\right) \leq L(x+y)$
$\leq \log_2 3 \left(\max\left(L(x), L(y)\right) + 1\right)$

(E4) $L(x-y) \leq \log_2 3 \max\left(L(x), L(y)\right)$

Remark: $\log_2 3 = 1.58496250...$, $\log_3 2 = 0.63092975...$

As for this L, we have also obtained the following theorem as an extension form of Euler's function φ.

Theorem. 8. (*Miyata–Yamashita*, [11], [12]) *Let* **P** *be a set of prime numbers and* $\mathbf{P} \to \mathbf{N}$ (*natural numbers*) *be a function such that* $1 \leq f(p) < p \in \mathbf{P}$. *If*

$$\varphi_f(x) = x \prod_{i=1}^{r} \frac{f(p_i)}{p_i}, \quad x = p_1^{e_1} p_2^{e_2} ... p_r^{e_r}$$

and

$$L_{\varphi f}(1) = 0$$
$$L_{\varphi f}(x) = L(\varphi_{\varphi f}(x)) + \#\{p \in f^{-1}(1) : p \mid x\}.$$

then

$$L_{\varphi f}(xy) = L_{\varphi f}(x) + L_{\varphi f}(y).$$

The φ_f in the above theorem is a formal generalization of Euler's function by f. Also, according to the symbol of this theorem, $L(x) = L_\varphi(x)$.

1.2 Extensibility of $L(x)$

L defined on the natural numbers can naturally be extended on $\mathbf{Z} \setminus \{0\}$ via $L(-1) = 0$, $L(-x) = L(x)$. For $L(0)$, if we define, for example, $L(0) = \infty$, it can also be is defined on $\mathbf{Z}$. Therefore, if we define $L\left(\dfrac{x}{y}\right) = L(x) - L(y)$ for $\dfrac{x}{y} \in \mathbf{Q}^\times = \mathbf{Q} \setminus \{0\}$, then we have a natural extension to $\mathbf{Q}$. In other words, the following holds:

Proposition. 9. *The L in Definition 1 can be naturally expanded on rational* numbers **Q** and the properties of Proposition 2 are also inherited.

Can this L (here is where we part ways with the world of Euler's function φ) be expanded to a number $\mathbf{Q}[\sqrt{-1}]$ which is obtained by adding $\sqrt{-1}$ to real numbers **R** and **Q**, or complex number **C**, while maintaining the properties of Proposition 2?

Let us calculate by assuming the properties of Proposition 2. If we do some calculations with irrational numbers then,

- $L(\sqrt{2}) = L(2^{1/2}) = \frac{1}{2}L(2) = \frac{1}{2}$
- $L\left(\frac{1}{\sqrt{2}}\right) = L(2^{-1/2}) = -\frac{1}{2}L(2) = -\frac{1}{2}$
- $L(2^{\sqrt{2}}) = \sqrt{2}L(2) = \sqrt{2}$
- $L(2^{\pi}) = \pi L(2) = \pi$

When observing this situation, in order for L to be welldefined even on **R**, the range must be at least **R**.

In addition, let us continue to observe **C** as well.
If

$$\omega = \cos\left(\frac{2\pi}{n}\right) + \sqrt{-1}\sin\left(\frac{2\pi}{n}\right) \ (n \in \mathbf{N})$$

then from

$$nL(\omega) = L(\omega^n) = L(1) = 0$$

we obtain

$$L(\omega) = 0.$$

In addition, if we let $\zeta = \cos \alpha + \sqrt{-1} \sin \alpha)$, and then take β as $\alpha\beta = 2\pi$, then

$$\beta L(\zeta) = L(\zeta^\beta) = L(1) = 0 \ \text{より} \ L(\zeta) = 0$$

Then, it will be $L(w) = 0$ for the point w on the unit circle of a complex plane, and the arbitrary z of **C** has the form $z = |z|w$. Therefore, we can obtain

$$L(z) = L(|z|w) = L(|z|) + L(w) = L(|z|).$$

However, there remain issues as to whether L can continue or extend in a well-defined manner from **Q** to **R** and **R** to **C** (including handling of transcendental numbers).

2. abc Conjecture for the Derived Logarithmic Function L

2.1 On the *abc* conjecture for L

Regarding this L, we have provided an *abc* conjecture (L version *abc* conjecture) pertaining to this derived logarithmic function L of Euler's function.

Conjecture. (Yamashita–Miyata [14])
Let a, b, c be coprime. If $a + b = c$, then
$$\max\{L(a), L(b), L(c)\} < 2 \cdot L\left(\mathrm{rad}\,(abc)\right).$$
Regarding this conjecture, we confirmed the correctness up to $c < 2^{30}$ by computer verification (Miyata-Yamashita [16]), and by touching lightly on the proof of the polynomial version *abc* conjecture by Stothers ([8]). The results we obtained were as follows.

Theorem. 10. (Yamashita–Miyata [14]) *Let a, b, c be coprime. If $a + b = c$, then*
$$\max\{L(a), L(b), L(c)\} < 2 \cdot L(\mathrm{rad}\,(abc)).$$
The condition of Theorem 10 where $\varphi(a) + \varphi(b) = \varphi(c)$ is feasible, (a, b, c), is called **primitive φ–triple** (Miyata–Yamashita [17]). Yamashita–Miyata have argued regarding the feasibility status of primitive φ–triple, and it is predicted to exist infinitely many times, and it is also known that the probability of existence of primitive φ–triple differs greatly due to the even/odd of c (Yamashita–Miyata [17]).

2.2 Cases other than primitive φ–triple

In Theorem 10 we asserted that our conjecture is correct in the case of primitive φ–triple (Yamashita–Miyata [11]). However, what about cases other than primitive φ–triple?
Let p and q be coprime, and assume
$$\frac{q}{p} = \frac{\varphi(a) + \varphi(b)}{\varphi(c)}$$
If so, then the following theorem holds.

Theorem. 11. *Let a, b, c be coprime. If $a + b = c > 2$, then under the following*

condition (*)
we obtain

(*) $\max(L(p), L(q)) \leq (2 - \log_2 3) L(\mathrm{rad}(abc))$

$\max\{L(a), L(b), L(c)\} < 2 \cdot L(\mathrm{rad}(abc))$.

Proof. When simultaneously both $a + b = c$ and $p\varphi(a) + p\varphi(b) = q\varphi(c)$, then we obtain

$$ac\left(q\frac{\varphi(c)}{c} - p\frac{\varphi(a)}{a}\right) = bc\left(p\frac{\varphi(b)}{b} - q\frac{\varphi(c)}{c}\right)$$

Then if we assume

$$q\frac{\varphi(c)}{c} - p\frac{\varphi(a)}{a} = 0$$

then

$$aq\varphi(c) = cp\varphi(a) = (a+b)\varphi(a)$$

On the other hand, $q\varphi(c) = p\varphi(a) + p\varphi(b)$ results via
(# 1) $a\varphi(b) = b\varphi(a)$
However it must be $a|\varphi(a)$ because $(a, b) = 1$ and it must be $a = 1$. Meanwhile, if $a = 1$, then it is $\varphi(b) = b$ via (# 1), therefore $b = 1$, resulting in a contradiction in $2 < c = a + b = 1 + 1 = 2$. Therefore,

$$q\frac{\varphi(c)}{c} - p\frac{\varphi(a)}{a} \neq 0.$$

From which follows:

$$\frac{a}{b} = \frac{p\frac{\varphi(b)}{b} - q\frac{\varphi(c)}{c}}{q\frac{\varphi(c)}{c} - p\frac{\varphi(a)}{a}}$$

$$= \frac{\mathrm{rad}(abc)\left(p\frac{\varphi(b)}{b} - q\frac{\varphi(c)}{c}\right)}{\mathrm{rad}(abc)\left(q\frac{\varphi(c)}{c} - p\frac{\varphi(a)}{a}\right)}$$

$$= \frac{p\left(\mathrm{rad}\,(abc)\frac{\varphi(b)}{b}\right) - q\left(\mathrm{rad}\,(abc)\frac{\varphi(c)}{c}\right)}{q\left(\mathrm{rad}\,(abc)q\frac{\varphi(c)}{c}\right) - p\left(\mathrm{rad}\,(abc)\frac{\varphi(a)}{a}\right)}$$

Then, if we note the fact that with $k = a, b, c$ then

$$\mathrm{rad}\,(abc)\frac{\varphi(k)}{k} \in \mathbf{N}$$

(hereinafter, rad (abc) will be denoted as rad*), then

$$a \mid p\left(\mathrm{rad}*\frac{\varphi(b)}{b}\right) - q\left(\mathrm{rad}*\frac{\varphi(c)}{c}\right).$$

Therefore,

$$L(a) \leq L\left(p\left(\mathrm{rad}*\frac{\varphi(b)}{b}\right) - q\left(\mathrm{rad}*\frac{\varphi(c)}{c}\right)\right).$$

If the domain of L is expanded $\mathbf{Q}$ and we note that

$$L\left(\frac{\varphi(k)}{k}\right) = \begin{cases} -1 & (k:\mathrm{even}) \\ 0 & (k:\mathrm{odd}) \end{cases}$$

regarding $k = a, b, c$, we can then use Proposition 7 (E4), which results in the following right side of the above equation:

$$L\left(p\left(\mathrm{rad}*\frac{\varphi(b)}{b}\right) - q\left(\mathrm{rad}*\frac{\varphi(c)}{c}\right)\right).$$

Simply, if we denote as rad* $\frac{\varphi(k)}{k} = C(k)$ ($k = a, b, c$) then

$$L(a) \leq \log_2 3 \cdot \max(L(pC(b)), L(qC(c)))$$

$$\leq \log_2 3\left(\left(\frac{2}{\log_2 3} - 1\right)L(\mathrm{rad}*) + \max(L(C(b)), L(C(c)))\right)$$

$$\leq \log_2 3\left(\left(\frac{2}{\log_2 3} - 1\right)L(\mathrm{rad}*) + L(\mathrm{rad}*)\right)$$

$$= 2L(\mathrm{rad}*) = 2L(\mathrm{rad}\,(abc))$$

In the case of primitive φ–triple, since $L(p) = L(q) = L(1) = 0$, then the conditions of Theorem 11 are satisfied and it can then be obtained as a corollary.

Corollary. 12. (Theorem 10) *If a* primitive φ-triple *then*
$$\max\{L(a), L(b), L(c)\} < 2 \cdot L(\text{rad}(abc)) /$$

3. Computer Verification of the Conjecture

3.1 The difficulty of computer verification for $c \leq N = 10^{10}$

For our conjecture, computer experiments have confirmed that the conjecture is true for $c < 2^{30}$ (Miyata–Yamashita [15]), but with $c \geq 2^{30}$ and above it is difficult to verify using a typical PC environment.

Generally, the problem of finding $\varphi(x)$ for x is called an RSA problem, and if $\varphi(x)$ is easily obtained, the RSA public key encryption problem terminates, hence this is a very challenging problem.

Since it is necessary to repeatedly calculate $\varphi(x)$ to calculate $L(x)$, finding $L(x)$ involves more difficulty than the RSA problem.

On the other hand, if $L(x)$ is found for all x where $O(N \log \log N)$, it is known that time complexity $O(N \log \log N)$ can be used [15]. With that method, $L(x)$ can be obtained with $O(\log \log N)$ per each case.

However, this method requires a storage area for $O(N)$ which amounts to 4 GB of memory for $N = 10^9$.

In order to execute $N = 10^{10}$ in the same way (since the integers to be handled exceed 32 bits, it would mean using a 64-bit integer type), 80 GB of memory is required, which is impossible to execute on a typical PC.

As follows, verification was performed at $c \leq N = 10^{10}$ for $(1, b, c)$. The verification results are shown in Table 1, and $q(1, b, c)$ in the Table is called a quality of $(1, b, c)$, expressed as

$$q(1, b, c) = \frac{L(c)}{L(\text{rad}(bc))}.$$

The verification environment was as follows:
- PC: Acer Veriton X4620G
- OS: Windows 8.1 Pro
- CPU: Intel Core i5-3340 CPU (3.10GHz)
- RAM: 12.0GB
- Language: Java 9.0.1 (64-bit) Java (TM) SE Develoment Kit 9.0.1 (64-bit)
- Software: Eclipse

Execution time: 36 minutes 54 seconds

3.2 Computer verification for $c < 10^{10}$ regarding $(1, b, c)$

3.2.1 memoization

In the verification of $(1, b, c)$, $L(x)$ and $L(\text{rad}(x))$ were calculated in advance for $x \leq 10^8$ using the Miyata–Yamashita method ([15]). As necessary, for reference, memoization was implemented. The storage area required for this is about 800 MB.

To obtain $L(x)$ for $x > 10^8$, the function was first factorized into prime numbers by trial division to obtain $\varphi(x)$, and then the memo could be referenced with values less than 10^8. When $x > 10^8$, we sought to the greatest extent possible not to evaluate $L(x)$.

3.2.2 Finding the maximum prime of c

In the verification algorithm, for $S = 10^6$, the calculation was performed by dividing 10^{10} into segments of size S.

For example, for the k–th segment, calculation is performed for $c = kS + 1, kS + 2, \ldots, (k + 1)S$, and then, using the segmented sieve algorithm, the largest prime factor of each c was sought.

If $S \leq \sqrt{N}$, $N(\text{i.e.}, O(S \log N)$ per each one), $O(S \log N)$ is sufficient for the calculation amount. Also, the storage area was $O(S)$ (in reality, $16S$ bytes = 16 MB required).

Let p be the largest prime factor of and $c = xp$. If $p < 10^8$, $L(c)$ and $L(\text{rad}(c))$ can be computed at high speed.

The reason being, if $p > 100$ then $x < 10^8$, it is therefore sufficient to merely reference the memo for both $L(x)$ and $L(p)$ because $L(c) = L(x) + L(p)$.

On the other hand, if $p < 100$, c can be factorized into prime numbers at high speed because it is rendered with the product of small prime numbers less than 100.

3.3 $(1, b, c)$–triple determination

Definition. 13. *Let* $1 + b = c$. $(1, b, c)$ *that satisfy*

$$\frac{L(c)}{L(\operatorname{rad}(abc))} \geq 1.25$$

is called $(1, b, c)$-**triple**.
In this verification, we will judge whether each c is

$$\frac{L(c)}{L(\operatorname{rad}(p-1)) + L(\operatorname{rad}(c))} \geq 1.25$$

Determination is conducted as follows, with p being the maximum prime factor of c, and q being the maximum prime factor of $c - 1$.

3.3.1 Case $p \geq 10^8$

If $c = p$, then $L(p) / (L(\operatorname{rad}(c-1)) + L(p)) < 1$.
If $c = xp$, then $1 < x < 100$. Therefore,

$$\frac{L(c)}{L(\operatorname{rad}(c-1)) + L(\operatorname{rad}(c))}$$

$$\leq \frac{L(x) + L(p)}{2 + L(p)}$$

$$= 1 + \frac{-2 + L(x)}{2 + L(p)}$$

$$\leq 1 + \frac{-2 + \log_2 10^2}{2 + \log_3 10^8} < 1.248.$$

Therefore, in this case, $(1, c - 1, c)$ does not become a triple.

3.3.2 Case $p < 10^8$ and $q < 10^8$

In this case, $L(c)$, $L(\operatorname{rad}(c))$, $L(c - 1)$, $L(\operatorname{rad}(c - 1))$ can be calculated at high speed. So we actually calculate as

$$\frac{L(c)}{L(\operatorname{rad}(c-1)) + L(\operatorname{rad}(c))}$$

and then we simply need to investigate whether it is 1.25 or higher or not.

3.3.3 Case $p < 10^8$ and $q \geq 10^8$

Since $L(q) \geq \log_3 10^8$, then we first seek out

$$\frac{L(c)}{L(\operatorname{rad}(c)) + 1 + \log_3 10^8}$$

If this is not 1.25 or higher, then we can determine that is not a triple.
If not, then we calculate $L(c-1)$ and $L(\text{rad}(c-1))$ while factorizing into prime numbers, then determine whether it is

$$\frac{L(c)}{L(\text{rad}(c-1))+L(\text{rad}(c))} \geq 1.25$$

or not.

By the way, the number of cases where it was necessary to calculate $L(c-1)$ and $L(\text{rad}(c-1))$ by prime factorization was only several hundred times out of $c \leq 10^{10}$. Of those, those that were 1.25 or higher more were 0 times.

3.3.4 The reason for a threshold of 1.25

There are three reasons why we used 1.25 as the sieving threshold for the verification algorithm.

Reason1: The lower the threshold, the higher the number of corresponding triples. And, for this study, we were not interested in small triples.

Reason2: Our conjecture was

$$\frac{\max\{L(c-1), L(c)\}}{L(\text{rad}(c-1))+L(\text{rad}(c))} < 2$$

but the enumeration is

$$\frac{L(c)}{L(\text{rad}(c-1))+L(\text{rad}(c))} \geq 1.25.$$

If there is a c such that

$$\frac{\max\{L(c-1), L(c)\}}{L(\text{rad}(c-1))+L(\text{rad}(c))} \geq 2,$$

then it will be

$$\frac{L(c)}{L(\text{rad}(c-1))+L(\text{rad}(c))} \geq 2\log_3 2 > 1.26$$

which means that it will always be included in this enumeration. Therefore, setting the threshold to 1.25 makes it possible to verify that there is no counterexample.

Reason3: As a practical reason, we tried memoization for 10^8 or less as we wanted to be able to be execute this verification using a personal computer of ordinary specifications. (10^9 is impossible to do without a slightly high-performance personal computer.)

4. Summary and Future Issues

In this study, we examined the domain extensibility of $L(x)$, further improved results using primitive φ–triple, and showed our conjecture is correct for non-primitive φ–triples as long as certain conditions were met.

In terms of verifying our conjecture, we focused on $(1, b, c)$ and verified that our conjecture is correct for $C \leq 10^{10}$.

In terms of future issues, we still need a proof for our conjecture's feasibility, but we also need to verify our conjecture. For the time being, we will further increase N until $c \leq N$. However, of note are the following:
- In the case of $(1, b, c)$, we will increase the evaluation accuracy of the inequality in Section 4.5.1 and lower the sieve threshold to below 1.248.
- We will optimally apply the inequality condition of Theorem 11 to the verification algorithm.

This paper is a partial addition to [19].

Notes

*1. Yamashita showed that k according to a different definition from theirs was completely logarithmic in his high school days ([5]). After that, in 1977, during correspondence with Professor Saburo Uchiyama (Tsukuba University) (Yamashita-Uchiyama, Uchiyama-Yamashita [6],[7]) he learned for the first time of Pilali ([1],[2]), Shapiro ([3]), and Murányi's work ([4]). However, at this timing, facts in a perfect logarithmic form were not known in academic circles. It was not perfectly logarithmic in the first edition of Shapiro's textbook in 1983 ([9]). The first time it become known that it was perfectly logarithmic in academic circles was in the note made by Prasad, et al. ([10]).

References

[1] Pillai Sivasankaranarayana S. : *On some functions connected with* $\varphi(n)$, *Bull.*

Amer. Soc., 35, 6 (1929), 832–836
[2] Pillai Sivasankaranarayana S. : *On a function connected with $\varphi(n)$*, Bull. Amer. Soc., 35, 6 (1929), 837–841
[3] Shapiro, H. : *An arithmetic function arising from the φ function*, Amer. Math. Monthly, 50 (1943), 18–30
[4] Murányi, Aladár. : *Az Euler-félé φ -függvény iterálásával nyert számelméleti füuggvényröl*, Mat. Lapok 11 (1960), 47–67
[5] Yamashita M. → Yamamoto, S. : *On the Euler's function, 1971.12.23* (*private communication*)
[6] Yamashita, M. → Uchiyama, S. : *On a derived logarithmic function of an Euler function, 1977.9.10*, (*private communication, Uchiyama, S.=Uchiyama, Saburo* [*Prof., Univ. of Tsukuba*])
[7] Uchiyama, S. → Yamashita, M. : *Re: On a derived logarithmic function of an Euler function, 1977.9.12*, (*private communication*)
[8] Stothers, W. W. : *Polynomial identities and hauptmoduln*, Quarterly J. Math. Oxford, 2 32 (1981), 349–370
[9] Shapiro, Harold N.: *Introduction to the Theory of Numbers*, John Wiley & Sons, New York et al.,(1983) [3. Arithmetic Functions §3.7 The Euler Function. Exrcise] 17 (77–78)]
[10] Prasad, V. Siva Rama–Rangamma M.–Fonseca Phil. : *On functions arising form generalized Euler functions*, Indian J. pure appl. Math., 18(10), (1987), 941–946
[11] Miyata D.–Yamashita M. : *A generalization of Yamashita's note on derived logarithmic functions of Euler functions*, 2001.12.14, (unpublished)
[12] Miyata D.–Yamasita M. *Note on derived logarithmic functions of Euler's functions, Proceedings of Autum meeting*(*App. Math.*), Math. Soc. of Japan, 2004.9, (in Japanese)
[13] Miyata D.–Yamashita M.–Tomonaga Shoji: *On a derived logarithmic function of a generalized Euler's function*, A research meeting involving MEXT (The Ministry of Education, Culture, Sports, Science and Technology) and special university educational members (Kochi University of Technology adopted), Kochi University of Technology, 2004.10.23 (in Japanese)
[14] Yamashita M.–Miyata D.: *On the abc conjecture for a derived logarithmic function of the Euler function*, Proceedings of 1st CCATS2015 IEEE (International Conference on Computer Application & Technologies 2015), Session 7(9.2), Kunibiki Messe (Matsue), 2015.8.31–9.2
[15] Miyata D.–Yamashita M.: *Enumeration of abc–triples in a derived logarithmic function of Euler's function*, Japan Personal Computer Application and Technology Society's 1st Workshop for "Mathematical Science and Computers" (2015), Japan Personal Computer Application and Technology Society, Rissho University, 2016.3.18, JPCATS research report "Mathematical Science and Computers" Vol. 3 E-ISSN 2188-1685, 23-24, (in Japanese)
[16] Yamashita M.–Miyata D.: *Feasibility status of $\varphi(a) + \varphi(b) = \varphi(c)$ and abc*

conjecture of a derived logarithmic function of Euler's function, Proceedings of the 1st International ICT Application Research Society Conference (2016) (online edition: ISSN 2432-7956), International ICT Application Research Society, Rissho University Shinagawa Campus, S3-4, 2017.3.12, (in Japanese)

[17] Miyata D.–Yamashita M.: *High speed enumeration of abc-triples in a derived logarithmic function of Euler's function*, Journal of International Society for ICT Utilization Journal, Volume 1, No. 1, International ICT Application Research Society, 111-116 (2017.6.30), (in Japanese)

[18] Fjita N.–Miyata D.–Yamashita M.: *On the enumeration of $(1, b, c)$–triples in the Yamashita-Miyata conjecture*, Proceedings of the Annual meeting 2017 (International ICT Application Research Society), D2-5, IIARS, 2017.12.09, 192-196, (in Japanese)

[19] Yamashita M.–Miyata D.–Fujita N.: *On the abc conjecture of a derived logarithmic function $L(x)$ of Euler's functionannd its computer verification*, Faculty of Geo-environmental Science, Rissho University, Geo-environmental Research, No. 20, (2018), 143-149, (in Japanese)

Calculation Results

b	c	$q(1, b, c)$
$2 \cdot 3^7$	$5^4 \cdot 7$	1.667
$19 \cdot 509^3$	$2^{19} \cdot 3^4 \cdot 59$	1.647
$3 \cdot 5^5 \cdot 47^2$	$2^{18} \cdot 79$	1.643
$3^9 \cdot 7^2 \cdot 197$	$2^7 \cdot 5^7 \cdot 19$	1.6
$3^{16} \cdot 7$	$2^3 \cdot 11 \cdot 23 \cdot 53^3$	1.563
$2^4 \cdot 3^7 \cdot 547$	$5^8 \cdot 7^2$	1.538
$3^2 \cdot 7$	2^6	1.5
$3^3 \cdot 7 \cdot 19 \cdot 73$	2^{18}	1.5
$11^4 \cdot 47$	$2^{15} \cdot 3 \cdot 7$	1.5
$2^{11} \cdot 3^3 \cdot 19$	$5^4 \cdot 41^2$	1.5
$5^4 \cdot 367$	$2^{15} \cdot 7$	1.417
$31 \cdot 127^2$	$2^5 \cdot 5^6$	1.417
$7^2 \cdot 127 \cdot 337$	2^{21}	1.4
$2^6 \cdot 3 \cdot 5 \cdot 7 \cdot 13^4 \cdot 17$	239^4	1.4
$3^7 \cdot 13 \cdot 23^2$	$2^9 \cdot 5^4 \cdot 47$	1.375
$7^2 \cdot 43^4$	$2 \cdot 5^4 \cdot 13^3 \cdot 61$	1.353

The abc Conjecture of the Derived Logarithmic Functions of Euler's Function and Its Computer Verification

b	c	$q(1, b, c)$
$5^4 \cdot 19 \cdot 15541$	$2^{24} \cdot 11$	1.35
$3^{13} \cdot 1277$	$2^3 \cdot 19^2 \cdot 89^3$	1.35
$2^3 \cdot 7^5 \cdot 13^2 \cdot 109$	$3^3 \cdot 11^3 \cdot 41^3$	1.35
$2^5 \cdot 3^2$	17^2	1.333
$2^5 \cdot 3 \cdot 5^2$	7^4	1.333
$3^2 \cdot 5 \cdot 7 \cdot 13$	2^{12}	1.333
$3^4 \cdot 79$	$2^8 \cdot 5^2$	1.333
$5 \cdot 11^3$	$2^9 \cdot 13$	1.333
$2^6 \cdot 3^2 \cdot 5 \cdot 29$	17^4	1.333
$2^5 \cdot 3 \cdot 5 \cdot 7 \cdot 29^2$	41^4	1.333
$5^3 \cdot 7^4 \cdot 11$	$2^{13} \cdot 13 \cdot 31$	1.333
$7^4 \cdot 2399$	$2^{10} \cdot 3^2 \cdot 5^4$	1.333
$2^5 \cdot 3^3 \cdot 7 \cdot 13 \cdot 307$	17^6	1.333
$3^7 \cdot 53 \cdot 131^2$	$2^{20} \cdot 7 \cdot 271$	1.333
$3^9 \cdot 5^4 \cdot 709$	$2^6 \cdot 53 \cdot 137^3$	1.333
$2^6 \cdot 3^{10} \cdot 331$	$17^5 \cdot 881$	1.318
$7^2 \cdot 71^2 \cdot 223$	$2^{15} \cdot 41^2$	1.316
$2^{14} \cdot 8111$	$3^5 \cdot 5^7 \cdot 7$	1.313
$7^3 \cdot 487$	$2 \cdot 17^4$	1.308
$7^2 \cdot 13^2 \cdot 186391$	$2^{26} \cdot 23$	1.304
$19^3 \cdot 23^2 \cdot 1613$	$2^{19} \cdot 3 \cdot 61^2$	1.304
$2^{12} \cdot 5^3$	$3^5 \cdot 7^2 \cdot 43$	1.3
$31^3 \cdot 79^2$	$2^{16} \cdot 2837$	1.3
$3^7 \cdot 11 \cdot 19^2 \cdot 31$	$2^{18} \cdot 13 \cdot 79$	1.3
$3^2 \cdot 7^3 \cdot 19^4$	$2^{13} \cdot 49109$	1.3
$7^4 \cdot 13 \cdot 23^2 \cdot 59$	$2^4 \cdot 3^6 \cdot 17^4$	1.3
$5 \cdot 139^3$	$2^7 \cdot 3 \cdot 11^2 \cdot 17^2$	1.294
$2^7 \cdot 3 \cdot 5^2 \cdot 7^4$	4801^2	1.294
$2^3 \cdot 3^7 \cdot 5^4 \cdot 7$	$13^2 \cdot 673^2$	1.294
$2 \cdot 3 \cdot 281^3$	$7^5 \cdot 89^2$	1.294

b	c	$q(1,b,c)$
$3 \cdot 157 \cdot 3323^2$	$2^{25} \cdot 5 \cdot 31$	1.292
$3^5 \cdot 5$	$2^6 \cdot 19$	1.286
$3^7 \cdot 13 \cdot 17$	$2^{13} \cdot 59$	1.286
$2^3 \cdot 3^3 \cdot 5 \cdot 7^3 \cdot 127$	19^6	1.286
$3^6 \cdot 5^3 \cdot 4003$	$2^{17} \cdot 11^2 \cdot 23$	1.286
$3^{14} \cdot 311$	$2^{15} \cdot 5 \cdot 7 \cdot 1297$	1.286
$3^6 \cdot 5 \cdot 493291$	$2^{18} \cdot 19^3$	1.286
$2^{10} \cdot 3 \cdot 5^2 \cdot 43 \cdot 1321$	257^4	1.28
$2^7 \cdot 3^2 \cdot 5 \cdot 29 \cdot 41761$	17^8	1.28
$23^2 \cdot 109 \cdot 491$	$2^{20} \cdot 3^3$	1.278
$3 \cdot 43 \cdot 127$	2^{14}	1.273
$3^5 \cdot 5 \cdot 7^2$	$2^4 \cdot 61^2$	1.273
$2 \cdot 3^3 \cdot 11^3$	$5^5 \cdot 23$	1.273
$7^2 \cdot 17^3 \cdot 2143$	$2^{22} \cdot 3 \cdot 41$	1.273
$47^3 \cdot 53 \cdot 109$	$2^{22} \cdot 11 \cdot 13$	1.273
$19 \cdot 37^3 \cdot 937$	$2^{22} \cdot 5 \cdot 43$	1.273
$5^3 \cdot 71^2 \cdot 2971$	$2^{17} \cdot 3^3 \cdot 23^2$	1.273
$13^3 \cdot 43 \cdot 163^2$	$2^7 \cdot 5^7 \cdot 251$	1.273
$2^4 \cdot 3^2 \cdot 5^3 \cdot 7 \cdot 17^2 \cdot 109$	251^4	1.273
524287	2^{19}	1.267
$3 \cdot 7^3 \cdot 11^3$	$2^9 \cdot 5^2 \cdot 107$	1.267
$3^4 \cdot 37 \cdot 79 \cdot 173$	$2^{16} \cdot 5^4$	1.263
$3^8 \cdot 7 \cdot 937$	$2^{10} \cdot 5^2 \cdot 41^2$	1.263
$3 \cdot 5 \cdot 7 \cdot 11^3 \cdot 317$	$2^{18} \cdot 13^2$	1.263
$2^4 \cdot 3^2 \cdot 7 \cdot 11 \cdot 13^2 \cdot 79$	23^6	1.263
$3^6 \cdot 17^3 \cdot 71$	$2^{12} \cdot 7^3 \cdot 181$	1.263
$3^3 \cdot 5^2 \cdot 7^3 \cdot 5779$	$2^{22} \cdot 11 \cdot 29$	1.261
$2^{14} \cdot 7^4 \cdot 13^2$	$17^3 \cdot 29^2 \cdot 1609$	1.261
19^3	$2^2 \cdot 5 \cdot 7^3$	1.25
$3^4 \cdot 7 \cdot 11^2$	$2^{10} \cdot 67$	1.25

The abc Conjecture of the Derived Logarithmic Functions of Euler's Function and Its Computer Verification

b	c	$q(1,b,c)$
$3^5 \cdot 643$	$2 \cdot 5^7$	1.25
$5 \cdot 7^4 \cdot 19$	$2^8 \cdot 3^4 \cdot 11$	1.25
$3 \cdot 5^2 \cdot 11 \cdot 31 \cdot 41$	2^{20}	1.25
$5 \cdot 29 \cdot 47^3$	$2^9 \cdot 3^5 \cdot 11^2$	1.25
$2^4 \cdot 5^2 \cdot 7^2 \cdot 13^2 \cdot 29$	$3^8 \cdot 11^4$	1.25
$5^9 \cdot 163$	$2^4 \cdot 3^3 \cdot 23 \cdot 179^2$	1.25
$3^2 \cdot 7 \cdot 11 \cdot 31 \cdot 151 \cdot 331$	2^{30}	1.25
$3^8 \cdot 13^2 \cdot 2311$	$2^{18} \cdot 5^2 \cdot 17 \cdot 23$	1.25
$2^2 \cdot 5^4 \cdot 17^3 \cdot 211$	$3^3 \cdot 7^3 \cdot 23^4$	1.25

Characteristics of the Potential Temperature Distribution Along Mountain Slopes Experiencing Cross-Mountain Air Currents in the Winter Season

Yasushi Watarai[1]
Yoshinori Shigeta[2]
Kiyotaka Nakagawa[3]

Abstract

In winter, northwesterly winds in the vicinity of Japan are predominant in the winter pressure distribution pattern that characterizes the climate of the environs of Japan, and on the Kanto Plain cross-mountain air currents frequently occur in winter because the winds pass over the Joshin'etsu mountainous region. A detailed analysis of the cross-mountain air currents is important to understanding the climate in the northwestern inland region of the Kanto Plain on the leeward side. In addition, little research has been conducted on the role of the gap flow in regard to the winter cross-mountain air currents. To address this shortage, advanced meteorological observation was carried out along the channel traversing the Joshin'etsu mountainous region, and that data was used to research the characteristics of the surface atmosphere along the mountain slopes when winter cross-mountain air currents blow. As a result, in the case in which cross-mountain air currents were not blowing, the potential temperature along the mountain slope tended to rise with altitude, in both the Sea of Japan side and Pacific Ocean side. However, in the case in which cross-mountain air currents were blowing, the potential temperature distribution was nearly uniform on the slope of the leeward, Pacific Ocean side, regardless of elevation. The case in which cross-mountain air currents were blowing had characteristics similar to foehn. This also suggests an impact by gap winds that pass through the Uonogawa-Tonegawa channel.

Introduction

The northwestern inland region of the Kanto Plain, which lies between Kumagaya and Maebashi, comprises a semi-basin-like land formation bordered by mountains on three sides: the Taishaku Mountains and the Ashio Mountains to the north, the Echigo Mountains to the northwest, and the Kanto Mountains to the west, southwest, and south. Its climate is massively influenced by these mountain regions. For example, this region experiences intense heat frequently as the weather becomes hotter during the warmer months of the year (May to September), and is one of the areas of Japan where high or extremely high temperatures occur quite frequently; it is considered that it is caused by the inland location, which lessens the impact of sea breezes, and the topographical factors, which include the influence of valley wind circulation and cross-mountain air currents induced by the surrounding mountains. When a record high temperature occurred in Kumagaya on 16 August 2007 (a daily maximum air temperature of 40.9°C), the development of northwesterly foehn winds across the Echigo Mountains was cited as one factor behind this (Shinohara et al., 2009; Watarai et al., 2009; Takane and Kusaka, 2001).

Because a typical sea-level pressure pattern frequently observed in winter around Japan comprises high pressure to the west and low pressure to the east, northwesterly monsoon winds tend to develop on the Kanto Plain on many days during winter. In these cases, it is considered that the air temperature and surface wind in the northwestern inland region of the Kanto Plain are affected by the cross-mountain air currents, which traverse the Echigo Mountains located on the windward side of the plain. When particularly powerful northwesterly winds blow in certain regions, these are referred to as *karakkaze* or *akagi-oroshi* (descending air currents from mountains). Miya and Kusaka (2009) undertook a climatological analysis of *karakkaze* based on the Automated Meteorological Data Acquisition System (AMeDAS) data for 15 winters in order to observe the characteristics of these air currents. The data when the *karakkaze* is blowing showed a clear diurnal variation of wind velocity (strong during the daytime and weak during the nighttime), a drop in relative humidity, an increase in solar radiation, and relatively weakening of the atmospheric stability level. It was suggested that the *karakkaze* follows the characteristics of foehn winds, and surface winds grow stronger in the daytime by heat convective mixing.

As has been explained in detail by Saito (1994), the two-dimensional behavior of the atmosphere when air currents traverse mountains will vary depending on the wind velocity to the windward side, the height of the mountain and the static stability. However, actual mountain regions are not perfectly two-dimensional, and cross-mountain air currents exhibit three-dimensional behavior due to topographical influences. When fully stable stratification develops in the atmosphere, air currents that circumvent the mountains in a horizontal direction frequently develop, and air currents that follow the paths of the saddle-shaped recesses and channels in mountain ranges grow stronger. Saito (1992) carried out numerical experiments on the cross-mountain air currents that traverse mountain ranges possessing saddle-shaped recesses, which revealed a tendency for particularly powerful descending air currents to develop to the leeward side of such saddle-shaped recesses. The kinds of effects brought about by air currents that emerge from channels in this manner have also been noted in foehn winds in the Alps. In a review by Drobinski et al. (2007), who compiled the results of a series of intensive observations and model research studies looking at foehn winds in the Alps, shows instances of gap winds forming in the channels of certain alpine valleys (shallow foehn) as the initial stage of a foehn wind, before transitioning into cross-mountain air currents (deep foehn) that cross the ridgelines at the center of the mountains, and instances in which temperatures rise markedly due to compensatory air flows from the upper atmosphere, which develop due to the dispersal of shallow foehn wind at the exit point of valley. In the case of the northwestern inland region of the Kanto Plain, channels where the development of gap winds has been suggested are found in the mountain regions, such as the Uonogawa-Tonegawa channel which cuts across the Echigo Mountains, and the Chikumagawa-Usuigawa channel in the Kanto Mountains. However, little research focusing on the role of these channels in relation to cross-mountain air currents has been undertaken.

In order to investigate in detail the structure and formation mechanisms of cross-mountain air currents and gap winds, which affect the northwestern inland region of the Kanto Plain regardless of the season, it is important to advance research through a combination of finely-detailed spatio-temporal observations and numerical simulations of the nearby Joshin'etsu mountainous region. However, it has to be admitted that obtaining sufficiently detailed observation data for the Joshin'etsu mountainous region from the existing meteorological observation network is no easy task, and a limited range of meteorological elements are available to be used. Therefore, our research group has expanded the spatio-temporally dense network of surface meteorological observation along the channels that traverse the Joshin'etsu mountainous region in particular, and carried out a series of observations based on this network, under the Rissho University Joshin'etsu Mountainous Region Meteorological Observation Project. The objective of this paper is to clarify the characteristics of the surface atmosphere along the slopes of such channels during the winter season, both when cross-mountain air currents are blowing and when no such currents are blowing, based on our data.

1. Overview of the Observations and Data Used

1.1 Advanced meteorological observations from the Joshin'etsu mountainous region

As set out previously, our research group conducted advanced meteorological observations from the Joshin'etsu mountainous region. As these observations were intended to target the cross-mountain air currents that cut in a traverse line across the Joshin'etsu mountainous regions as well as gap winds, we developed the surface observation network by setting out two observation lines which followed major channels that were relatively large in scale and which more or less intersect at the main ridgelines of the mountain range. One observation line followed a course of traverse along a channel passing from Uonogawa on the Sea of Japan side through Tonegawa on the Pacific Ocean side, and straddling Mikunitoge (hereinafter referred to as the "Uonogawa-Tonegawa line"), while the other observation line followed a course of traverse along a channel that passes from Chikumagawa on the Sea of Japan side through Usuigawa on the Pacific Ocean side, and straddling Usuitoge (the "Chikumagawa-Usuigawa line"). A total of 24 observation sites were set up, comprising 16 points along the Uonogawa-Tonegawa line, seven points along the Chikumagawa-Usuigawa line and one point close to the summit of Mt. Akagi, which is located in the far northwest of the Kanto Plain. Three elements were noted in the observation: temperature, relative humidity and atmospheric pressure. We envisaged that conserved values such as potential temperature and equivalent potential temperature could be derived from the simultaneous observation of these meteorological elements, enabling conjectures to be formed about the behavior of the atmosphere close to the surface level. Shigeta et al. (2013) may be referred to for a more detailed overview of the observation.

1.2 Data used

Out of the 24 meteorological observation sites in the Joshin'etsu mountainous region, data were used from a total of 16 observation sites along the Uonogawa-Tonegawa Line (shown in open circles in Fig. 1). The data cover a four-month period over winter from December 2013 to March 2014, and include three meteorological elements (temperature, relative humidity and atmospheric pressure) sampled at 10-minute intervals.

This study conducted an analysis of two cases (26 and 28 February 2014) in which the daytime temperatures were elevated markedly above temperatures for normal years during times when the northwestern Kanto Plain experienced sunny weather. As there was no wind data among our observation items, we used data for surface wind direction and wind velocity that had been observed at the Maebashi Local Meteorological Observatory and at the AMeDAS observation sites (Numata, Minakami, Yuzawa, Koide and Nagaoka), near the Uonogawa-Tonegawa Line. We also referred to data on temperature, relative humidity and sunshine duration taken from the Maebashi Local Meteorological Observatory. The relative positions of our observation sites compared to the various Japan Meteorological Agency weather stations and AMeDAS sites are shown in Fig. 1. Finally, we also confirmed the stratification on the Sea of Japan side (Wajima) and the Pacific Ocean side (Tateno) on the two dates in question by using radiosonde observation values provided via the University of Wyoming website.

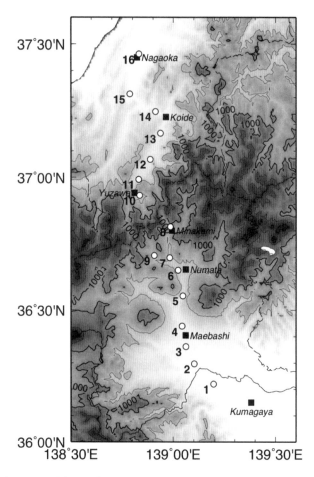

Fig. 1 The locations of the 16 observation sites (represented here by open circles) out of the advanced meteorological observation network in the Joshin'etsu mountainous region whose data was used in this study. The figures here show the number of each observation site. The isolines show the elevation (the isolines being taken at 500m intervals), and the dashed lines show the prefectural boundaries. The black squares represent the weather offices of the Japan Meteorological Agency and AMeDAS sites which are close to observation sites.

2. Results

2.1 Surface potential temperature distribution during the winter of 2013–2014

Fig. 2 shows the mean surface potential temperature distribution over a four-month period from December 2013 to March 2014, created based on the advanced meteorological observation data for the Joshin'etsu mountainous region. Comparing the data for the slope on the Pacific Ocean side (shown below the central bold line in Fig. 2) and that for the slope on the Sea of Japan side (shown above the same line), some major differences are apparent in the characteristics of the potential temperature distribution along these slopes. On the slope on the Pacific Ocean side, the potential temperature is approximately the same at elevations of 100m to 500m, the central area of the slope, particularly during the daytime. It is evident that on the Pacific Ocean side at elevations of less than 600m the tendency is that the lower the elevation of the slope, the higher the potential temperature tends to become, with potential temperatures in the plains area where the elevation is below 100m being somewhat higher than in the central areas of the slopes, while the potential temperatures in areas of the slopes above 500m in elevation are somewhat lower than in the central areas. Conversely, on the Sea of Japan side, in areas of the slope with altitudes of 100m or above the tendency is that the higher the elevation, the higher the potential temperatures tend to be.

Fig. 2 shows the mean values throughout the whole period, including sunny days and stormy days. With "sunny days" being defined as those with eight or more hours of sunlight and "cross-mountain air current days" defined as those days in which the prevailing wind pattern was west-northwest to north-northwest and in which the daily mean wind velocity was 3m/s or more, 51 days out of a total of 121 days across the period corresponded to such a definition (42% of the total), based on observation values from the Maebashi Local Meteorological Observatory. When we created a composite figure for the potential temperatures only for the cross-mountain air current days, the characteristics were almost the same as in Fig. 2 (figure omitted).

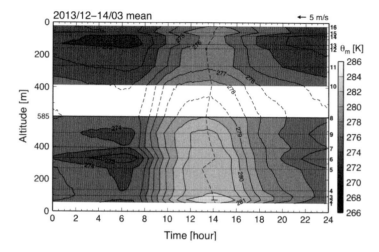

Fig. 2 Mean potential temperature distribution for four-month period from December 2013–March 2014 based on the advanced surface observation data along the Uonogawa-Tonegawa channel. The vertical axis shows the elevation in line with the course of traverse, with the area above the central bold line being the Sea of Japan side, and the area below this line being the Pacific Ocean side. The dashed line connects together the maximum values for potential temperature throughout the day.

2.2. Case of February 26, 2014

On February 26, 2014, there was fairly light wind, the prevailing wind direction was northwest, and the daily mean wind velocity was 2.2m/s at the Maebashi Local Meteorological Observatory. Fig. 3 (a) shows a surface weather chart for 09:00 on February 26. A migratory anticyclone covered much of the Japanese archipelago centering on the point to the immediate north of the Noto Peninsula, and conditions across this region (excluding Kyushu and the Nansei Islands) developed under the influence of the high atmospheric pressure. The environs of the Kanto region experienced high atmospheric pressure throughout the day, resulting in sunny weather. The graph indicated in gray in Fig. 4 shows the air temperature and relative humidity at Maebashi. The air temperature at Maebashi fell to almost 0°C at around 6:00 in the morning, but then rose at sunrise to reach a daily maximum temperature of 13.1°C (deviation from normal year: +2.8°C), which was recorded

Characteristics of the Potential Temperature Distribution Along Mountain Slopes Experiencing Cross-Mountain Air Currents in the Winter Season

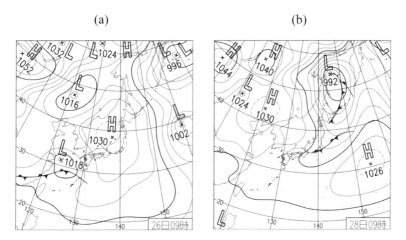

Fig. 3 Surface weather charts for (a) February 26, 2014 and (b) February 28, 2014 (taken from the Japan Meteorological Agency). Both taken at 09:00 (AM).

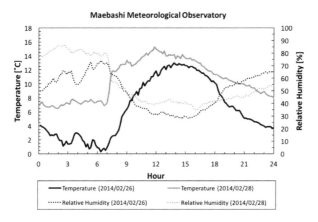

Fig. 4 Temporal change in the surface air temperature (represented by solid lines) and relative humidity (dotted lines) taken from the Maebashi Local Meteorological Observatory for February 26, 2014 (gray lines) and February 28, 2014 (black lines).

at 14:37. Following this, the air temperature fell gradually from evening through the night, following a pattern of diurnal variation that is typical for a sunny day. The relative humidity level was inversely correlated with the air temperature, with a daily minimum humidity level of 27% reached at 14:43.

Fig. 5 shows a vertical profile based on the radiosonde data gathered for 09:00 on 26 February at Wajima on the Sea of Japan side and Tateno on the Pacific Ocean side. An inversion layer at 800–900 hPa was observed, with the air in the layers above this being extremely dry. This could be a subsidence inversion layer with a migratory anticyclone. There is a tendency for the equivalent potential temperature and saturation equivalent potential temperature to increase at the higher levels of the atmosphere, indicating an extremely stable state in the atmosphere. It is evident that the vertical profiles for Wajima and Tateno are extremely similar, and that there are few differences in the stratification of the lower atmosphere for the Sea of Japan side and that for the Pacific Ocean side, while the horizontal potential temperature gradient is extremely small.

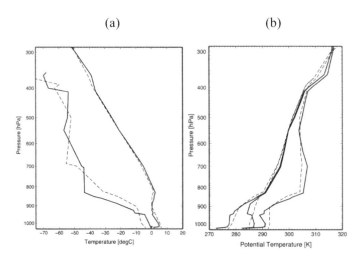

Fig. 5 Vertical profiles at Wajima (solid line) and Tateno (dashed line) at 09:00 on February 26, 2014. (a) shows the air temperature and frost point (from the center-right side of the chart), and (b) shows the potential temperature, equivalent potential temperature and saturated equivalent potential temperature from left side of the chart.

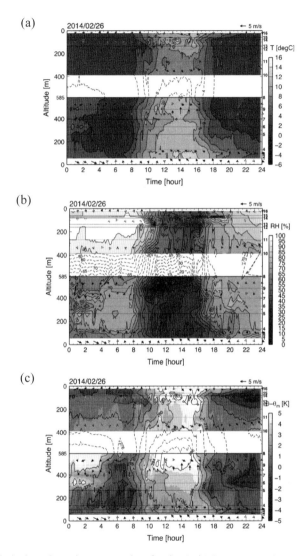

Fig. 6 Isopleths based on observation data for the Joshin'etsu mountainous region on February 26, 2014, with (a) showing the surface air temperature, (b) the relative humidity and (c) the potential temperature. The vertical axis is the same as in Fig.2. The arrows show the hour-by-hour values for surface wind taken from the observatories and AMeDAS sites which are closest to the course of traverse.

The isopleths for the temperature, relative humidity and potential temperature taken from the observation data from the Joshin'etsu mountainous region are shown in Fig. 6. Looking at the surface air temperature (Fig. 6a), the figure shows a tendency for temperatures to be somewhat higher for the plains area where the elevation is below 100m, compared to the slopes above this elevation during both daytime and nighttime. However, for the slopes at elevations of approximately 100–400m, a more or less uniform temperature distribution is found, and the disparity between the Sea of Japan side and Pacific Ocean side is small at the same level of elevation. Overall, lower values are observed for the relative humidity for the slopes on the Pacific Ocean side than for the Sea of Japan side (Fig. 6b), but at elevations of approximately 400m and above during the daytime, slopes on both sides are characterized by extreme dryness. Looking at the potential temperature distribution (Fig. 6c) derived from the air temperature and atmospheric pressure values taken from the observation data, a tendency for the potential temperature to rise as the elevation grows higher can be observed on both slopes (a point which differs from the mean distribution graph for the four-month period; Fig. 2), with a distribution pattern that is close to symmetry with respect to the ridgeline. The surface air on the slopes during the daytime is almost isentropic, but the potential temperature is somewhat higher at elevations of approximately 400m and above. Based on the fact that this region corresponds to the air zone of extreme dryness, it is suggested that this is due to the effect of the downward wind which accompanies the migratory anticyclone. In the isopleths, the surface wind at the meteorological observation sites and the AMeDAS observation sites is recorded together with the elevation at the observation sites; looking at the surface wind during the daytime, some elements are observed to converge in the mountain range on the slopes for the surface wind, based on which it is suggested that valley wind circulation has developed. However, due to the suppression created by the downward wind with high pressure, it is surmised that in the formation of the valley wind circulation is weak, and that the circulation is low in height if these are formed.

2.3 Case of February 28, 2014

On February 28, 2014, two days after the first case, it was a sunny day with 9.2 hours of sunlight at the Maebashi Local Meteorological Observatory, and the prevailing wind direction, daily mean wind velocity, and daily maximum wind velocity showed at north-northwest, 4.4m/s, and 8.6m/s (measured at 14:02; wind direction at north-northwest), respectively. Fig. 3 (b) shows the surface weather chart for 09:00 on February 28: two low-pressure points to the north and south (with the south point dissipating by 09:00) passed by the environs of Japan before shifting to an atmospheric pressure distribution pattern that is typical for winter. There was slight precipitation until 4:00 at Maebashi due to the influence of the stationary front that developed to the south of Kanto region at 09:00. Although the precipitation then dissipated, considerable cloud cover persisted throughout the entire day (daily mean cloud cover: 9.5). However, as stated previously, the sunshine duration for the day was long at 9.5 hours, and most of the cloud cover was light in degree throughout the day. A northwest to north-northwest wind blew throughout almost all the day from around 8:00 onwards; i.e., a cross-mountain air current was predominant in the northwestern Kanto Plain. The black lines in Fig. 4 show the air temperature and relative humidity at Maebashi on 28 February. The diurnal air temperature range at Maebashi on 28 February was smaller than on 26 February; this is due to the fact that, on 28 February the daily maximum air temperature at 15.5°C was higher than on 26 February, the air temperature did not fall in the morning on this day due to heat remaining from the previous day, and the effects of greater cloud cover throughout the day. Another notable feature was the somewhat rapid rise in air temperature at a rate of 4.7°C/hour between 7:00 and 8:00, at the same time as a fall in relative humidity at a rate of 22%/hour. Based on the fact that the northwesterly cross-mountain air current became prominent more-or-less between the boundaries of this timeframe, it is surmised that there is a relationship between these developments.

According to the vertical profile (Fig. 7) for 09:00 on 28 February, the lower troposphere can be divided into a lower humid layer and an upper dry layer at 750hPa. This characteristic is observed both at Wajima on the Sea of Japan side and at Tateno on the Pacific Ocean side. At Tateno, the areas close to the surface under 1,000hPa were mostly saturated, and it can be assumed that clouds were found there. In addition, when the potential temperature profiles at Wajima and Tateno are compared, there is a disparity of approximately 1,000m in height, for example, 290K being located at approximately 800hPa in Wajima but at approximately 900hPa in Tateno. This suggests that there is a large horizontal gradient for potential temperature for the Sea of Japan side and the Pacific Ocean side, with this characteristic being observed

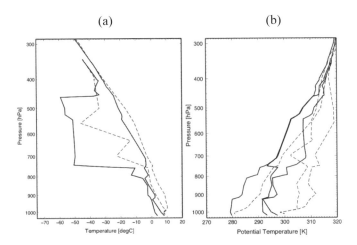

Fig. 7 Vertical profiles at Wajima (solid line) and Tateno (dashed line) at 09:00 on 28 February 2014. (a) shows the air temperature and frost-point (from the right side of the chart), while (b) shows the potential temperature, equivalent potential temperature and saturated equivalent potential temperature from left side of the chart.

around the 1,000 to 400hPa layer.

Fig. 8 shows the isopleths for the temperature, relative humidity and potential temperature along the mountain slopes on February 28. There is a major contrast between the Sea of Japan side and the Pacific Ocean side for both temperature (Fig. 8a) and relative humidity (Fig. 8b), with low temperature and high humidity on the Sea of Japan side compared to high temperature and low humidity on the Pacific Ocean side. The values for the Pacific Ocean side show a distribution pattern in which the lower the altitude, the higher the temperature and lower the humidity, particularly during the period throughout the day from 08:00 onwards. In the distribution patterns for potential temperature (Fig. 8c), the potential temperatures for each slope are similar during the daytime regardless of the height on the slope, but there is a major disparity in potential temperature between the Pacific Ocean side and the Sea of Japan side, with that for the Pacific Ocean side being higher by approximately 10K. When the potential temperature for the slopes is compared with that for the plains area, on the Sea of Japan side of the plain, the plains area is somewhat lower than that of the slope, whereas on the Pacific

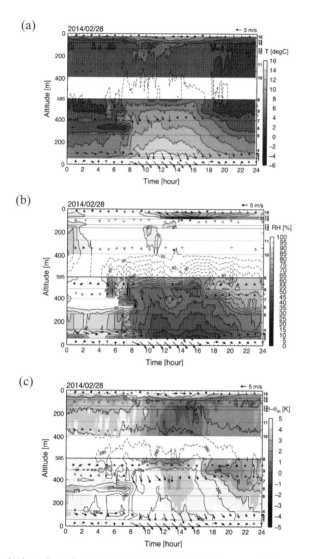

Fig. 8 Isopleths based on observation data for the Joshin'etsu mountainous region on February 28, 2014, with (a) showing the surface air temperature, (b) the relative humidity and (c) the potential temperature. The vertical axis is the same as in Fig. 2. The arrows show the hour-by-hour values for surface wind taken from the observatories and AMeDAS sites which are closest to the course of traverse.

Ocean side of the plain, the potential temperature for the plains area is somewhat higher than that of the slope, resembling the characteristics of the mean winter values which were observed in Fig. 2. However, the contrast between the Sea of Japan side and the Pacific Ocean side is emphasized more clearly when the potential temperature distribution for February 28 is compared with the mean winter potential temperature. Looking at surface winds, for the Pacific Ocean side, a somewhat strong wind moving towards the plains was observed in the timeframes and heights where the potential temperature was approximately uniform to the slope, and the development of a katabatic wind and an adiabatic heating effect accompanying this is surmised. Conversely, the winds on the slope on the Sea of Japan side remained quiet throughout the day. Based on this, it is speculated that the cross-mountain air current of February 28 gave rise to a blocking effect in the lower layers on the Sea of Japan side throughout the day from 08:00 onwards and to a dynamic foehn wind effect accompanying this, which blew downwards along the slope on the Pacific Ocean side.

Fig. 9 (a) shows the observation values from the Maebashi Local Meteorological Observatory for the distribution pattern for surface air temperature and surface wind at 08:00 on February 28 immediately after an abrupt rise in the air temperature and a fall in relative humidity were observed, and Fig. 9 (b) shows how surface air temperature rose during the one-hour period from 07:00 to 08:00 on 28 February. These graphs are based on the surface observation values taken from the weather stations of the Japan Meteorological Agency and AMeDAS data, but the data for surface air temperature and disparities in surface air temperature was created by using air temperature data taken from the surface observation sites (represented by square symbols on the figure) in the Joshin'etsu Mountainous Region Meteorological Observation Project. Looking at the surface temperature at 08:00 on February 28 (Fig. 9a), the high-temperature zone is seen to spread from the Tonegawa channel into the northwestern Kanto Plain region in a northwest-to-southeast direction. This high-temperature zone develops in response to the zone developed when the northwesterly surface wind blows relatively strongly. In addition, this zone also accords closely to the zone in which the rise in air temperature over the previous one-hour period as shown in Fig. 9 (b) occurs at a rate of over 2°C/hour, suggesting that a foehn phenomenon has developed in accordance with a cross-mountain katabatic wind. In central Saitama Prefecture, the rise in air temperature was particularly

Characteristics of the Potential Temperature Distribution Along Mountain Slopes Experiencing Cross-Mountain Air Currents in the Winter Season

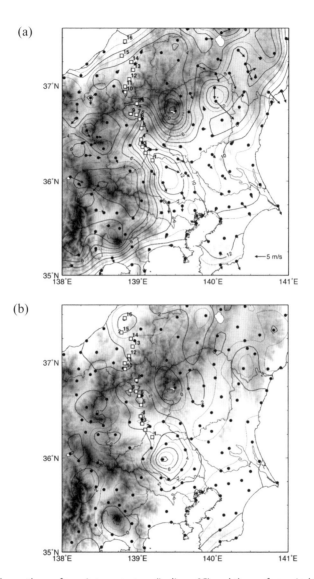

Fig. 9 (a) shows the surface air temperature (isolines; °C) and the surface wind (arrows) at 08:00 on February 28, 2014, and (b) shows the distribution of the extent of the rise in surface air temperature from 07:00 to 08:00 on February 28, 2014 (°C/hour).

marked with temperatures exceeding 12°C at 08:00 on February 28, a rise in air temperature of 4°C/hour. Looking at the surface wind in Fig. 9 (a), the surface wind emerging from the valley at Tonegawa can be observed to be greatly dispersed in a horizontal direction near central Saitama Prefecture. It is possible that the rise in temperature has become particularly marked in this region due to the addition of what has been referred to as the shallow foehn, but further investigations are required to examine this.

3. Summary

The objective of this study was to clarify the characteristics of the surface atmosphere along the mountain slopes in two cases showing markedly high temperatures in the daytime in the northwestern inland region of the Kanto Plain over the winter of 2013–2014, using original surface observation data. We investigated two cases: that of February 26, 2014 in which a cross-mountain air current did not become predominant under the influence of a migratory anticyclone, and that of February 28, 2014 in which a cross-mountain air current did become predominant under a sea-level pressure pattern typical for winter. It is speculated that on February 26 a downward wind by the anticyclone and a low-level valley wind circulation appeared, and that on February 28 a dynamic foehn wind was observed due to the blocking effect on the windward side of the mountains.

Investigations based on a combination of numerical models are an effective way to examine questions such as the kind of behavior seen in the atmosphere on and around the mountain slope, and whether this exhibits the kind of characteristics possessed by the shallow foehn wind observed in the Alps in which the wind selects a channel as the course of traverse. As this study analyzed only one example of each type (one in which a cross-mountain air current was predominant and one in which no such current was predominant), it is necessary to conduct further case study analyses and statistical analyses to ascertain whether the characteristics that became evident in this study are generally applicable or not. We hope to consider this issue in the future.

Acknowledgements

This study forms part of the outcomes of the Rissho University Joshin'etsu Mountainous Region Meteorological Observation Project.

Notes

1. Yasushi Watarai, Faculty of Geo-environmental Science, Rissho University
2. Yoshinori Shigeta, Faculty of Environmental Studies, Tottori University of Environmental Studies
3. Kiyotaka Nakagawa, Faculty of Geo-environmental Science, Rissho University

References

Drobinski, P., R. Steinacker, H. Richner, K. Baumann-Stanzer, G. Beffrey, B. Benech, H. Berger, B. Chimani, A. Dabas, M. Dorninger, B. Dürr, C. Flamant, M. Frioud, M. Furger, I. Gröhn, S. Gubser, T. Gutermann, C. Häberli, E. Häller-Scharnhost, G. Jaubert, M. Lothon, V. Mitev, U. Pechinger, M. Piringer, M. Ratheiser, D. Ruffieux, G. Seiz, M. Spatzierer, S. Tschannett, S. Vogt, R. Werner and G. Zängl, 2007: Föhn in the Rhine Valley during MAP: A review of its multiscale dynamics in complex valley geometry. *Q. J. R. Meteor. Soc.*, 133, 897 – 916.

Miya, Y. and H. Kusaka (2009). Climatological study of Karakkaze wind over the Kanto Plain, focusing on the vertical structure. *Geographical Review of Japan*, 82, 346 – 355 (in Japanese).

Saito, K. (1992). Shallow water flow having a lee hydraulic jump over a mountain range in a channel of variable width. *J. Meteor. Soc. Japan*, 70, 775 – 782.

Saito, K. (1994). On cross-mountain air currents (focusing on downslope winds). *Tenki*, 41, 731 – 750 (in Japanese).

Shigeta, Y., Y. Watarai and K. Nakagawa (2013). Construction of regional weather observation network with the aim of elucidating the mechanism of the formation of the intense heat generated in the northwestern Kanto Plain. *Symposium Proceedings of the Academic Meeting of the Association of Japanese Geographers in Spring 2013*, 7-10 (in Japanese).

Shinohara, Y., K. Mashimo, M. Sakurai and T. Sunaga (2009). Two instances of high temperatures in the summer of 2007 with daily maximum air temperatures exceeding 40.9°C in the Kanto region: Replication of daily maximum temperatures using the Japan Meteorological Agency Non-hydrostatic Model (JMANHM) and discussion of the causes of the high air temperatures. *Tenki*, 56, 543 – 548 (in

Japanese).

Takane, Y. and H. Kusaka (2011). Formation mechanisms of the extreme high surface air temperature of 40.9°C observed in the Tokyo metropolitan area: Considerations of dynamic foehn and foehnlike wind. *J. Appl. Meteor. Climatol.*, 50, 1827 – 1841.

Watarai, Y., K. Nakagawa and Y. Fukuoka (2009). Numerical simulation of the intense heat over the Kanto Plain in 15–16 August 2007, using the meteorological model. *Japanese Journal of Biometeorology*, 46, 35 – 41 (in Japanese).

The Promotion of Social Inclusion by Adopting of the Private Finance Initiative on a Correctional Institution[*1]

Yumiko Kamise[2]
Naoya Takahashi
Emi Yano

Abstract

This study focuses on two questionnaire surveys that were conducted about the adoption of the Private Finance Initiative (PFI prison) method in Japan as a new correctional system. For study 1, a Web questionnaire was administered to residents of within a 30 km zone of Tokyo as well as those in Yamaguchi Prefecture to determine familiarity and resistance to the PFI prison systems. For study 2, a questionnaire survey was administered to residents of a neighborhood near a PFI prison in Mine city. The results showed that the attitudes toward the PFI prison were more positive in this area. Furthermore, contact with the correctional systems promoted residents' acceptance of prisoners and former prisoners. Finally, we discuss social and institutional support and contact with social systems to promote social inclusion.

Introduction

In this study, we focused on the opening of a new correctional institution in Mine City, Yamaguchi Prefecture through a public finance initiative (PFI). We conducted two surveys, in order to determine how the adoption of a new social system for correctional treatment changed the attitude of the local residents toward the correctional institution, inmates, and former inmates. Based on the survey results, we considered the issues of social and institutional support and contact in social policies aimed at social inclusion.

Reducing stereotypes and biases, and social inclusion

In research on stereotypes and biases, the issue of how the strong negative emotions and severe discriminatory behavior toward a specific group of people can be reduced and changed has drawn much interest in recent years (Hodson & Hewstone, 2013). A string of research efforts on social exclusion such as Baumeister & Leary (1995) has contributed to the accumulation of knowledge showing that the social exclusion of specific people leads to the deterioration of society overall (Ura, 2009). This research indicates that it is important not only to prevent stigmatization and discriminatory behavior, but also to actively consider ways of ensuring social inclusion for people that tend to be discriminated against and excluded. Social inclusion is a concept that is the opposite of social exclusion, and has become the new principle in social welfare policy that aims to resolve the problem of social exclusion by fostering social acceptance of those that have been excluded from society as members of society (Nihanda, 2007). Social inclusion has even been identified as a policy approach that could overcome the structures and factors behind social exclusion (Cabinet Office, 2011).

Judging from the findings of research on stereotyping and biases, social inclusion has important implications as a social policy. In the context of intergroup contact, social and institutional support has been identified as effective in reducing negative stereotypes and biases (Allport, 1954; Hodson, 2008). Social and institutional support refers to the unambiguous and consistent endorsement of appropriate inclusion policies by those in authority (for example, the school head-teachers and their staff, the politicians implementing new legislation, and the judges monitoring its administration) (Brown, 2010). Brown (2010) points out that this social and institutional support is important for the promotion of greater contact between groups, because those in authority can be penalized and rewarded as they work to meet the goal of reducing prejudice; peoples' prejudiced beliefs can be changed to avoid dissonance caused by forced contact; and over the long term, it leads to a new social climate in which more tolerant norms can emerge. However, while the provision of social and institutional support has been described as one of the essential conditions for effective contact, there is very little empirical research in this area (Brown, 2010). In fact, it is not fully understood what productive social and institutional support is, nor how it relates to contact in terms of reducing stereotypes and prejudice.

Background to the establishment of correctional institutions employing PFI

The current study focuses on private finance initiative correctional institutions (PFI prisons), as a case study for social policy attempting to promote social inclusion. The PFI prison method was launched in 2007 under the government's new criminal justice policy. We consider the impact that the opening of such a prison has had. Japan's conventional correctional institutions have been primarily run by government employees. However, PFI prisons represent a new approach in which prison guards, who are government employees, and private-sector employees cooperate together. In the past, Japan's prisons have not actively disclosed any information on their operations or internal affairs, which gave the general public biased images and led to the assumption that they were "unwanted facilities" (Nishida, 2012). This negative attitude toward prisons was one factor that prevented social inclusion for former inmates (Nishida, 2012). In response, the government carried out various reforms aimed at ensuring correctional institutions are open to, understood and supported by the general public. One of these reforms was the opening of the first PFI prison (Ministry of Justice, 2003). In recent years, the Japanese government has tried to make various administrative initiatives easier for the public to understand and more transparent (Cabinet Office, 2014). The approach of a correctional institution opens to and understood by the public, based on the principle of PFI prisons, is a way to make the current conditions and initiatives for correctional treatment more transparent.

Social inclusion is part of the principle behind PFI prisons. In line with this principle, inmates are actively given support so they can reintegrate into society. For example, inmates receive education by earning qualifications and are given support in finding employment after their release. This sets PFI prisons apart from general prisons. In addition, PFI prisons strive to coexist harmoniously with the local community through initiatives such as employing local residents and using local crops. This is intended to erase the image of prisons as unwanted facilities.

The potential to change attitudes through contact

Until now, whether or not opening PFI prisons actually affects the attitude of residents toward the institution and toward inmates and former inmates has not been confirmed. However, the findings of social psychology suggest that this policy would change residents' attitude toward correctional treatment. One reason for this is that opportunities to interact with the institution are provided after it is established. At PFI prisons, various initiatives are taken so that residents have many opportunities for direct contact with the institution, compared to conventional correctional institutions (Nishida, 2012; University of Shimane PFI Research Group, 2009). Each institution has different characteristics, but all PFI prisons conduct programs to encourage the local community to actively interact with the institution. This includes employment of local residents as private-sector employees in the prison, opening the hospital, cafeteria and other facilities inside the prison to the public, and holding tours and sports events, also open to the public. Moreover, in places where the local government attracted a PFI prison, the local government's newsletters and local newspapers actively provide information on the institution's events.

The findings of research into stereotypes and prejudice show that direct and indirect contact with stigmatized groups provides opportunities to realize that the stereotype and reality do not match and thereby reduce bias (Brown, 2010). It is difficult for citizens and inmates to have direct contact in a correctional institution, and considering approaches to contact in PFI prisons in a way that is in line with previous research is also difficult. However, it is possible to provide information on the correctional institution to residents via facility tours and employing private-sector employees, thereby giving citizens opportunities to confront the mismatch between their stereotypes and reality. Given this, contact with the institutions in various forms is expected to change residents' attitudes about the institutions in a positive way. Moreover, if the relationship between residents' contact with institutions after they were opened and their attitude can be elucidated, we can posit the need to establish a system, in other social inclusion policies, for residents to interact with the institution after it is opened.

The potential of orientation programs to change attitudes

Another reason that opening PFI prisons is expected to change residents' attitudes toward correctional treatment is that when PFI prisons are attracted by the local government, the national and local (city) governments regularly hold orientation sessions for the local residents, and the process leading up to the opening and the significance of the opening are broadly disclosed to residents (Nishida, 2012). These orientations, where the city and national governments with authority explain the intended policy unambiguously and consistently to the residents, play a role in demonstrating social and institutional support—a factor discussed in contact theory.

Moreover, it is also important to note that these orientation sessions are intended to explain the administration's decision-making process and the intention behind the policy. In research on social policy, "the availability of information to the general public and clarity about government rules, regulations, and decisions" (Asian Development Bank, 1995) is known as "transparency," and is a requirement of democratic governments (Hood, 2006). Grimmelikhuijsen & Welch (2012) explain administrative transparency in three dimensions: decision making, policy information, and policy outcome. In the case of research on Japan's administration such as Kim (2014) and Aoki (2005), the importance of transparency in administrative activities has been demonstrated in specific cases. Aoki (2005) states, in a case study focusing on local cooperation in public projects, that residents' evaluations of information disclosure on projects and the appropriateness of the government's response are related to the extent to which residents' accept the public project.

Social and institutional support is a prerequisite to the occurrence of contact, but thus far its relationship with contact has not been adequately discussed. This is likely related to the fact that much of the previous research, such as Lucker, Rosenfield, Sikes, & Aronson (1976), examining the effect of contact was modeled on cooperative learning within the classroom, in which teachers facilitate student contact. However, in the example of PFI prisons that we examined in this study, the administration could not mandate that residents interact, and contact did not necessarily begin at the launch of the system. That said, this study hypothesized that, even in these conditions, residents' contact with the institution would be encouraged if orientation sessions gave them an understanding of the institution's policy and they felt that the institutional support was clear. Based on this hypothesis, this study identified the residents' evaluation of the orientation sessions as one of the factors encouraging contact after the institution's opening and examined the relevant correlations.

Impact on attitude toward inmates and generalized former inmates

Improving the approaches of correctional institutions alone is not enough to ensure the social inclusion of former inmates. This requires that civilians agree with the provision of job training to inmates to support their social rehabilitation and accept former inmates as members of their community.

Research on stereotypes and prejudice has identified cases in which changes in the stereotypes that occur due to direct and indirect contact with a stigmatized person can be generalized to other members of the stigmatized group as well (Kamise, Oda, Miyamoto, 2002; Yamauchi, 1996). As a result, changes in the attitude of local residents toward prisons, prompted by the opening of a PFI prison, may change the attitudes of local residents to inmates and former inmates (hereafter, "(former) inmates") positively in general. If this correlation could be clearly shown, it would show that the social significance of PFI prisons lies not only in their ability to coexist with the local community, but also in their effectiveness in promoting the social inclusion of (former) inmates.

Objective of this study

Based on the aforementioned issues, this study focused on the Mine Rehabilitation Program Center in Mine City, Yamaguchi Prefecture, which is Japan's first PFI prison. A questionnaire was given to neighboring residents on their attitudes toward the institution before and after opening. The first objective of this study was to clarify whether the actual opening of the PFI prison changed residents' attitudes toward the institution.

Our second objective was to consider how residents' evaluation of the orientation sessions given by the administration and contact with the institution after opening affected their attitudes toward the institution and generalized (former) inmates.

The general public's attitude toward PFI prisons, including its awareness, has not been adequately studied previously. By determining the extent to which neighboring residents knew of the Mine Rehabilitation Program Center and identifying the general awareness and level of aversion to the institution as a baseline, we would be able to more accurately understand the impact of the PFI prison in the region. To this end, we conducted an online survey of people living within 30 kilometers of Tokyo, where there are no PFI prisons in residential areas, and people in Yamaguchi prefecture, excluding Mine City, to determine awareness and aversion (Study 1). Subsequently, we carried out a survey of residents living near the PFI prison and carried out a comparative analysis of the surveyed items (Study 2).

Study 1

The objective was to identify awareness and aversion to PFI prisons in areas other than those near PFI prisons. The survey targeted residents in Yamaguchi Prefecture, excluding the region targeted in the Study 2 survey (Mine City) and residents in the Tokyo metropolitan area, where no PFI prisons are located.

Method

Participants

The online survey targeted men and women from the ages of 20 to 69 living within 30 kilometers of Tokyo and in Yamaguchi Prefecture (excluding Mine City) from among monitors registered with survey services (INTAGE Inc. and Yahoo! Research; the number of registered monitors totaled 953,039 as of January 2010). A total of 3,513 requests with survey questionnaires were sent out after allocating evenly across the region, gender, and age. Among the 1,383 responses collected (a response rate of 39.4%, compared to the number of requests), 1,356 responses (from 639 men and 717 women) were analyzed after excluding incomplete responses and responses from prison officers. Looking at respondent profiles, 47.1% were men and 52.9% were women, while 20.2% were in their 20s, 19.5% in their 30s, 19.8% in their 40s, 21.1% in their 50s and 19.3% in their 60s. 52.5% were from the Tokyo metropolitan area and 47.5% were from Yamaguchi Prefecture.

Survey period

The survey was carried out from January 28 to February 1, 2010.

Survey questions

In addition to basic attributes, the following items were included in the questionnaires. Since all four of the current PFI prisons are known as "rehabilitation program centers," the subject institution was called a "rehabilitation program center" in our questionnaires.
1. Awareness of the institution
Respondents were asked whether they had ever heard of a national institution called a "rehabilitation program center," to which they replied "yes" or "no."
2. Aversion to the institution
Respondents were given a brief explanation of rehabilitation program centers, and were asked to indicate their level of aversion to the construction of rehabilitation program centers in Japan generally, and to the prospect of a center being constructed in their own neighborhood, by indicating one of four levels: "strong resistance," "moderate resistance," "low resistance" or "no resistance."

Results and discussion

When asked whether they had heard of rehabilitation program centers, 19.5% of respondents in Tokyo had, and 30.4% of respondents in Yamaguchi Prefecture had. There was a gap between the regions ($\chi^2(1)=21.65$ $p<.001$), but overall recognition was only 20–30%. When asked whether they felt aversion, when combining those who felt "strong resistance" and "moderate resistance," about 30% of respondents felt aversion about their construction in Japan (34.1% for Tokyo and 28.0% for Yamaguchi Prefecture; $\chi^2(1)=6.02$ $p<.05$). About 50% felt aversion about the prospect of the construction of a center in their neighborhood (56.5% and 46.4%, respectively; $\chi^2(1)=13.63$ $p<.001$).[4] Given these results, we can conclude that PFI prisons are not well known in regions in which these institutions have not been built and that about half of the respondents feel aversion to the thought of a center opening up in their neighborhood.

Study 2

In Study 2, people living around the Mine Rehabilitation Program Center were given questionnaires with the objective of determining how their attitude toward the center changed before and after it was opened. In this study, aversion to the center was the focus as a representative indicator for attitudes, and changes in aversion before and after opening were compared. The second objective was to consider how their evaluation of the orientation sessions and their contact with the center after opening affected their present attitude toward the center and generalized (former) inmates in general.

In line with these objectives, in this study, respondents were asked whether they were aware of the Mine Rehabilitation Program Center to determine the level of awareness in the surrounding area, and those who were aware were asked about their aversion when they first heard that the center would be opened (level of aversion before opening). They were then asked about their present level of aversion to the center (level of aversion after opening) to compare the two.

Respondents were asked about their awareness of regional revitalization, their evaluation of the center's opening and security worries, and awareness of risks to measure their present attitude toward the center, irrespective of aversion. Questions about their attitude toward generalized (former) inmates were also set. There were also questions about their evaluation of the orientation sessions and their contact with the center, since these factors could also have an impact. The correlations were then analyzed. Their evaluation of the orientation sessions was measured by asking whether the respondents felt that the national and local (city) governments had provided adequate briefings before the center was opened and whether they had been able to adequately understand the briefing. This is in line with the discussion of transparency dimensions by Grimmelikhuijsen & Welch (2012) and Aoki's survey items (2005).

Contact with the center after opening was measured by asking whether the respondent had experienced direct contact such as tours, indirect contact with information via the media, and interaction with a person involved outside of the center—covering three forms of contact. Since the correlation between the factors was not clear enough initially, we performed an exploratory analysis of the correlation by ordering the factors chronologically, with aversion to the center before opening coming first, followed by the evaluation of the orientation sessions, contact with the center after opening, attitude toward the center after opening, aversion to the center after opening, and attitudes toward generalized (former) inmates.

Existing research on residents' attitudes toward institutions involving risks has indicated that the background of receptivity to the institution differs depending on how far away they live from the institution (Kimura and Furuta, 2003; Okamoto and Miyamoto, 2004). In our research on PFI prisons, differences in the respondents' proximity to the institution may have affected their attitudes toward the center and changes in their attitude. As a result, when analyzing the responses of neighboring residents, we compared residents in Toyotamae district, where the center was opened, to residents in the Omine district, which is adjacent to the Toyotamae district.

Method

Procedures

Study 2 was carried out with a paper questionnaire distributed individually and returned by mail.

1. Regions surveyed and participants
The survey region comprised Toyotamae district, where the Mine Rehabilitation Program Center was built, and the Omine district, which is adjacent to the Toyotamae district. The survey was addressed to the head of the household and his/her spouse in households in these districts (480 households in Toyotamae and 3,173 households in Omine). All of the heads of household identified by the Local Resident Section of the Mine City Hall were targeted for this survey. The questionnaire for the spouse was enclosed with the questionnaire for the head of household.

2. Survey method
Using Mine City's Public Relation system, an envelope containing the questionnaires for the head of household and the spouse and return envelopes was distributed. The head of household and spouse were asked to return their questionnaires in separate envelopes (they were mailed to a survey company in Tokyo). If the head of household was not married, he or she was asked to enclose a blank survey with the head of household's survey and mail it back. We published an article on Mine City's newsletter released on the first day of the survey period asking that residents cooperate with the survey.

3. Survey period
The survey was conducted from January 15 to January 30, 2010.

4. Number of responses
The number of survey responses totaled 1,608 for heads of household and 1,540 for spouses. When excluding blank surveys, the return rate was 40.1%.

5. Number of respondents targeted for analysis
A total of 2,643 responses from 1,486 heads of household and 1,157 spouses were analyzed, after excluding responses from former public employees working at the center and incomplete responses. Looking at respondent profiles, 45.9% of respondents were men, 52.5% were women and 1.6% were gender unspecified. By age, 9.3% were from people in their 30s or younger, 10.6% from people in their 40s, 19.0% from people in their 50s, 28.5% from people in their 60s, 31.0% from people in their 70s or above, and 1.6% were age unspecified. By residential area, 14.0% were from Toyotamae district, 82.0% were from Omine district and 4.0% were other or unspecified.

Survey questions

In addition to attributes, the survey included the following questions.[5]

1. Awareness of the institution
Respondents were asked whether they had ever heard of the "rehabilitation program center" in Toyotamae district, Mine City to which they replied "yes" or "no."

2. Aversion to the institution before opening
First, respondents were asked whether they had resided in the region since before February 2006, when preparations had begun for the opening of this center. Second, those who replied they had lived there were then asked to indicate their level of aversion when they had first heard that a rehabilitation program center would be opened in Mine City, by indicating one of four levels from "strong resistance" to "no resistance."

3. Evaluation of orientation sessions
Respondents were asked about the city government's and center's (national

government's) measures in the period leading up to the opening of the institution in three items—"the city government's prior explanation to residents was adequate," "the center's prior explanation to residents was adequate" and "I understood the location of the center before it was opened." They were asked to respond with one of four answers, from "I agree" to "I do not agree."

4. Direct and indirect contact with the institution after it was opened
Respondents were given five items—"I read the information on the center provided to residents," "I toured the center," "I have used the cafeteria and martial arts dojo in the center," "I have been to the Mine Center's exhibition and sale of products" and "I have seen news on the center in the newspaper, television and/or magazines"—and were asked to select all of the items that applied to them.

5. Personal interaction with a person involved outside of the institution
Respondents were asked whether family members or acquaintances worked at a job or was involved in activities related to the center, by selecting any of six items that applied to them, such as "an acquaintance is/was a government employee at the center" and "an acquaintance is/was a private-sector employee at the center." [6]

6. Aversion to the institution at present (after opening)
Respondents were asked to indicate their level of aversion they felt now about the Mine Rehabilitation Program Center, by selecting one of four answers from "strong resistance" to "no resistance."

7. Perceived regional activation
Respondents were asked about any changes in the region they experienced after the center's opening, by selecting any of three items that applied to them: "the local population has increased," the number of students at the local elementary and middle schools has increased," and "job opportunities for local people have increased."

8. Evaluation of the institution opening and worries
Respondents were asked to choose any of the 12 items that describe their current thoughts about the institution, including "thanks to the center, there has

been progressing in inmates' social rehabilitation," and "I am worried that an inmate might escape."

9. Perceived risk
Respondents were asked to indicate the level of risk (danger) they feel the Mine Rehabilitation Program Center could cause to their own and their families' health and safety, by selecting one of four answers that most closely matched their feelings, from "very dangerous," "dangerous," "somewhat dangerous," to "virtually no danger." Respondents were asked to choose "I don't know" if they could not choose any of these four answers.

10. Attitude toward generalized (former) inmates
Eight items designed to assess the respondents' attitude toward generalized (former) inmates were given, including "It is difficult for former inmates to find a job" and "When inmates are released, the national government should actively help them find work." Respondents were asked to choose from four answers, from "I agree" to "I do not agree."

Results

Awareness of the institution

Awareness of the center was 98.7% ($N=2,458$), with 99.7% awareness in Toyotamae and 98.5% in Omine ($\chi^2(1)=3.415$ $p<.1$). This is high compared to awareness in Tokyo (19.5%) and Yamaguchi (30.4%) in Study 1.

Changes in the level of aversion to the institution

If we look at the aversion to the institution before opening, we find that 51% of respondents felt aversion (total of those who felt strong resistance and moderate resistance), and 48.9% did not feel aversion (total of those who felt low resistance and no resistance), which is about evenly divided. This is a significant difference when compared with the results in Study 1, in which 56.5% in Tokyo and 46.4% in Yamaguchi felt aversion toward the prospect of the construction of an institution in their neighborhood ($\chi^2(2)=13.720$ $p<.001$). However, after residual analysis, the levels in the Mine region were not significant.

At the same time, the aversion group fell sharply to 13.6% after opening (present). The score was added up by assigning one point for "no resistance" and four points for "strong resistance" (and two and three points for the answers in between), and the difference of the average score was calculated by totaling both districts to determine the gap from before and after the center was opened. This showed that points were significantly lower ($t(2176)=42.94$ $p<.001$) after opening ($M=1.75$ $SD=0.77$) than before opening ($M=2.48$ $SD=0.91$).

When we look at this by district, we find that aversion was significantly higher in Toyotamae both before (Toyotamae $M=2.73$ $SD=1.03$; Omine $M=2.43$ $SD=2.43$; $t(381.111)=4.781$ $p<.001$) and after (Toyotamae $M=1.86$ $SD=0.87$; Omine $M=1.73$ $SD=0.74$; $t(446.700)=42.63$ $p<.001$) the center was opened.

Evaluation of orientation sessions

The responses to the three items assessing the government's orientation sessions were quantified by giving four points to the answer "4. I agree" and one point to "1. I disagree" (and three and two points to the answers in between). The simple sum of the answers to the three items was the score for "evaluation of orientation" ($\alpha=.841$). The average of the total of both districts was $M=7.83$ and $SD=3.06$, with the median exceeding six points. A comparison of the gap by district shows that the score ($t(2142)=2.86$ $p<.01$) was significantly higher for Toyotamae ($M=8.28$, $SD=2.91$) than for Omine ($M=7.75$, $SD=3.05$).

Direct and indirect contact with the institution after opening

When asked about contact with the center, the responses were as follows: "I have seen news on the center in the newspaper, television and/or magazines" (71.8%), "I read the information on the center provided to residents" (32.2%), "I toured the center" (23.4%), "I have been to the Mine Center's exhibition and sale of products" (15.1%) and "I have used the cafeteria and martial arts dojo in the center" (14.0%). Of these, the number of times "newsletter" and "news" were selected was designated as the score for "indirect contact" and the number of times "tours," "center use" and "exhibition and sale" were selected was designated the score for "direct contact." The gap by district was significantly higher for the Toyotamae in the case of direct contact (Toyotamae M=1.17 SD=1.12; Omine M=0.41 SD=0.79; $t(425.803)$=1.59 p<.001). There was no significant difference between the districts in terms of indirect contact (Toyotamae M=1.02 SD=0.73; Omine M=1.05 SD=0.68; $t(2456)$=0.73 ns).

Personal interaction with a person involved outside of the institution

Responses about whether family members or acquaintances worked at a job or were involved in activities related to the center were as follows: "A family member is/was a government employee at the center" (1.3%), "an acquaintance is/was a government employee at the center" (4.7%), "a family member is/was a private-sector employee at the center" (4.7%), "an acquaintance is/was a private-sector employee at the center" (28.2%), "a family member is/was an educator/volunteer at the center " (2.5%), and "an acquaintance is/was an educator/volunteer at the center" (13.8%). The number of responses to these six items was the score for "personal interaction with a person involved." A review of the gap between scores by district shows that the score ($t(460.003)$=6.62 p<.001) was significantly higher for Toyotamae (M=0.82 SD=0.82) than for Omine (M=0.51 SD=0.71).

Perceived regional activation

When asked about local changes, a higher percentage (33.8%) agreed that "the number of students at the local elementary and middle schools has increased," followed by "the local population has increased" (32.3%) and "job opportunities for local people have increased" (30.4%). The number of respondents who agreed with these three items was the score for "awareness of regional revitalization." A comparison of the gap between districts showed that the score ($t(477.001)$=9.46 p<.001) was significantly higher for Toyotamae (M=1.49 SD=1.14) than for Omine (M=0.88 SD=1.07).

Evaluation of the institution opening and worries

When using mathematical quantification theory class III to classify the 12 items that describe respondents' current evaluation and security worries, the responses can be divided into three groups. The first group consists of five items such as "I want the center to keep the same acceptance criterion (only first-time offenders with light crimes)" (54.4%) and "I want the benefits obtained by the city and prefecture as a result of the center's opening to be shared more with the local community" (38.4%).[7] This group of items concerns ways in which residents want the center to improve so that they can coexist more easily, and was given the name "requests for better coexistence with the institution." The second group consists of four items: "the center contributes to the country and society" (31.2%), "I want the center to continue operating" (26.1%), "the center is a better place to rehabilitate inmates than a regular prison" (22.3%), and "the social rehabilitation of inmates has been promoted thanks to the center" (11.5%). These items indicate "perceived contribution to society." The third group consists of the three items: "I am worried about inmates escaping" (16.2%)," "I am concerned that people who disturb the public order are coming into our community" (15.2%) and "I am concerned that having the center here hurts the community's image" (8.2%). This group is called the "anxious about security situation" group. The number of responses to the item in each group was added up to produce group scores for "requests for better coexistence," "perceived contribution to society" and "anxious about security situation."

A review of the gap between group scores by district showed that the score for "requests for better coexistence" ($t(2456)=5.00\ p<.001$) was significantly higher for Toyotamae ($M=1.86\ SD=1.26$) than for Omine ($M=1.51\ SD=1.20$). There was no significant difference in the scores for "anxious about security situation" (Toyotamae $M=0.467\ SD=0.88$; Omine $M=0.39\ SD=0.77$; $t(462.110)=1.59\ ns$) and "perceived regional activation" (Toyotamae $M=0.89\ SD=1.16$; Omine $M=0.92\ SD=1.21$; $t(2456)=0.42\ ns$).

Perceived risk

When asked about the center's risk in four levels from 4, "very dangerous" to 1, "virtually no danger," the results were $M=1.47\ SD=0.74$,[8] excluding an optional response of "I don't know." There was no significant difference between districts (Toyotamae $M=1.50\ SD=0.84$; Omine $M=1.47\ SD=0.73$; $t(385.021)=0.583\ ns$).

Attitude toward generalized (former) inmates

The eight items designed to assess the respondents' attitude toward generalized (former) inmates were quantified by assigning four points to the answer "I agree" and one point to "I disagree" (and three and two for the answers in between). We carried out a factor analysis (maximum likelihood method) for these eight items and identified two factors by looking at a scree plot and interpreting the factors. The total variance explanatory rate for the two factors before rotation is 53.2%. As a result of pattern matrix after Promax rotation, we determined that the items that had a high load on the first factor were items expressing acceptance of inmates and former inmates, such as "when inmates are released, the national government should actively help them find work" and "the public should accept former inmates without looking at them differently."[9] As a result, we named the first factor "receptive attitude toward generalized (former) inmates." The items that had a high load on the second factor were "it is difficult for former inmates to find a job" and "former inmates tend to repeat similar crimes after they are released," and this factor was named "negative attitude toward generalized (former) inmates."[10] Using the items with absolute values for loads of 0.40 or higher for each factor, two scales were created through the simple sum of the responses: "receptive attitude" (five items, $\alpha=.69$) and "negative attitude" (three items, $\alpha=.71$). When examining the difference between the averages of the district, we did not find any significant difference for either the receptive attitude (Toyotamae M=14.70 SD=2.85; Omine M=14.81 SD=2.78; $t(2329)$=0.635 ns) or the negative attitude (Toyotamae M=9.75 SD=1.68; Omine M=9.97 SD=1.77; $t(2405)$=0.845 ns).

Analysis of correlations between factors

We carried out a covariance structure analysis to determine how other factors affected attitudes toward the institution after opening and attitudes toward generalized (former) inmates. When carrying out the analysis, aversion to the institution before opening was given precedence, followed by the evaluation of the orientation sessions, contact with the institution after opening, attitudes toward the institution after opening (perceived regional activation, requests for better coexistence, perceived contribution to society, anxious about security situation, perceived risk), aversion to the institution after opening, and attitude toward generalized (former) inmates in general (receptive attitude, negative attitude).[11] A covariance structure analysis using AMOS was carried out on the premise that the chronologically prior factors would affect all of the subsequent factors.[12, 13]

At this point, we set a latent variable that we called "contact with the institution," consisting of "direct contact," "indirect contact" and "personal interaction with a person involved" for contact with the institution after opening. Since "anxious about security situation" and "perceived risk" measure similar trends, a latent variable consisting of these two was designated generally as "anxiety."

The results of analysis thus far had indicated attitudes toward the institution differ depending on the district, so a covariance structure analysis was carried out by district. We repeated analysis in which we eliminated paths that were not significant for either district in order to raise the model's relevance.

Figure 1 shows the results of the analysis. For both districts, the "evaluation of orientation sessions" showed a positive path to "contact with the institution" and a negative path to "requests for better coexistence." Then, "contact with the institution" showed a positive path to "perceived contribution to society," "requests for better coexistence" and "perceived regional activation," and it indicated a negative path to "aversion after opening" and a positive path to "receptive attitude."

If we look at the key differences between districts, we find that the significant differences observed in the Omine district alone showed a positive path from "aversion before opening" to "aversion after opening," a negative path from "aversion after opening" to a "negative attitude," a negative path from "evaluation of orientation sessions" and "contact with the institution" to "anxiety," a negative path from "anxiety" to "receptive attitude," a positive path from "anxiety" to "negative attitude," a positive path from "requests for better coexistence" to "negative attitude," and a negative path from "perceived contribution to society" to "negative attitude."

The significant difference observed in the Toyotamae district alone was a positive path from "evaluation of orientation sessions" to "perceived regional activation" and a negative path from "requests for better coexistence" to "receptive attitude."[14]

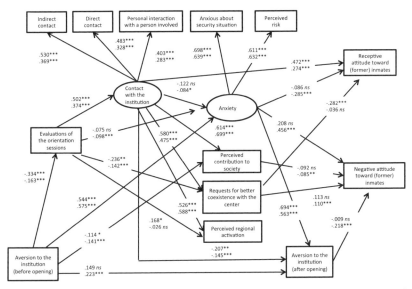

Fig. 1 Backdrop to attitude toward generalized (former) inmates and PFIcorrectional institution (covariance structure analysis using AMOS)

Top path coefficient values are for Toyotamae district where the center was opened ($N=268$), and the bottom path coefficient values are for Omine district adjacent to the district where the center was opened ($N=1665$).
Toyotamae; $\chi^2(52)=78.290$, $p < .05$, GFI=.958, AGFI=.926, CFI=.956, RMSEA=.044, AIC= 156.290, CAIC=335.339
Omine; $\chi^2(52)=253.600$, $p < .001$, GFI=.977, AGFI=.961, CFI=.941, RMSEA=.048, AIC= 331.600, CAIC=581.886
* $p < .05$ ** $p < .01$ *** $p < .001$

Discussion

Current status of awareness of PFI prisons

This study focused on the example of PFI prisons as one kind of social policy aimed at promoting social inclusion, and considered the impact of their opening.

The general awareness of PFI prisons has not been previously studied, but we discovered that, in regions that did not have PFI prisons locally, awareness was only 20–30% (Study 1). Even in Yamaguchi Prefecture, where the Mine Rehabilitation Program Center is located, awareness was low in places far from the district in which it was opened, which indicates that the general public is not yet very familiar with this policy, which was launched in 2007. However, awareness was over 90% in neighboring districts (Study 2), confirming that the existence of the institution is well known among residents. Moreover, 70% of residents had encountered media information about the center, and 20% had toured the center, which confirms that residents obtained information on the institution both directly and indirectly. Moreover, the percentage of respondents who indicated "an acquaintance is/was a private-sector employee at the center" or "an acquaintance who is/was an educator/ volunteer at the center" was 30% and 10%, respectively, showing that they had many opportunities to interact with people involved with the institution, even outside of the institution. In addition, the score for the evaluation of the government's orientation sessions exceeded the median value. These results show that, with the opening of a PFI prison, an attempt to make the current status of remediation and initiatives more transparent has had a certain amount of impact in neighboring areas.

Changes in aversion to PFI prisons

One goal of this study was to demonstrate whether the opening of a PFI prison changed neighboring residents' attitude toward the institution. In Study 2, we considered changes with a focus on aversion. The results showed that about half of respondents felt aversion to the institution before opening. This was about the same as the percentage of respondents from the area with no such institution who indicated aversion when asked about the prospect of a PFI prison opening in their neighborhood (Study 1). Although the Mine Rehabilitation Program Center was opened because it was attracted by Mine City, our results show that the initial aversion was not markedly lower compared to the other region. At the time of the survey two years after the institution had opened, however, only about 10% of respondents indicated aversion. Therefore, we conclude that the residents' attitude toward the institution changed in a more positive direction after it was opened. One qualification we must report is that this study assessed aversion to the institution before opening using the recall method, which may have affected the results. Future research should include longitudinal and other studies that track changes in attitude over time.

Background of changes in attitude toward the institution and generalized (former) inmates

The second objective of this study was to consider the impact that the evaluation of the administration's orientation and contact with the institution after opening had on present attitudes toward the institution and generalized (former) inmates. The results of the covariance structure analysis showed that a good evaluation of the orientation encouraged contact with the institution after opening, and also that this contact led to a reduction in present aversion to the institution as well as a more receptive attitude toward generalized (former) inmates. Based on contact theory, we predicted that stereotypes and prejudice toward prison and (former) inmates would be reduced when a social policy aiming for social inclusion set the contact. Overall, this study confirmed the expected effect of contact along with social and institutional support.

Approach to social and institutional support and theoretical position

Up until this point, there has not been adequate consideration of the questions of how social and institutional support can be conveyed in social policy, or how a clear expression of support is related to contact. The current study positions the orientation sessions as the forum in which social and institutional support is expressed in social inclusion policy regarding PFI prisons. A good evaluation of this orientation promoted contact with the institution, which indicates that holding this orientation and explaining the decision process and intentions is one way of conveying social and institutional support.

In theoretical research on contact thus far, the focus has been on situations in which an authority figure has significant influence, as in a cooperative learning situation, but mandating contact is difficult in actual social policy. This study has social significance in that it shows a practical example of social and institutional support in a real situation where contact cannot be compensated or mandated. The result showed that the provision of social and institutional support could bring people into contact with objects of prejudice and actually reduce their stereotypes and prejudice. Moreover, there is theoretical significance even in laying out the process by which social and institutional support encourages contact, which has not been adequately considered in contact theory.

In the context of social policy research thus far, the transparency of administrative procedures and results disclosure has been widely discussed, and in recent years Japan's national government has stressed the need to make its administrative initiatives transparent by communicating more succinctly with the public. However, the results of this study suggest that even when the administration uses orientations to disclose information and thus ensure transparency and residents gain understanding, this alone is not enough to change residents' attitudes. When building new social systems to promote social inclusion, the administration's initiatives must not only be made transparent and social and institutional support made clear; the new social system itself must also always include mechanisms that involve the general public.

However, the current study did not elucidate the psychological processes by which the demonstration of social and institutional support promotes contact. It did, however, identify a good evaluation of the orientation sessions as a factor that encouraged contact and considered this correlation. Still, in future research, it will be important to consider the process by which, depending on the policy approach, social and institutional support subsequently modifies the effect of mandatory contact. We believe that the relationship between social and institutional support and contact in social inclusion policies should be considered in a multifaceted way.

Effect and limits of contact

The results of the correlation analysis show a direct path in which contact with the institution reduces aversion to the institution and leads to a more receptive attitude toward generalized (former) inmates. The reason that the direct impact was strong, regardless of other attitude factors, may have been that aversion to the institution before opening was based on a lack of knowledge about correctional treatment. The general public was unfamiliar with this type of correctional institutions. Learning more about it via tours and the media directly reduced aversion to the institution and encouraged a more receptive attitude toward generalized (former) inmates. However, this point has to be confirmed in conjunction with changes in the amount of knowledge.

At the same time, contact made people more aware of the institution's contribution to society and its role in regional activation. Contact with the institution deepened understanding about the policy's intent. However, we did not find that perceived contribution to society and perceived regional activation had a significant impact on aversion to the institution and attitudes toward the generalized (former) inmates. Frequently, when opening risk-related institutions, the merits to the region are stressed in convincing the public. However, this study suggests that stressing these positive effects is unlikely to change individuals' stereotypes and prejudices. In particular, anxiety is closely related to aversion to such institutions, which means that the approach to contact should take into consideration approaches for reducing anxiety. Regarding the limits to contact indicated in this study, they may be related to individual problems with this case study, so a detailed analysis involving a comparison to another PFI prison opened in another region, is essential.

In addition, our research suggested the negative aspects of contact with PFI prisons. The contact led to stronger requests for better coexistence with the institution, which heightened the residents' negative attitude toward (former) inmates and reduced their receptive attitude. Contact stimulated residents' interest in a symbiotic relationship with the institution, but the feeling that the institution is responsible for ensuring a smooth coexistence may have made them more resistant to changes in attitude. When considering effective contact in social policy, future research should elucidate the effect of social and institutional support, but also relationship factors such as equal status and cooperation, which have been considered in previous studies on contact theory, and how they impact the relationship between the administration and residents.

Differences by district

A comparison of the psychological process causing changes in attitude by district revealed partial discrepancies. This confirmed that when attempting social inclusion as a social policy, it is important to keep in mind that effective processes differ depending on the region. For example, in the Omine district, which is adjacent to the institution, aversion to the institution before opening determined aversion after opening. We believe this is because in the Omine district overall, evaluation of the orientation sessions and contact with the institution were low overall. There is room to consider techniques to improve direct and personal contact and ways to demonstrate social and institutional support using means other than orientations with residents living far from the institution. In the Toyotamae district, good impressions of the orientation and contact did not result in a path to reduced anxiety. Moreover, the paths from anxiety to a receptive attitude toward generalized (former) inmates and to a negative attitude were not significant. The approach to orientations and contact should be adjusted so that they mitigate the anxiety felt by residents living closer to the institution and lead to a change in attitude toward inmates and former inmates.[15]

Limitations of this study and future issues

In this research, we attempted to broadly consider anything that could be seen as contact with the institution. For this reason, we included not only contact requiring voluntary action on the part of residents, such as center tours, in the types of contact we measured, but also activities that were more passive, such as watching news on television, and activities affected by the activity of people other than the individual concerned, such as contact with acquaintances who worked at the institution as private-sector employees. Future research is needed to elucidate the properties of these contacts. Also, it is necessary to clarify the relationship between these properties of contact, social and institutional support, and attitude change in more detail.

In closing, we would like to note that this effort toward greater transparency around correctional institutions has only just begun in Japan with the opening of a few PFI prisons. Even in the case of conventional correctional institutions whose information disclosure and coexistence harmoniously with the community have not yet been examined, there is room to discuss the possibility of improving transparency and enhancing contact in the future. Also, the social integration of former inmates relates to the total correctional system including institution and process, such as offender rehabilitation facilities. It requires consideration of the integration process after release as it relates to the provision of social and institutional support and contact.

Notes

* This paper is a translation of "*Kanminkyodo keimusho kaisetu niyoru shakaiteki housetsu sokusin no kento*" by Yumiko Kamise, Naoya Takahashi, Emi Yano (2017) (*The Japanese Journal of Psychology*, Volume 87, No. 6, 579-589). It has gotten consent for translation and publishing from the Japanese Psychological Association and all authors. When it was translated, the person cited in the acknowledgement was changed from original article, and a new key word (contact

hypothesis) was added.
1. Study 1 was conducted as a part of the intramural joint research project "The relationship between worries to risk facilities and stereotypes towards offenders" by Edogawa University in 2009. Part of Study 1 was reported at the 77th Annual Convention of the Japan Association of Applied Psychology in 2010. Study 2 was conducted as a part of the project "Gender Equality and Multicultural Conviviality in the Age of Globalization" by the School of Law Tohoku University GCOE program. Part of Study 2 was reported at the 51th Annual Conference of The Japanese Society of Social Psychology in 2010.
2. When carrying out the survey for Study 2, we received cooperation from the citizens in Mine City and others involved. We also benefited significantly from the assistance provided by Professor Minoru Saito at Kokugakuin University, Fumiya Tezuka, former warden of the Mine Rehabilitation Program Center, and Satoshi Yoshino of the Ministry of Justice's Correction Bureau. We would like to take this opportunity to express our sincere gratitude for their assistance.
3. "The Rehabilitation Program Center is a correctional institution run with private-sector cooperation in which government employees work together with private-sector employees. It is also known as a 'private finance initiative prison (PFI prison).' The first such institution was opened in Mine City, Yamaguchi Prefecture in 2007, followed by institutions in Hyogo Prefecture, Tochigi Prefecture, and Shimane Prefecture."
4. The breakdown of the group of people feeling aversion to the construction of PFI prisons throughout Japan is as follows. In Tokyo, 4.1% felt "strong resistance" and 30.1% felt "moderate resistance." In Yamaguchi, 1.2% felt "strong resistance" and 26.7% felt "moderate resistance." The breakdown of the group of people feeling aversion to the construction of PFI prisons in the region in which they live is as follows. In Tokyo, 11.1% felt "strong resistance" and 45.4% felt "moderate resistance." In Yamaguchi, 7.5% felt "strong resistance" and 39.0% felt "moderate resistance."
5. Before these survey questions were prepared, in August 2009 we held a semi-structured interview with four neighboring residents, four private-sector employees, and four government employees, requesting their thoughts on the Mine Rehabilitation Program Center, and we reflected the results in preparing the questions.
6. We also asked about the respondent's own contact (such as "I am/was a private-sector employee at the center"), but the percentage to which this applied was less than 5% in all cases and thus was excluded from the scope of analysis for this study.
7. In addition, "the inmates' life at the center is too comfortable" (33.2%), "I want the inmates to contribute to the community outside of the center as well, for example by cleaning and gardening in the city" (17.2%) and " interaction between the center and the community should be more active" (13.6%).

8. 3.2% of the number of effective responses ($N=72$)
9. Other items that had a high load on the first factor were: "the majority of inmates reflect deeply on their own crimes," "former inmates do not repeat their crime if they can find a job after being released," and "job training for inmates is a waste of money" (reverse-scored item). Other items that had a high load on the second factor were: "it is difficult for former inmates to find a job," "public opinion is biased against people who have been in prison" and "former inmates tend to repeat similar crimes after they are released."
10. The correlation in the scoring for "receptive attitude" and "negative attitude" was $r(2398)=-.110$ ($p<.001$). There was a negative correlation, but the value was low, which suggests that different aspects are measured, rather than that the aspects that "receptive attitude" and "negative attitude" measure are contrasting. Clarifying the structure of attitudes toward generalized (former) inmates is a topic for future research.
11. In order to confirm that an increase or decrease in evaluations of the orientation sessions encouraged to contact, the overall group was separately divided into those with low evaluation and those with high evaluation of the orientation, based on the average evaluation score of the orientation, and a t-test was carried out to look for differences in the average of the contact score (simple sum of the direct contact score, indirect contact score, personal interaction with a person involved). This showed that the group with the high assessment had a significantly higher contact score at the 0.1% level.
Also, we divided the group based on the average of contact score into those with low contact and those with high contact. We carried out 2 (evaluation low vs. high) × 2 (contact low vs. high) ANOVA for each of the scores measuring the attitude toward the center after opening. The results did not indicate any significant interaction effect between evaluation and contact. Nevertheless, when looking at the two districts separately, we found a significant interaction in the 5% level in the Toyotamae district for "requests for better coexistence with the center" and "negative attitude." The post-hoc tests showed that when evaluation of the orientation sessions was low and contact was high, requests for better coexistence with the institution were higher, and when evaluation and contact were both high, negative attitudes toward generalized (former) inmates were lower. As noted in the discussion, a consideration of the process in which social and institutional support adjusts the effect of contact is an issue for the future.
12. "Awareness of the institution" was excluded from the factors, since over 90% of respondents were aware of it.
13. The sense of aversion to the institution after opening could be thought of in a wider sense as part of the attitudes toward the institution after opening. However, we thought that the overall aversion to the institution is being expressed after evaluating various aspects of the institution including the anxiety and perceived regional activation. Therefore, we presumed that the attitude toward the

institution after opening (perceived regional activation, requests for better coexistence with the institution, perceived contribution to society, anxious about security situation, perceived risk) preceded the aversion to the institution after opening.

14. In this research, hypotheses about how district differences regarding changes in attitude would manifest were not made in advance. Therefore, we carried out covariance structural analyses by district and focused on the relations between factors in each district. However, in regards to Figure 1, when carrying out multiple group structural equation modeling and testing the difference between parameters (the model fit when combining both districts is $\chi^2(104)=331.992$ $p<.001$, GFI=.975, AGFI=.956, CFI=.945, RMSEA=.034, AIC=487.992), we found a significant difference (5% level) in multiple path coefficients (aversion before opening to evaluation of orientation, evaluation of orientation to contact with the institution, evaluation of orientation to perceived regional activation, contact with the institution to perceived contribution to society, contact with the institution to requests for better coexistence with the institution, contact with the institution to perceived regional activation, anxiety to receptive attitude toward generalized (former) inmates, anxiety to negative attitude toward generalized (former) inmates, and requests for better coexistence with the institution to receptive attitude toward generalized (former) inmates)). In this research, we did not carry out a comparative analysis of the path coefficient by district, but we believe that the model's precision, including district gaps, was enhanced by these results.

15. In the Omine region, low aversion to the institution after opening also lowered the negative attitude toward generalized (former) inmates. A negative attitude toward generalized (former) inmates included statements asking about social bias against former inmates. The more that a respondent felt aversion to the institution, the more likely he/she was to answer that the struggles of the (former) inmate were that inmate's own responsibility and that social biases were not related. However, this relation was not observed in the Toyotamae district. The measurements of the negative attitude and the context for the differences in these districts must be further examined.

References

Asian Development Bank (1995, August). *Governance: Sound development management*. Asian Development Bank. Retrieved from http://www.adb.org/sites/default/files/institutional-document/32027/govpolicy.pdf

Allport, G. (1954). *The nature of prejudice*. Cambridge, MA: Addison-Wesley.

Brown, R. (2010). *Prejudice*: *Its social psychology* (2nd ed.). West Sussex, UK:

Wiley-Blackwell.
Aoki, T. (2005). An empirical study on fair process effect. *Journal of Japan Society of Civil Engineers*, *12*, 1–8.
Baumeister, R. F., & Leary, M. R. (1995). The need to belong: Desire for interpersonal attachments as a fundamental human motivation. *Psychological Bulletin*, *117*, 497–529.
Grimmelikhuijsen, S. G., & Welch, E. W. (2012). Developing and testing a theoretical framework for computer-mediated transparency of local governments. *Public Administration Review*, *72*, 562–571.
Hodson, G. (2008). Interracial prison contact: The pros for (social dominant) cons. *British Journal of Social Psychology*, *47*, 325–351.
Hodson, G., & Hewstone, M. (2013). *Advances in intergroup contact*. New York: Psychology Press.
Hood, C. (2006). Transparency in historical perspective. In C. Hood & D. Heald (Eds.), *Transparency: The key to better governance?* (pp.3–23). Oxford, UK: Oxford University Press.
Ministry of Justice (2003, December 22). Recommendations from Administrative Reform Council: Toward correctional facilities understood and supported by the public. Retrieved from http://www.moj.go.jp/content/000001612.pdf
Kamise, Y., Oda, K., & Miyamoto, S. (2002). Changing stereotypes of visible disabilities: An experiment with E-mail communication, *Bulletin of Edogawa University (Information and Society)*, *12*, 91–100.
Kim, G. (2014). A political and administrative analysis on conflict management of local governments: Case studies of general waste incineration facilities of Suginami ward and Musashino city in Tokyo. *Sociotechnica*, *11*, 55–69.
Kimura, H. & Furuta, K. (2003). What factors affect decision for or against nuclear policy?: Comparative analysis focusing on region and knowledge. *Sociotechnica*, *1*, 307–316.
Lucker, G. W., Rosenfield, D., Sikes, J., & Aronson, E. (1976). Performance in the interdependent classroom: A field study. *American Educational Research Journal*, *13*, 115–123.
Cabinet Office (2014). Promoting 'visibility' of the status of women's activity in companies. *Kyodo Sankaku*, *66*, 2–7.
Nishida, H. (2012). *New Form of Prison: PFI Prisons Take Up the Challenge of Creating the Future*. Shogakukan-Shueisha Productions Co., Ltd.
Nihanda, S. (2007). Social Inclusion and Human Rights Policy. In Japan Social Inclusion Promotion Association (Eds.), *Social inclusion: Prescription for an unequal society* (pp. 2–14). Chuohoki Publishing Co., Ltd.
Okamoto, K., & Miyamoto, S. (Eds.) (2004). *Public opinion on nuclear power after JCO accident*. Nakanishiya Shuppan.
University of Shimane PFI Research Group (Eds.) (2009). *New initiative with PFI correctional facilities: Challenges and issues for Shimane Asahi Rehabilitation*

Center. Seibundoh.

Prime Minister of Japan and his Cabinet (2011, May 31). Basic approach to promoting social inclusion measures: Basic policies. Retrieved from http://www.kantei.go.jp/jp/singi/housetusyakai/kettei/20110531honbun.pdf

Ura, M. (2009). *Behavioral science of social exclusion and acceptance: Isolation created by society and emotions.* SAIENSU-SHA Co., Ltd.

Yamauchi, T. (1996). *Psychology of prejudice resolution.* Nakanishiya Shuppan.

Mental Health in Local Public Employees Affected by the Great East Japan Earthquake[1]

Naoya Takahashi[2]
Takeshi Furuya[3]
Shigeki Sakata[4]

Abstract

The Great East Japan Earthquake was a complex disaster with a variety of destructive effects, including tsunami damage and damage due to the nuclear power plant accident. Local public employees who work for disaster-struck municipalities, while themselves disaster victims, are engaged in unimaginably difficult work including disaster relief and recovery. This study presents the outcomes of a two-stage panel survey on mental health conducted once in 2015 and once in 2016. The subjects were 672 local public employees in one disaster group that suffered tsunami damage and another disaster group that suffered damage from the nuclear disaster. Results showed the high-risk rate on the Impact of Event Scale-Revised (IES-R) was 11.9% for the tsunami-disaster group and 31.4% for the nuclear-accident group at Time 1. At Time 2, it was 8.9% for the tsunami-disaster group and 27.2% for the nuclear-accident group. From Time 1 to Time 2, the high-risk rate significantly decreased in both groups, but the percentage of high-risk persons remained elevated in the nuclear-accident group. In addition, factors predicting high risk for mental health issues by group were examined by logistic regression analysis. As a result, it was shown that the risk of traumatic stress and psychiatric disorders was increased by the occurrence of burnout as a result of high stress due to work experience after the disaster. Based on these results, future issues concerning stress care for local disaster public employees were discussed.

Introduction

This paper presents a quantitative study at two points in time of the mental health of local public employees affected by the Great East Japan Earthquake.

1. Great East Japan Earthquake and disaster workers

The Great East Japan Earthquake was a massive magnitude 9.0 earthquake that struck off the Pacific Coast of the Tohoku region on March 11, 2011. The earthquake triggered powerful tsunami waves that caused catastrophic damage to the Pacific coast of Japan from Tohoku to the Kanto region. The tsunami also reached the Fukushima Daiichi Nuclear Power Plant run by the Tokyo Electric Power Company (TEPCO), where it disabled the emergency generators that would have provided power necessary to cool the reactors. The insufficient cooling led to an accidental release of radioactive material. This accident was rated the highest Level 7 on the International Nuclear and Radiological Event Scale (INES). As a result, the victims of the Great East Japan Earthquake suffered the consequences of a massive, complex disaster composed of a natural disaster (the earthquake and subsequent tsunami) and a technological disaster. This posed new challenges for disaster research conducted in Japan. In other words, due to the complex disaster composed of a massive earthquake, a tsunami, and a nuclear accident, the victims who lived in municipalities in the area of the nuclear power plant were not allowed to return to their homes and were forced to live as evacuees in temporary housing. It was reported that 50,641 people were still living as evacuees as of February 2018, seven years after the disaster. In August 2013, Fujimori and Omori (2014) surveyed disaster victims who were forced to leave their homes as a result of the release of radioactive material from the Fukushima Daiichi Nuclear Plant and were living as evacuees in temporary housing built in Aizu Wakamatsu City in August 2013. They reported that an overwhelming number of the victims of the complex disaster had nothing to live for, had a low level of satisfaction with their living conditions, and experienced life stress. They also reported that 78.4% of victims had high risk of mental health issues as screened by the General Health Questionnaire – 28 (GHQ28).

As outlined above, the negative impact of this complex disaster on the mental health of people was identified, and specific recovery measures are discussed in this study. For instance, a research group at the Fukushima

Medical University conducted a survey targeting 210,000 people (the Fukushima Health Management Survey, implemented in cooperation with Fukushima Prefecture). The survey findings indicate that the K6 high-risk rate was 14.6% in 2011, 11.7% in 2012, and 9.7% in 2013 (Yagi A., et al., 2015). These results are valid at a K6 cutoff point of 13 points. This research group reports that a score of 17 points was set as a standard for providing assistance.

In complex disasters, however, the people providing professional assistance in the event of such disasters also experience strong stress. According to Matsui (2005), victims of critical incident stress can be classified into four categories: victims of 1st order (primary victims), victims of 1.5th order, victims of 2nd order (secondary victims), and victims of 3rd order. In this classification, local public employees fall into the category of secondary victims. They are considered "professional disaster workers" and their job is considered "an occupation that involves frequent disaster relief and assistance work." The category of professional disaster workers who are secondary victims also includes firefighters, journalists, and nurses. For these occupations, surveys and research, as well as stress care programs are already being provided. (Matsui, 2005; Journalists' Critical Incident Stress Research Group, 2011)

2. Mental health of local public employees affected by the Great East Japan Earthquake

Local public employees have the following characteristics in Japan. Decentralization under the public administration system in Japan has not advanced, so local governments have low discretion with regard to recovery and reconstruction. Additionally, despite the fact that local public employees play an important role in the management of shelters in the event of a natural disaster and in the post-disaster reconstruction, they tend to be viewed in a negative way by citizens as compared with other categories of disaster workers. Research also points out that local public employees are exposed to the following "three layers" of distress: (1) local public employees are disaster victims themselves; (2) local governments affected by disasters are centers for provision of support to disaster victims and for reconstruction efforts, so the workload of local public employees dramatically increases; and (3) complaints from ordinary disaster victims and local residents also increase

(Wakashima and Noguchi, 2013). Furthermore, it can also be pointed out that citizens affected by a disaster demonstrate low levels of understanding of the distress experienced by local public employees, and priority is given to measures for the mental health of ordinary victims, so it is somewhat difficult to implement measures for the mental health of local public employees.

There is little research that uses a standardized measurement scale to examine the mental health of local public employees affected by complex disasters among studies targeting disaster workers suffering from critical incident stress. Furthermore, there is almost no organized research into the mental health status of local public employees in disaster areas who have been exposed to complex disasters, and this issue is without elucidation. A study by Kuwahara, Takahashi and Matsui (2014, 2015) can be cited as one of the few survey and research efforts to examine the mental health of employees of local governments in the aftermath of the Great East Japan Earthquake. In that study, the authors carried out surveys of employees in three local governments in Miyagi Prefecture, and the results showed that the rate of respondents in the high-risk category of the Impact of Event Scale-Revised Japanese version (IES-R-J) a self-report measure that assesses subjective distress caused by traumatic events) two years and four months after the Great East Japan Earthquake was 23.2%, which is almost on the same level as the rate in the surveys conducted one year and four months earlier (Kuwahara, et al., 2014, 2015). Research has also revealed that support from supervisors and colleagues and gratitude that citizens express to public employees who perform their duties define the sense of growth of public employees after a disaster (Kuwahara, et al., 2013, 2014). According to the report from another survey of local public employees in Miyagi Prefecture (Suzuki, Kim & Fukazawa, 2013), 9.6% of respondents in the top 10% of the K6 questionnaire had a score of 10 points or higher. The situation in the areas affected by the Great East Japan Earthquake, however, differs significantly depending on the location, so while there are local governments such as Miyagi Prefecture, which was the target of a series of surveys such as those outlined above, and where recovery and reconstruction activities are steadily advancing, there are also local governments where entire towns are still evacuated as a result of the nuclear accident. Therefore, in some areas the situation is still far from post-traumatic growth, and it is difficult to examine the issue of mental health uniformity in a uniform manner.

Against this backdrop, this study was performed to clarify the mental health status of local government employees affected by the Great East Japan Earthquake, by type of disaster. Specifically, we measured the mental health of local public employees in areas affected by the tsunami and in areas affected by the nuclear accident at two successive times using standardized scales, analyzed the changes between the two periods, and identified predictors of mental health between these two periods. As factors to predict mental health, we chose and analyzed the following three exploratory factors based on past research on critical incident stress of firefighters: social support, workplace climate, and burnout.

Method

We conducted the following two surveys on a commission by the Fund for Local Government Employees' Accident Compensation. In the analysis of this research, we used panel data adjusted to the following surveys at two points of time.

1. First survey

(1) Procedures

From November 2014 through January 2015, among local governments participating in initiatives to deal with stress after the Great East Japan Earthquake implemented by the Fund for Local Government Employees' Accident Compensation, we conducted a questionnaire survey of local public employees at two local governments in areas that were affected by the tsunami in Iwate Prefecture (tsunami-disaster group) and two local governments in areas that were forced to evacuate entire towns in Fukushima Prefecture (nuclear-accident group). The questionnaires were distributed at workplaces and collected in sealed envelopes at the workplaces. The questionnaires were distributed to the subjects via the divisions in charge of general affairs at each local government. The number of distributed questionnaires was 1,050 for the tsunami-disaster group and 305 for the nuclear-accident group. The survey was conducted in a format asking respondents to enter their names in order to enable cross-referencing with the responses in a second follow-up survey. The filled-out questionnaires were enclosed in sealed envelopes and returned to the divisions in charge of general affairs at each local government.

The divisions collected all envelopes and submitted them in one batch to the survey staff. All collected questionnaires were accepted as valid responses, and the unanswered and wrongly answered questions were processed as missing values. The number of valid respondents from the tsunami-disaster group was 739 people, and from the nuclear-accident group was 234 people, for a total of 973 people for both groups.

(2) Survey content used in the analysis

(i) Indicators concerning mental health
We used the following indicators to measure mental health: K6 for screening for mental disorders such as depression and anxiety disorder (Furukawa, T, et al., 2003); the 12-item General Health Questionnaire (GHQ-12), which measures mental health status (Narita K, et al., 2001); and the Japanese version of the Impact of Event Scale-Revised (IES-R-J), which measures levels of traumatic stress caused by disasters (Asukai, et al., 2002).

(ii) Details of workplace experience from the time of the earthquake until the time of implementation of the survey
We asked about the participants' experience at work in the aftermath of the Great East Japan Earthquake. We used the items regarding troubles at work specified by Tanno, Yamazaki, and Matsui (2012), and added to them three more items based on the content of pilot interview that we conducted with local government employees.

(iii) Social support
We used the items formulated by Hatanaka, et al., (2010) in order to question the subjects regarding social support from supervisors and colleagues at the workplace.

(iv) Characteristics of respondents
Demographic variables: gender, age, current lifestyle, current living arrangement
Basic information regarding work: years of continuous employment, years of work at the current division, overtime work hours per month for the month with the largest number of overtime work hours in the past one year, workplace position, availability or lack of work from before the earthquake,

content of work.

2. Second survey

(1) Procedures

From January through April 2016, among local governments that participated in the first survey, we distributed questionnaire surveys at the workplace of employees of one local government in Iwate Prefecture that was affected by the tsunami disaster and two local governments in areas that were forced to evacuate entire towns in Fukushima Prefecture. The completed surveys were collected in sealed envelopes at the workplace. The questionnaire surveys were distributed to the subjects via the divisions in charge of general affairs at each local government. The number of distributed questionnaires was 750 for the tsunami-disaster group and 305 for the nuclear-accident group. The survey was conducted in a format that asked respondents to enter their names to enable cross-referencing with the responses in the first survey. The filled-out questionnaires were enclosed in sealed envelopes and returned to the divisions in charge of general affairs at each local government. The divisions submitted all collected envelopes in one batch to the survey staff. In the collected questionnaires, the unanswered and wrongly questions were processed as missing values. The number of valid respondents from the tsunami-disaster group was 657 people, and from the nuclear-accident group was 235 people, for a total of 892 people.

(i) Indicators concerning mental health
We used the same three indicators as in the first survey.

(ii) Social support
As in the first survey, we questioned the subjects regarding social support from supervisors and colleagues.

(iii) Burnout
We used the Japanese version of the burnout scale developed by Kubo (1998) to measure burnout tendencies. This scale is composed of three aspects: depersonalization, decline in the sense of personal accomplishment, and emotional exhaustion.

3. Cross-referencing of responses

Based on the entered names, we compared and cross-referenced the responses in the two surveys. The responses which we were able to cross-reference totaled 672 (494 people in the tsunami-disaster group and 178 in the nuclear-accident group). The data provided by these 672 people was used in the analysis reported in this paper.

Results

1. Demographic characteristics of the respondents

Looking at the demographic characteristics of the respondents, the gender composition was approximately 70% male and 30% female, and there were no differences among groups in terms of gender (Table 1). The average age of the respondents was 43.78 years (SD10.49) in the tsunami-disaster group and 42.94 years (SD11.61) in the nuclear-accident group (t (286) = 0.84, $n.s.$). As for their current lifestyle, respondents living alone accounted for approximately 15% of the tsunami-disaster group and approximately 40% of the nuclear-accident group (Table 2). As for the current living arrangements, in the tsunami-disaster group more than 70% of the respondents lived in their own homes, while nearly 60% of the respondents in the nuclear-accident group lived in rented housing (Table 3).

Table 1—Composition of respondents by gender

	Male		Female	
	n	(%)	n	(%)
Tsunami-disaster group	336	(68.2%)	157	(31.8%)
Nuclear-accident group	125	(70.2%)	53	(29.8%)

Fisher's exact test, $n.s.$

Table2—Respondents' lifestyle

	Living alone		Other	
	n	(%)	n	(%)
Tsunami-disaster group	77	(15.7%)	415	(84.3%)
Nuclear-accident group	73	(41.0%)	105	(59.0%)

Fisher's exact test, $p < .001$

Table 3—Respondent's living arrangements

	Temporary housing		Rented housing		Own homes		Other	
	n	(%)	n	(%)	n	(%)	n	(%)
Tsunami-disaster group	7	(1.4%)	75	(15.2%)	365	(74.2%)	45	(9.1%)
Nuclear-accident group	2	(1.1%)	101	(57.1%)	37	(20.9%)	37	(20.9%)

$\chi^2(3)=162.79$, $p < .001$

Looking at the basic information regarding work, the average number of years of continuous employment was 17.47 years in the tsunami-disaster group (SD10.49) and 14.35 years in the nuclear-accident group (SD12.61), indicating that the average number of years of continuous employment was longer in the tsunami-disaster group than in the nuclear-accident group (t (295) = 2.87, $p < .05$). The number of years of continuous employment at the current division was 48.25 months in tsunami-disaster group (SD 44.79) and 31.14 months in the nuclear-accident group (SD 45.30), indicating that the number of years of continuous employment at the current division was longer in the tsunami-disaster group than in the nuclear-accident group (t (440) = 3.55, $p < .001$). The number of overtime work hours for the month with the largest number of overtime work hours in the past one year was 41.78 hours in the tsunami-disaster group (SD 34.74) and 25.33 hours in the nuclear-accident group (SD 43.51), indicating that the number of overtime work hours per month was longer in the tsunami-disaster group than in the nuclear-accident group (t (489) = 4.05, $p < .05$). As for the position of the respondents, for both areas approximately 10% were employed in managerial positions and approximately 70% were employed in general positions (Table 4). As for the availability or lack of work before the earthquake, in the tsunami-disaster group, approximately 80% of the respondents were employed prior to the earthquake, while in the nuclear-accident group, after the earthquake the ratio of employed respondents was only a bit over 30% (Table 5). As for the content of work of the respondents, in the tsunami-disaster group, the ratio of respondents engaged in ordinary work duties was high, at over 70%, while in the nuclear-accident group, the ratio of respondents engaged in disaster response and operations for residents affected by the disaster had increased to over 30% (Table 6).

Table 4—Respondents' position

	Managerinal positions		General positions		Other	
	n	(%)	n	(%)	n	(%)
Tsunami-disaster group	44	(9.0%)	360	(73.5%)	86	(17.6%)
Nuclear-accident group	23	(13.1%)	125	(71.0%)	28	(15.9%)

$\chi^2(2)=2.46$, n.s.

Table 5—Availability or lack of work before the earthquake

	Work before the earthquake		Work after the earthquake	
	n	(%)	n	(%)
Tsunami-disaster group	383	(78.0%)	108	(22.0%)
Nuclear-accident group	113	(63.8%)	64	(36.2%)

Fisher's exact test, $p < .001$

Table 6—Content of work of respondents

	Disaster-response operations related to the earthquake, tsunami, and nuclear accident		Response operations for residents affected by the disaster		Other ordinary work duties	
	n	(%)	n	(%)	n	(%)
Tsunami-disaster group	72	(15.2%)	42	(8.8%)	361	(76.0%)
Nuclear-accident group	42	(25.5%)	53	(32.1%)	70	(42.4%)

$\chi^2(2)=72.50, p < .001$

2. Mental health and social support by location and timing

We matched the results of the IES-R-J and K6 questionnaires conducted at two points in common to the original paper and assigned points to them. As for the GHQ12, we used the 0-0-1-1 method to assign points. We also assigned points to supervisor and colleague support in line with the original paper. With regard to these indicators, we conducted two-way mixed design (disaster group x timing) analysis of variance in order to check for significant differences by disaster-group and survey timing (Table 7). The results demonstrated that both the timing and type of disaster group had a significant main effect with regard to IES-R-J, K6, and GHQ12, and that points at Time 2 were lower than Time 1. Additionally, the points on all indicators were higher in the nuclear-accident group than in the tsunami-disaster group. With regard to the two indicators for social support, there was no significant difference by timing and disaster group.

Table 7—Mental health indicators and social support by disaster group and timinig

		n	Time1 M	(SD)	Time2 M	(SD)	Time F(df)	group F(df)	Interaction F(df)
IES-R	Tsunami-disaster group	460	10.60	(11.44)	9.27	(11.26)	7.56**	76.81**	0.03
	Nuclear-accident group	154	20.52	(17.11)	19.34	(18.10)	(1)	(1)	(1)
K6	Tsunami-disaster group	480	5.66	(5.53)	5.00	(5.23)	23.63**	22.27**	3.07†
	Nuclear-accident group	173	8.11	(6.05)	6.72	(5.68)	(1)	(1)	(1)
GHQ-12	Tsunami-disaster group	465	3.78	(3.52)	3.44	(3.43)	11.33**	18.21**	1.27
	Nuclear-accident group	161	5.17	(3.85)	4.50	(3.68)	(1)	(1)	(1)
Boss support	Tsunami-disaster group	476	7.99	(2.55)	7.99	(2.62)	2.40	0.01	2.51
	Nuclear-accident group	165	7.82	(2.56)	8.19	(2.46)	(1)	(1)	(1)
Colleague support	Tsunami-disaster group	477	8.10	(2.48)	8.21	(2.45)	0.65	0.12	0.04
	Nuclear-accident group	165	8.19	(2.41)	8.25	(2.47)	(1)	(1)	(1)

$p < .01**, p < .10†$

3. High-risk ratio in mental health indicators by disaster group and timing

Cut-off values were established in the three mental health indicators used in this research. In the IES-R, the cut-off value was 24/25, and subjects with results of 25 points or higher were conceived as high-risk subjects (Asukai, et al., 2002). Results over 24/25 points and over 15 points in the K6 were conceived as cut-off values with an over 50% probability of mental disorder (Furukawa et al., 2003). As for the GHQ12, according to a study by Honda, S. et al., (2001), information is available that supports conceiving of subjects with four or more points in the GHQ12 as high-risk subjects. Subjects with values higher than the cut-off values for each indicator were perceived as high-risk subjects, and subjects with values lower than the cut-off values were perceived as low-risk subjects. Then, we calculated the ratio of the two groups by disaster group and survey timing (Table 8).

Table 8—High-risk ration in mental health indicators by disaster group and timing

		Time1 High-risk	Time2 High-risk
IES-R ($25\leqq$)	Tsunami-disaster group	11.9%	8.9%
	Nuclear-accident group	31.4%	27.2%
K6 ($15\leqq$)	Tsunami-disaster group	7.8%	5.0%
	Nuclear-accident group	15.9%	10.9%
GHQ12 ($4\leqq$)	Tsunami-disaster group	44.1%	39.5%
	Nuclear-accident group	61.8%	54.4%

Overall, the ratios of high-risk subjects from Time 1 to Time 2 in all indicators were declining, but in the nuclear-accident group the high-risk subjects remained at a higher value.

In order to analyze the changes in the risk ratios for mental health indicators depending on the survey implementation time by location, we also cross-referenced the values for Time 1 and Time 2, established four groups, and calculated the ratios for each group (Figure 1).

As for the breakdown of IES-R high-risk subjects in Time 2, in the tsunami-disaster group, the percentage of respondents who remained at high risk was 5.2%, while the percentage of respondents who became high risk at Time

2 was 3.7%. In the nuclear-accident group, the percentage of respondents who remained at high risk was 21.4%, while the percentage of respondents who became high risk at Time 2 was 5.2%.

As for the breakdown of K6 high-risk subjects in Time 2, in the tsunami-disaster group, the percentage of respondents who remained at high risk and was 2.5%, with the same percentage becoming high risk at Time 2. In the nuclear-accident group, the percentage of respondents who remained at high risk was 7.5%, while the percentage of respondents who became high risk at Time 2 was 2.9%.

As for the breakdown of GHQ12 high-risk subjects in Time 2, in the tsunami-disaster group, the percentage of respondents who remained at high risk was 28.2%, while the percentage of respondents who became high risk at Time 2 was 11.6%. In the nuclear-accident group, the percentage of respondents who remained at high risk was 46.0%, while the percentage of respondents who became high risk at Time 2 was 8.7%.

In all three mental health indicators, in the tsunami-disaster group, there were numerous low-risk respondents at both points in time, while in the nuclear-accident group the rate of high-risk respondents was significantly higher at both points in time.

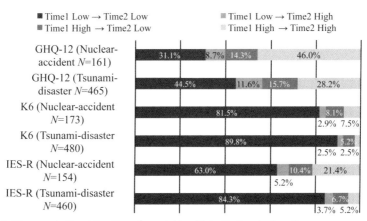

Fig. 1 Changes in the risk ration of mental health indicators by location

4. Experience at work from the time of the disaster until present day

As for the 16 items that we asked about regarding experience at work from the time of the disaster until the present day, we conducted a factor analysis using the major factor method and promax rotation. The results indicated that one item, "solidarity among employees was reinforced" did not demonstrate a high load in any of the factors. We therefore removed this item and repeated the factor analysis, extracting three factors (Table 9). The pre-rotation eigenvalues were, in decreasing order, 7.24, 1.50, and 1.08, and the cumulative eigenvalue was 61.32%. The first factor was interpreted as a factor that demonstrates deterioration of the workplace atmosphere due to stricter control and instructions by supervisors, and we named it "Management-caused deterioration of atmosphere." The second factor was interpreted as a factor that demonstrates confusion of employees due to increased workload and chaos after the disaster, and we named it "Fatigue and exhaustion." The third factor was interpreted as a factor that demonstrates communication problems among fellow employees, and we named it "Workplace communication problems." We conducted simple addition of items that demonstrated high load in all factors and established them as indicators.

Table 9—Factor analysis results for experience at work after the disaster

		F1	F2	F3
Q16_12	Instructions and reprimands from supervisors increased	.858	-.074	-.059
Q16_9	Management and instructions were strict	.830	.100	-.116
Q16_11	I was often scolded over problems and responsibilities	.815	-.010	.025
Q16_10	Mistakes and troubles at the workplace increased	.553	.098	.178
Q16_8	I did not receive fair evaluation of my work	.528	.048	.180
Q16_7	The workplace atmosphere deteriorated	.488	-.036	.328
Q16_2	Hardships increased due to manpower shortage	-.002	.853	-.033
Q16_1	It was physically hard	.022	.826	-.127
Q16_3	There was prolonged confusion at the workplace	.017	.739	.020
Q16_4	I felt inexperienced in the work	.000	.403	.219
Q16_5	I felt a gap between my ideal with regard to work and the reality	.015	.398	.339
Q16_15	I had fewer colleagues with whom I could speak openly	.016	-.118	.857
Q16_16	The number of new colleagues increased and communication became more difficult	.037	-.100	.856
Q16_14	There was less time to discuss with colleagues	-.056	.174	.658
Q16_6	The number of new colleagues increased and I had difficulties with education and information transfer	.045	.198	.476
	[Correlation between factors] F1		.722	.637
	F2			.590

Regarding the three indicators for experience at work from the disaster until the present day, all comparisons between locations demonstrated significant differences, and all three indicators were higher in the nuclear-accident group than in the tsunami-disaster group (Table 10).

Table 10—Experience at work by disaster group

		N	Average Value	Standard deviation	t value (df)
Management-caused deterioration of atmosphere	Tsunami-disaster group	477	12.85	3.55	-3.26**
	Nuclear-accident group	166	13.92	3.80	(641)
Fatigue and exhaustion	Tsunami-disaster group	482	14.30	2.98	-3.89**
	Nuclear-accident group	173	15.46	3.51	(266)
Workplace communication problems	Tsunami-disaster group	482	9.14	2.46	-5.22**
	Nuclear-accident group	172	10.36	2.70	(279)

$p < .01$**

5. Burnout

As for burnout, we created the following three indicators in line with the original paper: depersonalization, decline in the sense of personal accomplishment, and emotional exhaustion. A comparison between disaster groups with regard to these three indicators demonstrated significant differences in depersonalization and emotional exhaustion. The points for depersonalization and emotional exhaustion were higher in the nuclear-accident group than in the tsunami-disaster group (Table 11).

Table 11—Burnout by disaster group

		N	Average Value	Standard deviation	t value (df)
Depersonalization	Tsunami-disaster group	474	1.97	.81	-3.44**
	Nuclear-accident group	173	2.22	.85	(645)
Decline in the sense of personal accomplishment	Tsunami-disaster group	475	3.74	.77	.07
	Nuclear-accident group	171	3.74	.77	(644)
Emotional exhaustion	Tsunami-disaster group	478	2.59	.98	-2.25*
	Nuclear-accident group	175	2.79	1.06	(651)

$p < .01$**, $p < .05$*

6. Analysis of factors to predict high risk at Time 2

In order to identify the variables for the high-risk ratio at Time 2, we conducted a logistic regression analysis by disaster group. The criterion variables were set as high-risk ratios in IES-R, K6, and GHQ12 at Time 2. The explanatory variables were social support and experience at work at Time 1, social support and burnout at Time 2, and high-risk ratios in IES-R, K6, and GHQ12 at Time 1. As an analysis method, we used the step-up procedure by Ward. See the tables below for the analysis results by disaster group (tsunami-disaster group shown in Table 12, nuclear-accident group shown in Table 13).

In the tsunami-disaster group, the relative risk equivalent to the IES-R high risk at Time 2 was 15 times higher when the risk was high at Time 1, and 2.5 times higher when depersonalization points were high. The relative risk equivalent to the K6 high risk at Time 2 was 13 times higher when the risk was high at Time 1, 5.7 times higher when depersonalization points were high, and 0.7 times higher when supervisor support was high at Time 2. The relative risk equivalent to GHQ12 high risk at Time 2 was 3.2 times higher when emotional fatigue was high, 1.8 times higher when the sense of personal accomplishment was low, 0.23 times higher when the risk was low at Time 1, and 0.9 times higher when the support from colleagues was high at Time 2. This indicates that in the tsunami-disaster group, with regard to the IES-R and K6, the high risk and depersonalization at Time 1 were risk factors. On the other hand, despite the fact that the GHQ12 has risk impact at Time 1, immediate decline in the sense of personal accomplishment and emotional fatigue were identified as risk factors. Social support was barely a resiliency factor.

Table 12—Factors predicting high risk in the tsunami-disaster group

		Time2 IES-R High risk					Time2 K6 High risk					Time2 GHQ12 High risk			
		β	SE	Wald	df	Estimated odds ratio	β	SE	Wald	df	Estimated odds ratio	β	SE	Wald	df	Estimated odds ratio
Time1	Supervisor support															
	Colleague support															
	Management-caused deterioration of atmosphere															
	Fatigue and exhaustion															
	Communication problems at the workplace															
Time1	Low risk															
	High risk	2.74	.42	43.01	1**	15.45	2.59	.65	16.02	1**	13.35	-1.45	.25	32.61	1**	.23
Time2	Supervisor support						-.36	.14	6.37	1**	.70	-.11	.05	3.84	1*	.90
	Colleague support															
	Depersonalization	.92	.22	17.39	1**	2.52	1.73	.34	26.54	1**	5.65					
	Decline in the sense of personal accomplishment											.59	.18	10.87	1**	1.80
	Emotional exhaustion											1.15	.16	51.16	1**	3.17
	Invariable	-8.01	.88	83.50	1**	.000	-8.57	1.54	31.14	1**	.00	-4.12	1.00	16.84	1**	.02

$p < .01**$

Table 13—Factors predicting high risk in the nuclear-accident group

		Time2 IES-R High risk					Time2 K6 High risk					Time2 GHQ12 High risk				
		β	SE	Wald	df	Estimated odds ratio	β	SE	Wald	df	Estimated odds ratio	β	SE	Wald	df	Estimated odds ratio
Time1	Supervisor support															
	Colleague support															
	Management-caused deterioration of atmosphere															
	Fatigue and exhaustion															
	Communication problems at the workplace															
Time1	Low risk															
	High risk	3.27	.53	38.68	1**	26.31	2.98	.97	9.42	1**	19.78	-2.75	.66	17.60	1**	.06
Time2	Supervisor support															
	Colleague support															
	Depersonalization						1.56	.70	5.02	1*	4.75					
	Decline in the sense of personal accomplishment															
	Emotional exhaustion						1.32	.67	3.88	1*	3.75	2.68	.52	26.69	1**	14.55
	Invariable	-5.77	.86	44.92	1**	.003	-15.67	3.54	19.66	1**	.00	-6.21	1.35	21.19	1**	.00

$p < .01**$

In the nuclear-accident group, the relative risk equivalent to the IES-R high risk at Time 2 was 26 times higher when the risk is high at Time 1. The relative risk equivalent to the K6 high risk at Time 2 was 20 times higher when the risk was high at Time 1, 4.8 times higher when depersonalization points were high, and 3.8 times higher when the emotional fatigue was high. The relative risk equivalent to GHQ high risk at Time 2 was 15 times higher when emotional fatigue was high and 0.06 times higher when the risk was low at Time 1. This indicates that in the nuclear-accident group, for all indicators, high risk at Time 1 was a risk factor, and in the K6 and GHQ12 emotional fatigue is a strong risk factor. Depersonalization was a risk factor only in the K6.

The analyses displayed in Table 12 and Table 13 demonstrated that high risk at Time 1 and burnout at Time 2 strongly predicted high risk at Time 2. We, however, could not clearly analyze the relative impact of Time 1 factors and Time 1 high-risk background factors. So, as a supplementary analysis, we conducted a discriminant analysis of the changes in risk from Time 1 through Time 2 by setting four groups as criterion variables and using social support, work experience, and burnout at two points in time as explanatory variables.

In the tsunami-disaster group, the results of a discriminant analysis using the stepwise method with four groups with regard to the IES-R as criterion variables demonstrated that fatigue and exhaustion and depersonalization were selected as significant explanatory variables. Higher fatigue and exhaustion signified H→L, higher depersonalization signified L→H, and when both depersonalization and fatigue and exhaustion were high, the outcome was likely to be H→H (discriminant rate 50.3%). The results of a discriminant analysis using the stepwise method with four groups with regard to the K6 as criterion variables demonstrated that workplace communication problems and burnout depersonalization were selected as significant explanatory variables. Higher workplace communication problems signified H→L, and when both depersonalization and workplace communication problems were high, the outcomes were likely to be, respectively, L→H and H→H (discriminant rate 66.5%). The results of a discriminant analysis using the stepwise method with four groups with regard to the GHQ12 as criterion variables demonstrated that fatigue and exhaustion, decline in the sense of personal accomplishment, and emotional exhaustion were selected as significant explanatory variables, higher fatigue and exhaustion signified H→L, and when both decline in the sense of personal accomplishment and emotional exhaustion were high, the outcomes were likely to be L→H and H→H (discriminant rate 50.8%).

In the nuclear-accident group, the results of a discriminant analysis using the stepwise method with four groups with regard to the IES-R as criterion variables demonstrated that only depersonalization was selected as a significant explanatory variable. Higher depersonalization signified H→H, H→L, and L→H (discriminant rate 50.0%). The results of a discriminant analysis using the stepwise method with four groups with regard to the K6 as criterion variables demonstrated that management-caused deterioration of environment and depersonalization were selected as significant explanatory variables, higher depersonalization signified L→H, and when both management-caused deterioration and depersonalization were higher, the outcome was H→L and H→H (discriminant rate 70.4%). The results of a discriminant analysis using the stepwise method with four groups with regard to the GHQ12 as criterion variables demonstrated that only emotional exhaustion was selected as a significant explanatory variable, higher emotional exhaustion signified H→L and H→H (discriminant rate 39.8%).

Discussion

1. Mental health of local public employees

The aggregate results of the basic characteristics of the respondents indicated that local public employees, particularly those in the nuclear-accident group, perform numerous disaster-related work duties even today, which suggests that employees recruited before the disaster are mixed with employees recruited after the disaster. The results also indicated that local public employees in the nuclear-accident group still have an unstable livelihood, living alone or in rented housing.

This survey was implemented at two points in time after the Great East Japan Earthquake, three years and nine months after the disaster and four years and ten months after the disaster. The results indicate that even today, the ratio of respondents at high risk of PTSD at Time 2 was 27.2% in the nuclear-accident group and 8.2% in the tsunami-disaster group. In comparison with the 23.2% of local public employees with IES-R high risk at two years and four months after the disaster in the coastal areas of Miyagi Prefecture, according to a study by Kuwahara, et al. (2015), it can be claimed that local public employees in the nuclear-accident group are at a higher risk of traumatic stress. As for the values in the tsunami-disaster group, since more time has passed after the disaster than in the study by Kuwahara, et al. (2015), the ratio of respondents at high risk was less than 10%, so it can be claimed that the risk of traumatic stress for the tsunami-disaster group has stabilized.

As for the K6 scores that measure probable cases of depression and anxiety disorders, the results indicate that at Time 2, 10.9% of the respondents in the nuclear-accident group and 5.9% of the respondents in the tsunami-disaster group show possible symptoms of depression and anxiety disorders. If we take into consideration the results of Furukawa, et al. (2003), according to which the K6 cut-off values suggest a 10% prevalence rate, although the values in the nuclear-accident group are higher than those in the tsunami-disaster group, it is impossible to conclude that these figures represent high risk.

Additionally, the scores in the GHQ12, which serves as an indicator of mental health, suggest that the share of respondents at high risk in the nuclear-accident group and the tsunami-disaster group at Time 2 is, respectively, 55% and 40%, which indicates that although local public employees in both the nuclear-accident group and the tsunami-disaster group suffer from mental ailments, they continue to perform their duties.

2. What causes deterioration in the mental health of local public employees?

The IES-R risk for both the nuclear-accident group and the tsunami-disaster group was defined by the high risk at Time 1, and the combined results of the logistic regression analysis of the tsunami-disaster group and the supplementary analysis of the nuclear-accident group indicate that burnout depersonalization is a factor that increases the risk. In the tsunami-disaster group, higher exhaustion and fatigue indicate higher risk at Time 1, while prolonged burnout depersonalization can be interpreted as a factor that increases the risk at Time 2.

The K6 risk for both the nuclear-accident group and the tsunami-disaster group was defined by the high risk at Time 1 and burnout depersonalization.

In the tsunami-disaster group, support from supervisors was a resiliency factor, and in the nuclear-accident group, emotional exhaustion was a risk factor. If these results are considered in combination with the results of the supplementary analysis, it becomes clear that in the tsunami-disaster group, workplace communication problems increased the risk at Time 1, while prolonged burnout depersonalization can be interpreted as a factor that increases the risk at Time 2. In the nuclear-accident group, management-caused deterioration of atmosphere increased the risk at Time 1, and depersonalization can be interpreted as a factor that increases the risk at any point in time.

As for the GHQ12 risk, in both groups, low risk at Time 1 reduced the risk at Time 2. In the tsunami-disaster group, fatigue and exhaustion increased the risk at Time 1 and triggered a decline in the sense of personal accomplishment with burnout and emotional exhaustion, thus increasing the risk at Time 2. In the nuclear-accident group, emotional exhaustion increased the risk at Time 2.

3. Conclusions and limitations

The first conclusion of the present research is that, as demonstrated by the GHQ12, approximately half of the local public employees affected by the disaster continue to perform their duties while struggling with mental health issues. Local public employees are essential for citizen services and basic local government operations, so going forward it will be necessary to continue to address the deterioration of the mental health of these employees adequately. This suggests that, as argued by Matsui (2005), it is necessary to consider care for local public employees dealing with critical incident stress caused by natural disasters.

The second conclusion is that, of all local public employees affected by natural disasters, local public employees in areas affected by a nuclear accident in particular are at a high risk of post-traumatic stress. Previous research with ordinary citizens as subjects has been suggesting a decline in stress values, and against this backdrop, the high levels of traumatic stress risk among local public employees in areas affected by the nuclear accident indicate that it is essential to implement continuous traumatic stress care in areas affected by nuclear accidents. Also, traumatic stress for local public employees caused by natural disasters normally is more difficult to see than it is for other disaster rescue workers, which may suggest that local public employees have not been provided with psychological education.

The third conclusion is that, against the backdrop of the risk of post-traumatic stress, mental disorders and mental health, the experience of work during that period becomes a remote stressor, and as high stress conditions persist, burnout also advances and in turn the risk of mental health disorders further increases. This indicates that it is necessary to advance not only direct intervention with regard to mental health, but also intervention with regard to organizations and workplaces. For instance, it will be necessary to provide training for employees who work in proximity with employees demonstrating mental health disturbances on how to deal with them, or how to implement smooth communication between supervisors and subordinates in the process of work, as well as training for employees in managerial positions.

The limitations of the present research are listed here. The first limitation is that the research does not provide a sufficient understanding of stressors because its focus is on gaining insight into stress response. This research makes it possible to confirm whether local public employees demonstrate stress response, but the research does not clarify what the stressor (the burden that causes stress reaction) is. It is important to examine and clarify whether stress is caused by work duties after disasters, by personal relations at the workplace, or whether disasters themselves cause psychological trauma to local public employees. It is believed that such research will make a difference in post-disaster mental health care. The second limitation is the necessity of being mindful of the fact that, even if employees are evaluated as being at high risk, this evaluation does not address whether these employees actually demonstrate symptoms of work-related suffering, anxiety disorder or depression. It is possible that the employees may not suffer from functional disorders, and it is essential to examine in detail each individual case to determine how to handle personal circumstances. Therefore, it will become necessary to explore institutional care and response.

Notes

1. The details of this research were presented at the 2017 International Society for Traumatic Stress Studies 33rd Annual Meeting. We would like to express our gratitude to the respondents who participated in this survey despite the severe environment. The two sets of survey data in the present research were collected

through commissioned research from the Fund for Local Government Employees' Accident Compensation (FY 2014 Principal Investigator Tatsuo Fujimori, FY 2015 Principal Investigator Naoya Takahashi), and are published with permission.
2. Rissho University, Faculty of Psychology.
3. Rissho University, Faculty of Psychology.
4. Tokai University, Department of Psychological and Social Studies.

References

Asukai, N., Kato, H., Kawamura, N., Kim, Y., Yamamoto, K., Kishimoto, J., Miyake, Y., Nishizono-Maher, A. (2002). Reliability and validity of the Japanese-language version of the Impact of Event Scale-Revised (IES-R-J): Four studies on different traumatic events. *The Journal of Nervous and Mental Disease*, *190*, 175-182.

Fujimori, T., Omori, T. (2014). Research on preference behavior and mental health of long-term evacuees after a nuclear accident. Tobacco Academic Studies Center Grant-Supported Research Report, 161-181.

Furukawa, T., Ono, Y., Uda, H., Nakane, Y. (2003). Research on short screening of mental disease in the general population. FY2002 Health and Labour Sciences Research Grant (Health and Labour Sciences Special Research Project), Research on mental health issues and actual status of infrastructure for countermeasures, Research Cooperation Report.

Hatanaka, M., Matsui, Y., Ando, K., Inoue, K., Fukuoka, Y., Koshiro, E., & Itamura, H. (2010). Traumatic stress in Japanese broadcast journalists. *Journal of Traumatic Stress*, *23*, 173-177.

Honda, S., Shibata, Y., Nakane, Y. (2001). Screening for psychiatric disorders that uses the 12-item General Health Questionnaire (GHQ-12), *Journal of Health and Welfare Statistics*, *48 (10)*, 5-10.

Kubo, M. (1998). The relation between stress and burnout. *A Japanese Association of Industrial/Organizational Psychology Journal*, *12*, 5-15.

Kuwahara, Y., Takahashi, S., Matsui, Y. (2014). Post-traumatic growth of local government officers in earthquake damaged area of Japan, *Tsukuba Psychological Research*, *47*, 15-23.

Kuwahara, Y., Takahashi, S., Matsui, Y. (2015), Post-traumatic stress in local public officers in Earthquake damaged area of Japan, *Japanese Journal of Traumatic Stress*, *13*, 161-170.

Matsui, Y. (2005). Care for critical incident stress. *Brain Publishing.*

Narita, K. (2001). The multidimensionality of the 12 item version of the General Health. Bulletin of Tokyo Gakugei University, Series 1, science of education, *52*, 115-127.

Suzuki, Y., Kim, Y., Fukazawa, M. (2013). Mental health and stress factors of Miyagi Prefecture employees after the Great East Japan Earthquake, Health and Labour Sciences Research Grant (Comprehensive Research on Disability Health and Welfare (Mental Disorders Field)), Study for creation and evaluation of guidelines for monitoring and countermeasures to mental diseases caused by large-scale disasters and crime damage. Research Committee Report.

Tanno, H., Yamazaki, T., Matsui, Y. (2012). Stress-responses of caregiving staffs in the 2007 Niigataken Chuetsu-oki Earthquake (2) – Results of questionnaire survey conducted in one year after disaster, *Japanese Journal of Disaster Medicine*, *17*, 431-437.

Wakashima, K., Noguchi, S. (2013). Psychosocial support for local public employees (1) – the approach to Ishinomaki City Hall employees. Hasegawa, K. Wakashima., K. (editor), *Disaster Psychosocial Support Guidebook*. Kaneko Shobo pp. 76-91.

Yagi, A., Maeda, M., Ueda, Y., Oikawa, Y., Otoji, M., Kashiwazaki, Y., Yabe, H., Yasumura, S., Abe, M. (2015), Support in "Survey on mental health and lifestyle habits": "Fukushima Health Management Survey," *Japanese Journal of Traumatic Stress*, *13*, 84-88.

Contributors

Noboru Saito, Ph.D., President of Rissho University
Hideichi Sakazume, Ph.D., Professor Emeritus, Rissho University
Hiroki Takamura, Ph.D., Professor Emeritus, Rissho University
Kazunori Sasaki, M.A., Lecturer, Faculty of Buddhist Studies, Rissho University
Fumio Shoji, Ph.D., Lecturer, Faculty of Buddhist Studies, Rissho University
Shumbun Homma, Ph.D., Lecturer, Faculty of Buddhist Studies, Rissho University
Fumiko Kohama, Ph.D., Professor, Faculty of Letters, Rissho University
Atsushi Iwamoto, Ph.D., Associate Professor, Faculty of Letters, Rissho University
Mika Takiguchi, Ph.D., Lecturer, Faculty of Letters, Rissho University
Yasuhiro Maruyama, Ph.D., Associate Professor, Faculty of Law, Rissho University
Ju Kaneko, M.A., Professor, Faculty of Social Welfare, Rissho University
Yoriko Okamoto, Ph.D., Associate Professor, Faculty of Social Welfare, Rissho University
Yukie Sugano, Ph.D., Professor, Department of Childhood Studies, Aoyama Gakuin Women's Junior College
Reika Shouji, Ph.D., Associate Professor, Graduate Faculty of Interdisciplinary Research Faculty of Education, University of Yamanashi
Chie Takahashi, Associate Professor, Faculty of Letters, Tohoku Gakuin University
Akiko Yagishita-Kawata, Japan Organization for Employment of the Elderly, Persons with Disabilities and Job Seekers
Yayoi Aoki, Professor, Faculty of Childhood Education, Hosen College of Childhood Education
Ayuchi Ishikawa, Chita Welfare Consultation Center
Miyako Kamei, Associate Professor, Department of Early Childhood Education and Care, Shohoku College
Manabu Kawata, Ph.D., Associate Professor, Faculty of Education, Hokkaido University

Osamu Suda, Ph.D., Emeritus Professor, Tokyo Metropolitan University
Michinori Yamashita, M.S., Professor, Faculty of Geo-Environmental Science, Rissho University
Daisuke Miyata, M. Eng., Professor, Faculty of Commerce and Economics, Chiba University of Commerce
Natsumi Fujita, B.S., Fujitsu Marketing Ltd./External Researcher, Faculty of Geo-Environmental Science, Rissho University
Yasushi Watarai, Ph.D. in Science, Associate Professor, Faculty of Geo-Environmental Science, Rissho University
Yoshinori Shigeta, Ph.D. in Science, Associate Professor, Faculty of Environmental Studies, Tottori University
Kiyotaka Nakagawa, D. Sc., Professor, Faculty of Geo-Environmental Science, Rissho University
Yumiko Kamise, Ph.D., Professor, Faculty of Psychology, Rissho University
Naoya Takahashi, Ph.D., Associate Professor, Faculty of Psychology, Rissho University
Emi Yano, Master of Laws, Professor, Graduate School of Law, University of the Ryukyus
Takeshi Furuya, Ph.D., Professor, Faculty of Psychology, Rissho University
Shigeki Sakata, M.A., Part-time Lecturer, Department of Psychological and Social Studies, Tokai University

The Rissho International Journal of Academic Research in Culture and Society 2
The Academic Canon of Arts and Humanities, and Science

発行日	2019 年 3 月 20 日　初版第 1 刷
編集	立正大学学術英文叢書編集・刊行委員会
発行	立正大学 〒 141-8602　東京都品川区大崎 4-2-16 電話 03-3492-2681（代表）
発売	株式会社平凡社 〒 101-0051　東京都千代田区神田神保町 3-29 電話 03-3230-6570（代表） 　　 03-3230-6573（営業）
装丁	馬面俊之
印刷	株式会社東京印書館
製本	大口製本印刷株式会社

落丁・乱丁本のお取り替えは平凡社読者サービス係までお送り下さい（送料小社負担）。
Ⓒ立正大学 2019 Printed in Japan
ISBN978-4-582-47442-8
NDC 分類番号 040.3　A5 判（21.6cm）　総ページ 372